MYSTERY TRAIN

MYSTERY TRAIN

GREIL MARCUS was born in San Francisco in 1945. Among his books are *Lipstick Traces* (1989), *Dead Elvis* (1991), *The Old Weird America* (1997), *The Shape of Things to Come* (2006), *Bob Dylan by Greil Marcus* (2010), *The Doors* (2011), and *The History of Rock 'n' Roll in Ten Songs* (2014). He is the editor of *Stranded* (1979), *Psychotic Reactions and Carburetor Dung* by Lester Bangs, with Sean Wilentz *The Rose & the Briar*, and with Werner Sollors *A New Literary History of America* (2009). Since 2000 he has taught at Berkeley, Princeton, Minnesota, NYU, and the New School in New York. In 1989 he was a curator of the exhibition *On the Passage of a Few People Through a Brief Moment in Time: The Situationist International 1957–1972* at the Centre Pompidou in Paris, the ICA in London, and the ICA in Boston; in 1998 he curated the exhibition *1948* at the Whitney Museum in New York, and in 2014 Festival Albertine at the French Embassy in New York. He is the author of one rock 'n' roll song, "I Can't Get No Nookie," which, as recorded in 1970 by the Masked Marauders, fraudulently reached #123 in the "Bubbling Under" section of the *Billboard* charts, after which it was attacked by Dean Burch, then head of the FCC, as an example of "obscenity on the air." He was a member of the Critics Chorus of the Rock Bottom Remainders until the ignominious dissolution of the all-author rock 'n' roll band in 1996.

Greil Marcus writes a monthly column for the *Barnes & Noble Review*. He lives in Oakland with his wife, Jenny Marcus.

MYSTERY TRAIN

IMAGES OF AMERICA IN ROCK 'N' ROLL MUSIC

GREIL MARCUS

SIXTH REVISED EDITION

FABER & FABER

This sixth, revised edition first published in the UK by
Faber & Faber Ltd, Bloomsbury House
74–77 Great Russell Street, London WC1B 3DA
and in the USA by
Plume, a member of
Penguin Group (USA) LLC
Previously published in a Dutton Edition

Printed in the UK by CPI Group (UK) Ltd, Croydon CR0 4YY

A CIP record for this book is available from the British Library

ISBN 978–0–571–32317–3

FSC
www.fsc.org
MIX
Paper from
responsible sources
FSC® C101712

2 4 6 8 10 9 7 5 3 1

To Emily and Cecily
and in memory of my dear friend and editor, Bill Whitehead

CONTENTS

AUTHOR'S NOTE

Writing these opening notes reminds me of the prefaces to the American history books that were written during World War II, when the authors, looking back for the meaning of the Revolution or the Civil War or whatever, drew modest but determined parallels between their work and the struggle. They were affirming that their work was part of the struggle; that an attempt to understand America took on a special meaning when America was up for grabs. Those writers were also saying—at least, this is what they now say to me—that to do one's most personal work in a time of public crisis is an honest, legitimate, paradoxically democratic act of common faith; that one keeps faith with one's community by offering whatever it is that one has to say. I mean that those writers were exhilarated, thirty years ago, by something we can only call patriotism, and humbled by it too.

Well, I feel some kinship with those writers. I began this book in the fall of 1972, and finished it late in the summer of 1974. Inevitably, it reflects, and I hope contains, the peculiar moods of those times, when the country came face-to-face with an obscene perversion of itself that could be neither accepted nor destroyed: moods of rage, excitement, loneliness, fatalism, desire.

Like a lot of people who are about thirty years old, I have been listening and living my life to rock 'n' roll for twenty years, and so behind this book lie twenty years of records and twenty years of talk. Probably it began when a kid pushed a radio at me and demanded that I listen to a song called "Rock Around the Clock," which I disliked at the time and still do. I know the music came together for me in high school, thanks to my cruising friend, Barry Franklin. We spent years on the El Camino, driving from Menlo Park to San Francisco to San Jose and back again, listening to Tom Donahue and Tommy Saunders on KYA, trying to figure out the words to "Runaround Sue" and translating "Little Star" into French. Later, we followed the sixties trail to college, Beatles shows, and Dylan concerts.

About a month before the Beatles hit I met my wife, Jenny, who confirmed my enthusiasms and who has always kept them alive; it means more to me to say that this book wouldn't have been written without her than to say that it couldn't have been.

The time I have spent talking rock 'n' roll with my friends Bruce Miroff, Langdon Winner, Ralph Gleason, Ed Ward, Michael Goodwin, and many more, has gone into this book; so has talk with my brothers Steve and Bill, with teachers and students, and with my daughter Emily, who picked "Mystery Train" as her favorite song at the age of two. My daughter Cecily is not as yet so discriminating, but I have hopes. As much as anything, rock 'n' roll has been the best means to friendship I know.

I have been writing about the music since 1966—professionally, for publication, since 1968. Before I got up the nerve to see my efforts in print I put together a book of pieces by myself and some friends; one of them, Sandy Darlington, taught me a lot about music and a lot more about writing. After the book was finished I took over Sandy's music-space in the San Francisco *Express-Times*, then edited and inspired by Marvin Garson. Until the events of Peoples' Park sent it reeling into mindlessness, the *Express-Times* was the best underground newspaper in America, and I've always been proud to have been part of it. When it changed I moved across town to *Rolling Stone*, where I wrote and edited for a year. In 1970 I left, and ultimately ended up with *Creem*, a magazine that seemed like a place of freedom and was. *Creem* gave me the chance to try out many of the ideas that eventually found their way into this book.

There would be little to those ideas without the study I did in American political thought and American literature with three Berkeley teachers: John Schaar, Michael Rogin, and Norman Jacobson. And there are a few books that mattered a great deal to the ambitions of my own book, and to its content: D. H. Lawrence's *Studies in Classic American Literature*, Leslie Fiedler's *Love and Death in the American Novel*, James Agee's *Let Us Now Praise Famous Men*, Pauline Kael's *I Lost It at the Movies*, Alexis de Tocqueville's *Democracy in America*, and, in a way that is still pretty mysterious to me, Ernest Hemingway's short stories.

Many people helped me in many ways while I was writing: Mary

Clemmey, Greg Shaw, Richard Bass, Pat Thomas, Ms. Clawdy, Bill
Strachan of Anchor Press, and Wendy Weil. Jenny Marcus, Peter Guralnick, Bruce Miroff, Bob Christgau, and Dave Marsh read every page
of the manuscript, and made it far better than it would have been without their help.

Bob and Dave deserve special thanks. They have been part of my
work from beginning to end; they encouraged it, at times inspired it,
always cared about it. No critic could ask for better colleagues, and no
one could ask for better friends.

And I owe as much to my editor, Bill Whitehead. Without his commitment to the book, mine would have faded out a long time ago.

What I have to say in *Mystery Train* grows out of records, novels,
political writings; the balance shifts, but in my intentions, there isn't
any separation. I am no more capable of mulling over Elvis without
thinking of Herman Melville than I am of reading Jonathan Edwards
(not, I've been asked to point out, the crooner mentioned in the Randy
Newman chapter, but the Puritan who made his name with "Sinners In
the Hands of an Angry God") without putting on Robert Johnson's
records as background music. What I bring to this book, at any rate, is
no attempt at synthesis, but a recognition of unities in the American
imagination that already exist. They are natural unities, I think, but
elusive; I learned, in the last two years, that simply because of those
unities, the resonance of the best American images is profoundly deep
and impossibly broad. I wrote this book in an attempt to find some of
those images, but I know now that to put oneself in touch with them is
a life's work.

Berkeley, August 9, 1974

INTRODUCTION
TO THE 2015 EDITION

Every seven or eight years, I've had the privilege, thanks to the publisher that, under different names, has stayed with *Mystery Train* for four decades, to dive into the Notes & Discographies back sections of the book and again take up the story it tried to tell. Of the six principals in the book—Harmonica Frank, Robert Johnson, the Band, Sly Stone, Randy Newman, and Elvis Presley—Garth Hudson and Robbie Robertson of the Band, Sly Stone, and Randy Newman are still alive, though only Newman performs in anything like the way that he did when this book first appeared. But there are always reissues to chronicle, and often there's music that was never heard in its time. New books, sometimes shaping an old tale in a new way, sometimes working from discoveries that upend what everybody thought they knew, are always appearing. There are movies inspired by the music traced in these pages. Novels. Poems. Plays. Countless new songs from the handful that are followed here.

The great surprise I found, when I began to look at where those once fugitive, once looming figures stood today, was that the one who seemed most culturally alive—the one who was, after however many years, most the subject of a real and ongoing conversation—was Robert Johnson, the Mississippi blues singer who has been dead since 1938. When I wrote about him in 1975, almost nothing certain was known about him. But the discovery and publication, soon after that, of the facts about the identity of this once almost absolutely crepuscular artist did nothing to still the voices hiding in his songs—to fix *their* identity. For that matter the facts of Johnson's identity—his birth, real name, life, travels, death, even imposture—are probably more in dispute today than they have ever been, to the point that some people who have devoted a good part of their lives to the search for Robert Johnson now seem to be arguing that he may have never existed at all. Johnson may have a greater presence today than he has ever had. He may have a greater hold on the imaginations of individuals and the common, constructed memory, which is to say the story we tell each other about who we are and where we came from. That is partly because of the re-release of Johnson's music in 2011, to mark the putative centennial of his birth, in a form so clear and deep it was less that he seemed to step into the present than that he was able to transport any listener into the Texas hotel rooms where he recorded almost eighty years ago, because of the issue by Dogfish Head Brewery in that same year of "Robert Johnson's Hellhound on My Ale," or because in 2012 the president of the United States sang Robert Johnson's "Sweet Home Chicago" to close a celebration at the White House. But if Johnson's presence in culture were that simple it wouldn't exist.

I thank the people at Plume who have made this edition possible: editors Matthew Daddona and Philip Budnick, managing editor Norina Frabotta, senior production editor Lavina Lee, designer Eve Kirch, and for the cover the design firm the Heads of State, and proofreader Jennifer Rappaport.

Wendy Weil, who died suddenly in 2012, guided this book through many editions. I was in the Bill Clinton Library in Little Rock when her associate Emily Forland called with the news, and the version of the American story in the library, the Civil Rights Movement plaques marking vicious attacks on citizens witnessing and making history at the same time, the museums and blues lines painted on the windows of restaurants on President Clinton Avenue brought home, like a building collapsing, how central Wendy was to the books that, with her soft-spoken, often quizzical advice, I've had the chance to write. I am lucky now to continue to work with Emily Forland, now with Brandt & Hochman, and as well with her colleagues Emma Patterson, who was also with Wendy, and Marianne Merola and Henry Thayer. They are the quickest people I have ever known in publishing, and the sunniest.

Oakland, February 1, 2015

INTRODUCTION
TO THE 2008 EDITION

When I took the title of Elvis Presley's last single for Sun Records as the title for this book, I had no argument to make for it. The words had an echo in them, that was all I knew.

More than thirty years later, I know one thing more: it's been a good train to hitch a ride on. Over time, the idea or the image of the song has surfaced again and again, as a kind of talisman—of, I think, the need or the wish for mystery itself, as a dimension of life too often missing. I first noticed that this train was still running in 1986, with Thurston Moore's slow chant "Mystery train / Three-way plane" in Sonic Youth's "Expressway to Yr. Skull," the sound blowing up in a tiny nightclub but those first two words as clear as a fire alarm. That same year, I came across Lynn Turner's Harlequin Intrigue novel *Mystery Train* discarded on a beach. The jacket showed a clean-cut young man apparently attempting to rescue a clean-cut young woman, who seemed about to pitch off the back of a railcar. In the lower right-hand corner was a smaller picture of a dead woman facedown in a creek. Cut in under the first woman's windblown hair was an insert promising "SPECIAL OFFER WIN A GREAT PRIZE See inside No Purchase Necessary." The prize was detailed on the inside cover: "Lots of money." In 1989 there was Jim Jarmusch's film *Mystery Train*—three stories about foreign visitors holed up in the same Elvis-haunted Memphis hotel on the same night, but with the train that brings two Japanese rockabilly fans into town taking a turn that wasn't in the script. In the middle of the night, an Italian woman is awakened by a befuddled Elvis ghost; she asks him what he's doing in her room. "I don't rightly know, ma'am," he says; then he vanishes. The actor was Stephen Jones, perhaps the least convincing Elvis impersonator in the history of Western civilization, though a few years later Jones got his hands on American history, the real thing, when his wife, Paula—fronting for a slew of heavily funded right-wing groups—filed a sexual harassment suit against another sometime Elvis impersonator, a better one, especially in 1992, when he was elected president of the United States.

"Mystery train"—it was a phrase that, once Elvis made it a metaphor for fate and desire, became a signpost, a doorway to a better world, a key to the truth, a philosopher's stone. Even in the fifties, Janis "The Female Elvis" Martin was asking the other Elvis for a ride on his mystery train, in her hands an image Elvis would not have likely associated with schedules and conductors; in 1969, in "Rock Is Dead," a miserable studio jam not released until 1997, Jim Morrison found his one moment of lucidity when he stumbled onto the long black train. From the Soft Boys to the Blake Babies to Ashtray to the Waco Brothers, from Robert Zimmerman in Hibbing, Minnesota, in 1958 (with his band the Golden Chords and their "Mystery Train" rewrite "Big Black Train") to Bob Dylan in Los Angeles in 1981 (a hammering version of the real thing, with saxophone and female shouters), as band after band has found itself scavenging pieces of the tune, ringing small changes on a song that, the performances seemed to say, was too big for them, you could hear the twentieth century itself riding the song's rails—riding them straight into the next century, where, as I write, in 2007, Bruce Springsteen is calling down the talisman, "searching for a mystery train" in a "Radio Nowhere" determined to give up no such thing. "'It takes a worried man to sing a worried song,' sang the Carter Family in the Victor studios one Saturday evening on May 24, 1930," the late Charles K. Wolfe wrote in the notes to the 1995 Carter Family reissue *Worried Man Blues*, speaking of the earliest recording of the folk ballad that Sam Phillips and Junior Parker would rewrite as "Mystery Train." "The record wouldn't be released until November of that fall—it would be one of their last really big hits for some time—and by then more than a few listeners were nodding their heads in sad appreciation of the lyrics. Out in the Midwest over a million farm families were being devastated by the drought . . . President Hoover was admitting that over four million other Americans were now unemployed, but denying that the government should offer direct aid to them. Across the South as furniture store owners wheeled Victrolas out on their sidewalks to play the new Carter Family records, families with grim faces and patched clothes gathered and listened."

"It takes a worried man to sing a worried song," David Thomas sang in his tune "Enthusiastic" in 1984; in 1995 he was writing liner notes for his band Pere Ubu's *Ray Gun Suitcase*. "That's the way it goes at the lost, last outpost of American folk culture," he said, thinking back to the time he'd spent at the Days Inn on Brooks Road in Memphis, during Elvis Week '93. The delirium of the notes is more frantic, less happily wishful, than the delirium in Thomas's voice as the record begins: "I want to hang around inside your Greyhound terminal . . . I want to ride the baggage car of your old mystery train." "No, I say to you," Thomas continued in his notes, "You be the judge—Oh, citizens, how CAN I leave the Right Here, the Right Now when clearly it's all happening RIGHT HERE RIGHT NOW? And gathering momentum—in the moment—moving in processions—in the moment—to the climactic candlelight walk on Graceland—in the moment . . ."

Is this where the train ends up? In no way—it can go in any direction, and off the tracks. In 2005 a video showing contractors working for Aegis Defence Services firing indiscriminately on cars and civilians as their huge vehicles pounded down Baghdad streets streamed over the Internet, with Elvis's "Mystery Train" pounding even harder in the background. Who understood the song? Who didn't? The train less crosses any map than leaves one in its wake, and on that map any place can disappear and reappear as readily as any other. Taking its title from the radioactive suitcase in Robert Aldrich's fantastically paranoid Cold War thriller *Kiss Me Deadly*, Pere Ubu boards a train that passes through a modern nation as if it were an ancient land, all ruin and portent, prophecy and decay. Thus the train makes the familiar strange, unseen—new.

I wrote this book—in the mid-'70s, just about the time Pere Ubu was coming together in Cleveland as a dada experiment, as a punk band—out of a conviction that, in their music or in their public lives, a few blues and rock 'n' roll performers had at once drawn upon and transfigured certain bedrock, ineradicable strains of American experience and identity. The blues singer Robert Johnson died in 1938, Elvis Presley died in 1977, the medicine-show artist Harmonica Frank died in 1984, the careers of the Band and Sly and the Family Stone effectively ended soon after this book was published, with only the discomforting Randy Newman pressing on—but the premise of the book remains the same. Few if any performers have carried it forward more completely than Pere Ubu, even if their music is far less at home in a romantic America, in the spiritualist historiscapes of Thomas Hart Benton, than in some Midwestern downtown so commonplace it can't even hold a name, in Edward Kienholz's seedy hotel rooms and rotting boarding houses, where chances are nothing will happen and anything can. "It was chance that we stopped at the Days Inn, Brooks Road," Thomas concluded in his *Ray Gun Suitcase* notes, with the Greyhound terminal and the mystery train still ready for him when he's ready to get out of town. "The Elvis people last night were saying, 'No it was fate.' But I know it was an accident. Like driving down a backroad out in the country and going through a ghost town and you think, 'This is the way it used to be,' and you never forget the sight because it's a perfectly shaped moment in time and space and like a vision of the distant future that will never be and you know it as you dream it, and you think, 'We can renovate one of these old store fronts and move out here,' and, of course, you know you never will but the vision has power because it answers a need. Some people find what they need in the darkness. Some people are transfixed by light. We checked in and we'll check out."

In this edition, the main text is little changed from what it was when the book was first published, in 1975. The "Notes and Discographies" section that follows has continued to grow; it has been completely revised and rewritten, with the expanding and contracting arcs of each performer's career followed as closely as I could manage. I have the chance, too, to thank some people who were not involved with this book when it first appeared, but who have helped keep it before the public: at the Wendy Weil Agency, Emma Patterson and Emily Forland; at the David Higham Agency, Anthony Goff and Georgia Glover; at La Nouvelle Agence, Mary Kling; at Paul & Peter Fritz, Peter Fritz and Christian Dittus; in Japan, over nearly thirty years, the infinitely resourceful Toru Mitsui; at Plume, Emily Haynes and Nadia Kashper; at Penguin in the U.K., Tony Lacey and Rosie Glaisher; at Rowohlt, Nikolas Hansen and Klaus Humann; at Rogner & Bernhard, Klaas Jarchow, Birgit Politycki, and Antje Landshoff; at Ullstein, Dorle Maravilla; at Nijgh & Van Ditmar, Vic van der Reijt; at Editions Allia, Gérard Berréby and François Escaig; Eric Vigne at Folio; at Faber and Faber, Lee Brackstone; and going back through many projects and almost as many publishers, Jon Riley. I thank as well Fritz Schneider, a fine translator, a great correspondent, and a shaming fact-checker; Chuck Death and Colin B. Morton; John Rockwell; Cecil Brown; John Bakke; and the late Ray Johnson. Along with many others they helped make the good luck I've had.

Berkeley, August 7, 2007

PROLOGUE

Our story begins just after midnight, not so long ago. *The Dick Cavett Show* is in full swing.

Seated on Cavett's left is John Simon, the New York Critic. On Cavett's right, in order of distance from him, are Little Richard, Rock 'n' Roll Singer and Weirdo; Rita Moreno, Actress; and Erich Segal, Yale Professor of Classics and Author of *Love Story*. Miss Moreno and Mr. Segal adored *Love Story*. Mr. Simon did not. Little Richard has not read it.

Cavett is finishing a commercial. Mr. Simon is mentally rehearsing his opening thrust against Mr. Segal, who is very nervous. Miss Moreno seems to be falling asleep. Little Richard is looking for an opening.

Mr. Simon has attacked Mr. Segal. Mr. Segal attempts a reply but he is too nervous to be coherent. Mr. Simon attacks a second time. Little Richard is about to jump out of his seat and jam his face in front of the camera but Mr. Simon beats him out. He attacks Mr. Segal again.

"NEGATIVE! NEGATIVE NEGATIVE NEGATIVE!" screams Mr. Segal. He and Simon are debating a fine point in the history of Greek tragedy, to which Mr. Simon has compared *Love Story* unfavorably.

"'Neg-a-tive,'" muses Mr. Simon. "Does that mean 'no'?"

Mr. Segal attempts, unsuccessfully, to ignore Mr. Simon's contempt for his odd patois, and claims that the critics were wrong about Aeschylus. He implies that Simon would have walked out on the *Oresteia*. Backed by the audience, which sounds like a Philadelphia baseball crowd that has somehow mistaken Mr. Simon for Richie Allen, Segal presses his advantage. Little Richard sits back in his chair, momentarily intimidated.

"MILLIONS OF PEOPLE WERE DEEPLY MOVED by my book," cries Segal, forgetting to sit up straight and slumping in his chair until his body is near parallel with the floor, "AND IF ALL THOSE PEOPLE LIKED IT—" (Segal's voice has now achieved a curious tremolo) "*I MUST BE DOING SOMETHING RIGHT!*"

The effort has exhausted Segal, and as he takes a deep breath Little Richard begins to rise from his seat. Again, Simon is too fast for him. Simon attempts to make Segal understand that he is amazed that anyone, especially Segal, takes this trash to be anything more than, well, trash.

"I have read it and reread it many times," counters Segal with great honesty. "I am always moved."

"Mr. Segal," says Simon, having confused the bull with his cape and now moving in for the kill, "you had the choice of acting the knave or the fool. You have chosen the latter."

Segal is stunned. Cavett is stunned. He calls for a commercial. Little Richard considers the situation.

The battle resumes. Segal has now slumped even lower in his chair, if that is possible, and seems to be arguing with the ceiling. "*You're* only a critic," he says as if to Simon. "What have *you* ever written? What do you know about art? Never in the history of art . . ."

"WHY, NEVER IN THE HISTORY!"

The time has come. Little Richard makes his move. Leaping from his seat, he takes the floor, arms waving, hair coming undone, eyes wild, mouth working. He advances on Segal, Cavett, and Simon, who cringe as one man. The camera cuts to a close-up of Segal, who looks miserable, then to Simon, who is attempting to compose the sort of bemused expression he would have if, say, someone were to defecate on the floor. Little Richard is audible off-camera, and then his face quickly fills the screen.

"WHY, YES, IN THE WHOLE HISTORY OF AAAART! THAT'S RIGHT! SHUT UP! SHUT UP! WHAT DO YOU KNOW, MR. CRITIC? WHY, WHEN THE CREEDENCE CLEARWATER PUT OUT WITH THEIR 'TRAVELIN' BAND' EVERYBODY SAY WHEEE-OOO BUT I KNOW IT CAUSE THEY ONLY DOING 'LONG TALL SALLY', JUST LIKE THE BEATLES ANDTHESTONESANDTOMJONESANDELVIS—I AM ALL OF IT, LITTLE RICHARD HIMSELF, VERY TRULY THE GREATEST, THE HANDSOMEST, AND NOW TO YOU (to Segal, who now appears to be *on* the floor) AND TO YOU (to Simon, who looks to Cavett as if to say, really old man, this *has* been fun, but this, *ah, fellow* is becoming a bit much, perhaps a commercial is in order?), I HAVE WRITTEN A BOOK, MYSELF, I AM A WRITER, I HAVE WRITTEN A BOOK AND IT'S CALLED—

"'HE GOT WHAT HE WANTED BUT HE LOST WHAT HE HAD'! THAT'S IT! SHUT UP! SHUT UP! SHUT UP! HE GOT WHAT HE WANTED BUT HE LOST

WHAT HE HAD! THE STORY OF MY LIFE. CAN YOU DIG IT? THAT'S MY BOY
LITTLE RICHARD, SURE IS. OO MAH SOUL!"

Little Richard flies back to his chair and slams down into it.
"WHEEEEE-OO! OOO MAH SOUL! OO mah soul . . ."

Little Richard sits with the arbiters of taste, oblivious to their bitter
stares, savoring his moment. He is Little Richard. Who are they? Who
will remember Erich Segal, John Simon, Dick Cavett? Who will care?
Ah, but Little Richard, Little Richard *himself!* There is a man who
matters. He knows how to rock.

A phrase that Little Richard snatched off Erich Segal stays in my
mind: "Never in the history—*in the whole history of art* . . ." And that was
it. Little Richard was the only artist on the set that night, the only one
who disrupted an era, the only one with a claim to immortality. The
one who broke rules, created a form; the one who gave shape to a vitality that wailed silently in each of us until he found a voice for it.

He is the rock, the jive bomber, the savant. "Tutti Frutti" was his
first hit, breaking off the radio in 1955 to shuffle the bland expectations
of white youth; fifteen years later the Weirdo on the *Cavett Show*
reached back for whatever he had left and busted up an argument about
the meaning of art with a spirit that recalled the absurd promise of his
glory days. "I HAVE WRITTEN A BOOK, MYSELF, AND IT'S CALLED . . ."

Listening now to Little Richard, to Elvis, to Jerry Lee Lewis, the
Monotones, the Drifters, Chuck Berry, and dozens of others, I feel a
sense of awe at how fine their music was. I can only marvel at their
arrogance, their humor, their delight. They were so sure of themselves.
They sang as if they knew they were destined not only to survive a few
weeks on the charts but to make history; to displace the dreary events
of the fifties in the memories of those who heard their records; and to
anchor a music that twenty years later would be struggling to keep the
promises they made. Naturally, they sound as if they could care less, so
long as their little black 45's hit number one and made them rich and
famous. But they delivered a new version of America with their music,
and more people than anyone can count are still trying to figure out
how to live in it.

Well, then, this is a book about rock 'n' roll—some of it—and America.
It is not a history, or a purely musical analysis, or a set of personality
profiles. It is an attempt to broaden the context in which the music is
heard; to deal with rock 'n' roll not as youth culture, or counterculture,
but simply as American culture.

The performers that I have written about appeal to me partly because they are more ambitious and because they take more risks than most. They risk artistic disaster (in rock terms, pretentiousness), or the alienation of an audience that can be soothed far more easily than it can be provoked; their ambitions have a good deal to do with Robbie Robertson's statement of his ambitions for the Band: "Music should never be harmless."

What attracts me even more to the Band, Sly Stone, Randy Newman, and Elvis, is that I think these men tend to see themselves as symbolic Americans; I think their music is an attempt to live up to that role. Their records—the Band's *Big Pink*, Sly's *There's a riot goin' on*, a few of Randy Newman's tunes, Elvis Presley's very first Tennessee singles—dramatize a sense of what it is to be an American; what it means, what it's worth, what the stakes of life in America might be. This book, then, is an exploration of a few artists, all of whom seem to me to have found their own voices; it is rooted in the idea that these artists can illuminate those American questions and that the questions can add resonance to their work.

The two men whose tales begin the book—white country hokum singer Harmonica Frank and black Mississippi blues singer Robert Johnson—came and went before the words "rock 'n' roll" had any cultural meaning at all. Both men represent traditions crucial to rock 'n' roll, and both are unique. They worked at the frontiers of the music, and they can give us an idea of what the country has to give the music to work with—a sense of how far the music can go. Harmonica Frank sang with a simple joy and a fool's pride; he caught a spirit the earliest rock 'n' roll mastered effortlessly, a mood the music is always losing and trying to win back. Robert Johnson was very different. He was a brooding man who did his work on the darker side of American life; his songs deal with terrors and fears that few American artists have ever expressed so directly. In this book, Frank and Johnson figure as metaphors more than musical influences. Their chapters are meant to form a backdrop against which the later chapters can take shape, a framework for the images the other artists have made.

The Band, Sly Stone, Randy Newman, and Elvis Presley share unique musical and public personalities, enough ambition to make even their failures interesting, and a lack of critical commentary extensive or committed enough to do their work justice. In their music and in their careers, they share a range and a depth that seem to crystalize naturally in visions and versions of America: its possibilities, limits, openings, traps. Their stories are hardly the whole story, but they can tell us how much the story matters. That is what this book is about.

> ... to be an American (unlike being English or French
> or whatever) is precisely to *imagine* a destiny rather than
> to inherit one; since we have always been, insofar as we
> are Americans at all, inhabitants of myth rather than
> history ...
>
> LESLIE FIEDLER, "Cross the Border, Close the Gap"

It's easy to forget how young this country is; how little distance really separates us from the beginnings of the myths, like that of Lincoln, that still haunt the national imagination. It's easy to forget how much remains to be settled. Since roots are sought out and seized as well as simply accepted, cultural history is never a straight line; along with the artists we care about we fill in the gaps ourselves. When we do, we reclaim, rework, or invent America, or a piece of it, all over again. We make choices (or are caught by the choices others have made) about what is worth keeping and what isn't, trying to create a world where we feel alive, risky, ambitious, and free (or merely safe), dispensing with the rest of the American reality if we can. We make the oldest stories new when we succeed, and we are trapped by the old stories when we fail.

That is as close as I can come to a simple description of what I think the performers in this book have done—but of course what they have done is more complex than that.

In the work of each performer there is an attempt to create oneself, to make a new man out of what is inherited and what is imagined; each individual attempt implies an ideal community, never easy to define, where the new man would be at home, where his work could communicate easily and deeply, where the members of that ideal community would speak as clearly to the artist as he does to them.

The audiences that gather around rock 'n' rollers are as close to that ideal community as anyone gets. The real drama of a performer's career comes when the ideal that one can hear in the music and the audience that the artist really attracts begin to affect each other. No artist can predict, let alone control, what an audience will make of his images; yet no rock 'n' roller can exist without a relationship with an audience, whether it is the imaginary audience one begins with, or the all-too-real confusion of the audience one wins.

The best popular artists create immediate links between people who might have nothing in common but a response to their work, but the best popular artists never stop trying to understand the impact of their work on their audiences. That means their ideal images must change as their understanding grows. One may find horror where one expected only pleasure; one may find that the truth one told has become a lie. If the audience demands only more of what it has already accepted, the artist has a choice. He can move on, and perhaps cut himself off from his audience; if he does, his work will lose all the vitality and strength it had when he knew it mattered to other people. Or the artist can accept the audience's image of himself, pretend that his audience is his shadowy ideal, and lose himself in his audience. Then he will only be able to confirm; he will never be able to create.

The most interesting rock 'n' rollers sometimes go to these extremes; most don't, because these are contradictions they struggle with more than resolve. The tension between community and self-reliance; between distance from one's audience and affection for it; between the shared experience of popular culture and the special talents of artists who both draw on that shared experience and change it—these things are what make rock 'n' roll at its best a democratic art, at least in the American meaning of the word democracy. I think that is true because our democracy is nothing if not a contradiction: the creed of every man and woman for themselves, and thus the loneliness of separation, and thus the yearning for harmony, and for community. The performers in this book, in their different ways, all trace that line.

If they are in touch with their audiences and with the images of community their songs hint at, rock 'n' rollers get to see their myths and parables in action, and ultimately they may even find out what they are worth. When the story is a long one—a career—they find the story coming back to them in pieces, which of course is how it was received.

Here is where a critic might count. Putting the pieces together, trying to understand what is novel and adventurous, what is enervated and complacent, can give us an idea of how much room there is in this musical culture, and in American culture—an idea of what a singer and a band can do with a set of songs mixed into the uncertainty that is the pop audience. Looking back into the corners, we might discover whose America we are living in at any moment, and where it came from. With luck, we might even touch that spirit of place Americans have always sought, and in the seeking have created.

Ancestors

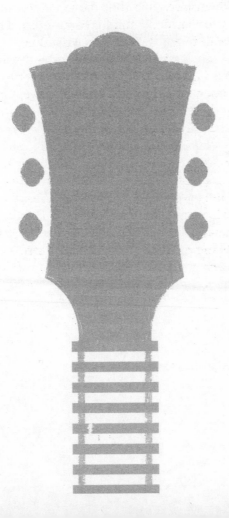

HARMONICA FRANK
1951

In 1951 Sam Phillips was the owner of a shoestring operation that cut records by young black blues singers in Memphis, Tennessee. A few years later he would shape the careers of such founding rockers as Elvis Presley, Carl Perkins, Roy Orbison, and Jerry Lee Lewis; today, he counts his money. But at least one writer has stepped forward to call him "America's Real Uncle Sam," a title he might like.

Phillips was raised on a plantation in Alabama; when he was a little boy an old black man named Uncle Silas Payne would take him aside and sing him the blues, playing Jim to Sam's Huck. In the fifties, bored by the music business and itching for something new, it would be quite natural for Phillips to look for someone to complete a role that was sketched out in his own past. "If I could find a white man who had the Negro sound and the Negro feel," he was saying in those days (as Huck Finn met the Riverboat Gambler), "I could make a billion dollars." Harmonica Frank Floyd, a white man in his early forties, who held a harmonica in one side of his mouth and sang out of the other, was Sam Phillips's first try.

Harmonica Frank was never famous. Born in 1908 in Toccopola, Mississippi, a short ways from Elvis Presley's birthplace in Tupelo, he was a drifter, who left home at the age of fourteen and bummed his way around the country for the next forty years, a man who came up with his own idea of the country's music, black and white.

In 1973, an old man, Frank wrote: "Just one thang I would love to say the first time I played a rock and roll tune on my oath I had never heard no one else do that type therefore I am almost sure I am the originator of rock and roll regardless of what you may have heard at the time I could not read or write music but now I can I am truly a hillbilly from the state of miss but have traveled all over played in old time vaudeville shows medicine shows on the streets barber shops court house lawns auctions sales woodman halls radios television you name it I've played it comedy fire eaters with carnivals tricks or magic so at least I'm an old showman picked cotton picked fruit dug mussel shells in Ark pan some gold in calif one time on KELW in Hollywood with Bustie steel and log cabin wranglers . . .

". . . You see I played rock and roll before I ever heard of elvis presley I saw him in memphis before he ever made a record with sam phillips on north main in memphis tennessee . . ."*

Frank cut many sides in 1951 for Phillips, who leased a few to Chess, the Chicago blues label. They didn't sell. Phillips recorded two more tunes and put them out as a single on his own Sun label in 1954, just before Elvis Presley's first record was released, but the disc went nowhere.

Harmonica Frank's music was a joke, mostly, because there was a little more money for a street-singer who could make people laugh. Yet there was an edge to Frank's music, a fool's resistance to the only role he knew; and that, along with the vitality and invention of the sounds Frank made, was a key to the inarticulate desires shared by Sam Phillips and the impatient new audience whose presence he sensed. "Old Sam Phillips only had one thing to tell me," Harmonica Frank says today. "Said it over and over. 'Gimme something different. Gimme something unique.'"

In his own way Harmonica Frank was as much a maniac as Little Richard. He sounded like a drunken clown who's seen it all, remembers about half of that, and makes the rest up. He put together a style of country rock that did not really find an audience until years later, when Bob Dylan caught the same spirit and much of the sound with "Mixed-Up Confusion," his first single, a lot of the *Freewheelin'* album, and his "I Shall Be Free" songs. In a broader sense Frank can be heard every time a rocker's secret smile breaks open: when Randy Newman sings from the bottom of a bottle, or when Levon Helm gurgles "Hee, hee!" in the middle of "Up on Cripple Creek," the Band's sexiest song.

Harmonica Frank was perhaps the first of the rock 'n' roll vocal contortionists—like Buddy Holly, Clarence "Frogman" Henry, and Bob Dylan—whose mission in life seemed to be the willful destruction of the mainstream tradition of popular singing and the smooth and self-assured way of life it was made to represent. Frank screeched, he bellowed, croaked, cackled, and moaned, carrying his songs and never mind about the tune. He was a noisemaker.

* From a letter Frank wrote to Greg Shaw.

What matters about Frank is the sense of freedom he brought to his music: a good-natured contempt for conventional patterns of life combined with a genius for transforming all that was smug and polite into absurdity. The result was a music of staggering weirdness, dimly anchored by the fatalism of the blues and powered by the pure delight of what was soon to be called rock 'n' roll. Frank wasn't sexy, like the rockabilly singers who were to make Sam Phillips's fortune; he was more like a dirty old man. He was ribald, and he had a flair. "I am," he growled in one of his numbers, "a howling tomcat."

His only Sun single was his best—"The Great Medical Menagerist," a wonderful talking blues, backed by "Rockin' Chair Daddy," a first-rate piece of nonsense that really does set the stage for rock 'n' roll. Here he reaches for falsettos, talks to himself, corrects himself, roaring into town

Rock to Memphis, dance on Main
Up stepped a lady and asked my name
Rockin' chair daddy dont have to work
I told her my name was on the tail of my shirt!

and pounding away to the finish: "Never been to college, never been to school, if you want some rockin' I'm a rockin' fool!"

"The Great Medical Menagerist" is simply a triumph. Probably a miniature autobiography, it is a catalogue of all the prim and decent people Frank made asses of, and of the jobs his fun cost him. The first lines have the perfection of myth:

Ladies and gentlemens, cough white dodgers and
little rabbit twisters, step right around closely,
tell ya all about a wonderful medicine show I
useta work with . . .

"We have Doctor Donicker here with us," he drawls, too sly to believe, "the Great Medical Menagerist . . . *of the world.*" That little pause charges the performance with wit and even menace; Frank sings with a squeak. Frank barely lets on that the menagerie is none other than Doctor Donicker's audience, which is to say, his.

His most compelling record was "Goin' Away Walkin'," one of the sides on Chess. It is a classic country blues, and a kind of final statement. If the form is blues, though, the spirit and the sound come from the high, lonely whine of the white mountain music that goes back to the Revolution. The notes seem to hang in the air like ghosts; the song is bitter, unrepentant, and free. "I ain't gonna get married," Frank Floyd sings. "I ain't gonna settle down. I'm gonna walk this highway, till my whiskers drags the ground."

That was his promise, and he kept it. Of all the characters who populate this book, only Harmonica Frank did more than keep the legend of Huckleberry Finn alive—he lived it out. He showed up, made his records, and lit out for the territory, banging his guitar and blowing his harp, dodging Greyhounds and working the fields, setting himself free from an oppression he never bothered to define.

His humor, his cutting edge, came like Twain's from that part of the American imagination that has always sneered at the limits imposed by manners; the strain that produced both obscenity and the tall tale, two forms of a secret revolt against the Puritans who founded the country and against the authority of their ghosts. It is a revolt against the hopeful morality of Twain's aunts and the tiresomeness of Ben Franklin doing good and being right; a revolt against pomposity, and arrogance.

And this revolt is powerful stuff, after all. How long would Ahab have lasted if he'd been up against a howling weirdo like Harmonica Frank instead of a dumb Christian like Starbuck?

A DIGRESSION THAT MAY PROVE
WORTHWHILE TO THOSE READERS
WHO DO NOT SKIP IT

Our latest Ahab almost had it both ways, because there was a lot of Harmonica Frank in Lyndon B. Johnson, once President of All the People; one of America's secrets is that the dreams of Huck and Ahab are not always very far apart. Both of them embody an impulse to freedom, an escape from restraints and authority that sometimes seems like the only really American story there is. That one figure is passive and benign, the other aggressive and in the end malignant; the one full of humor and regret, and the other cold and determined never to look back; the one as unsure of his own authority as he is of anyone else's, the other fleeing authority only to replace it with his own—all this hides the common bond between the two characters, and suggests how strong would be a figure who could put the two together. For all that is different about Ahab and Huck Finn, they are two American heroes who say, yes, they will go to hell if they have to.

The obsessiveness and the wish for peace of mind that most easily set Ahab and Huck off from each other—on the surface, anyway— are cornerstones of how rock 'n' roll works and what it is for, but we will find the two spirits together more often than not.

LBJ had his year on the road, quitting college and hoboing his way out to California, digging ditches and washing dishes, finally coming home after having gone far enough to say, years later, that any member of his generation that hadn't been a communist or a dropout wasn't worth a damn. Deeply contemptuous of Eastern gentility (and attracted by it too), Johnson coupled a devastating talent for obscenity that no Easterner could match with an image of himself as a latter-day Pecos Bill; the American, Johnson might have been telling us, is alive only as long as he is uncivilized. Thus Johnson carefully received his guests on the toilet—the "donicker"—because it threw them off guard. Bob Dylan was pouting that even the President of the Yew-Nited States had to stand naked, but LBJ was way ahead of him: he forced heads of state to strip for a swim and got the upper hand. He showed his scar and the *New York Review of Books* never forgave him. He told them his name was on the tail of his shirt.

But Johnson's best defense was his verbal obscenity, that side of Huck that Twain left out of the book and kept for himself.

Norman Mailer was the only one of Johnson's adversaries who understood this side of the man, and so he took LBJ on with *Why Are We in Vietnam?* It was the most gloriously obscene book Mailer could write, a book whose hero was in fact a Texas Huck on his way to becoming a Texas Ahab, changing fast from a reckless kid into a killer. The job, Mailer knew, was to find the sources of Johnson's power—not merely his political power, but his personal strength. That meant Mailer had to understand the language LBJ really spoke, and then beat him at his own game. And so the obscenity of Mailer's book, at first so funny, so full of honest rebellion, becomes more and more cruel, until finally it is part and parcel with brutality, and murder.

But Mailer didn't win the fight with Lyndon Johnson. The richest, riskiest passages of his book cannot compare with the off-hand remark Johnson made when he was asked why he had not told the people more about Vietnam: "If you have a mother-in-law with only one eye, and that eye is in the middle of her forehead, you don't keep her in the living room."*

If anything could redeem the arrogant obsessions of the man who introduced us to the obscenity of the burnt baby, it was a style of personal obscenity. This allowed Johnson to transcend, for a time, the

* Cited in David Halberstam, *The Best and the Brightest* (New York: Random House, 1972).

self-righteousness (and righteousness pure and simple) of those who vilified him with every obscenity at *their* command. After all, compared to the crowds who hounded him with their mechanical chants, Lyndon Johnson was a poet.

Perhaps, if the political language of America was as free as its secret language, LBJ could have made King Shit a title to be reckoned with. Perhaps, in the presidential election of our dreams, he could have beaten even Lenny Bruce.

And maybe he would have kept Harmonica Frank on retainer, down there on the LBJ ranch.

Harmonica Frank's music, like LBJ's language, has a spirit that occasionally emerges to redeem those impulses in American life that are cold, bitter, and corrupt—just as that book about a river and a raft was meant to displace Mark Twain's dread of what, hard into the Gilded Age, the country seemed eager to believe it was all about. The idea that the two Americas are separable, I suppose, is the heart of our romanticism.

A good part of the impact of rock 'n' roll had to do with its anachronistic essence, the way it seemed to come out of nowhere— the big surprise that trivialized the events that governed daily life. Rock 'n' roll gave the kids who had seen no alternative but to submit to those events a little room to move. Any musicologist, neatly tracing the development of the music, can tell us that rock 'n' roll did not come out of nowhere. But it sounded as if it did. It was one of those great twists of history that no one anticipated—no one, that is, except a few men like Sam Phillips, who were looking for it, looking for something to break the boredom they felt when they turned on the radio.

Harmonica Frank was part of Phillips's quest for the weird, and weird it had to be if it was to crack the ice that was seeping into Memphis in 1951. When Phillips looked at his town he must have seen the thousands of good country people, the people who worked hard and prayed harder, who had migrated to Memphis after World War II. They wanted a home that was safe, orderly, and respectable, and as far as the old wide-open riverboat town was concerned, they were perfectly satisfied to visit it in a museum. There was a sense that life was set in a pattern; winding down.

"It seemed to me that Negroes were the only ones that had any freshness left in their music," Phillips has said of those days when he was looking for a white man. Maybe it was a white man who sounded like a cross between a barnyard and a minstrel show—Harmonica

Frank, say, maybe a cocky kid, child of those new Memphians, who sang a new kind of blues. Certainly it had to be someone who toyed with race, the deepest source of limits in the South.

The alternative for Phillips, as a record producer, was the white country music of the Carter Family, Jimmie Rodgers, Hank Williams, Patsy Cline. But leaving aside the fact that Phillips was not likely to make a billion dollars on it, there was a problem with that music. It so perfectly expressed the acceptance and fatalism of its audience of poor and striving whites, blending in with their way of life and endlessly reinforcing it, that the music brought all it had to say to the surface, told no secrets, and had no use for novelty. It was conservative in an almost tragic sense, because it carried no hope of change, only respite. By the early fifties this music was all limits. Country music was entertainment that made people feel better, as all true American folk music is before it is anything else, but at its deepest country music was a way of holding on to the values that were jeopardized by a changing postwar America. Country music lacked the confidence to break things open because it was not even sure it could find space to breathe. Hank Williams was eloquent, but his eloquence could not set him free from the life he sang about; he died proving it, overdosing in the back of a car, on his way to one more show.

Phillips had not even worked out the sound he wanted; it was music toward which he was only groping, and most important, ready to accept. Frank Floyd, a white man with some life in him, whose music wasn't exactly blues but was too strange to peddle as anything else, couldn't have sounded less like Hank Williams (though he might have picked up some of his twinkle from Jimmie Rodgers, whom he met on the road years before). Maybe Frank's music was something that would make people take notice if they heard him on the radio, which they rarely did; whatever it was, it was music to turn things around a bit—a clue to what Phillips was looking for, to what made rock 'n' roll happen and to what keeps it alive.

What Phillips was looking for was something that didn't fit, that didn't make sense out of or reflect American life as everyone seemed to understand it, but which made it beside the point, confused things, and affirmed something else. What? The fact that there *was* something else.

What finally arrived was a music of racial confusion, Huck and Jim giving America's aunt the slip, no dead-end "white Negroes" but something new, men like Harmonica Frank and Elvis Presley, whose styles revealed possibilities of American life that were hardly visible anywhere else with an intensity and delight that had no parallel at all.

The music unleashed by Elvis, Little Richard, and the rest of the early rockers was a thrill, and it was also unnerving. I recall hearing Little Richard's "Rip It Up" for the first time, loving the sound but catching the line, "Fool about mah money dont try to save," and thinking, well, that *is* foolish. Had Harmonica Frank's "Rockin' Chair Daddy" been on my radio, I would have been appalled that anyone could skip college *and be proud of it.*

I know that when Elvis was drafted I felt a great relief, because he made demands on me. It was close to what I felt when the politics of the sixties faded—an ambivalent feeling of cowardice and safety. I loved his records—"Hound Dog" was the first I ever owned; "All Shook Up" the first I bought; and "(You're So Square) Baby I Don't Care" (the title may sum up this dilemma) my first private treasure, a record I loved that no one else seemed to like.

But I didn't like—that is, didn't understand—what the Big E did to the girls I went to school with or the way he looked on the cover of his first album, demented, tongue hanging down his chest, lost in some ecstasy completely foreign to me. What was this? Harmonica Frank wasn't the source of this confused delight, not in terms of musicology anyway, because almost no one ever heard him. But he was in on it: he helped Sam Phillips open the doors the King walked through. More than that, he was a harbinger of a certain American spirit that never disappears no matter how smooth things get.

ROBERT JOHNSON
1938

When the train
Left the station
It bad two lights on behind
When the train left the station
It bad two lights on behind
Well, the blue light was my blues
And the red light was my mind.
All my love's
In vain.

ROBERT JOHNSON, "Love in Vain"

You know how it feels—you understand
What it is to be a stranger, in this unfriendly land.

BOBBY "BLUE" BLAND, "Lead Me On"*

It may be that the most interesting American struggle is the struggle to set oneself free from the limits one is born to, and then to learn something of the value of those limits. But on the surface, America takes its energy from the pursuit of happiness; from "a love of physical gratification, the notion of bettering one's condition, the excitement of competition, the charm of anticipated success" (Tocqueville's words); from a memory of open spaces and a belief in open possibilities; from the conviction that you *can* always get what you want, and that even if you can't, you deserve it anyway.

Most of the big shore places were closed now and there were
hardly any lights except the shadowy, moving glow of a ferryboat
across the Sound. And as the moon rose higher the inessential
houses began to melt away until gradually I became aware of the
old island here that had flowered once for Dutch sailors' eyes—a
fresh, green breast of the new world. Its vanished trees, the trees
that had made way for Gatsby's house, had once pandered to the
last and greatest of human dreams; for a transitory enchanted moment man must have held his breath in the presence of this continent, compelled into an aesthetic contemplation he neither
understood nor desired, face to face for the last time in history
with something commensurate to his capacity for wonder.

No one ever captured the promise of American life more beautifully
than Fitzgerald did in that passage. That sense of America is expressed
so completely—by billboards, by our movies, by Chuck Berry's refusal
to put the slightest irony into "Back in the U.S.A.," by the way we try
to live our lives—that we hardly know how to talk about the resentment and fear that lie beneath the promise. To be an American is to feel
the promise as a birthright, and to feel alone and haunted when the
promise fails. No failure in America, whether of love or money, is ever
simple; it is always a kind of betrayal, of a mass of shadowy, shared
hopes.

Within that failure is a very different America; it is an America of
desolation, desolate because it is felt to be out of place, and it is here
that Robert Johnson looked for his images and found them.

Robert Johnson was a Mississippi country blues singer and guitarist,
born in 1911; he was murdered, by a jealous husband, in 1938. He died
in a haze: if some remember that he was stabbed, others say he was
poisoned; that he died on his hands and knees, barking like a dog; that
his death "had something to do with the black arts."

Nearly forty years after his death, Johnson remains the most emotionally committed of all blues singers; for all the distance of his time
and place, Johnson's music draws a natural response from many who
outwardly could not be more different from him. He sang about the
price he had to pay for promises he tried, and failed, to keep; I think the
power of his music comes in part from Johnson's ability to shape the
loneliness and chaos of his betrayal, or ours. Listening to Johnson's
songs, one almost feels at home in that desolate America; one feels able
to take some strength from it, right along with the promises we could
not give up if we wanted to.

Like Charley Patton, Tommy Johnson, Son House, or Skip James—the men who worked out the country blues form in the late teens and twenties—Robert Johnson sang an intense, dramatic music, accompanied only by his guitar. He put down twenty-nine of his songs for the old Vocalion label in 1936 and 1937; his songs lasted, in the work of other bluesmen, long after Johnson was dead, and in the early sixties Johnson's original versions began to appear on albums. Today Johnson's presence can be felt behind many of the best modern guitar players; in a more subtle and vital way, his presence can be felt behind many of our best singers. And a good musical case can be made for Johnson as the first rock 'n' roller of all. His music had a vibrancy and a rhythmic excitement that was new to the country blues. On some tunes—"Walking Blues," "Crossroads Blues," "If I Had Possession Over Judgment Day"—Johnson sounds like a complete rock 'n' roll band, as full as Elvis's first combo or the group Bob Dylan put together for *the John Wesley Harding* sessions, and tougher than either. Johnson's way of looking at things, though, is just beginning to emerge.

I have no stylistic arguments to make about Johnson's influence on the other performers in this book, but I do have a symbolic argument. It seems to me that just as they all have a bit of Harmonica Frank in their souls, the artistic ambitions of the Band, Sly Stone, and Randy Newman can at times be seen as attempts to go part of the way into the America Robert Johnson made his own; that since his journey into that America knew few limits, his music can help us understand the limits of other artists and the risks they take when they try to break through them.

And as for Elvis Presley—well, his first music might be seen as a proud attempt to escape Johnson's America altogether.

Johnson's vision was of a world without salvation, redemption, or rest; it was a vision he resisted, laughed at, to which he gave himself over, but most of all it was a vision he pursued. He walked his road like a failed, orphaned Puritan, looking for women and a good night, but never convinced, whether he found such things or not, that they were really what he wanted, and so framing his tales with old echoes of sin and damnation. There were demons in his songs—blues that walked like a man, the devil, or the two in league with each other— and Johnson was often on good terms with them; his greatest fear seems to have been that his desires were so extreme that he could satisfy them only by becoming a kind of demon himself. When he sings, so slowly, in "Me and the Devil Blues,"

Early this morning
When you knocked upon my door
Early this morning
When you knocked upon my door
I said, Hello, Satan
I believe it's time, to go

the only memory in American art that speaks with the same eerie resignation is that moment when Ahab goes over to the devil-worshiping
Parsees he kept stowed away in the hold of the *Pequod.* That is a remarkable image, but Johnson's images were simply part of daily life.

Me and the devil, was walking side by side
Oooo, me and the devil, was walking side by side
I'm going to beat my woman, until I get satisfied

It may seem strange that in the black country South of the twenties
and thirties, where the leap to grace of gospel music was at the heart of
the community, the blues singers, in a twisted way, were the real Puritans. These men, who had to renounce the blues to be sanctified, who
often sneered at the preachers in their songs, were the ones who really
believed in the devil; they feared the devil most because they knew him
best. They understood, far better than the preachers, why sex was man's
original sin, and they sang about little else.

This side of the blues did not come from Africa, but from the Puritan
revival of the Great Awakening, the revival that spread across the American colonies more than two hundred years ago. It was an explosion of
dread and piety that Southern whites passed onto their slaves and that
blacks ultimately refashioned into their own religion. The blues singers
accepted the dread but refused the piety; they sang as if their understanding of the devil was strong enough to force a belief in God out of their
lives. They lived man's fear of life, and they became artists of the fear.

Or perhaps that is not the truth; perhaps Robert Johnson was very different from other blues singers. For all his clear stylistic ties to Son House,
Skip James, and others, there are ways in which he stands apart. Part of this
is musical—it has to do with the quality of his imagery, his impulse to
drama, the immediacy of his singing and guitar playing—but mostly it is
Johnson's determination to go farther into the blues than anyone else, and
his ability, as an artist, to get there. Anyone from Muddy Waters to Mick
Jagger to Michael Jackson could put across the inspired pornography of
Johnson's "Terraplane [a good, rough car of the thirties] Blues"—

I'm gonna get deep down in this connection
Keep on tangling with your wires
I'm gonna get deep down in this connection
Keep on tangling with your wires
And when I mash down on your little starter—
Then your spark gonna give me fire

—but as for "Stones in My Passway," which was the other side of sex, no one has been fool enough to try.

Few men could brag like Robert Johnson: "Stuff I got'll bust your brains out, baby," he sang in "Stop Breakin' Down Blues," "it'll make you lose your mind." Women crowded around him at the back country juke joints to find out if it was true, and no doubt it often was. But such tunes gave way to songs like "Phonograph Blues," where Johnson sings, with far too much emotion it seems, about his broken record player. "What evil have I done . . . what evil has the poor girl heard." That one line shows us how far he is trying to go.

The poor girl is the phonograph, softly personified; she refuses to play Johnson's wicked records and breaks down. With a blazing insistence, Johnson intensifies his personification, unveils his metaphors. At once, you see him struggling with his machine, and in bed with his girl. The records are his sins; the phonograph his penis. The song ends as a confession that the sins his records embody have made him impotent.

What Johnson found on his road was mostly this: ". . . the sense that life is essentially a cheat and its conditions are those of defeat, and that the redeeming satisfactions are not 'happiness and pleasure' but the deeper satisfactions that come out of struggle." So wrote Fitzgerald to his daughter, about what he had found in Lincoln and Shakespeare and "all great careers." His words make good company for Stanley Booth's: "The dedication [the blues] demands lies beyond technique; it makes being a blues player something like being a priest. Virtuosity in playing blues licks is like virtuosity in celebrating the Mass, it is empty, it means nothing. Skill is a necessity, but a true blues player's virtue lies in his acceptance of his life, a life for which he is only partly responsible. When Bukka White sings a song he wrote during his years on Parchman Prison Farm, 'I wonder how long, till I can change my clothes,' he is celebrating, honestly and humbly, his life."

When acceptance and celebration mean the same thing, or when the two words must fill the same space in the mind at once, we can begin to grasp the tension and the passion of Robert Johnson's music— because when one accepts one's life by celebrating it, one also asks for something more. In Johnson's blues the singer's acceptance is profound, because he knows, and makes us see, that his celebration is also a revolt, and that the revolt will fail, because his images cannot deny the struggles they are meant to master.

> It is obvious that man dwells in a splendid universe, a magnificent expanse of earth and sky and heavens, which manifestly is built upon a majestic structure, maintains some mighty design, though man himself cannot grasp it. Yet for him it is not a pleasant or satisfying world. In his few moments of respite from labor or from his enemies, he dreams that this very universe might indeed be perfect, its laws operating just as now they seem to do, and yet he and it somehow be in full accord. The very ease with which he can frame this image to himself makes the reality all the more mocking ... It is only too clear that man is not at home in this universe, and yet he is not good enough to deserve a better.
>
> PERRY MILLER, on the Puritan view of the world*

When Robert Johnson traveled through the Deep South, over to Texas and back to Memphis, into the Midwest and up to Chicago, across the border to Canada and back to Detroit to sing spirituals on the radio, to New York City (the sight of this primitive blues singer gazing up at the lights of Times Square is not only banal, it is bizarre), to the South again, he was tracing not only the miles on the road but the strength of its image. It was the ultimate American image of flight from homelessness, and he always looked back: the women he left, or who left him, chased him through the gloomy reveries of his songs, just as one of them eventually caught up. Like a good American, Johnson lived for the moment and died for the past.

Sometimes the road was just the best place to be, free and friendly, a good way to put in the time. In "From Four Until Late" there is even a girl waiting at the other end.

> *When I leave this town,*
> *I'm gonna bid you fair, farewell*
> *When I leave this town,*
> *I'm gonna bid you fair, farewell*
> *And when I return again,*
> *You'll have a great long story to tell.*

* From *The New England Mind: The Seventeenth Century* (Boston: Beacon Press, 1968).

There is the grace and bitterness of "Rambling on My Mind" (which Johnson played with his walking bass figure that was to define Chicago blues, making the song sound just like a man pushing himself down the highway, half against his will); the slow sexual menace of "Traveling Riverside Blues"; the nightmare of "Crossroads," where Johnson is sure to be caught by whites after dark and does not know which way to run; there is always one more "strange man's town," one more girl, one more drink; there is the last word of "Hellhound on My Trail."

> *I got to keep moving, I got to keep moving*
> *Blues falling down like hail, blues falling*
> *down like hail*
> *Blues falling down like hail, blues falling down*
> *like hail*
> *And the days keep on 'minding me*
> *There's a hellhound on my trail*
> *Hellhound on my trail, hellhound on my trail*

It wasn't the open road, to say the least; more like Ishmael falling in behind funeral processions, because they made him feel more alive, and on good terms with death. You could imagine what the two travelers would have to say to each other: *This is no way for a young man to act!*

That spirit gives us what might be Johnson's most American image, these lines from "Me and the Devil Blues"—most American because, as a good, defiant laugh at fate, they are vital not only beneath the surface of American life, but on it. They are often called in as proof of Johnson's despair, and they are part of it, but also his most satisfied lines, a proud epitaph:

> *You may bury my body, down by the highway side*
> *Babe, I don't care where you bury my body when*
> *I'm dead and gone*
> *You may bury my body, ooooo, down by the*
> *highway side*
> *So my old evil spirit*
> *Can get a Greyhound bus, and ride.*

Robert Johnson had a beautiful high voice, a tragic voice when he meant it to be. In "Walking Blues" he wakes up to find that his woman has left him without even his shoes. He is plainly in awe of this woman ("Well!" he sings to himself, "she's got Elgin movements, from her head down to her toes . . . From her head down to her toes!"); when he says the worried blues are the worst he ever had, he's still too full of admiration for that woman to make you believe him.

So he will sing, with a distracted, comic determination:

Lord I—feel like blowin' my, old lonesome home
Got up this morning, my little Bernice was gone
Now, up this light, ooooo, my lonesome home

and then with utter grace his voice rises, almost fades away, and there is a soft moan that could echo in your heart for a long time, a melancholy too strong to step around:

Well, I got up this morning . . . all I had, was gone.

Johnson was in his mid-twenties when he sang these songs (Don Law, the great recording engineer who handled the sessions, thought of him as a teenager). Johnson didn't have the worldly dignity of Son House or Skip James. Neither House nor James ever sounds confused; they sing as men who live deeply, but within limits. In Johnson's voice, there is sometimes an element of shock—less a matter of lost innocence than of innocence willfully given up and remembered anyway.

Johnson seemed to take more pure pleasure out of making music than any other Delta singer; there is rock 'n' roll fun in his guitar playing you can hear anytime you like. He was, I think, working out a whole new aesthetic that rock 'n' roll eventually completed: a loud, piercing music driven by massive rhythms and a beat so strong that involvement was effortless and automatic. Yet Johnson also had more to say than other singers. His music was half seduction, half assault, meant to drive his words home with enormous force. His technique was not only more advanced, it was deeper, because it had to be.

Only his weakest songs move on an even keel; the greatest shudder and break and explode, or twist slowly around quietly shaking strings into a kind of suspension, until Johnson has created a mood so delicate and bleak one feels he cannot possibly get out of his song alive. Johnson's most distinctive performances have the tension that comes when almost everything is implied, when the worst secrets are hiding in plain talk. With "Come on in My Kitchen" Johnson plays out the sound of a cold wind on his guitar, and his voice rides it; there is a stillness in the music. The loneliness is overpowering and the feeling of desolation is absolute. The most prosaic lines take on the shape of pure terror.

When a woman gets in trouble
Everybody throws her down
Looking for her good friend
None can be found.
You better come on, in my kitchen
There's going to be rain in our door.

It was songs like this one—the combination of voice, guitar, words, and the mythical authority that comes when an artist confirms his work with his life—that made Eric Clapton see Johnson's ghost, and his own, in Jimi Hendrix's death. "Eric wanted to do a Robert Johnson," one of Clapton's friends said when Hendrix died. "A few good years, and go."

Johnson's music is so strong that in certain moods it can make you feel that he is giving you more than you could have bargained for—that there is a place for you in these lines of his: "She's got a mortgage on my body, a lien on my soul." It is no exaggeration to say that Johnson changed the lives of people as distant from each other as Muddy Waters, who began his career as a devoted imitator; Dion, who made his way through the terrors of his heroin habit with Johnson's songs for company; and myself. After hearing Johnson's music for the first time—listening to that blasted and somehow friendly voice, the shivery guitar, hearing a score of lines that fit as easily and memorably into each day as Dylan's had—I could listen to nothing else for months. Johnson's music changed the way the world looked to me. Over the years, what had been a fascination with a bundle of ideas and dreams from old American novels and texts—a fascination with the foreboding and gentleness that is linked in the most interesting Americans—seemed to find a voice in Johnson's songs. It was the intensity of his music that changed fascination into commitment and a bundle of ideas into what must serve as a point of view.

But commitment is a tricky, Faustian word. When he first appeared Robert couldn't play guitar to save his life, Son House told Pete Welding; Johnson hung out with the older bluesmen, pestering them for a chance to try his hand, and after a time he went away. It was months later, on a Saturday night, when they saw him again, still looking to be heard. They tried to put him off, but he persisted; finally, they let him play for a lull and left him alone with the tables and chairs.

Outside, taking the air, House and the others heard a loud, devastating music of a brilliance and purity beyond anything in the memory of the Mississippi Delta. Johnson had nothing more to learn from *them*.

"He sold his soul to the devil in exchange for learning to play like that," House said.

*   *   *

Well, they tell a lot of stories about Robert Johnson. You could call that one superstition, or you could call it sour grapes. Thinking of voodoo and gypsy women in the back country, or of the black man who used to walk the streets of Harlem with a briefcase full of contracts and a wallet full of cash, buying up souls at $100 a throw, you could even take it literally.

If there were nothing else, the magic of Johnson's guitar would be enough to make that last crazy interpretation credible. But in a way that cannot be denied, selling his soul and trying to win it back are what Johnson's bravest songs are all about, and anyone who wants to come to grips with his music probably ought to entertain Son House's possibility. I have the feeling, at times, that the reason Johnson has remained so elusive is that no one has been willing to take him at his word.

Let us say that Johnson sought out one of the Mississippi Delta devil-men, or one of the devil-women, and tried to sell his soul in exchange for the music he heard but could not make. Let us say he did this because he wanted to attract women; because he wanted to be treated with the kind of awe that is in Son House's voice when he speaks of Robert Johnson and the devil; because music brought him a fierce joy, made him feel alive like nothing else in the world. Or let us say that the idea of the devil gave Johnson a way of understanding the fears that overshadowed him; that even if no deal was made, no promises passing from one to another, Johnson believed that his desires and his crimes were simple proof of a consummation quite beyond his power to control; that the image of the devil appealed to Johnson when he recognized (singing, "I mistreated my baby, but I can't see no reason why") that his soul was not his own, and, looking at the disasters of his life and the evil of the world, drew the one conclusion as to whom it did belong.

Blues grew out of the need to live in the brutal world that stood ready in ambush the moment one walked out of the church. Unlike gospel, blues was not a music of transcendence; its equivalent to God's Grace was sex and love. Blues made the terrors of the world easier to endure, but blues also made those terrors more real. For a man like Johnson, the promises of the church faded; they could be remembered— as one sang church songs; perhaps even when one prayed, when one was too scared not to—but those promises could not be lived. Once past some unmarked border, one could not go back. The weight of Johnson's blues was strong enough to make salvation a joke; the best he could do was cry for its beautiful lie. "You run without moving from a terror in which you cannot believe," William Faulkner wrote in one of his books about the landscape he shared with Robert Johnson, just about the time Johnson was making his first records, "toward a safety in which you have no faith."

We comfort ourselves that we do not believe in the devil, but we run anyway; we run from and straight into the satanic images that press against the surface of American life. I think of Robert Mitchum, the mad preacher in *Night of the Hunter*, with LOVE tatooed between the knuckles of his right hand, HATE tatooed between the knuckles of his left—and he seems, again, like the legacy of the men who began the American experience as a struggle between God and the devil, the legacy of a Puritan weirdness, something that those who came after have been left to live out.

The dreams and fears of the Puritans, those gloomy old men, are at the source of our attempts to make sense out of the contradictions between the American idea of paradise and the doomed facts of our history; they emerge when "solving problems" is not good enough or even the point, when the hardest task is not to denounce evil, but to see it.

Unlike Fitzgerald's Dutch sailors, the Puritans did not take their dreams from the land; they brought them along. They meant to build a community of piety and harmony, what their leader, John Winthrop, called "a city on a hill"—an idea, in its many forms, that we have never gotten over, nothing less than America as the light of the world. They had a driving need to go to extremes, as if they could master God and the devil if only they could think hard enough; that, and a profound inability to make peace with the world as they found it. They failed their dreams, and their community shattered. "This land," Winthrop wrote before he died, "grows weary of her inhabitants."

The Puritans came here with a Utopian vision they could not maintain; their idea was to do God's work, and they knew that if they failed, it would mean that their work had been the devil's. As they panicked at their failures, the devil was all they saw. Their witch trials were a decadent version of their America—shlock, as it were, but their biggest hit.

Their initial attempts to shape America, and their failures, set the devil loose in the land—as a symbol of uncontrollable malevolence, of betrayal, of disaster, of punishment. Just as the Puritans' failures and compromises anticipated our own, there is something in us that responds, not always quite consciously, to the original image of American failure—to the terror that image can speak for.

If the presence of that image has been felt from the Puritans' day to ours, it is, perhaps, because that image is a way of getting to the idea of an American curse. The image of the devil is a way of comprehending the distance between Fitzgerald's shining image of American possibility and his verdict on its result; it is a way of touching the sense (there in Fitzgerald's beautiful image of America as "an aesthetic contemplation [man] neither understood nor desired") that America is a trap: that its promises and dreams, all mixed up as love and politics and landscape, are too much to live up to and too much to escape. It is as if to be an American means to ask for too much—not even knowing one is asking for too much—and to trade away one's life to get it, whatever it is; as if this is what makes America special, vital, murderous, and noble.

The Puritan devil endures as a face on the betrayal of the promises we mean to keep; the Puritan commitment to extremes, the willingness to live in a world where the claims of God and the devil are truly at odds, has lasted as a means to comprehend the depths of the promise and the failure alike.

This world may have survived most completely in the tension between the blues and the black church. Robert Johnson inherited this world, and, as a black blues singer, he made a new kind of music out of it. The image of the devil was played out within the matrix of Johnson's struggle with women, and with himself. It was a drama of sex, shot through with acts of violence and tenderness; with desires that no one could satisfy; with crimes that could not be explained; with punishments that could not be escaped.

The most acute Americans, in the steps of the old Puritans, have been suspicious, probing people, looking for signs of evil and grace, of salvation and damnation, behind every natural fact. Robert Johnson lived with this kind of intensity, and he asked old questions: What is our place in the world? Why are we cursed with the power to want more than we can have? What separates men and women from each other? Why must we suffer guilt not only for our sins, but for the failure of our best hopes?

This is a state of mind that gives no rest at all. Even if you have sold your soul to the devil, you cannot rest with him; you have to keep looking, because there is never any end to the price you have to pay, nor any certainty as to the form that price will take. Every event thus becomes charged with meaning, but the meaning is never complete. The moments of perfect pleasure in Johnson's songs, and the beauty of those songs, remind one that it is not the simple presence of evil that is unbearable; what is unbearable is the impossibility of reconciling the facts of evil with the beauty of the world.

This shadow America comes to a verge with "Stones in My Passway." It is the most terrifying of Johnson's songs, perhaps because his desolation can no longer be contained in the old, inherited image of the devil—those lines from "Me and the Devil Blues" seem suddenly almost safe, comfortable, the claims of a man who thinks he knows where he stands. In "Stones in My Passway" terror is too ubiquitous to have a face: it is formless, elusive, overpowering.

A few months before he recorded "Stones in My Passway," Johnson sang these astonishing lines:

> *If I bad possession, over Judgment Day*
> *If I bad possession, over Judgment Day*
> *Then the woman I'm lovin', wouldn't have no right to pray*

No right to pray—that is a staggering demand to make on life; it is to ask for the same power the devil has over one who has sold his soul. "Stones in My Passway" is the song of a man who once asked for power over other souls, but who now testifies that he has lost power over his own body, and who might well see that disaster as a fitting symbol of the loss of *his* soul. There is no way to "know"; there are no Gothic images in this song. The idea simply takes shape as the song draws in all the echoes of hellhounds, devils, the weirdness of blues walking like a man, draws in those images and goes past them. If those images were a means to expression, they are no longer necessary—they are no longer good enough.

Because not even his body is his own, Johnson cannot satisfy his woman. Because that matters more than anything else in his life, that fact, as a symbol, expands to create more facts, more symbols. Finally, with stones in every passway and no way clear, there is a way in which the singer's life is resolved: he has seen all around his life, for as long as he can hold onto the image. Because the stakes of the song are so high, every word and every note is fashioned to carry the weight of what Johnson wants to say. The four knife-stroke notes that open the song are like a warning; the song is stark. It communicates so directly any distance between the singer and the listener is smashed.

> *I got stones in my passway*
> *And my road seems dark as night*
> *I got stones in my passway*
> *And my road seems dark as night*
> *I got pains in my heart—*
> *They have taken my appetite.*

The tune darts forward on a high, almost martial rhythm; one shattering note freezes the music and the image just before the last line of each verse. "Shock technique," a friend called it.

My enemies have betrayed me
Have overtaken poor Bob at last
My enemies have betrayed me
Have overtaken poor Bob at last
And there's one thing certain—
They have stones all in my passway.

If the passway is in his body, immediately it must stand for every invisible trap on the road; if the stones are at first the most direct, physical description of the sexual collapse that has made Johnson afraid to look his lover in the face, those stones must be made to stand for the men who will soon block the way to his lover's door.

I'm crying please—please, let us be friends
And when you hear me howlin' in my passway, rider
PLEASE *open your door and let me in.*

The song is enormous. I cannot put it any other way. The image of the words is subsumed into Johnson's singing, his guitar, into the eerie, inevitable loudness of the song. The music has its claims to make: no matter how low you set the volume, the music creeps up louder, demanding, and the only way to quiet this music is to shut it off.

I got three lanes to truck on
Boys, please don't block my road
I got three lanes to truck on
Boys, please don't block my road
But I been 'shamed by my rider—
I'm booked and I got to go.

"Stones in My Passway," like a few others of Johnson's songs—"Love in Vain," "Come on in My Kitchen," "Me and the Devil Blues"—is a two-minute image of doom that has the power to make doom a fact. One hardly knows if it is the clarity of the world Johnson revealed in his music, or Johnson's resilience as he made his way through that world that is most exhilarating; but that so many people—people who have never left the American mainstream that Johnson was never part of—respond to his music is perhaps not such a mystery. Because of our faith in promises, the true terror of doom is in the American's natural inability to believe doom is real, even when he knows it has taken over his life. When there is no way to speak of terror and no one to listen if there were, Johnson's songs matter.

What Robert Johnson had to do with other bluesmen of his time is interesting to me, but not nearly so interesting as what Johnson has to do with those discovering him now, without warning and on their own. The original context of Johnson's story is important, and it is where his story is usually placed; but a critic's job is not only to define the context of an artist's work but to expand that context, and it seems more important to me that Johnson's music is vital enough to enter other contexts and create all over again. Off in the Netherlands to teach college, my friend Langdon Winner wrote back:

> . . . the truth of the matter is that in my first months here I found out a lot more about America than I did about Holland. Hundreds of things which are second nature to us just do not play a part here. Dissatisfaction, for example. Dutch musicians know the techniques pioneered by America's black masters. But they are not interested in extremes of rage, ecstasy, dissipation, or religious enlightenment. And this sums up the place: While jazz has long been popular in the Netherlands, *the blues has never arrived.* How can you understand Aeschylus, Augustine, Shakespeare, and Nietzsche if you can't listen to Robert Johnson in your own time?

Which is to say that if Robert Johnson is an ancestor, or even a ghost, he is really a contemporary.

It is the inescapable pull of Johnson's music that gives us Mick Jagger singing "Love in Vain" in the middle of a rock 'n' roll show—and a rock 'n' roll show is a celebration that is rooted in Little Richard's kind of revolt, or in Harmonica Frank's, far more than it is in Robert Johnson's. Robert Johnson is a presence these days, as rock 'n' roll fans find the world less of a home than it used to be, and yet accept more and more their inability to do anything about their displacement; Johnson is a sort of invisible pop star. He has caught up with us.

The music that is animated by Robert Johnson today is not really found in new rock 'n' roll versions of his songs; Johnson's spirit is not so easy to capture. All of Eric Clapton's love for Johnson's music came to bear not when Clapton sang Johnson's songs, but when, once Johnson's music became part of who Clapton was, Clapton came closest to himself: in the passion of "Layla" and "Any Day." Finally, after years of practice and imitation, Johnson's sound was Clapton's sound: there was no way to separate the two men, nor any need to. And perhaps to keep the story straight, there is, in "Layla," one lost echo buried under Clapton's screams and who knows how many guitars: "Please don't say / You'll never find a way / And tell me, all my love's in vain."

This music sounds like real Delta blues to me, forty years after: Duane Allman's solos on Boz Scaggs's "Loan Me a Dime"; Sly Stone's "Thank you for talkin' to me Africa"; Randy Newman's "God's Song"; much of the Rolling Stones' music from *Let It Bleed* to *Exile on Main Street*; Bob Dylan's "All Along the Watchtower"; Eric Clapton's "Layla." If someone were to ask me where Johnson's spirit had found a home, I would play these songs.

All the beauty of the world and all the terror of losing it is there in Eric Clapton's rock 'n' roll; Robert Johnson's music is proof that beauty can be wrung from the terror itself. When Johnson sang his darkest songs, terror was a fact, beauty only a glimmer; but that glimmer, and its dying away, lie beneath everything else, beneath all the images that hit home and make a home. Our culture finds its tension and its life within the borders of the glimmer and the dying away, in attempts to come to terms with the betrayal without giving up on the promise. And so at the borders of Elvis Presley's delight, of his fine young hold on freedom, there is, in his "Peace in the Valley," a touch of fear, of that old weirdness:

> *And I'll be changed*
> *Changed from this creature*
> *That I am**

And at another frontier there is Robert Johnson, pausing for a moment in "Hellhound on My Trail," frightened, running down his road, but glancing over his shoulder with a smile:

> *If today was Christmas Eve, if today was Christmas Eve*
> *And tomorrow was Christmas Day*
> *If today was Christmas Eve*
> *And tomorrow was Christmas Day*
> *Aw, wouldn't we have a time, baby?*

---

* Copyright 1939 by Hill and Range Songs, Inc. Copyright renewed 1966 and assigned to Hill and Range Songs, Inc. Used by permission.

Inheritors

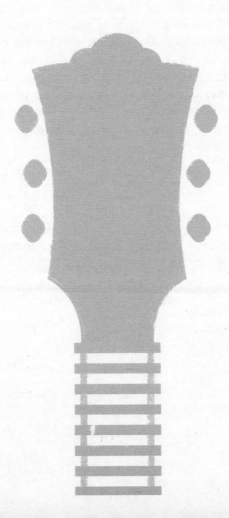

THE BAND

Pilgrims' Progress

The Band—four Canadian rockers held together by an Arkansas drummer—staked their claim to an American story from the beginning. The story had its veils, but the fact of the story was plain. "This is *it*," my editor Marvin Garson said in the spring of 1969, as he sent me off to cover the Band's national debut in San Francisco. "This is when we find out if there are still open spaces out there."

Marvin was a New Yorker; living in California sometimes made him talk like Natty Bumppo, but his words were accurate. By out there he meant right here, and he was talking about the Band because it was obvious they were committed to the very idea of America: complicated, dangerous, and alive.

Their music gave us a sure sense that the country was richer than we had guessed; that it had possibilities we were only beginning to perceive. In the unique blend of instruments and good rhythms, in the shared and yet completely individual vocals, in the half-lost phrases and buried lyrics, there was an ambiguity that opened up the world with real force. The songs captured the yearning for home and the fact of displacement that ruled our lives; we thought that the Band's music was the most natural parallel to our hopes, ambitions, and doubts, and we were right to think so. Flowing through their music were spirits of acceptance and desire, rebellion and awe, raw excitement, good sex, open humor, a magic feel for history—a determination to find plurality and drama in an America we had met too often as a monolith.

The Band's music made us feel part of their adventure; we knew that we would win if they succeeded and lose if they failed. That was what Marvin Garson meant. It was a good feeling.

CROSSING THE BORDER

When the Band surfaced in 1968 with *Music from Big Pink* they had been playing rock 'n' roll music for more than half as long as there had been such a thing. What mattered most, though, was that they had put in their years together, as a group. A rock 'n' roll group is a banding together of individuals for the purpose of achieving something that none of them can get on their own: money, fame, the right sound, something less easy to put into words. But what begins as a marriage of convenience sometimes takes on its own value. An identity comes into being that transcends individual personalities, but does not obscure them—in fact, it is the group, sometimes only the group, that makes individuals visible. The Beatles, after all, were the most satisfying and complex testament to the limits of self-reliance most of us have ever known; they were also proof of the limits of a common bond. Groups are images of community. That the Band had created itself through the years, and had come to our attention bent on demonstrating just what their years together had been worth, was perhaps the most potent image of all.

Like John Lennon and Paul McCartney, Booker T. & the MG's, Bob Dylan, and a few thousand others, drummer Levon Helm, guitarist Robbie Robertson, piano man Richard Manuel, bass Rick Danko, and organist Garth Hudson started out in the high school bands that appeared overnight in the flash of the first great rock explosion.* Still in their teens in the early sixties, they came together in Toronto as the Hawks, back-up band for Ronnie Hawkins, a small-time Arkansas rockabilly singer who had brought Levon north with him around 1958.

Hawkins, though he brushed the charts twice in 1959—with a Chuck Berry remake and an R&B cover—was too little and too late to pass for the next Elvis Presley; his task was to keep himself alive. In the U.S.A. he was one of too many; in Canada, where authentic American rockers were a solid commercial rarity, Hawkins could bill himself "The King of Rockabilly" and get away with it. Sometimes he liked to call himself "Mr. Dynamo." It was, as so many have testified, better than working.

Ronnie Hawkins was a windjammer in the grand style. He claimed to have picked cotton right alongside Bo Diddley; to have made the first

---

* The names of those bands are too good to leave out: the Robots, the Consuls, Thumper and the Trombones (Robbie); Paul London and the Capers, later changed to "Kapers" (Hudson); the Rockin' Revols (Manuel); and the Jungle Bush Beaters. The last was Levon's original Marvel, Arkansas, outfit—and as the soubriquet of a bunch of Southern white boys chasing the blues across the tracks, it's rock 'n' roll poetry if anything is.

rock 'n' roll record of all, back in 1952 (no one, so far as I know, has ever found it, but Hawkins, keeping his story straight, says it was the first version of "Bo Diddley"); to have passed up a chance for stardom when he graciously offered the sure-hit "It's Only Make Believe" to his old pal Conway Twitty; to know more back roads, back rooms, and backsides than any man from Newark to Mexicali. His singing was only fair, though in one sense it was quite distinctive: Hawkins is the only man I have ever heard who can make a nice sexy song like "My Gal Is Red Hot" sound sordid. "None of us rock 'n' rollers could understand all that fuss about Jerry Lee Lewis marrying a thirteen-year-old girl," he is reputed to have said. "All us Southern cats knew she was only twelve."

Hawkins was no fool; he needed a band to carry him, and when the razorbacks he had imported began to scatter, he and Levon recruited the Canadian kids one by one. As characters in the classic bildungsroman that tells of the wise old philosopher who initiates innocent young boys into the mysteries of life, Hawkins and his Hawks played their way through the collected works of Gene Vincent, Chuck Berry, Larry Williams, Fats Domino, and the rest, filling out their shows with tunes about the whores they met.

Robbie wrote his first song, "Hey Boba Lu," which Hawkins recorded; on stage, Manuel and Levon handled most of the singing. "When Ronnie sang," Robbie remembers fondly, "we had to count out the beat for him. It was, 'Oh, Carol—one, two, three, *four*— Don't let him steal . . .'"

The Hawks were looking for their music. When Robbie was fifteen Levon took him into the South, with hopes of putting the Bush Beaters back together. That came to nothing, but the trip changed something in Robertson; just what it was is elusive even to him, but listening to the man retrace his steps, one gets the sense that an enormous creative ambition was set free when he discovered that the place that had put magic into his life was real. There had been the music, of course—rock 'n' roll from Memphis, rock 'n' roll from New Orleans—and Robbie already had the beginnings of his idea that the land makes the music. But there were also the family histories and local legends Levon had told him; the inexplicably exciting foreign names, suddenly right there on billboards and coming over the drifting Southern radio dial in between the fiddles and sermons, names like "Dr. Pepper" and "Ko-Ko bars"; there was the fact of seeing people, black and white, living out the sounds he had heard on his records. The reality only made the magic that much more fierce. Here was a different world, with more on its surface than Canada had in its abyss; you could chase that world, listen to it, learn from it. Perhaps you could even join it.

Before too long, Howlin' Wolf, Junior Parker, Bobby Bland, and other bluesmen were climbing the Hawks' charts, and Hawkins' repertoire no longer seemed so romantic. Robbie had tried to get Jimmy Ray Paulman, Hawkins' original guitarist, to teach him how to play—Paulman, with a good eye for the competition, told the kid to get lost—but now Robbie was in a position to feel the competition himself. For a white boy, that meant James Burton, star of "Suzie Q" and hero of Ricky Nelson's hits; Roy Buchanan, the lonesome master of the blues; Lonnie Mack, who sang from the church and played straight from the alley. To live up to all that Levon had shown him, and to satisfy his own brash self, Robbie had to be better than any of them.

He was listening hard to Wolf's guitarists: Willie Johnson on "How Many More Years" and Hubert Sumlin on "Wang-Dang-Doodle." Johnson and Sumlin had created a guitar style so chaotic and fast it demanded a rhythm section as quick as it was hard just to keep a performance from flying to pieces. There was none of the polite formality of a band setting up a solo, taking turns; there was no showcasing. Wolf's best records came on like three-minute race riots. The drums, bass, piano, and harp converged on the beat, hammering, shoving; for a moment they let the beat take the song, let you think you had the sides sorted out and the picture clear, and then the guitarist leaped in, heaved himself through the crowd like a tornado, and the crowd paid no attention and went right on fighting. This was the sound the Hawks were after, and on an unbelievably demonic recording of Bo Diddley's "Who Do You Love," they got it. Hawkins' vocal (his only real claim to greatness, but it will do) was one ghastly scream; Robbie fought back with a crazed, jagged solo that to this day has never been matched. It is still possibly the most menacing piece of rock 'n' roll ever made.

The Hawks, however, did not need their front man—fooling around in the studio after the dry sessions for Hawkins' *Mojo Man* LP, Levon took over the mike for Bobby Bland's hard-rocking "Further on Up the Road" and Muddy Waters's slow and sexy "Nineteen Years Old," and the group left behind the most exciting white blues recordings since the early days of Elvis Presley. "White blues" doesn't really describe the music—though they were white, and the songs were blues—Levon's singing and Robbie's guitar playing fell into no genre. This wasn't like the early Paul Butterfield Band, or John Hammond, Jr., to be judged on how precisely the white music matched the sound of the black idols. The Hawks were a long way past questions of technique; the problem was to find out what they could do with that technique.

Unfortunately, they were making music in a vacuum; in America, those great sides were never released, not that they would have fit the commercial demands of the radio anyway. Like most of the best bands forming at the time, the Hawks were a walking jukebox that played only other people's hits, and the jukebox was a few years out of date to boot. Over in Hamburg, the Beatles too were jamming out five sets a night, as John Lennon shouted "Dizzy Miss Lizzy" with a toilet seat around his neck; Van Morrison and the Monarchs were peddling their Ray Charles imitations to homesick GIs in Germany; the Rolling Stones were up all night trying to figure out how Sonny Boy made his harp sound like that; Elvis was having fun in Acapulco; and Creedence Clearwater, calling themselves the Blue Velvets, were scuffling up and down the road from Sacramento to San Jose, fighting a battle of the bands with Peter Wheat and the Breadmen while John Fogerty scribbled the bayou fantasies that would lift him out of a world he hated. In the early sixties, rock 'n' roll was a waiting game.

After a year or two apprenticed to Hawkins, Levon led the Band out on their own as Levon and the Hawks, sometimes as the Crackers, sometimes as the Canadian Squires. They traveled Hawkins' circuit of honky-tonks and dives—a tough, loud band that played, as Garth Hudson once put it, "for pimps, whores, rounders, and flakeouts." "We had one thing on our minds," Robbie says. "Stomp."

They cut occasional 45's, whenever they found someone to let them into a studio: "Go Go Liza Jane," the old folk song; a good hard punchout of a record called "Leave Me Alone"; an odd, churchy paean to "this righteous land" with the even odder title of "The Stones I Throw (Will Free All Men)"—crude stuff, but hopeful. "Down in L.A., you know they got everything," Levon sang on "Uh-Uh-Uh." "Moved out there, became the new Southern King."

This was not earthshaking. By 1965 the Beatles and the Stones were running the scene, and from their name to their nightclubs, the Hawks were an anachronism. Still, they built up a vague word-of-mouth reputation on the East Coast; eager to take on the world with a new sound and perhaps feeling a bit anachronistic himself, Bob Dylan got in touch. The combination clicked: suddenly Dylan was singing like a demon, and the Hawks—never introduced, always anonymous—twisted around him with a noise that not even they could have been prepared for. The Hawks backed Dylan through the rough, mean tours of 1965 and 1966, and the Stones sat in the audience. The Hawks left the stage as the best band in the world.

Levon, a pro when Bob Dylan was still hard at work scaring his high school principal, did not go along; the Hawks, after all, had been *his* band.

But when the Canadians followed Dylan to Woodstock once the tours were over, Levon joined up again, and the Band made a second founding.

Out of all this they fashioned a music that sounded not at all like what had preceded it; they seemed to draw less on their old music than on the friendship they had discovered making it. Calling themselves "The Band" was proof of their arrogance, but there was a depth of experience in their music that could not be denied, and the fans they won had no wish to deny it. It was, in fact, precisely what a lot of people were looking for.

In 1968 rock 'n' roll was coming out of its San Francisco period— psychedelic music, rebel energy, Father-Yes-Son-I-Want-To-Kill-You, drum solos, drug visions, bright and happy dancing crowds—a fabulous euphoria in the middle of a war, innocence and optimism running straight into the election of Richard Nixon. It had been a fine time, with many chances taken and many chances blown, but it was over, it was soft underneath the flash and it had exhausted itself. There was a peculiar emptiness in the air, and in the music; *Sgt. Pepper*, generally enshrined a year earlier as the greatest achievement in the history of popular music— by some, in the history of Art—now seemed very hollow, a triumph of effects. The Yippies showed up to take over the politics of the decade, and defrauded them. There were heroes and heroines of the era just past who had only a year or two to live; some of the political heroes had already been murdered. We had gone too far, really, without getting anywhere.

With Bob Dylan, the Band had seen much of this world from the inside, seen it as it was born, even helped bring it into being; but they came through on the other side, in a place very much of their own making. They stepped out, very consciously, as an alternative.

The pictures inside *Big Pink*—of the Band, their friends and relatives, and their ugly but much-loved big pink house—caught some of what they had to say. Against a cult of youth they felt for a continuity of generations; against the instant America of the sixties they looked for the traditions that made new things not only possible, but valuable; against a flight from roots they set a sense of place. Against the pop scene, all flux and novelty, they set themselves: a band with years behind it, and meant to last.

Many young Americans had spent the best part of the decade teaching themselves to feel like exiles in their own country; the Band, particularly songwriters Robbie Robertson and Richard Manuel, understood this, and were sure it was a mistake. They had come here by choice, after all. They had fallen in love with the music, first as they sought it out on the radio and on records, later as they learned to play it, and, wonder of wonders, define it. Coming out of Canada into the land that had kicked up the blues, jazz, church music, country and western, and a score of authentic rock 'n' roll heroes, playing their way up and down the spine of the continent, they fell in love with the place itself.

They felt more alive in America. They came to be on good terms with its violence and its warmth; they were attracted by the neon grab for pleasure on the face of the American night, and by the inscrutable spookiness behind that face. American contradictions demanded a fine energy, because no one could miss them; the stakes were higher, but the rewards seemed limitless. The Band's first songs were a subtle, seductive attempt to get this sense of life across. Their music was fashioned as a way back into America, and it worked.

STRANGER BLUES

With *Music from Big Pink*, the Band presented a rough moral drama. It had none of the mythic clarity of, say, John Ford's movies; it came through a modern haze, something like Robert Altman's *McCabe and Mrs. Miller*, obscure in its plots, dialogue hard to catch, communicating with a blind humor and a cryptic intensity nothing in rock 'n' roll has ever remotely touched.

They began with "Tears of Rage," an eerie invocation of Independence Day, dragging the organ and their secretive horns across a funeral beat, changing the Fourth of July into an image of betrayal, and of loneliness: America betrayed by those who would no longer be part of it. The Band made a claim to an identity others no longer wanted, and the album opened up from there. In its stories, its feel for place and language, its music, and most of all in its quest, this was an American mystery.

The liveliest songs (half Robertson's, half Manuel's, and all of a piece) shared an oddly familiar actor: the voice of "Lonesome Suzie," "Caledonia Mission," "To Kingdom Come," "We Can Talk About It Now," "Chest Fever," "The Weight," and "Long Black Veil."* His part

---

* This last, a modern country tune in the guise of an old Kentucky murder ballad, was not the Band's song, but it fits in perfectly with the rest. "This Wheel's on Fire" and "I Shall Be Released" (the former by Dylan and Danko and the latter by Dylan) don't fit in, not because the lyrics are out of place but because as performances the songs are not emotionally convincing, and the quality of emotion is what makes Big Pink a great album, not merely an interesting one. The music and the singing sound strained, contrived, probably because the Band felt obligated to replace the original arrangements they had worked out with Dylan when the songs were first put down on the famous Basement Tape. "Tears of Rage" is another Basement composition, but it works, perhaps because it was so necessary to what the Band was after; but the other two sound like filler on a record that needs nothing of the sort.

is taken by Levon (gutty, carnal, bewildered, always hanging onto the end of his rope), Rick Danko (quivering, melancholy, hesitant), Manuel (the Band's great sentimentalist, devastated and bursting with joy by turns), Robbie (anxious, yelping), or the four of them at once; but as I hear them now, years after I thought I knew this record, the vocals, like the writing, complete a single story.

The hero of this story (such as I find him, and I ought to note that I am setting the story down—or, if you like, making it up—simply as I hear it, without much regard for song sequence, cross-checked lyrics, or other formalities) has *Big Pink* pretty much to himself. He almost disappears on the next album, *The Band*, returns with *Stage Fright*, loses his voice on *Cahoots*, and perhaps hits the end of his road with Richard Manuel's singing on a handful of the rock 'n' roll classics that make up *Moondog Matinee*. To follow his trail is to leave out a good bit of what the Band has done—wonderful tunes like "Get Up Jake" and "Strawberry Wine," and their work with Bob Dylan. But there is a storyteller in their music, and in one form or another, his tale is the one I'm after, because it seems to be the one the Band tells best: the story of the worried man.

"Delivered Under the Similitude of a Dream, Wherein Is Discovered the Manner of His Setting Out, His Dangerous Journey, and Safe Arrival at the Desired Country," as John Bunyan put it. That, really, is only the beginning of his adventure.

He first appears on *Big Pink* as a wanderer, a quester, hoping to brazen his way through a strange land and learn something. He lives by his wits, moving across the territory explored by Robert Johnson and Harmonica Frank, taking his spirit from the best of both men.

To use a dark old word the worried man would recognize, these two men are his familiars. Like Johnson, he is obsessed by choices he never asked for, because he sees too clearly to avoid the guilt and fear that worm out of the Bible he carries in his carpetbag; like Harmonica Frank, he is saved by his sense of humor, and he refuses to take his fears too seriously.

The combination gives us a resurrection shuffle: prophecy, cut with jive. "Been sittin' in here for so darn long, waitin' for the end to come along," he complains in "To Kingdom Come"—Judgment Day is supposed to deliver the answers he wants, but unlike some people he will meet in *Big Pink*, he can't hang around forever. He moves on, but before he is even out of the song a stranger appears to suggest that it might be wiser for him to turn back. "'Tarred and feathered, thistles and thorns—One or the other,' he kindly warned." Well, that's not much of a choice—what else can you show me? The seeker knows the stakes are high, but he can't believe the game is fixed. He keeps looking, scared to death and full of optimism—careful to watch out for himself, once he's fallen into a trap. The devil might be anywhere—though, thanks to the touch of Harmonica Frank in the story, the devil comes on like the Headless Horseman—so the quester only wants to do the right thing; given the clutch of all-too-human doomsters that fly through the album, he'd better. "Time will tell you well," he offers hopefully, "if you truly, truly fell."

And so he dives headlong into a Gothic world of tricksters, fortune tellers, mummers, lunatics, witch doctors, cops, and lovers, struggling to find a home at the heart of that world. The music, like the character it shapes, is full of chance, uncertainty, and humor; the sound of *Big Pink* is one version of the quester's struggle, and of the world that makes his struggle interesting.

That sound is an uncanny blend of ancient folk songs, New Orleans jazz, postwar blues, white gospel groups, the Monotones, and Motown; and these sources are only a few of the obvious, picked almost at random. Al Kooper, reviewing *Big Pink* in 1968, heard the Beach Boys, the Association, the Swan Silvertones (*black* gospel), Hank Williams, the Beatles, Bob Dylan, and the Coasters. He's right, of course: *Big Pink* music is as dense as it is elusive. All those people are in it, and anyone's listening will turn up dozens more. The richness of *Big Pink* is in the Band's ability to contain endless combinations of American popular music without imitating any of them; the Band don't refer to their sources any more than we refer to George Washington when we vote, but the connection is there. The Band's music on *Big Pink* is personal, their own invention, but not merely personal; it is an unpredictable resolution of a common inheritance, something we shared in pieces. This was a new sound, but you could recognize yourself in that sound. *That* connection is what gives this music its natural authority, and makes it so exhilarating.

There are times when Richard Manuel sounds like the ghost of Johnny Ace (that sweet-voiced fifties R&B singer who died in a game of Russian roulette)—Johnny Ace condemned to haunt a gloomy radio, from which "Pledging My Love," the first posthumous rock 'n' roll hit, issues every time you spin the dial. There are times when the tone is desperate, close to the panicky feeling Marvin Gaye got on "I Heard It Through the Grapevine." But more often than not, the music is simply ominous.

This has to do, I think, with Robbie's hide-and-seek guitar, Garth Hudson's slithery organ, and the Band's collective sense of timing—

which is really a sense of freedom. In most blues or rock bands, each musician has to give something up in order to make a performance work; the men in the Band played and sang with second sight, and they made no concessions at all. The beat is tough, but open; fast little riffs shoot out from behind vocals without warning; vocals twist around seemingly random chords. The parts combine to pull the listener into a labyrinth, with no idea of what might be lurking around the next turn.

When the music is most exciting—when the guitar is fighting for space in the clatter while voices yelp and wail as one man finishes another's line or spins it off in a new direction—the lyrics are blind baggage, and they emerge only in snatches. This is the finest rock 'n' roll tradition ("I learned the words to Little Richard's songs the best I could and what I couldn't figure out didn't matter," Robbie said once), but on *Big Pink* such a style also seems to link up with an older tradition: the instinct of the American artist to put his story in disguise, to tell his tale from the shadows, probably because that is where he usually finds it. Those who mean to seduce do not announce their intentions through megaphones.

On the other hand, those who are too subtle wind up plying their seductions in the mirror. If *Big Pink* wasn't good to hear from a distance, no one, certainly myself included, would ever bother to get close to it. The first virtue of the album is that the danger, promise, and craziness of the quester's adventure come across directly in the music; not only can't you understand the words, you don't have to. Garth Hudson's satanic organ playing (straight out of *Sunset Boulevard*, with Erich von Stroheim at the pipes) is the key to "Chest Fever"—the words couldn't be, no one has ever deciphered them anyway. You don't need to analyze the lyrics of "The Weight" to understand the burden Miss Fanny has dropped on the man who sings the song; as Jon Carroll has written, Levon Helm is the only drummer who can make you cry, and drums are all he needs to get across the weary, fated sense of a situation that simply cannot be escaped. We never find out who Miss Fanny is, let alone what the singer is supposed to do for her; but the music, not to mention the singing, is so full of emotion and complexity it makes "the weight"—some combination of love, debt, fear, and guilt—a perfect image of anyone's entanglement.

So the story is revealed, and concealed, in flashes, dreams, pieces of unresolved incident, rumbles of doubt exiting through a joke. Yet if the music is part of the story, it is also the landscape against which the story takes place. Blurred at the edges and unsure of its center, this America is still a wilderness—the moral, social wilderness that is left even when the natural wilderness is gone. Excited and intrigued by the place for just that reason, the worried man has to get on without maps.

He has, however, brought along a lot of time-honored, prudent advice; unfortunately, it's never equal to the imprudent dilemmas life persists in forcing upon him. "Be careful what you do, it all comes back on you," he says, poking his head out of the mad confusion of "To Kingdom Come" (recalling, perhaps, a Sunday School lesson); but a few songs later, stuck in "The Weight" and surrounded by the suddenly comic riddles first set out in Robert Johnson's "Me and the Devil Blues," this is not quite good enough. Miss Fanny has given him his job, packed him off "with her regards for everyone," and since that phrase is as mysterious to him as it is to us, all he can do is stick out his hand and hope that whoever grabs it will eventually let go.

> *I picked up my bag, I went looking for a place to hide*
> *Then I saw Carmen and the devil, walking side by side*
> *I said, Hey, Carmen, come on, let's go downtown*
> *She said, I gotta go, but my friend can stick around.**

The sound of the quester's voice tells us that his first desire is simply to be left alone—left alone by friends, enemies, neighbors, women, relatives, dogs, good and evil—but he was born with his eyes and ears wide open, and he misses nothing. He can't stop asking questions (which is not to say that there aren't times when he wouldn't mind stopping—the golden calf that chases him through "To Kingdom Come" is not his idea of a good time); with nothing but the best intentions, he stumbles into everything in his way. And because he is fascinated by everything the rest of us take for granted, he finds himself caught up with his fellow men and women, and inevitably, their troubles become his own.

Looking for salvation, he ends up trying to save others: the woman of "Caledonia Mission" (she lives hidden behind a wall, and the city has a lock on her gate), "Chest Fever" ("She drinks from the bitter cup," he declares; "I'm trying to get her to give it up"), the daughter in "Tears of Rage," and many more. Whether he succeeds is never made clear, but what is clear is that his salvation is tied to theirs.

There is Lonesome Suzie, for one; an outcast, or maybe an aging spinster, in the timeless and mythical American town in which *Big Pink* seems to be set. She dearly needs a friend, and though the quester isn't

* Copyright © 1968 & © 1969 by Dwarf Music. Used by permission of Dwarf Music.

willing, he thinks, in Manuel's wonderful phrase, that maybe he can loan her one. But that, he knows, only makes him one of the confidence men his search has bound him to unmask, and so he gives in: "I guess just watching you / Has made me lonesome too."

The whole of *Big Pink*, and perhaps the best of what the Band has had to say over the years, seems to dovetail into those modest lines. The man who lives them feels like part of the crowd, and he is only too happy to fade into it; but he recognizes himself in everyone he meets, and so he is drawn out of himself and into the world. He takes his vitality from that paradox. To survive it, he can't afford to be anyone's fool; to make it worth his considerable trouble, he needs a talent for friendship that is as deep as it is broad. "Save your neck, or save your brother," he shouts a couple of years later in "The Shape I'm In," just out of jail and searching for his woman. "Looks like it's one or the other." But it's one more false choice, one more denial of the fraternity he feels in spite of himself, and he can't rest with it. Maybe that's why he sounds so desperate; even running for his life, his mind is on the people he leaves behind.

Now, taken all at once, this is a remarkable figure: the Band's re-creation of an American original, the democratic man—trapped, against his better judgment, in a hilarious and scarified re-creation of a very old American idea: this is a joint-stock world. A joint-stock world is open to devils and angels alike; all barriers are betrayals, and the man who sees only himself sees nothing at all.

This is the possibility the Band pursue through the tangles of the country itself. The extraordinary diversity of the place, and the claim of every man and woman to do just as they please, make a joint-stock America both necessary and hard to find; the man who looks for it has a right to be worried.

America has a lot of mottoes—common slogans, because they sum up how individuals act among themselves. "We Must All Hang Together, Or We Shall All Hang Separately" is a sentimental favorite, but the edge goes to "Don't Tread On Me"—which is to say that the man who wants to hang together had best take care not to give the good people he meets an excuse to string him up. America, as the quester finds it in his songs, is not a very friendly place. It is suspicious of itself. Most people no longer even know that they have brothers to save, and if they do, "brother" means men, but not women; the young, but not the old; blues singers, but not country singers; Northerners, but not Southerners; whites, but not blacks; or a general vice versa. The man who tells this story becomes who he is, the one who reaches out, because he responds so deeply to the yearning for unity and affection that these facts hide. Perhaps because he comes from outside, he can see the country whole, just as those who have always lived there see it only in pieces. His job, as in "The Weight," no longer a matter of isolated predicament but of vocation, is to drag that affection out into the open, even if it comes hard, as his did.

The song for that is "We Can Talk About It Now," a wonderful Richard Manuel tune that sounds like the best merry-go-round in the world. Full of exultation, exhortation, smiles, and complaints, it is the song of a man who has gone far enough to have become a part of what he sings about. "It's safe now," he says, "to take a backward glance."

> *It seems to me, we've been holding something*
> *Underneath our tongues*
> *I'm afraid if you ever got a pat on the back*
> *It would likely burst your lungs*
> *Whoa—stop me, if I should sound*
> *Kinda down in the mouth*
> *But I'd rather be burned in Canada*
> *Than to freeze here in the south!**

If his quest has taught him anything, it is that if he wants to find a home in this country he will have to make it himself, and that means breaking through to the warmth others hide, just as Lonesome Suzie broke through to him. The pure joy of the music unveils the depth of emotion that's his to win; and that must have been the treasure he was after from the beginning, whether he knew it or not. He had to learn, in John Barth's line, that the key to the treasure is the treasure—that to be free is not to get what you want or to settle for what you've got, but to begin to know what you want and to feel strong enough to go after it. So now, out of the claustrophobia of *Big Pink*, he has a glimpse of what he wants. For a moment, to say yes is to say everything.

> *We can talk about it now*
> *It's the same old riddle, always starts from the middle*
> *I'd fix it but I don't know how*
> *Well, we could try to reason*
> *But you might think it's treason*
> *One voice for all*
> *Echoing around the hall,* ECHOING, *echoing around the hall!**

* Copyright © 1968 & © 1969 by Dwarf Music. Used by permission of Dwarf Music.

The song is loose and rangy, and the song has plenty of room in it: room for doubt, and room for doubt to turn into love without any explanation at all; room for arguments interrupted by a bottle, room for friends and strangers, room for escape and room for homecoming. For its moment, the song—a free and friendly conversation between the men in the Band and anyone who might care to listen—is that one voice.

The song creates, out of words and music, a big, open, undeniable image of what the country could sound like at its best, of what it could feel like. One good burst of rock 'n' roll blows the trail clean, and the people our man has seen and the places he has been look brand-new.

"Dontcha see," he shouts, in an extraordinary flash of vision, that seems to reveal the secret America holds, even as it hints at deeper secrets, "there's no need to slave."

"The whip," he sings, "is in the grave."

THIS RIGHTEOUS LAND

Those lines, I think, deserve a pause—there is no bottom to them. Nothing I know captures with such mystery and clarity the circle traced by American optimism, and by the dread that optimism leaves behind and inevitably meets again. You couldn't ask for a more perfect statement of the conviction that America is blessed, or of the lingering suspicion that it is cursed. When the two ideas come together—in a story, a voice, or a group—all things seem possible. The lines touch both sides of the country's soul at once; the tension they create can push out the limits of what an artist can accomplish, for just so long as the spirit of the lines can support their contradictions. By contradictions I mean that a paradise is made out of a line that turns on the image of a whip; by spirit I mean the joy one feels when Richard Manuel shoots the line across Levon's drums—and the way Levon sounds like a man calling a town meeting to order with a gavel in each hand.

When the spirit fades, those lines will contract, and trap the man who sings them. But until then, what they bring is freedom, and the space to use it. The result is *The Band.*

That second album—arriving in 1969, soon after the group went out on the road on their own for the first time since Levon and the Hawks broke up—is the map *Big Pink*'s quester was missing. The new songs roll right over the surface of American life, proof of how magnificent that surface can be.

Turn the sound up, and the music rocks like "Blue Suede Shoes"; keep it quiet, and it sounds as folksy as an old Charlie Poole 78. The good eye of the last record is still working, but instead of probing the dark for phantoms, there is a loving feel for detail, for nuance. With its warm, happy vocals, and an irresistible snapping rhythm square in the middle of almost every tune, *The Band* is the testament of a man who has come up from a netherworld for a breath of air, a man who can now afford to have himself a good, long look around.

The worried man is a settler now, here to stay, complete with wife and kids, and the album opens with his wife holding a gun on him. As he pleads and jokes with her, trying to explain himself (No matter what you think, honey, I didn't do it), he is drawn back to the days when all he wanted was a place to come home to. He remembers his hard times, his fears, how close he came to giving up the ghost; he thinks he just may have to hit the road again if she doesn't put that gun away. By the time his reverie is finished the fight is over—still, he wouldn't mind knowing where she hid the pistol . . .

The song is called "Across the Great Divide," an appropriate beginning for an album Robbie once said the Band could have called *America*—might as well kick it off right there where the water runs both ways. But there is more to it than that.

The Band gives author's credit to the land because while we usually read our own meanings into the landscape—when we don't miss it altogether—they know that at our best we live and speak according to the metaphors of the land. The land—the image of a place like "The Great Divide," the simple fact that there is such a phenomenon—attracts the Band. The symbol seems full of meaning—the Great Divide is where the two sides of the country separate, but it is also where the two sides meet. If we look into this double metaphor, we can understand the ambitions of *The Band* clearly. That first song and those that follow are meant to cross the great divide between men and women; between the past and the present; between the country and the city; between the North and the South; between the Band and their new audience. The worried man steps back, once he has shown up to play the theme song: he wants to celebrate the country he has discovered, and he celebrates by letting the country speak for itself, in as many voices as can be crammed onto a twelve-inch disc. At home here now, the man from *Big Pink* can sit back and listen with the rest of us.

The songs, mostly by Robbie, are classics now; "Up on Cripple Creek," "Rag Mama Rag," "The Night They Drove Old Dixie Down," "King Harvest (Has Surely Come)" made up the heart of the Band's stage show for years. What they say was clear the moment they were released, and I have nothing to add to that. Their power, though, is too great to take for granted.

The songs were made to bring to life the fragments of experience, legend, and artifact every American has inherited as the legacy of a mythical past. The songs have little to do with chronology; most describe events that could be taking place right now, but most of those events had taken on their color before any of us was born. There is a conviction here that every way of life practiced in America from the time of the Revolution on down still matters—not as nostalgia, but as the necessity of someone's daily life—and the music, though it never bends to any era, never tries for any quaint support of a theme, seems as if it would sound as right to a gang of beaver trappers as it does to us. There is no feeling of being dragged back into the past for a history lesson; if anything, the past catches up with us. Robbie put his stories on the surface, but they hit home because they draw the traces of that legacy out of each of us, bringing them to the surface of our own lives.

"The Night They Drove Old Dixie Down," for one—written for Levon, who sings it—is not so much a song about the Civil War as it is about the way each American carries a version of that event within himself. In this case it is a man named Virgil Kane, who makes no claim to speak for anyone else; but something in his tone demands that everyone listen.

In a few short verses, we learn a lot about him. He is a poor white farmer from the Confederate side of Tennessee, probably not more than twenty years old, a survivor of the attacks made by General Stoneman's cavalry on the Danville train he defended. With the war over, a glimpse of Robert E. Lee is worth as much to him as the memory of his brother, who died fighting for the sense of place Virgil Kane's war was all about. He wants us to understand that the war has cost him almost everything he has.

It is hard for me to comprehend how any Northerner, raised on a very different war than Virgil Kane's, could listen to this song without finding himself changed. You can't get out from under the singer's truth—not the whole truth, simply *his* truth—and the little autobiography closes the gap between us. The performance leaves behind a feeling that for all our oppositions, every American still shares this old event; because to this day none of us has escaped its impact, what we share is an ability to respond to a story like this one.

The scope of the album, words and music, is astonishing. In "King Harvest," probably Robbie's greatest song, we meet a man who might be Virgil Kane's grandson—or our contemporary, you can't tell. He works that same farm, but it fails and sends him into the bitter mills of the New South; when times are slow the mills shut down, and he runs into the arms of a union, hoping for one last chance. Yet wherever he is driven, he carries his roots with him like a conscience. He cannot escape the feel of the land any more than we can escape its myth.

"King Harvest" is the last number on the album; like "Dixie" or the desolate "Whispering Pines" (one of Richard Manuel's two contributions), the song is optimistic only because it is so full of desire. It goes against the usual playful, rocking grain of *The Band*, giving the music the tension it must have if it is to work as a version of our own roots, of our own conscience.

The distance between those songs of struggle is marked by a set of easy, honest affirmations that can be summed up in a dozen lines, but perhaps best by this one: "Life has been so good to us all." Jawbone, the Band's unregenerate thief, would say yes to that; certainly the trucker and his semipro girlfriend down in Lake Charles would, along with the little boy and his grandfather in "When You Awake" and the tired sailors of "Rockin' Chair." Even the people scrambling into the storm cellar in "Look Out Cleveland" and the lover stuck with a woman who only wants to dance would show up to sign that pledge. The man who sings "King Harvest" is alone, and he probably could not agree.

With that last reservation ahead of us we ride down the Mississippi, out to California, through the Midwest to Virginia, back again to Canada. We listen to fiddles, what sounds like an amplified jew's-harp, a rock 'n' roll band, laughing horns, good guitar, yodels, sniggers, snorts, and moans; along with the people we meet we take satisfaction in whiskey, in the grinning joys of miscegenation, in Garth Hudson's mad piano, trickling through the fast steps of "Rag Mama Rag." From song to song paradise means good times—and good times are where you find them.

> Up on Cripple Creek she sends me
> If I spring a leak, she mends me
> I don't have to speak, she defends me
> A drunkard's dream if I ever did see one!*

Again and again, the music creates that moment of shared recognition first confirmed in "Dixie"—the songs catch it in sex, in work, in failure, in the weather, in the choice of an instrument, in names lifted from half-forgotten Westerns, in the emotion of a vocal, in a memory of family life. The shifts between the songs finally let us understand that the man who sings "King Harvest" wants nothing more from his life than to sing a song like "Rag Mama Rag"; we understand that the voice of "Rag Mama Rag" is real because it has been shaped by the terrors of "King Harvest," and knows a chance to dance them away for what it's worth.

The album tells no lies. It touches the size and the age of the country, takes in its fabulous multiplicity, but that repeated moment links us to each part of the story even as it knits the songs into one.

For as long as that moment lasts, the story seems complete. Every character, every place, every event in the music looms up at once. Crossing the great divide, the Band left community in their wake.

EVEN STRANGER BLUES

The problem with community, as the Band was to discover when they finally followed their records into the country, is that you have to live in it. They had, in fact, made those first two albums from a distance—isolated in the musicians' haven of Bearsville/Woodstock and walled off from the crowd by their manager, Albert Grossman. *Big Pink* had been out for almost a year and *The Band* was in the can when the group arrived in San Francisco to meet their audience for the first time—people had gathered from all over the West to celebrate *them*.

No matter how many rave record reviews the Band might have read, until they stepped onto a stage there was no way they could have understood how fierce and intense the expectations of their audience would be. Their music had cut even more deeply than they could have hoped—to many, *Big Pink* was one of the memorable events of their lives, and the stakes of that first night were as high as they could be.

After hours of delays, excuses, promises, and interminable tuning up, the Band came on with Robbie dazed and sick, dragging along a hypnotist to cure him. The hypnotist stood on the stage conjuring up spells while the Band fell apart before the crowd's very eyes. They struggled through a handful of weak, ragged tunes, and then they turned and ran. The crowd's hopeful energy had been suspended between disappointment and desire, and it collapsed into fury. The Band's first concert ended with an outpouring of anger and rage unlike anything I have ever seen at a rock 'n' roll show.

Perhaps the crowd's reaction was vicious, but it was certainly real—a good measure of how much the Band had to live up to. They had it all the next night, playing on and on with a wild, raucous delight that finally climaxed with Little Richard's "Slippin' and Slid-in'," a number that the five had likely been playing—in afterschool pick-up bands, as the Hawks, up in Woodstock—since it came out in 1956. But we had loved the song as long as the Band had, and as Richard Manuel tossed off the unmistakable first notes of the tune the crowd began to dance and cheer. This was a common celebration now: as we made the old song new, what seemed most remarkable was the recognition that our links to the Band had been forged so long ago, and that our time together was just beginning.

Still, I think something of that initial disaster stayed with the Band. They made a number of cross-country tours after that, but if they never played as badly as they did that first night, they never played with the freedom of the show that followed either. Performing involved all the psychic risks they had faced and dodged in the adventures of *Big Pink*; performing also demanded new links, no matter how tenuous, to the America their audience lived in, which was very different from their own—a scary place, violent with blocked hopes and bad dreams, a place where roots were not enough, where a good concert by the Band was like shelter in the storm, a means to strength and pleasure. And they had aimed for more than that.

Sometimes, though, there was less. The Band began to hedge their bets. They called their next album *Stage Fright*, and both the new songs and the concerts of the time proved they meant it. *Stage Fright* was an album of doubt, guilt, disenchantment, and false optimism. The past no longer served them—the songs seemed trapped in the present, a jumble of desperation that was at once personal and social. The music at its best was still special, but in every sense, the kind of unity that had given force to those first two albums, and to the idea of the Band itself, was missing. Now, instead of hearing music that could not really be broken down, one picked at parts for satisfaction—Robbie's guitar and Garth's organ on "The Shape I'm In," Rick Danko's bass and fiddle on "Daniel and the Sacred Harp." Robbie had completely taken over the songwriting; the surprises of four voices wrestling for a lyric were abandoned for solo vocals. There was an edge of separation in the music: the worried man was back, drawing the shade on his window as the police wailed by in one tune, picked up for vagrancy himself in another, spinning a hilarious but ultimately unsettling tale of sin and damnation in a third. He still reaches out to others—*he* needs shelter now—but no one is there.

Facing an audience, the Band hid in their arrangements. The arrangements were tight, disciplined, precise; the open spirit of their music contracted. They were known to spend more time on testing the sound system than they did playing, but often they didn't play loud enough to come across. They presented perfect replicas of their records—to the point where Rick Danko would back off from the mike at the end of "When You Awake," imitating the studio fade—the surest way to please an audience without really moving it.

From the days when they had first paid out their money to hear Howlin' Wolf, there had been a side to the Band that was anarchic, risky, virtually out of control, and when they caught that spirit, they could take it farther than anyone else. Sometimes Robbie made his guitar sound like a musical equivalent of Jim Brown's big scene in *The Dirty Dozen*—that moment when he takes off on a broken-field run around a Nazi chateau, dropping a hand grenade down an air shaft every ten yards and grinning madly as explosions leap up behind him in sequence—but to bring such qualities into your music you have to touch such emotions in yourself. The Band saw chaos in the crowd, in the country, in the commercial pressures that were driving the five of them apart, driving at least one of them into dope and alcohol, and they stepped back.

Almost always, the numbers they had never recorded—Rick Danko's lovely country version of the Four Tops' "Loving You Is Sweeter Than Ever," or their hard rock assault on Marvin Gaye's "Baby Don't You Do It (Don't Break My Heart)"—were most vital, because you could hear them reaching for the songs and grabbing hold. But most of all they were looking for safety—they rarely cut loose, tried hard not to take chances. Their shows began to lose excitement, their music began to lose its drama, and the Band began to lose their audience.

Cahoots came out in 1971, but only the earlier songs gave any weight to the title—and the title was the best thing on the album. The songs were stiff and the music was constricted; all the humor and drive had gone. On *The Band* Robbie had breathed life into his characters in a line, and the singers made you care about them; here there were only abstractions and stereotypes, and the singers sounded as if they had no real connection to the words they were given.

The music no longer had any life of its own; it took its cues from the lyrics, and when the result wasn't flat, it was cute. "When I Paint My Masterpiece" was about an expatriate artist in Europe, so the tune featured a little Michel Legrand accordion; the utterly pointless "Shootout in Chinatown" came complete with Fu Manchu guitar, a touch so tasteless it verged on racism. The Band's ability to create a sense of place was reduced to a humorless presentation of fixed images. The failure of language made even the good ideas of the lyrics unsatisfying—made the truth sound false.

That sense of struggle and reward that bled through *Big Pink*, *The Band* and *Stage Fright*, the balance always changing, had collapsed into a nostalgic pastoralism in which few who had felt the strength of their best songs could believe. The last cut on *Cahoots*, a tribute to the white gospel communities of the South, was as sentimental in its performance as it was honest in its intent; hearing it after the strained failures of the rest of the album, I couldn't help but think of the studio happy ending that was tacked onto Fritz Lang's *You Only Live Once*, wherein Henry Fonda, having died tragically in the last shot, suddenly ascends to heaven with a bewildered smile on his face. *Cahoots* was a commercial disaster; the Band retreated even further, playing only an occasional concert, making no tours at all.

In the last week of 1971 they arranged a special set of shows in New York, and with a horn section unlike anything ever heard in rock 'n' roll to force their music past itself, the Band broke through and said their piece once more. Out of those nights came a magnificent live album, *Rock of Ages*—a claim that their music was meant to last, and certainly the best of it will. But as I listened to the live records when they were released in 1972—so full of playfulness and bite, blazing with soul and love—I was struck by how long it had been since the Band had put out a single new song that mattered.

The Band's vision of the country had darkened as they moved farther apart. If they were to keep the group they had made, they could not ask too much of it. The music seemed to say that they had lost their trust in the country, in themselves, and in each other—that they had to fight harder than they were able to touch the spirit that had made their work worth doing in the first place. Like most good American artists, and like their worried man, they had been romantics, but not fools; when the romance began to go, their talent for asking the right questions went with it. They still looked for community, but like many who cannot find it, they fell back into an even deeper privacy than they started out with. Because their dreams were too real and too beautiful to give up, they felt a sense of guilt; their withdrawal—a separation from the country, from their audience, and from each other—was a betrayal of those dreams.

They had closed out *Stage Fright* with a queer song that had all the warmth of "The Man Who Corrupted Hadleyburg," which it resembled: "The Rumor." The old quester who sings it is afraid now, and his voice is muted—no one else speaks at all. He sings to a crowd he has long since joined, but the bonds between them—of loyalty, affection, fascination—have faded away. When the singer first came to the country, he found it poisoned by suspicion and shame; he meant to change it, but instead, the country changed him.

Someone in the crowd has been harmed: "His name abused, his privacy refused." Why he has been harmed is not spelled out, probably no one really knows, and the mystery deepens the malevolence of the scene. "Feel the good," the seeker calls out, "hang down your heads / Until the fog rolls away—Let it roll away." He means it, but the words no longer mean what they might have, because the community can never be what it was. "He can forgive—and you can regret—but he can never, never forget." Not even the victim is known—the victim might be anyone, as might be the villain.

When the worried man looks into the crowd, as he must, for he has nowhere else to go, the people he sees will seem different to him, as he will to them. The whip will hang over them all.

Perhaps. The last song on *Rock of Ages* was the old Chuck Willis/ Jerry Lee Lewis hit, "(I Don't Want To) Hang Up My Rock and Roll Shoes," and it capped a New Year's Eve night when the Band and their fans had put themselves back in touch with each other. But as the Band left the stage, Robbie says, they felt a common sense of depression—no, they didn't wanna, and they weren't gonna, but the song, like so many, was complex in its context. The Band knew that when Chuck Willis's version was on the radio, he was in the grave; that while Jerry Lee kept his rock 'n' roll shoes, he lost his rock 'n' roll audience. The song was not a curse, but it wasn't the simple affirmation they had bargained for either. It simply raised questions they could not answer, about the cheers that had ridden them off the stage; reaching for the past had forced them to think about what they had left to do.

Many months later, in the fall of 1973, an article appeared in *Playboy*, measuring Richard Manuel for a straight-jacket; at the same time, the Band released *Moondog Matinee*, a collection of some favorite oldies. Manuel had been in bad shape for a long time; he had not finished a song of his own for years, but this was his album.

He sang about giving up the bottle in "Saved," and slowly pulled down his mask with "The Great Pretender." If that last had been more than a little overblown when the Platters first sang it in 1955, one would have thought that after nearly twenty years there would be nothing left of the song but nostalgia. Manuel transformed it into the truest kind of soul music; his singing made the Band's more predictable rockers sound tame by comparison.

The best of the album took the Band's tale back to its beginnings, and eased their special voice into its parts. "Third Man Theme," their little instrumental, had a quiet affection in its modesty and humor—the music asked for good times, perhaps for less than before, perhaps not. The finest cut of all, Manuel's gentle, utterly despairing version of Bobby Bland's "Share Your Love," was as lonesome a song as any can be. As he sang, surrounded again by the old simpatico of the Band, it seemed like the last word of that worried man. Share your love with me, share your love with me—what had he ever said but that, what else had anyone ever said to him?

THE WEIGHT

"It was a rowdy life," Robbie once recalled, thinking back over the years before *Big Pink*. "The places we played had tough audiences. They would throw things at you; they were rednecks. Fighting plays a big part in their life, you know—fighting and woman-stealing. And you fall in, you just do what the custom is. If they take off their shoes, you take off your shoes.

"We were all so young—we were sixteen, seventeen years old at the time. We played in joints. That's what they were. Some of it was great and some of it was scary and some of it was horrible, and some of it was very valuable to us, to this day.

"You see—instead of throwing a knapsack over your back and getting out on the highway, to learn about life, we were able to do it together. We were protected by one another. We were secured by one another."

Those are fine words. They tell us that the Band sought in America what they found among themselves: that their music and their stories were not only a version of America, but a reflection of their own unity. All those years on the road had given them their values; in a sense, community was only a projection of comradeship.

The group was its own joint-stock world, but it could not survive the honest demands of the greater joint-stock world that was the country itself. Every song on the first two albums had been written before the Band had played a single show in public; once they began to tour, the group, as men who contributed what was special about themselves to something bigger than any of them, began to fall apart. Richard

Manuel never wrote another song; the singers stopped calling out to one another across the verses; the uncanny sense of timing that had made the Band's early music move disappeared altogether. As the Band stepped back from their audience, you could feel the friendship go out of their sound.

In order to save the group, Robbie took it over. He took it over as lyricist, manager, strategist, savant, visionary, and spokesman. No one else in the Band ever gave an interview; after a time, the rock press began to celebrate Robbie as a genius and the Band as his foil, and the other members were not asked to talk. And yet, because the group was no longer truly whole, Robbie could not really draw on it; since his links to the country and to his audience were no longer strong, he could no longer see the country or his audience clearly. *Moondog Matinee*, for all of its satisfactions, had the melancholy tinge of a reunion—a feeling that became all the more unsettling when one realized the five men saw each other all the time.

Friendship, in the end, is not community, though it was the Band's sense of friendship that let them embody community—in their stories, in their music, in their ambitions. Friendship can be the means to community. But if one does not live in the world, then one will feed off the small world of friendship until there is nothing left.

When I went up to Woodstock to talk to Robbie late in 1972, he was ready to leave. The Band had been hiding out there for years, their houses squirreled off in the Catskills; I had never seen that part of the country before, and I understood how one could read its signs as a promise of peace of mind. Woodstock itself looked like the usual American idea of community—quaint, tasteful, small, homogeneous—but in fact it was more like a private club, inhabited by musicians, dope dealers, artists, hangers-on. The town made me nervous; it seemed like a closed, smug, selfish place.

I asked Robbie about his favorite cities. Montreal and New Orleans, he said, and he began to talk about the cultural confusion that he thought gave those cities their spirit—the mix of languages, customs, religions, music, food, architecture, politics. You could spend your whole life in one of those cities and be surprised every day. He had a house in Montreal—that was his wife Dominique's hometown—and they were going back. What that would mean for the future of the Band I didn't ask; the pastoral traps of Woodstock had already taken too much of the soul out of the group. That they had protected each other years ago was only half of their best music—the other half came from what they had protected themselves against: those rowdy audiences, scattered all over the country in dance halls and bars. "They take off their shoes, you take off your shoes"—in those days, the Band could not afford to keep their distance. They learned to lean on each other and to listen to the crowd; that, in a queer way, brought their commitment to friendship and their feel for community together.

Before I left Woodstock I sat and talked for a long time with Dominique Robertson. She told me about the struggles of the Quebec Separatist movement and what that fight meant to her, that she had tried to find someone to talk to when Trudeau imposed a terror on the people after Separatists kidnapped a government official, that no one in Woodstock had any idea there really was a world different from their own. There's nothing here but dope, music, and beauty, she said; if you're a woman, and you don't use dope and you don't make music, there's nothing here at all.

The Band did leave; they moved to Los Angeles, and early in 1974 they set out on a grand tour with Bob Dylan. With Dylan, they were once again the best rock 'n' roll band in the world; their own sets had all the old limits, and not a song was less than four years old. Still, there was a joy in their faces as they played that I had not seen since that great night in San Francisco.

America is a dangerous place, and to find community demands as much as any of us can give. But if America is dangerous, its little utopias, asking nothing, promising safety, are usually worse. "Look at this," Dominique said, taking in her house, the trees, the mountains. "It's beautiful. It's everything people ought to want, and I hate it." Then she grinned. "'This country life is killin' me,'" she sang, turning a song we had both heard too many times on its head. "I gotta find my way back to the city, and get some corruption in my lungs."

SLY STONE

The Myth of Staggerlee

I named my son Malik Nkrumah Staggerlee Seale. Right on, huh? Beautiful name, right? He's named after his brother on the block, like all his brothers and sisters off the block. Stagger*lee*.

Staggerlee is Malcom X before he became politically conscious. *Livin' in the hoodlum world.*

You'll find out. Huey had a lot of Staggerlee qualities. I guess I lived a little bit of Staggerlee's life too, here and there. That's where it's at. You move yourself up from a lower level to a higher level. And at one time brother Eldridge was on the block. He was Staggerlee.

"Staggerlee shot Billy . . ." Billy the *Lion*. "Staggerlee had a sawed-off shotgun and a Model A Ford and he owed money on that as well; his woman kicked him out in the cold 'cause she said his love was growin' old. Staggerlee took a walk down *Ramparts Street*, down where all them baaad son-of-a-guns meet. By the Bucket o' *Bluuuuuud.*" You know, the main drag? That's from Louisiana, Ramparts Street? Yeah, this is where Staggerlee's history is. Staggerlee is all the shootouts that went on between gamblers, and cats fightin' over women—the black community.

Staggerlee shot Billy, you know? "Shot that poor boy dead." Two black brothers fightin' each other. Billy the Lion was bad too. "Staggerlee walked into a bar and ordered . . . just to get a bite to eat. And he wound up with a glass of muddy water and a piece of rotten meat. He asked the bartender, did he know who he was? And the bartender says, 'I heard o' you across the way,' he says, 'but I serve *bad* son-of-a-guns *three* times a day.'" *Everybody's* bad, you see?

Something else, huh? That's *life*. And all the little Staggerlees, *a lot of 'em!* Millions of 'em, know what I mean?

And so I named that brother, my little boy, Staggerlee, because . . . that's what his *name* is.

BOBBY SEALE, from a jailhouse
interview with Francisco Newman, 1970.

STAGGERLEE

Somewhere, sometime, a murder took place: a man called Stack-a-lee—or Stacker Lee, Stagolee, or Staggerlee—shot a man called Billy Lyons—or Billy the Lion, or Billy the Liar. It is a story that black America has never tired of hearing and never stopped living out, like whites with their Westerns. Locked in the images of a thousand versions of the tale is an archetype that speaks to fantasies of casual violence and violent sex, lust and hatred, ease and mastery, a fantasy of style and steppin' high. At a deeper level it is a fantasy of no-limits for a people who live within a labyrinth of limits every day of their lives, and who can transgress them only among themselves. It is both a portrait of that tough and vital character that everyone would like to be, and just another pointless, tawdry dance of death.

Billy died for a five-dollar Stetson hat; because he beat Staggerlee in a card game, or a crap game; because Stack was cheating and Billy was fool enough to call him on it. It happened in Memphis around the turn of the century, in New Orleans in the twenties, in St. Louis in the 1880s. The style of the killing matters, though: Staggerlee shot Billy, in the words of a Johnny Cash song, just to watch him die.

Sometimes it was a cautionary tale, as in Mississippi John Hurt's version, recorded in 1928.

Po-lice officer, how can it be
You can 'rest everybody, but cru-el Stagolee
That bad man, Oh, cru-el Stagolee

Billy the Lion tol' Stagolee
Please don't take my life
I got two little babes, and a darlin' lovely wife
That bad man, Oh, cruel Stagolee

What I care about your two little babes
Your darlin' lovely wife
You done stole my Stetson hat
I'm bound to take your life
That bad man, Oh, cruel Stagolee

Boom-boom, boom-boom, went a .44
Well, when I spied ol' Billy the Lion
He was lyin' on the floor
That bad man, Oh, cruel Stagolee

Gentlemens of the jury, what you think of that
Stagolee shot Billy the Lion 'bout a five-dollar Stetson hat
That bad man, Oh, cruel Stagolee

If that was something like the original idea of the story, it didn't hold up very long. Usually, no white sheriff had the nerve to take Stack on, and he got away. When he didn't—when he was caught and hung—it was only for a chance to beat the devil. The song carried Staggerlee down to hell, where he took over the place and made it into a black man's paradise.

Innocent Billy was no longer seen as a helpless victim, but as a hapless mark. Staggerlee's secret admirers came out of the woodwork; the women (all dressed in red) flocked to his funeral (it was the best money could buy). Stagolee was a winner. "GO!" shouted Lloyd Price, caught up in the legend. "GO! GO! Stagger Lee!"

Nobody's fool, nobody's man, tougher than the devil and out of God's reach—to those who followed his story and thus became a part of it, Stack-o-Lee was ultimately a stone-tough image of a free man.

In the blues, Stack changed names, but little else. He was the Crawling Kingsnake; Tommy Johnson pouring Sterno down his throat, singing, "Canned heat, canned heat is killing me"; Muddy Waters's cool and elemental Rollin' Stone; Chuck Berry's Brown-Eyed Handsome Man; Bo Diddley with a tombstone hand and a graveyard mind; Wilson Pickett's Midnight Mover; Mick Jagger's Midnight Rambler.

Stack rode free as the Back Door Man in the deadly electric blues of Howlin' Wolf (" 'Cuse me for murder / First degree / Judge's wife cried, Let the man go free! / *I am* . . ."), and gave up the ghost, proud never to rest easy, in "Going Down Slow." Stagolee was a secret, buried deep in the heart as well as ruling the streets: in Bobby Marchan's "There Is Something on Your Mind," Stackerlee crawled out of a man who only wanted love and pulled the trigger that turned love into death. When the civil rights movement got tough, he took over. And Staggerlee would come roaring back on the screen in the seventies, as Slaughter, Sweet Sweetback, Superfly.

"Stagger Lee shot Billy . . ." The line echoes from Lloyd Price's rock 'n' roll hit through fifty years of black culture, passing, on its way back to its hidden source, thousands and thousands of Staggerlees and Billys. There is an echo for Jimi Hendrix, a star at twenty-four and dead at twenty-seven; for Sly Stone, "not," as was said of Bob Dylan once, "burning his candle at both ends, but using a blow torch on the middle"; for young men dead in alleys or cold in the city morgue; for a million busted liquor stores and a million angry rapes. Stack and Billy merge into a figure innocent on one level and guilty on another: into Robert Johnson, living from town to town and woman to woman, driven and searching for sin and peace of mind; into junkies twisted from their last OD's; into a young George Jackson, drunk and out for easy money, or his brother Jonathan, rising years later with a gun in his hand. Look and you will see King Curtis, stretched out dead in front of his house; Muhammad Ali; Rap Brown, so bad that Congress passed a law against him. Farther on are pimps like Big Red Little, Jack Johnson in a car full of white women, Sportin' Life steppin' out. It is an echo all the way back to the bullet that went through Billy and broke the bartender's glass, a timeless image of style and death.

SLY STONE

Born Sylvester Stewart in 1941, in Denton, Texas, Sly Stone grew up in Vallejo, California, a tough and grimy polyglot city on the north end of San Francisco Bay. He picked up guitar and drums as a kid, led his own gang into the streets, and played his part in the high school race riots that were endemic in the town. He made it into a few semipro bands in the early sixties; by the time he was nineteen, in 1964, he was producing small hits by local white club bands for Autumn Records, the label owned by the baron of San Francisco Top 40, Big Daddy Tom Donahue. This put Sly right in the mainstream of Bay Area rock 'n' roll; up until 1965, the local music scene pretty much came down to Donahue's kind of radio and the big package shows he and his partner, Bobby Mitchell, booked into the Cow Palace.

There was no big money; in fact, a lot of what there was never seemed to find its way from the distributors back to the company. The music that was going to put San Francisco on the rock 'n' roll map was taking shape; it would wipe out the tight, commercial sounds Donahue and Sly were after—that is, it would make them uncool.

Sly went to radio school and got a job on KSOL, the number two black station in the area. Fast on the air, he was a hit. A brilliant, kinetic DJ, he found the straight soul format a fraud on his taste, and salted it with Bob Dylan and the Beatles. At the same time, he was pulling a band together. There were whites as well as blacks, women—who played real instruments—as well as men: "The Family."

By early 1967 the hippie bands of the Haight had the ear of the nation, and San Francisco geared up for the crunch of the Summer of Love. The first hip FM rock station, led by Larry Miller and a reformed Tom Donahue ("Should I change my name?" he once asked his new listeners. "Send in your suggestions"), was breaking the Top 40 monopoly. *Sgt. Pepper* was on the way, as was the Monterey Pop Festival. It was a genuinely exciting time.

And it was a very white scene. If the Jefferson Airplane had little to say to blacks, the fact that they and bands like them brought a white audience into the Fillmore ghetto every weekend seemed unimportant, even if racial tensions were beginning to emerge in the Haight. No one knew what to say about that, so no one said anything, except that they sure dug spades.

Black music, led by Aretha Franklin, Wilson Pickett, and Sam and Dave, had hit a commercial peak and was approaching an artistic impasse, as inspiration turned into formula. Otis Redding became the white hope of the new rock 'n' roll fans, and at Monterey they would cover him with glory because he said they were all right. But six months later he was dead. A musical vacuum was opening up, and the racial contradictions of the counterculture were coming to the surface. There was no music to work out the contradictions, and no music to fill the vacuum.

It was at this point that Sly and the Family Stone emerged from the unhip white bars of Hayward and Redwood City—middle-class suburb towns—with a music they brashly called "a whole new thing," leaving behind (and picking up again on the radio) an audience of small-time boosters, bikers, college students, and the sons and daughters of transplanted Okies.

Sly had mastered the recording studio and a dozen instruments. He was tough and wily, already burned in the record business and determined never to let it happen again; a man out to build something worth the trouble it would take. He was bursting with ambition and ideas, the

wildest dresser rock 'n' roll had ever seen—which is saying something—
an outrageous showman whose style was a combination of Fillmore
district pimp gone stone crazy and Fillmore Auditorium optimism with
a point to it. A cultural politician of the first order, Sly was less interested in crossing racial and musical lines than in tearing them up.

In the manner of the very greatest rock 'n' roll, Sly and the Family
Stone made music no one had ever heard before.

In moments you could catch echoes of Sam Cooke, the Beatles, a lot
of jazz, and even a little surf music. Not just the singers but the whole
band seemed to find much of their inspiration in a few classic rock 'n'
roll songs, building off the furious vocal lines of the Silhouettes' "Get
a Job," the mad desire of Maurice Williams's "Stay," and the chaos of
Stevie Wonder's preteen apocalypse, "Fingertips." The band dismissed
the simple, direct sound of the black music of the day, from Stax to
James Brown, but took advantage of its rhythmic inventions; the Family Stone had much of the exhilaration of the white San Francisco
sound, along with the open spirit that sound was already beginning to
lose. And there was a keen ear for the hook lines and commercial punch
crucial to the charts of any rock era.

The whole was something other than its parts, perhaps because
what came across was not simply a new musical style, though there was
that, but a shared attitude, a point of view: not just a brand-new talk,
but the brand-new walk of young men and women on the move.

There was an enormous freedom to the band's sound. It was complex, because freedom is complex; wild and anarchic, like the wish for
freedom; sympathetic, affectionate, and coherent, like the reality of
freedom. And it was all celebration, all affirmation, a music of endless
humor and delight, like a fantasy of freedom.

They had hits: "Dance to the Music," "Stand!," "Everyday People,"
"Hot Fun in the Summertime," "Thank you falettinme be mice elf
Agin." A smash with black kids and white, these records had all the
good feeling of the March on Washington, and the street cachet that
march never had.

Sly's real triumph was that he had it both ways. Every nuance of his
style, from the razzle-dazzle of his threads to the originality of his music to the explosiveness of his live performance, made it clear he was his
own man. If the essence of his music was freedom, no one was more
aggressively, creatively free than he. Yet there was room for everyone
in the America of a band made up of blacks and whites, men and
women, who sang out "different strokes for different folks" and were
there on stage to show an audience just what such an idea of indepen-

dence meant. Vocals were demystified: everybody sang (even Cynthia Robinson, who screeched). When the band growled out "Don't Call Me Nigger, Whitey (Don't Call Me Whitey, Nigger)," they gave pleasure by using the insults for all they were worth, and at the same time showed how deeply those insults cut.

Sly was a winner. It seemed he had not only won the race, he had made up his own rules. Driving the finest cars, sporting the most sensational clothes, making the biggest deals and the best music, he was shaping the style and ambition of black teenagers all over the country— expanding the old Staggerlee role of the biggest, baddest man on the block. Sly was Staggerlee, and the power of the role was his, but he didn't have to kill anyone to get it.

RIOT

Motown raced to absorb Sly's new music, to catch up. They tightened his aesthetic and roared back up the charts with a revamped version of the Temptations and the new Jackson 5. Sly kept up the pace, breaking the color line at Woodstock and emerging as the festival's biggest hit. In early 1970 the band cut a new single, called "Everybody Is a Star," and it was their best—a lovely, awesomely moving statement of what the band was about and what it was for. A new album was on the way, Sly told an interviewer, "the most optimistic of all."

But something went wrong. Sly began to show up late for concerts, or not at all. That caused riots, including a very bad one in Chicago. Performances, when they came off, were often erratic, angry, or uncommitted. There was no new album; there was trouble with promoters; lawsuits; rumors of the band breaking up; rumors of bad dope, gangsters, extortion, death threats. Sly's manager said his client had a split personality.

Finally, in late 1971, the new record hit the stores. There was an American flag on the cover (flowers instead of stars) and happy pictures all over the rest of it (with odd, somber shots of Lincoln and the Gettysburg Address here and there). The album was called *There's a riot goin' on*, and the title cut was blank.

The record was no fun. It was slow, hard to hear, and it didn't celebrate anything. It was not groovy. In fact, it was distinctly unpleasant, unnerving. Many people didn't like it, wrote it off as a junkie bummer. If Robert Johnson were alive today there would be someone around to yell "Boogie!" at him.

There's a riot goin' on was an exploration of and a pronouncement on the state of the nation, Sly's career, his audience, black music, black politics, and a white world. Emerging out of a pervasive sense, at once public and personal, that the good ideas of the sixties had gone to their limits, turned back upon themselves, and produced evil where only good was expected, the album began where "Everybody Is a Star" left off, and it asked: So what?

The album contained, in a matrix of parody and vicious self-criticism, virtually all the images and slogans Sly had given to his audience. The new music called all the old music and the reasons for claiming it into question. Like *Bonnie and Clyde*, which angered critics in much the same way, *Riot* was, and is, a rough, disturbing work that can be ignored, dismissed, but never smoothed over.

Riot joined other pop reversals that confused and divided audiences and created new ones, pop acts that risked the destruction of the artist's audience. It was Sly's equivalent of Van Morrison's *Blowin' Your Mind*, his first solo album, where Van reached for the grotesque because it seemed the only rational description of everyday life; of Dylan's *John Wesley Harding*, in that Sly was escaping his own pop past and denying its value; of John Lennon's screaming break with the Beatles, though Sly worked with much greater sophistication and intelligence. Instead of merely orchestrating his confessions, Sly transformed them into a devastating work of art that deeply challenged anyone who ever claimed to be a part of his audience, a piece of music that challenges most of the assumptions of rock 'n' roll itself.

In an age when politics succeeds by confusing and obscuring matters of life and death, the strongest artists must claim those things as their own and act them out. Not many will ever have the nerve or the vision to do it, but at least for as long as it took to make *Riot*, Sly did.

Riot begins with a slow, stuttering beat, a chanting parody of "Stand!" As Sly comes in, wailing and groaning, half-satisfied, half-desperate, the question that comes through is whether it is worth standing up at all, or possible even if it is worth it. In another world, the man who sings this song did not merely "control the decisions that affected his life," to use a phrase from the decade this album left behind, he made them; now the words "control" and "decision" have lost their meaning. Tense, nervous, creepy, the song careens to an end, and it sets the tone. What follows is an expertly crafted and brilliantly performed review of folly, failure, betrayal, and disintegration—the confession of a man, speaking for more than himself, who has been trapped by limits whose existence he once would not even admit to, let alone respect: trapped by dope; by the weakness behind a world based on style; by the repression that sent black men and women into hiding, into exile, into the morgue; by the flimsiness of the rewards a white society has offered him. A testament to oppression, the music is, on first listening, itself oppressive.

The songs seem to wander, to show up and disappear, ghostly, with no highs or lows. At their kindest, they are simply ironic. Some, like "Africa Talks to You 'The Asphalt Jungle,'" are morbid: chased into hiding by the band, Sly shouts back, "Timmmmmberrr!" and the guitar mocks him into silence. "Brave and Strong" pleads for survival, but hints that only dope will get it.

Two tracks were released as singles—"Family Affair" and "Runnin' Away"—both were hits, and both had a deceptively easy movement. But the first was about finding your way back to mother and a marriage falling to pieces, and the second used a saucy female chorus to drive nails into a fool.

The album found its end with "Thank you for talkin' to me Africa," a reversal of "Thank you falettinme be mice elf Agin." There is no vocal music in rock 'n' roll to match it; the voices creep in and out of the instruments, cutting out in the middle of a line, messages from limbo, golem-talk. "I'm a-dyin, I'm-a-dyin," you can hear Sly wailing, and the only way to disbelieve is to stop listening. The song gathers up all the devastation of the rest of the album and slowly drives it home, grinds it in, and fades out.

This music defines the world of the Staggerlee who does not get away, and who finds hell as advertised. There is an enormous reality to the music: a slow, level sense of getting by. It is Muzak with its finger on the trigger; the essence of the rhythms James Brown has explored without the compensations of Brown's showmanship or his badass lyrics. It is a reality of day-to-day sameness and an absence of variety—like prison—that requires, if one is to endure it, either a deadening of all the senses, or a preternatural sharpening of them, so that the smallest change of mood or event can be seized on as representing something novel or meaningful.

In this sense, and only at the farthest margin, the music is part of the way out of the disaster it affirms. If you listen, you get sharper, and you begin to hear what the band is hearing; every bass line or vocal nuance eventually takes on great force. The disaster gains an emotional complexity, and you enter it. Finally, *Riot* bears the same relationship to most music as George Jackson's *Soledad Brother* does to *Confidential*. The second is easier to get into, but nothing is there.

Stand!, the brilliant album that preceded *Riot* (and literally turned black music inside out with its flash and innovation), had all the drive and machinery of a big semi-truck; listening to it put you in the driver's seat, made you feel like you owned the road. *Riot* is about getting off the truck. The mood is one of standing still; of performing every act with the care of one who is not sure his mind and his body will quite connect; of falling apart; of running, looking back, realizing you can be caught.

> *Lookin' at the devil,*
> *Grinnin' at his gun.*
> *Fingers start shakin',*
> *I begin to run.*
>
> *Bullets start chasin',*
> *I begin to stop.*
> *We begin to wrestle,*
> *I was on the top.*

"Thank you for talkin' to me Africa"

When the song was released a year earlier as "Thank you falettinme be mice elf Agin," it had a snappy rhythm. It was a winner's song, and neither the music nor the vocals left any doubt as to who was going to stay on top. On *Riot* the song comes slowly, emphasizing the thud of the bass guitar. The words are buried in a slurred half-chant; when Sly sings, "Thank you falettinme be mice elf Agin," the contempt in his voice is inescapable.

Notice how the song reads. The words Sly wrote for *Riot* are some of the most imaginative and forceful in all of rock 'n' roll. The images are perfectly developed; the songs achieve a tense and eerie balance, as each element of the music seems to pull more than its own weight. Not one image, not one note, is wasted. Nothing is gratuitous.

One song, "Poet," was called pretentious, because it said such things as, "I'm a songwriter, oh yeh a poet." The number is intentionally crude, but in the end such a song is pretentious only if it is false. And although for rock 'n' roll the terms themselves are probably false, the words of the songs on this album are better "poetry" than anything the "rock poets" have written. The rock poets are all of them white, of course, because the rock 'n' roll audience—and rock critics—often think in neat racial categories, and "black" does not fit into the "poetry" category. When Bob Dylan quipped that Smokey Robinson was America's greatest poet, most people thought that was some kind of joke.

Of all the nonsense that has been written about the poetry of Neil Young, Paul Simon, or even Bob Dylan, no one has ever said anything about Jimi Hendrix's "Little Wing." The poetry question, especially when we are dealing with a song, has to do with how a writer uses language—and his music will be part of his language—to make words do things they ordinarily do not do, with how he tests the limits of language and alters and extends the conventional impact of images, or rescues resources of language that we have lost or destroyed. The music on *Riot* mostly flattens out what Sly wrote, hiding it, telling the truth, but not quite out loud. The words peek out, and only occasionally do they hit you in the face.

> *Lookin' at the devil,*
> *Grinnin' at his gun.*
> *Fingers start shakin',*
> *I begin to run.*
>
> *Bullets start chasin'*
> *I begin to stop.*

The poetry of those lines is the use of the words "start" and "begin," which slow the usual pace of the violent images Sly is presenting. The eye is working here, taking in the scene from the edge of action; the description is minimal and the economy is absolute. The eye turns and the listener, or the reader, is given only a vague sense of physical motion, a whole body aware of itself with the precision of the eye in the first three lines. You feel the slowing down, the endless, instantaneous decisions and hesitations involved in turning to face the gun again. It all moves in pieces, and you are in the song, in the riot, breathing its risk.

Sly saw a band as the means by which each member finds his or her own voice; while he is the source of vision, the emotion of every singer, his included, has been authentic because that vision is shared. I think this is so because Sly's vision, whether one of affirmation, as it was in the sixties, or negation, as it is on *Riot*, is always an attempt at liberation.

It is Sly's musical authority that gives his singers freedom, that builds a home where freedom seems worth acting out. The singing on the Family's records—complex, personal, and unpredictable—really was something new. As opposed to the Temptations or the Jackson 5, whose records were not inspired by Sly's sound so much as they formalized it (just as earlier Motown imposed order on the risky spontaneity of gospel music), what you hear in Sly's music are a number of individuals who have banded together because that is the way they can best express themselves *as* individuals. It's the freedom of the street, not the church.

This was made explicit in "Everybody Is a Star." That meant not that everyone lives in the spotlight, but that every man and woman finds moments of visibility appropriate to what he or she has to give. On *Riot* Sly took this aesthetic—of the group that sings like a band plays—away from the context of celebration, which had seemed not only appropriate but necessary, and made it the means to a dramatization of events and moods that are bitter, mocking, and scary. Voices stretch words until they are drained of their ordinary meanings, just as the guitars, drums, bass, horns, and organ reduce the sensational clichés of the earlier music to bone. The superstar clothes are removed, piece by piece, and what is left, in a weird and modern way, is the blues.

The equality is still there: no one is a star.

With "Family Affair," so direct in its musical impact and so elusive in its meanings, Sly comes close to a conventional lead vocal, but here he needs the isolation of the spotlight because he is singing about the need to lean on other people.

> *Both kids are good to mom*
> *You see, it's in the blood*
> *Blood's thicker than the mud*

He sings from a distance, preaching, trying to explain something that matters. Some people give up on you; some don't, no matter what you do. Sometimes it's important to find out who's who. Sly presented this to the Top 40 audience like a philosophy lesson, holding out knowledge he had paid for.

> *You*
> *It's a family affair don't*
> *know*
> *who*
> *turned*
> *you*
> *in.*

With *Riot* Sly gave his audience—particularly his white audience—exactly what it didn't want. What it wanted was an upper, not a portrait of what lay behind the big freaky black superstar grin that decorated the cover of the album. One gets the feeling, listening, that the disastrous concerts that preceded and followed this record were not so much a matter of Sly insulting his audience as they were of Sly attacking that audience because of what the demands of the audience had forced him to produce. The concerts were an attack on himself as well, for having gone along with those demands and for having believed in them. All through *Riot* Sly turned on himself: "Must be a rush for me / To see a lazy / A brain he meant to be / Cop out?" He removed the question mark in the next verse, and ultimately covered the question with poison: "Dyin' young is hard to take / Sellin' out is harder."

Those last words were shoved under the graveyard chorus, "Thank you, falettinme be mice elf Agin," and it is not hard to see why this record was so hard to listen to, which is to say, hard to take.

The bonds of a peculiar aesthetic democracy held, one last time, to reveal a world of terror and falsehood, that moment when Staggerlee runs into the limits his role was meant to smash, the same limits that turned Selma into Attica and "Satisfaction" into "You Can't Always Get What You Want." The endless fantasies piled onto the Staggerlee myth over the years were simple proof of the force of those limits, of the need to transcend them, but the fantasy, remade again and again, had its own force: it created new Staggerlees.

Staggerlee is a free man, because he takes chances and scoffs at the consequences. Others, especially whites, gather to fawn over him, until he shatters in a grimy celebration of needles, juice, and noise. Finally he is alone in a slow bacchanal, where his buddies, in a parody of friendship, devote themselves to a study of the precise moment of betrayal. Out of this disaster the man who lives it sometimes emerges whole: Malcolm did. Sometimes he dies young; sometimes he cops out.

On the way to this silent riot Sly shouldered the racial and sexual fantasies of a huge audience and staggered under them, as if he were Staggerlee himself back from the dead to live up to his myth. The images of mastery, style, and triumph set forth earlier in Sly's career reversed themselves; his old politics had turned into death, his exuberance into dope, and his old music into a soundtrack for a world that didn't exist. As an artist, Sly used those facts to reverse the great myth itself.

The role is all too real. It was forced on Chuck Berry, who never wanted it, and he paid for it in prison; Hendrix resisted, but in the public mind, the role enclosed him anyway. *Riot* is the secret contained in the whole blazing tradition. Something more than a definition of the risks involved in getting your hands on Staggerlee's kind of freedom, more than an illustration of the neat duality of any cultural archetype, *Riot* claims the story.

When new roles break down and there is nothing with which to replace them, old roles, ghosts, come rushing in to fill up the vacuum. Whether or not he thought in these terms, Sly lived out one side of Staggerlee's life until the other side caught up, and took over. Once the first role broke down in the face of social and personal limits it could not countenance and still survive, the rage of Staggerlee intensified as his mastery was defrauded. Instead of breaking the bartender's glass Stack found himself aiming at the mirror behind the bar, and thus discovered that his target was himself.

SLY VERSUS SUPERFLY

The best pop music does not reflect events so much as it absorbs them. If the spirit of Sly's early music combined the promises of Martin Luther King's speeches and the fire of a big city riot, *Riot* represented the end of those events and the attempt to create a new music appropriate to new realities. It was music that had as much to do with the Marin shootout and the death of George Jackson as the earlier sound had to do with the pride of the riot the title track of this album said was no longer going on.

"Frightened faces to the wall," Sly moans. "Can't you hear your mama call? The Brave and Strong—Survive! Survive!"

I think those faces up against the wall belonged to Black Panthers, forced to strip naked on the night streets of Philadelphia so Frank Rizzo and his cops could gawk and laugh and make jokes about big limp cocks while Panther women, lined up with the men, were psychologically raped.

A picture was widely published. Many have forgotten it; Sly probably had not. This again is why *Riot* was hard to take. If its spirit is that of the death of George Jackson it is not a celebration of Jackson, but music that traps what you feel when you are shoved back into the corners of loneliness where you really have to think about dead flesh and cannot play around with the satisfactions of myth.

The pessimism of *Riot* is not the romantic sort we usually get in rock 'n' roll. Optimistic almost by definition, pop culture is always pointing toward the next thing and sure it is worth going after; rock 'n' roll is linked to a youthful sense of time and a youthful disbelief in death. Pop culture pessimism is almost always self-indulgent; not without the power to move an audience, but always leaving the audience (and the artist) a way out. In retrospect, records made in this spirit often seem like reverse images of narcissim. *Riot* is the real thing: scary and immobile. It wears down other records, turning them into unintentional self-parodies. The negative of *Riot* is tough enough to make solutions seem trivial and alternatives false, in personal life, politics, or music.

Rock 'n' roll may matter because it is fun, unpredictable, anarchic, a neatly packaged and amazingly intense plurality of good times and good ideas, but none save the very youngest musicians and fans can still take their innocence for granted. Most have simply seen and done too much; as the Rolling Stones have been proving for ten years, you have to *work* for innocence. You have to win it, or you end up with nothing more than a strained naïveté.

Because this is so pop needs an anchor, a reality principle, especially when the old ideas—the joy of the Beatles, the simple toughness of the Stones—have run their course and the music has begun to repeat its messages without repeating their impact. Rock 'n' roll may escape conventional reality on a day-to-day level (or remake it, minute-to-minute), but it has to have an intuitive sense of the reality it means to escape; the audience and the artists have to be up against the wall before they can climb over it. When the Stones made "Gimme Shelter," they had power because their toughness had taken on complexity: they admitted they had doubts about finding even something as simple as shelter, and fought for it anyway. But because the band connected with its audience when they got that across, and because the music that did it was the best they ever made, the song brought more than shelter; it brought life, provided a metaphor that allowed the Stones to thrive when Altamont proved toughness was not the point, and gave them the freedom to go on to sing about other things—soul survivors, suffocation, a trip down a moonlight mile.

Riot matters because it doesn't just define the wall; it makes the wall real. Its sensibility is hard enough to frame the mass of pop music, shuffle its impact, jar the listener, and put an edge on the easy way out that has not really been won. It is not casual music and its demands are not casual; it tended to force black musicians to reject it or live up to it. Some months after *Riot* was released—from the middle of 1972 through early 1973—the impulses of its music emerged on other records, and they took over the radio.

I don't know if I will be able to convey the impact of punching buttons day after day and night after night to be met by records as clear and strong as Curtis Mayfield's "Superfly" and "Freddie's Dead," the

Staple Singers' "Respect Yourself" and the utopian "I'll Take You There," the O'Jays' "Back Stabbers," War's astonishing "Slipping into Darkness" and "The World Is a Ghetto," the Temptations' "Papa Was a Rolling Stone," Johnny Nash's "I Can See Clearly Now," Stevie Wonder's "Superstition," for that matter the Stones' *Exile on Main Street* (the white *Riot)*—records that were surrounded, in memory and still on the air as recent hits, by Marvin Gaye's deadly "Inner City Blues," by the Undisputed Truth's "Smiling Faces Sometimes (Tell Lies)," by the Chi-Lites' falsetto melancholy, by *Riot* itself. Only a year before such discs would have been curiosities; now, they were all of a piece: one enormous answer record. Each song added something to the others, and as in a pop explosion, the country found itself listening to a new voice.

To me, the Temptations took the prize. Imagine—or simply remember—the chill of driving easily through the night, and then hearing, casually at first, then with interest, and then with compulsion, the three bass patterns, repeated endlessly, somewhere between the sound of the heart and a judge's gavel, that open "Papa Was a Rolling Stone." The toughest blues guitar you have heard in years cracks through the building music like a curse; the singer starts in.

More than one person I knew pulled off the road and sat waiting, shivering, as the song crept out of the box and filled up the night.

Four children have gathered around their mother to ask for the truth about their father, who has been buried that very day. They don't know him; he was just another street-corner Stagolee. So they ask. Was he one of those two-faced preachers, mama—"Stealing in the name of the Lord?"* A drunk? A hustler? A pimp? With another wife, more kids? They slam the questions into their mother, and all she can give them is one of the most withering epitaphs ever written, for them, as well as for him: "When he died, all he left us was alone."

Some thought "Back Stabbers" hit even harder. It moved with a new urgency, heading into its chorus with an unforgettable thump; it was like hearing the Drifters again, but the Drifters robbed of the pop optimism that let them find romance even in the hard luck of "On Broadway." The O'Jays sounded scared when they climaxed the song with an image that was even stronger than the music: "I wish somebody'd take/ Some a' these *knives* outta my back!'

Stevie Wonder reached number one with "Superstition"—his first time on top in ten years. It was the most ominous hard rock in a long

* A reference to Paul Kelly's single of the same name, which, along with Jerry Butler's "Only the Strong Survive," had opened up the new territory the Tempts were exploring.

while, a warning against a belief in myths that no one understood; Wonder made the old chicka-chicka-boom beat so potent it sounded like a syncopated version of Judgment Day.

All these records were nervous, trusting little if anything, taking *Riot*'s spirit of black self-criticism as a new aesthetic, driven (unlike *Riot*) by great physical energy, determined to get across the idea of a world—downtown or uptown, it didn't matter—where nothing was as it seemed. These black musicians and singers were cutting loose from the white man's world to attend to their own business—and to do that, they had to tell the truth. And so they made music of worry and confinement that, in their very different way, the Chi-Lites took to even greater extremes.

The Chi-Lites—like all the artists discussed here—had been around for many years, but they broke into the Top 40 in the seventies, with a dark chant called "(For God's Sake) Give More Power to the People." Stylistically, this was an old kind of record, but it was a new kind of politics; instead of a demand, or an affirmation, it was a plea, and a desperate one at that. The Chi-Lites' persona was open and vulnerable, the antithesis of machismo (something they explicitly dismissed with the great "Oh Girl"). Other hits—"A Lonely Man," "Have You Seen Her," and "The Coldest Day of My Life"—undercut the high-stepping burst of mastery on which Wilson Pickett and so many other black artists of the sixties had based their careers; the Chi-Lites made Pickett's old bragging music sound fake. Pickett had told his audience that ninety-nine-and-a-half won't do and made them believe it, but the Chi-Lites seemed ready to settle for a lot less—or to beg for something else altogether. The key to any black singer is in that old catch phrase about the way you talk and the way you walk; the Chi-Lites spoke softly and moved with great care.

This new music was a step back for a new look at black America; it was a finger pointed at Staggerlee and an attempt to freeze his spirit out of black culture. On many levels—direct, symbolic, commercial, personal—this music was a vital, conservative reaction to the radical costs Sly had shown that Staggerlee must ultimately exact. And since Stack was roaming virtually unchallenged in the new black cinema, this musical stance amounted to a small-scale cultural war.

All the new black movies—from *Hit Man* to *Trouble Man* to *Detroit 9000* to *Cleopatra Jones*—were cued by the reality behind one very carefully thrown-away line from *The Godfather* (a movie, it is worth remembering, that attracted millions of black Americans, even though it had no black characters, let alone any black heroes).

"They're animals anyway," says an off-camera voice, as the Dons make the crucial decision to dump all their heroin into the ghettos. "Let them lose their souls."

The Mafia may have missed the contradiction in that line, but Francis Coppola certainly did not; neither did the black men and women in the theaters. They suffered it; in *Lady Sings the Blues*, Diana Ross was stalking screens all over the country showing just what it meant. That audience had a right to revenge.

And so the fantasy went to work again. If that line had opened up the abyss, the old black hero shot up from the bottom and pushed in the white man instead. Stack slipped through the hands of the white sheriff, won his fight, got his girl, and got away.

Superfly summed up the genre; perhaps its first scene did, more than it was meant to. The hero, cocaine dealer Priest (played by Ron O'Neal, who looked uncomfortably like a not-very-black Sean Connery) stirs in the bed of his rich white mistress. Some black fool has made off with his stash. Priest chases him through the alleys, up the side of a building, and traps him in a tiny apartment. There, in full view of the man's family, Priest beats him half to death. This was John Hurt's Billy, but Lloyd Price's Stagger Lee.

Still, Priest is nervous. Hustling's all the Man has left us, he tells his partner, who thinks that's just fine; Priest wants out of the Life, but the invisible whites who run the show want him in—or dead. He bets everything on one last big deal. He turns on the pressure; one of his runners, Freddie, can't take it, and he panics and gets himself killed. Another man, a sort of father figure (who started Priest out peddling reefers when just a lad) is talked into the game, and he too loses his life to Priest's bid for freedom. Priest's partner weighs the odds and sells him out.

Moving fast, Priest penetrates the white coke hierarchy, takes out a first-class Mafia contract on Mr. Big to cover his bet, unmasks Mr. Big as a queer, and, with his money and his strong black woman, gets away clean. He turned up one movie later as a crusader for social justice in Africa, where life was simpler.

It was a fairy tale; but like most of the Staggerlee movies, *Superfly* had a soundtrack by an established soul singer, and in this case Curtis Mayfield's songs were not background, but criticism. (Mayfield had appeared in the picture singing in a dealers' bar, grinding out an attempted parody of his audience—but they thought it was a celebration.) His music worked against the fantasy, because to him one incident in the movie counted for more than all its triumphs: Freddie's dead. "Pushin' dope for *the Man!*" he sang, incredulous and disgusted. The movie hadn't even slowed to give Freddie an epitaph, but Mayfield clearly aimed his song at the hero as well.*

Superfly had a black director, Gordon Parks, Jr.; there was a surface ghetto realism, and there were touches of ambiguity, but the movie had Hollywood in its heart, and that was enough to smother everything else. Most of the pictures that followed simply shuffled *Superfly* clichés, but they kept coming.

Young black men began to imitate the movies, and real life put on its own endings. In the tiny black town of Brooklyn, Illinois, the mayor deputized a hustler named Bollinger to run a militant out of town (Priest had only contempt for black politics—not violent enough, he said, he'd deal with the Man his own way). With the competition out of business, Bollinger took over; he ran the town the way Capone ran Cairo, until another black man named Skinner—lacking the hustler's long coat and broad-brimmed hat—faced him down. Anyone doubting they had been to the movies can read the dialogue.

"'I guess you're lookin' for me,' said Bollinger calmly.

"'That's right,' replied Skinner. 'I'm lookin' for you, man. I know you've heard I'm the police chief now.'

"'I'm not giving up a goddamn thing,' said Bollinger."

Skinner shot Bollinger dead; then the hustler's girl stood over him. She said: "He lived like a man. He died like one too."†

The story out of Detroit was worse. A group of three young men—determined, like the heroes of so many new black movies, to clean the smack out of their neighborhood—began to lean hard on dealers and junkies. They were armed and violent. A run-in with STRESS (Stop Robberies Enjoy Safe Streets), the killer squad of the Detroit police, which the three men suspected had ties with the heroin trade, seemed inevitable. When it was over two cops were dead and the vigilantes were on the run. The youngest was caught in Detroit, and survived; his two comrades were tailed to Atlanta, set up, and executed. And all the while, in uptown movie houses across the country, Staggerlee killed and fucked and killed and fucked and the white sheriff near died of envy and Billy died to let Stack kill and fuck another day.

One movie was different, but it never found its audience, not among blacks, or whites either. *Across 110th Street* (directed by Barry Shear,

---

* Interestingly, these lyrics were not in the movie, even though the backing track was. Mayfield held off until the film was in the theaters, then wrote the words, released the record, and so took on the picture on his own turf: the radio. You could say he chickened out, and you could also say he was very smart.

†Dialogue quoted from "High Noon after Nightfall," *Time*, December 17, 1973.

who earlier made *Wild in the Streets*, the most paradoxical youth exploitation picture; written by Luther Davis) looked enough like all the
others to make it easy for nearly all critics to dismiss it. The film was
almost unbelievably violent, which gave reviewers license to attack it.
It began with the same clichés everyone else used, but intensified them
mercilessly. It pumped so much pressure into the world of the new
black movies that it blew that world apart.

Three black men—Jamaica, Superflake, and Dry Clean—murder a
pack of black and white Mafia bankers and make off with the week's
take for all of Harlem. They don't steal because they hate the mob; they
steal because they want the money. A Mafia lieutenant—played by Tony
Franciosa—is sent out to bring back the money and execute the thieves,
knowing full well he can forget his future if he fails. Anthony Quinn
plays a bought cop caught in the middle. He has to take the case straight
to make his pension, and a new black cop is keeping an eye on him, but
he has to do it without losing his payoff—or his life—to the Mafia
hirelings who control his district: a black man who runs a taxi company
and looks like Fats Domino risen from the swamp of evil, and his bodyguard, a Staggerlee who watches over the entire film with the cold eyes
of someone who sold his soul to the devil the day he was old enough to
know he had one.

You paid for every bit of violence, perhaps because the film refused
its audience the pleasures of telling the good guys from the bad guys,
and because the violence was so ugly it exploded the violence of the
genre. It wasn't gratuitous, but it wasn't "poetic" either. Every character
seemed alive, with motives worth reaching for, no matter how twisted
they might turn out to be; every character (save for Taxi Man and his
gunman) fled through the story scared half out of his wits, desperate for
space, for a little more time, for one more chance.

The thieves speed away from the litter of corpses, divide up the
money, and go into hiding. Superflake is too proud of himself to stay
holed up; good times are what it was all for, right? His best hustler's
clothes—tasteless Sly Stone, but gaudy—have been hanging for this
moment. Down at the best whorehouse in Harlem Superflake has a
dozen women and he's bragging.

Franciosa picks up the scent, and with Taxi Man's Staggerlee at his
side, his eyes glazing over with a sadism that masks his own terror, he rips
Superflake out of the whorehouse bar. When Quinn finds Superflake
crucified, castrated, and skinned alive, you realize that along with no
heroes, this movie may offer no way out. It was made to take your sleep.

Jamaica and Dry Clean pass the word and panic; they know that

Superflake had to finger them. Dry Clean shoves his money into a clothes bag from his shop and hails a cab for Jersey. The driver spots the markings on the bag, radios back to Taxi Man, and delivers Dry Clean straight to Franciosa at 110th Street—the border of Harlem and the one line the movie never crosses. Dry Clean breaks away; Franciosa traps him on a roof, ties a rope to his leg, and hangs him over a beam, dangling him into space. Staggerlee holds the rope; his eyes show nothing as he watches the white man torture the black. If Dry Clean talks, they say, they won't kill him; he is so scared he believes them. He talks, and the rope shoots over the side.

Jamaica and his girl meet in his wretched apartment (there is a little torn-out picture of Martin Luther King taped to the wall, a gray reminder of some other time) to plan an escape, or a better hideout. And in one of the most extraordinary scenes in any American movie, a death's-head reversal of every warm close-up you have ever seen, Jamaica begins to talk—about green hills and a blue sky; about quiet, rest, peace of mind; about going home. He has only killed nine men to get there. His face is scarred by smallpox; his eyes try hard to explain. Jamaica goes on; you don't hear him; the camera stays in tight. Every few seconds his whole face shudders, seems almost to shred, as a ghastly, obscenely complex twitch climbs from his jaw to his temple, breaks, and starts up again.

It is the visual equivalent of that last song on *Riot*, "Thank you for talkin' to me Africa," another reach for a home that isn't there. Like Sly's music, the scene is unbearably long, it makes you want to run, but each frame like each note deepens the impact, until everything else in the world has been excluded and only one artistic fact remains. Jamaica's twitch traces the fear of every character in the movie; it is a map of the ambiguities the other movies so easily shot away; and in this film, it is most of all the other side of Staggerlee's face, which never moves.

Finally, Franciosa, Quinn, and their troops converge on the abandoned tenement where Jamaica and his girl are hiding. Taxi Man gets word of the showdown. "Wanna watch," says Staggerlee. "No," says Taxi Man. "I know how it's gonna turn out."

A bullet cuts through the girl's forehead and pins her to the wall behind Jamaica. She stays on camera, standing up dead, a blank ugliness on her face. When Jamaica turns to see her you can feel the life go out of him, but he keeps shooting. Franciosa is killed; the cops take over. Jamaica flees to the roof with his gun and his bag of money, still firing. He kills more. Staggerlee, sent to cover for Taxi Man, watches from another rooftop. Jamaica falls, and in the only false moment in the picture, flings his money down to children in a playground. Staggerlee sets up a rifle, takes aim on Quinn, who has proved himself too weak to be worth the mob's time, and kills him.

In one way, then, this movie was like all the others: Staggerlee wins. But this time, the audience was not given the benefit of any masks; they had to take him as he came, and they were not about to pay money to see that.

Almost always, there is a retreat once something like the truth is out. Audiences respond to that moment of clarity, but they only want so much of it; scared of their own vision or not trusting their audiences, artists grow timid and hedge their bets. Follow hard rock with a ballad, follow a threat with reassurance. The O'Jays and their producers, Kenny Gamble and Leon Huff, put as much distance between themselves and "Back Stabbers" as they could with "Love Train" (the tough "992 Arguments" had died); the Temptations, as usual, copied themselves, with the horrendous "Ghetto" ("Hmmm, life sure is tough here in the ghetto"), and turned art into shlock in record time. The perfectly named Brighter Side of Darkness got a hit with "Love Jones," and made dope romantic. The restraint of the Chi-Lites became so stylized they went off the deep end with "We Need Order." The music seemed to lose its edge; it went bland, as if to prove that the only alternative to Stagolee was an imitation of white middle-class respectability.

At the core of the attempt to make artistic and commercial sense out of the world *Riot* revealed—and in terms of black music, almost invented—was a new triumph of black capitalism and controlled craftsmanship, a kind of poetic efficiency. Most of the records discussed here were created by producers, not groups, and while the producers would take virtually any risk to break onto the charts, their real ambition seemed to be to stay on the charts without taking any risks at all.

The team of Gamble and Huff, working out of Philadelphia, epitomized the style. Their records featured beautifully intricate hooks, a sophisticated blend of R&B force and mainstream strings, and irresistible internal riffs that stood up under hundreds of listenings, which meant that when the records got on the radio they stayed there. The Spinners' "I'll Be Around" (produced by Gamble-Huff disciple Thorn Bell) featured an up-and-down guitar line that could have carried a French lesson without losing any of its commercial force. But cultural force was something else again.

The new black hit factories—Willie Mitchell in Memphis with Al Green (who found his voice in the gap between Pickett's arrogance and the Chi-Lites' weakness), Lambert and Potter in Los Angeles with the Four Tops (whose "Keeper of the Castle" affirmed the family over hustling—or politics), and Gamble-Huff—spoke of consistency and stability as the crucial values. After that one burst of unity and vitality (which, if we call it a fad, will tell us how good fads can be), black music drifted back into something like a parallel of the most conventional black reality (save for Stevie Wonder and Marvin Gaye, who produced their own records with their own money, and kept moving). This was a limit not only on violence and excess, but on real cultural ambition: a black version of "benign neglect." Daniel Moynihan thought if you removed the promise you would remove the threat; here, the threat submerged, but so did the promise, because the paradox that gives *Riot* its tension is that Sly knows that Staggerlee holds the key to vitality as well as disaster.

What makes *Riot* truly bleak, after all, is not that Sly ever resists the role Staggerlee has carved out, not that he shrinks from its momentum, but that he cannot survive it. And it was this truth that made *Riot* so different from all the other records, no matter how good they were. The producers' singers moved easily from music that could have made history to music that merely reflected it; many even lost the energy that in popular music can usually be substituted for vision. They drifted, like all cultural reflections, into accommodation, into music for a new normalcy.

"An insufferable deadness had invaded our lives," Frank Kermode has written of the thirties, though his words do well enough for our own time. "We needed . . . to be violently stirred into life . . . intolerable social constraints grew daily upon us."

Nixon's rule made those lines seem quite familiar; their meaning has seeped down into our bones, like a secret second nature. It is a debilitating secret to which those who keep it can barely admit, because, in spite of all the clichés about how nothing can ever imprison an idea or a dream, dreams can be imprisoned inside those who once held to them.

Those dreams are worn down and dissolved as the world mocks them by its versions of reality; they are dissolved because the one who once felt alive because of them must live in that world. He or she does not conform to it, necessarily, but adjusts to it in a hundred ways every day: with every thought he turns away from, with every word she does not speak, with every fantasy of violence, liberation, or death that fades into the nightly dreams one does not understand and does not much want to.

Too much war and too much public crime have poisoned the country to be easily put to rest by any kind of reform or vengeance. There is simply too much to forget. Our politics have robbed the good words of ethics of their meaning; an impenetrable official venality has robbed the good ideas of the last few years of theirs. What, in the sixties, looked like a chance to find new forms of political life, has been replaced by a flight to privacy and cynicism; the shared culture that grew out of a love affair with the Beatles has collapsed (not without their help) into nostalgia and crackpot religion. The revisionists have already gone to work on the last decade—which was, no matter how smug, self-righteous, or naïve, a time of greater cultural and political freedom than most of us will likely know again. Those who, in Leslie Fiedler's words, "lived the mythic life of their generation," those who made it and were remade by it, can now hardly remember it.

Throughout the years of Nixon's ascendancy the *New Yorker* opened most issues with a page of unsigned commentary that tried to see through each week's dose of lies—the obvious lies told by those in power, and the more subtle, pathetic lies told by those who twisted to escape the first. It was something better than comforting to read that commentary every week, and something worse. There was satisfaction in knowing that someone had the will and the talent to work to find the truth no matter how pointless the effort seemed; there was a queasy disgust in knowing that someone else had to do that work for me. Whether my own talents were not up to the job, or my will too weak, didn't much matter. It was too easy to lose touch with rage, with a sense of what is good and evil, to lose touch with the idea that it is worth something to make, and try to live out, such a distinction.

These are politics of the freeze-out. They turn into a culture of seamless melancholy with the willful avoidance of anything—a book, some photographs, a record, a movie, even a newspaper—that one suspects might produce really deep feeling. Raw emotions must be avoided when one knows they will take no shape but that of chaos.

Within such a culture there are many choices: cynicism, which is a smug, fraudulent kind of pessimism; the sort of camp sensibility that puts all feeling at a distance; or culture that reassures, counterfeits excitement and adventure, and is safe. A music as broad as rock 'n' roll will always come up with some of each, and probably that's just as it should be.

Sometimes, though, you want something more: work so intense and compelling you will risk chaos to get close to it, music that smashes through a world that for all of its desolation may be taking on too many of the comforts of familiarity. Sly created a moment of lucidity in the midst of all the obvious negatives and the false, faked hopes; he made his despair mean something in the midst of a despair it is all too easy to think may mean nothing at all. He was clearing away the cultural and political debris that seemed piled up in mounds on the streets, in the papers, in the record stores; for all of the darkness of what he had to say and how he said it, his music had the kind of strength and the naked honesty that could make you want to start over.

A QUIET REBELLION

Sly clearly could not push *Riot* much farther, not without releasing a whole album of silence; and not, perhaps, without losing the audience he had worked to win. *Fresh*, the album that did follow, in 1973, showed Sly clicking his heels for Richard Avedon's camera, and the songs did their best to keep up with the title and the cover. "There's a mickie in the tastin' of disaster," was the first line of *Fresh*—Sly's instinctive paraphrase of Nietzsche's belief that he who gazes into the abyss will find the abyss looking back; that he who looks too long at monsters may well become one.

The music was good, but it lacked the fire of *Riot*, the tiny explosions of a bass riff or a horn part stuttering along vocal lines, ambushing words and transforming emotions. Save for "Que Sera, Sera," which Sly and Rosie Stone turned into a blues (this following months of bizarre rumors of a romance between Sly and Doris Day—"*Riot* or no *Riot*" said a friend, "he hasn't lost his sense of humor"), the music and the singing lacked risk. Most critics applauded Sly's step toward "a more positive" stance, but there was little on *Fresh* to prove that it was more than a stance.

Worse, the complexity of Sly's music, from "Everyday People" to *Riot*—the tension between the individual and the group, the tension of politics orchestrated in personal terms—was overtaken by a straightforward presentation of Sly's role, and the group now seemed little more than his servant. The album's hit, "If You Want Me to Stay," was a conventional comment on the ambiguities of stardom, and there were too many references to Sly's coke habit (switched to pep, he said), the time lag between LP's, and the like. Such subjects may have been meant to work outside the limited context of Sly's personal dilemma, but they did not connect. Still, there was "Que Sera"—and the album could be seen as an attempt to figure out how it would feel to live with honesty and energy in a country that had forced the recognitions of *Riot*, but that had more to show those who knew how to look.

A tour followed the release *of Fresh*—the first Sly and the Family Stone had made in two years (two original members had quit and been replaced)—and the show I saw in Berkeley in the summer of 1973 was both interesting and a fraud. It was Sly's homecoming concert, and he presented it as such; his last in the Bay Area had been a post-*Riot* shambles, with Sly walking off the stage after a few bitter minutes, shouting something about how the audience couldn't handle what he had to give them. He had played the Cow Palace then, which holds 16,000; the Berkeley Community Theatre was nearly full, but it seats only about 3,000.

Sly celebrated trumpet player Cynthia Robinson's birthday by bringing her mother out on stage; he talked quietly about his parents, smiling broadly, trying to get across how appropriate it seemed to him that his mother had given him the ideas for some of his best songs. That was interesting, and moving. It was the music that was a fraud.

The playing was mostly mechanical; as Dave Marsh, who walked out on a similar show in Long Island, put it, the songs were "a rehash of older, more frivolous material . . . also a rehash of the part of [the past] which is most insidious, bypassing the strength of songs like 'Everybody Is a Star' and 'Everyday People' for the relatively empty 'Stand!' and 'M'Lady.'" There was not a single tune from *Riot;* the only performance that had conviction was a stunning "Que Sera," which for a moment almost saved the show; and the concert ended, as all Sly's concerts ended back in the Woodstock days, with "I Want to Take You Higher," which was always facile and is now a stupid lie. It wasn't even an effective one; the audience probably wanted to go farther more than they wanted to be taken higher, and the old piece of frenzy fizzled out in three or four minutes, as if neither the audience nor the band had much heart for the deception.

"It's one thing to change on record, in private," Dave Marsh said to me when we compared notes on the tour. "It's something else to look all those people in the face and tell them the good old days are gone." Maybe so. Perhaps, if Sly had woven a new show out *of Riot* and *Fresh,* the next tour would have had him playing to empty seats. Neither record includes much of an obvious crowd pleaser, and something had already brought Sly down from the big arena to the theater.

Most of all, though, Sly seemed eager to say that *Riot* had been a bad dream best forgotten. But if the weakness and failure of nerve of the concert I saw is what really grows out of *Riot,* that only means that the world Sly discovered and made real on that record is as debilitating as he said it was.

*   *   *

Whether the retreat is one of vision, as I think it is in Sly's case, or of craftsmanship and accounting, as with many black record producers, Sly's truest work has its own momentum ("Never trust the artist, trust the tale," D. H. Lawrence wrote, noting that American artists, because they cannot escape their audiences, are always desperate to cover up whatever they reveal); Sly's work penetrates into black politics just as it changed black music and haunts black movies. The turnaround of the Black Panther party—from the politics of violent rhetoric and armed self-defense to the politics of elections and alliance with the black church—parallels the retreat of the black producers and of *Fresh*. The Panther retreat may produce the same kind of guarded success; it may also tell us how necessary such retreats are. But it is worth remembering that Eldridge Cleaver and Huey Newton fought a war over this change in politics—a very strange war.

After a murderous shootout provoked by the Oakland police in 1968, Cleaver was to be returned to prison as a parole violator. He was willing to stand trial, but he was convinced he would be killed in jail; he would not go back. And there was more to it. He told Gene Marine:

> When I went back to prison before, it didn't matter, you know? Nobody cared about me anyway, I was in the same prison, you know? The prison of being alone. Out or in, it didn't matter. But this time—this time I've found something, since I've been in the movement and working with all these cats. I've found people who really dig me, people I really dig. People care about me, people *like* me. I've never had that before, never at all. I can't go back in there now and leave that out here. I've got friends—I've got friends for the first time in my life, and man, I just don't think I can do without that anymore.*

Pushed into a corner, Cleaver jumped bail, escaped to Cuba, and eventually set up headquarters in Algeria. There, if the Panther newspaper is accurate, he terrorized his wife, took a new mistress, murdered a rival, and tumbled into fantasies of sweeping across America at the head of a guerilla gang. He denounced Newton, tried to seize the party from exile, and ordered his followers on the East Coast and in Los Angeles to put his vision into practice. The war for the party commenced; bodies began to turn up.

Newton and Seale had founded the Black Panthers (drawing up

* From Gene Marine, *The Black Panthers* (New York: Signet, 1969).

their statement of aims and demands while playing Dylan's "Ballad of a Thin Man" over and over) as a local self-defense organization, but the idea was irresistible and soon there were Panther chapters all over the country. As Bobby Seale says so well, Staggerlee was crucial to these new politics. A killer, a thief, setting himself up against his own people, plundering them to get what he wanted—they began there. They seized the fact of criminal violence, and tried to turn that fact into a political threat. Since no one doubted the fact was real, the threat was taken seriously.

Newton's idea came down to a new kind of power, growing out of the barrel of a gun that was good only as long as it didn't have to be fired, because once it was fired, the other side was going to win. The Panthers walked that fine edge, threatened by their own rhetoric, which called for actions they could not afford to take; their rhetoric won them some of the space necessary for action, but the police also forced them to live up to it. Police raids on chapter after chapter decimated the party; many of those who were left were junkies, hoods, and spies. Both Newton and Seale had been off the street while murder raps, ultimately tossed out, were hung over their heads; the party had lost its center. Either it changed drastically or it died, and once Newton got out of jail he moved to quiet it down and clean it out.

Cleaver, a confessed rapist who had spent nine years in California prisons, had been valuable to the Panthers not only because he was a superb recruiter and a good theorist, but because their politics were rooted in the streets. Newton's genius had been to bring Staggerlee into politics and there transform him; that also meant Newton had to risk him. Newton's careful arrogance and perfect nerve under the guns of San Francisco cops had inspired Cleaver to join the party, but Newton is a man of tremendous self-discipline; the demands his politics made on all party members were in some ways too much of a reflection of his own unquestionable ability to live up to them. Staggerlee was a mask Newton could put on at will; Cleaver was not always under control, and the myth held more traps for him. But he could take it farther, even as politics: he really was Staggerlee, and the explosive threat of his performance was vital to his role in the party.

Cleaver's worth lay in his ability to balance that role between his exploitation of it and it of him. In Algeria, cut off from the people who had changed his life, that balance shattered absolutely, and his old nemesis roared back with a vengeance. He had been a political man whose politics were rooted in a vitality and rage that had once come out in crime, but he emerged a criminal once again, out for blood.

There were no politics. The balance broke down because the political space necessary to it had been taken away, and what was left was murder, not for a five-dollar Stetson hat, but the old story all the same. Cleaver fell back to Staggerlee; he went all the way into his hands, and it may be that the only way he will ever get out will be with the epitaph John Hurt gave to his Stag-o-lee, the cruelest epitaph of all:

Standing at the gallows
Head way up high
At twelve o'clock they killed him
They was all glad to see him die.

And that is the context of *Riot.**

These events and Sly's understanding of his own career came together, as most likely they never will again, to form a music of extraordinary depth and power. Sly questioned his earlier music and our love for it; he implied that whatever the beauty of "Everybody Is a Star," that may have been only another way of saying that everybody is a mark. Sly's work was deeply personal and inescapably political; innovative and tough in its music; literate and direct in its words; a parody of the past and an unflinching statement about the present that its present has hardly contained.

Sly returned to the pop arena at a time when black music had remade itself on terms he had defined; he damned those terms and in-

* It was, I still believe, the context—but events have proved my comments on Newton and Cleaver more than a little naive.

After a bizarre incident in which he "arrested" fellow-fugitive Timothy Leary in Algiers, Cleaver fled to Paris, where he renounced politics for haberdashery—to wit, "Cleavers," pants cut with an "appurtenance" for genital display. Unable to interest a distrubutor in the latest in rapists' fashions, Cleaver negotiated with prosecutors back in Oakland, proclaimed himself a born-again Christian, returned to the U.S., and copped a plea to reduced charges stemming from the 1968 shootout—which, Cleaver now said, he had provoked. Free at last, he became a shill for the far right, ran unsuccessfully for office as a Republican, and in 1988 was convicted on charges of burglary and cocaine possession. He died in 1998.

Newton's story is worse. After the disintegration of the Black Panther Party in the early '70s, Newton received a Ph.D. from the University of California at Santa Cruz, and attempted to set up small-scale protection rackets in Oakland. Over the next years he was charged with many crimes, including the murder of a prostitute (he later admitted to friends that he had killed her, for no real reason, and also that he had ordered the murder of a Panther bookkeeper). He fled to Cuba; when he returned to face trial, an attempt was made to kill a witness; finally the charges were dismissed. Numerous further arrests followed—for drunk driving, weapons possession, and embezzlement—and Newton was briefly imprisoned for parole violations. He had become an alcoholic and a cocaine addict. On August 22, 1989, when for the first time in more than twenty years Newton was legally clean, he was shot to death by a crack dealer on a sidewalk in Oakland. He was 47.

vented new ones. He recognized the expectations of his audience, and moved to subvert them.

If after a time he allowed his audience to subvert his work, or simply played on and followed where his music led, *There's a riot goin' on* stands as a quiet, bitter, open act of rebellion. It is a rebellion the resolution of which depends as much on the audience as it does on Sly Stone, and a rebellion which as music or politics is not likely to work itself out for a long time. And if that musical insurrection can be captured in a line, it is probably a remark Josef von Sternberg once made: "Obviously, it is easier to kill than to create."

RANDY NEWMAN
Every Man Is Free

I believe . . . that to be very poor and very beautiful is most probably a moral failure much more than an artistic success. Shakespeare would have done well in any generation because he would have refused to die in a corner; he would have taken the false gods and made them over; he would have taken the current formulae and forced them into something lesser men thought them incapable of. Alive today he would undoubtedly have written and directed motion pictures, plays, and God knows what. Instead of saying, "This medium is not good," he would have used it and made it good. If some people called some of his work cheap (which some of it is), he wouldn't have cared a rap, because he would know that without some vulgarity there is no complete man. He would have hated refinement, as such, because it is always a withdrawal, and he was much too tough to shrink from anything.

RAYMOND CHANDLER, 1949,
from *Raymond Chandler Speaking*

POP

Chandler's statement, written in the midst of his failed attempts to do good work as a Hollywood screenwriter, tells us how completely he understood what it means to be an American artist. The momentum of democracy (of equality) (of conformity) that powers American life does not, as Tocqueville thought it might, bleed all the life out of culture; it has created a wholly new kind, with all sorts of new risks and possibilities. At its worst it can do just what Tocqueville expected, and there is always a good example around: *The Sound of Music* ("The audience," Pauline Kael wrote bitterly, "becomes the lowest common denominator of feeling—a sponge"); *Love Story*; the pop group "America" (Tocqueville smiling in his grave at the elegance of their conceit). There is, though, Chandler also wrote, "a vast difference between writing down to the public (something which always flops in the end) and doing what you want to do in a form that the public has learned to accept."

There have been great American artists who have worked beyond the public's ability to understand them easily, but none who have condescended to the public—none who have not hoped, no matter how secretly, that their work would lift America to heaven, or drive a stake through its heart. This is a democratic desire (not completely unrelated to the all-time number one democratic desire for endless wealth and fame), and at its best it is an impulse to wholeness, an attempt not to deny diversity, or to hide from it, but to discover what it is that diverse people can authentically share. It is a desire of the artist to remake America on his or her own terms.

This impulse powers the strongest popular artists as it powers pop culture itself. It is an urge to novelty and necessity; it exhausts most talents with terrific speed and goes on to something else.

The inability of the vital American artist to be satisfied with a cult audience, no matter how attentive, goes right back to the instinctive perception that whatever else America might be, it is basically *big*; that unless you are doing something big, you are not doing anything at all. The Beatles ("those imaginary Americans," Leslie Fiedler called them), madly in love with American popular culture and living out their own American dream, increased their ambitions as they got closer to their goals: first they wanted to be Eddie Cochran, then they decided they could be Elvis, and then they were on their own. They understood, finally, that they could affect the lives of kids all over the world. The fact that they succeeded tells us how much big pop ambitions are worth; everyone who might conceivably read this book has been changed for the better because of what the Beatles did.

When it is alive to its greatest possibilities—to disturb, provoke, and divide an entire society, thus exciting and changing a big part of society— pop says that the game of a limited audience is not really worth playing. It is as contradictory and as American as a politician who can't stand dissent, who gets and keeps his power by dividing the country and turning the country against itself, and then wants everyone to love him.

This is not simply a matter of the depth of the artist's idea, any more than the contours of American history really turn on how well Andrew

Jackson understood macroeconomics. What matters is the depth and breadth of response an artist can evoke in an audience, and whether or not that artist is really challenging the audience and not simply playing off its fears and weaknesses. In the case of someone extraordinary like Elvis Presley, or the Beatles, this process becomes its own idea—and a pretty deep one. But who knows if "Eight days a week is not enough to show I love you" is a deep idea, or a trivial one, or any kind of idea at all? And who cares? The joy of pop is that it can deliver you from such questions by its immediacy and provoke them by its impact.

Rock 'n' roll is a combination of good ideas dried up by fads, terrible junk, hideous failings in taste and judgment, gullibility and manipulation, moments of unbelievable clarity and invention, pleasure, fun, vulgarity, excess, novelty and utter enervation, all summed up nowhere so well as on Top 40 radio, that ultimate rock 'n' roll version of America. As one writer put it, describing a classic radio segue of a pimple commercial directly into Bob Dylan's "George Jackson": "Right on."

We fight our way through the massed and leveled collective safe taste of Top 40, just looking for a little something we can call our own. But when we find it and jam the radio to hear it again it isn't just ours— it is a link to thousands of others who are sharing it with us. As a matter of a single song this might mean very little; as culture, as a way of life, you can't beat it.

And what about Randy Newman, who is, unfortunately, somewhere else entirely (that is, buried on an occasional FM radio or in the back of someone's record collection)? "All combined," Newman is fond of saying, "my records have sold as many copies as James Taylor's last album sold in Des Moines. But I'm fantastically wealthy, so nothing matters." Spoken like a pop master: only money counts. But obviously if his public failure didn't bother him Newman wouldn't complain about it. To the degree that he knows his work is good he will want it to affect everyone in sight. And more than that, a singer whose songs contain an astonishing affection for every American from a middle-class couple wasting away in Florida to a rapist preying on their daughter cannot be satisfied with the attention of an elite, of critics and a few more, because a cult contradicts the best impulses of his work.

NEWMAN'S AMERICA, I

He is, all in all, one of the strangest performers to emerge in rock 'n' roll since the heady days of *Sgt. Pepper*. Born in 1943, raised in New

Orleans and then in Southern California, Newman was heir to both a family movie music dynasty (the most famous member was his Oscar-winning Uncle Alfred, whose credits are ubiquitous on late night TV), and along with everyone else his age, to rock 'n' roll. Fats Domino was his man.

Newman took up the piano, was classically trained at UCLA, and got a job with a music publishing company, hacking out songs for money. He made a lot, as he says, but since he didn't much like the way other people did his stuff, he began recording it himself.

Since the release of his first album, in 1968, Newman's singing has shifted from a style that could be called Jewish to one that can only be called black. He has become, as his producer Lenny Waronker likes to call him, "The King of the Suburban Blues Singers."

What Newman has taken from black singers is not what most rock 'n' roll singers have taken: assertiveness, aggression, melancholy, sexual power. His somnambulant personality determined his choice of a lazy, blurred sound, where words slide into each other, where syllables are not bitten off, but just wear out and dissolve. The blues practice of dropping a key word off the end of a line, to hint at ominous sexual mastery or knowledge too strong to put into words, becomes with Newman a wonderful throwaway, a surface lack of seriousness that at first hides, and after a few listenings intensifies, a sense of Newman's commitment to his material. It is as if Randy's real blues hero wasn't Howlin' Wolf, but Stepin Fetchit—and as if Randy had a pretty good idea of what secrets were hidden in the shuffle.

The movie music side of Newman's songs grows out of a tradition so well absorbed by generations of film fans that by now it seems completely American, regardless of its classy European antecedents. Listening to Newman, irrespective of the lyric of any particular song, you might see John Wayne in Monument Valley, Charles Boyer in a final clinch. Chances are it won't be anything so specific; you will hear a hundred movies whose titles you just cannot recall.

Newman's music is stronger than any to be found in those movies; his music is from a movie no one ever made, the score that was never quite written. It is everything that movie music aspired to, richer on his records because he is making records, not movies.

He uses the familiarity of the music to set us in the moods and situations the music automatically calls up; we respond in predictable ways to the music, and as we do, Newman's words and his singing pull us in other directions, or shift the story just enough to make it new. The music defines for us the way we want it to be, the way the movies have told us it is, and then Newman tells us how it looks to him. The tension that comes is almost never facile, because the movie dreams the music evokes are real to him too, and because he loves the music itself. It's not merely a device, but at the heart of the matter; not just half of his strategy, but half of his aesthetic.

When I saw Newman perform one night, I was startled by how many of his songs mattered to me. I was a casual fan, but after each number another came into my head that I had to hear. I hadn't been part of a rock 'n' roll audience that laughed so well since Dylan's tours in the mid-sixties (we forget how funny crowds found "Desolation Row," and how right they were).

Newman could put on the chill, too. He told an old man he ought to give it up and die; he made you feel, with "God's Song," that life is indeed a joke, and that all the laughs belong to its Author. Newman did his Southern California beach song—which must derive, somehow, from "Surf City"—about a girl who has fled from her graduation dance to offer herself to the gears of the beach-cleaning machine, which scoops her up along with the beer cans, candy wrappers, and condoms, like a California teenager hungry after a swim. He sang some of his easy-target tunes, like "Burn On," about the firetrap Cuyahoga River. Best of all was "Davy the Fat Boy," sung in the voice of "Davy's only friend," who has made a deathbed promise to the fat boy's parents to take care of the freak and keeps it by putting him into a sideshow. It reminded me of that unbearable climactic scene in von Sternberg's *Blue Angel*, where Emil Jannings—the fallen professor forced to stand before his ex-students imitating a chicken—holds his body like one enormous clubfoot, his face in a frozen mask of terror and madness, and produces a squawk that can shrivel the soul. As Davy's friend orders him to begin "his famous fat boy dance," Newman leaned back from his piano for a little ballet music, letting the audience see the scene as he did; and as the song ended, one of its lines echoed with a gruesome kind of love: *"You've got to let this fat boy in your life!"*

Newman had asked for requests, and I had yelled out for "Davy" because I had vaguely remembered being moved by it some years before. If I had remembered it better I probably would have kept my mouth shut.

Except in its weaker moments, this was not satire. It was a whole world, irresistibly funny and extremely uncomfortable, like W. C. Fields with the Hollywood varnish rubbed off. But the laughter was not smug, and the scariness of the songs was not smug on Newman's part, but simply presented as what he did for a living, what he did better than anyone else. When he sang his "Suzanne," the tale of a rapist picking a woman's number off a phone booth wall, you were caught up in the woman's terror and the rapist's crime. Both were real, both mattered.

The song was in the great rock 'n' roll tradition of answer records: in this case, an answer to Leonard Cohen's "Suzanne," the tender ballad of a river nymph, as erotic as a $500 book of pornographic etchings. Cohen's song screamed Poetry and Art; it virtually raped the listener with its mastery of the Higher Shlock. "This is not Leonard Cohen's 'Suzanne,'" Newman said. "It's on a somewhat lower moral plane, actually."

He said that with such modesty, fading his comment as if he were throwing away one of his best lines, that you had to think that sometimes, late at night when he couldn't make a song work, he might even believe it.

Newman is afraid of his sensibility, to the degree that he has to get it over to an audience. On one album he sang a version of that old Cotton Club favorite, "Underneath the Harlem Moon," all about the colored singing and dancing, summed up in the classic line: "That's why darkies were born." He sang it straight—beautifully, in fact—and you just couldn't tell. Where was he? Or more to the point, where did he put you? Here he was, a struggling singer whose only possible audience would be urbane, liberal rock 'n' roll fans, and he was unveiling . . . the charms of racism. He would not perform the song in front of an audience. "I was afraid someone might beat me up," he said. The night I saw him he sang his own "Yellow Man"; apparently no one had told him he was singing in a Chinese movie theater in the middle of the biggest Chinese community in the U.S.A. Or maybe he thought his height would save him. His distance from his material is always a bit uncertain.

If Newman's songs are the result of New Orleans R&B and an after-the-ball cul-de-sac of Hollywood movie music, they also grow out of a cul-de-sac pure and simple: Los Angeles, the Edge of America, the City of the Future. As an Angeleno, Randy Newman is something like Nathanael West on the verge of having a good time in spite of himself.

West thought Southern California was where America came to make its last stand, to reach for the last chance; inevitably betraying those hopes, Los Angeles became, to West and to Chandler and others, the place where those now resentful Americans would turn to fantasies of revenge, violence, and death. Looking for rebirth, dreamers found only that they felt older than they had seemed at home. These discrepancies—presented over and over again, in Chandler's *The Big*

Sleep and *Farewell, My Lovely*, in *Sunset Boulevard*, from a Holy Roller church in downtown L.A. to the Kirke Order of Dog Blood roaming the desert—created, against the backdrop of an industry based on the inexhaustibility of banal fantasy, a curious sort of moral ambivalence, a state of mind equally capable of producing commonplace boredom and uncommon crime. This ambivalence, I think, grows out of an attempt to come to terms with that sense of discrepancy: an aggressive and in many ways positive denial of the need for roots, a perception that everything that is old must be covered in neon and sandstone before anyone can be really free.

Once this is accomplished, of course, there is little left on which to base an idea of what that freedom could be for. People improvise; nothing seems completely out of the question. Some can endure, and use, this kind of freedom. Some can't; they lust after authority, and there are always too many to provide it: pimps, the Children of God, organized crime, weird figures of extraordinary charisma walking the street devouring souls.

Such a story is familiar enough. The same scared and lustful Americans who changed their names and killed for new lives in Chandler's books crawl through Ross MacDonald's; the rubber horse clumped at the bottom of a swimming pool in *Day of the Locust* was dumped into a bed in *The Godfather*. But because such a vision of Los Angeles pushed West and Chandler into a queer sort of Puritanism, they never noticed something else that matters about Southern California: its incredible exuberance, the talent of Southern Californians for enjoying themselves. It's a little too easy to look at the movement of the place and call it hysterical, too easy to quote Thoreau and pronounce that "the mass of men lead lives of quiet desperation," and think that you have told the whole truth. Put the Beach Boys of the early sixties up against West, and *he* sounds hysterical; there isn't a hint of their warmth and friendliness in his "definitive" book, but no one can tell me that "Fun, Fun, Fun" is a lie. The Beach Boys don't wipe out Chandler's world, but they enlarge it; and if finally the Beach Boys held hands with Charles Manson as the sixties ended, that only meant that they were as vulnerable to the L.A. of West and Chandler as they might have been to the Beach Boys'. You can say that the energy and pride the Beach Boys found cruising the strip in "I Get Around" was never meant to last, that it hardened and cracked like cheap Santa Monica stucco when they found out it was not enough and embraced the authority of the dread Maharishi. You can write their delight off to sun and money, but its value is still strong, still full of life. They felt free to enjoy themselves in every way imaginable, and that freedom from tradition, the freedom to invent, cuts deeply and all across the board. There's no way to separate the Beach Boys' smiling freedom from Manson's knife. Because this new world is a rich one, Randy Newman, as an artist, can work in it—he can laugh well and realize his fantasies of violence and death. "Suzanne" really is the other side of "Surf City"—or part of it.

Nathanael West was an Easterner; in spite of the fact that "West" was a name he chose, he was never at home in California—he was unable to imagine that anyone could be. But many Southern Californians, were they to be told that murder was the price of a way of life based on fun and fantasy, might still pay it. Newman accepts the deal because L.A. provides the indolence that suits his personality, and the risk that suits his art.

As an American artist, Newman represents some kind of opening up of the classic archetype of the keeper of the American imagination; and this too has a lot to do with the peculiar freedoms of Los Angeles. Most American critics—Nathaniel Hawthorne, say—throw up all sorts of horror and pretend they do so only to condemn it. If West, through his transplanted Easterner hero Tod Hackett, admitted complicity in the L.A. nightmare, he had to satisfy the guilt such a confession produced by destroying the city in a private apocalypse. Since Newman takes the moral shapelessness of his hometown as a given, such fantasies would be ridiculously melodramatic for him (they're more than a little ridiculous in West, too). Like the Beach Boys, Newman builds freedom out of what he's got; his humor is his version of the Beach Boys' open naïveté. Newman laughs all around his world, never at it. He is too at home in the place to feel guilty about it, and anyway, he is a rock 'n' roll singer, and such attitudes are not in the rock 'n' roll style. As with almost any popular art, the moment rock 'n' roll tries to criticize something, it becomes hopelessly self-righteous and stupid. It effectively criticizes by rendering a situation with such immediacy, or by affirming it to the point of such absurdity, that you can no longer take it straight. That is why there is no tougher antidrug song than the Velvet Underground's "Heroin," which also risks creating new addicts.

Perhaps because of the ambivalence of Southern California, Newman can sing with the same insulated force. He always writes, and what is harder, sings, in the voices of his characters (except when they are women, but he will manage that someday); no matter what grotesquerie is involved, he does not sing about, he sings *as*. He feels this is dangerous, which it is.

The imagination has fallen upon sorry days in post-Beatle rock 'n' roll. Audiences are no longer used to the idea that someone might make something up, create a persona and effectively act it out, the way Chuck Berry and Bob Dylan used to do. Audiences take everything literally, partly because sensitive personal confession, "honesty," and one-to-one communication between the singer and whoever is listening is so attractive and reassuring in times when pop culture and politics have lost their grander mythic dimensions, when there are no artists and no politics to create community, and every fan is thrown back on himself. Let me quote from a typical ad for a troubled troubador, supposedly appropriate to such times, presumably addressed to a troubled audience:

A few rare performers immediately become your friend the first time you listen to them. Jonathan Edwards is about to become your friend.

His songs are sensitive and warm, containing feelings and recollections which are sure to remind you of things in your life as well.

Jonathan Edwards. A new friend.

Courtesy Atlantic Records and Tapes, a Division of Warner Communications, the friendly giant conglomerate.

Note the style of the ad. The cadence is wonderfully smooth, caressing. The grammar is perfect, proper. The voice is fatherly. The whole thing is absolutely unbearable.

But it's always fun to fill in the blanks. Let's say:

A few rare performers immediately become your friend the first time you listen to them. Mick Jagger is about to become your friend.

His songs are loud, brutal, and mean, containing feelings you like to pretend you do not have, recollections you would like to forget, and temptations that up until now you have wisely avoided.

Mick Jagger. A new friend.

Courtesy Rolling Stones Records and Tapes, distributed by Atlantic Records and Tapes, a Division of Warner Communications . . . rock 'n' roll may have no center, but it is nothing if not pluralistic. Newman records for the same company, naturally.

Rock 'n' roll is suffering from that old progressive school fallacy that says if what you write is about your own feelings, no one can criticize it. Truth telling is beginning to settle into a slough where it is nothing more than a pedestrian autobiography set to placid music framed by a sad smile on the album cover. This is about as liberating as thinking typecast movie stars are "really like" the roles they play. In many cases, though, this *has* come to be true in rock 'n' roll: singers have dispensed with imagination and songs are just pages out of a diary, with nothing in them that could give them a life of their own. A good part of the audience has lost its taste for songs that are about something out there in the world that the singer is trying to make real—usually by convincingly assuming the burden of that reality; replacing such songs are tunes that desperately deny the world by affirming the joys of solipsism. The success of this genre, represented by no one so well as James Taylor (along with the Rowan Brothers, Shawn Phillips, "America," and many others who will no doubt be forgotten by the time this book is published), only reminds me of an old philosophy student joke: "Solipsism is great, everyone should try it." That was, actually, the cornerstone of Nixon's Second Inaugural: "What can I do for myself?"

As the members of an audience grow older, they lead less public lives. Their deepest affections shift from a multiplicity of friends—from the idea of friendship itself—to husbands, wives, children; they exchange the noisy heterogeneity of school for the quiet homogeneity of a job. They travel less freely, act less impulsively. If politics once meant the fellowship of the street or the political community of a campus for those who were lucky enough to have known such things, more and more politics comes to mean voting—the most solitary political act there is—or, at best, talk with a few friends. A life that was fluid with possibility can solidify into loneliness. One looks harder for the comforts of similarity, and shies from the risks of diversity. It becomes easy to think that nothing is new under the sun, or that if there is, that one can no longer be a part of what is new. Too much is settled.

If at its best rock 'n' roll *is* a kind of public life ("'School's Out' is my favorite song and I've been out of school for ten years!" my friend Simon Frith wrote. "What does that mean?"), the cults that have fragmented an audience potentially as big and broad as America itself speak for a less open life, as do the names of some successful post-Beatle record companies: Island, Shelter, Haven, Chrysalis, Asylum. Newman works against the limits of privacy, domesticity, and solipsism with his fantasies and the role playing of his songs, and yet he lacks the obsessive pop ambition to do more than that. Against the ideal community of music he feels the emotional and imaginative poverty of an America where men and women live estranged. But to drive the aesthetic of his fantasies into our heads would require him to value his music more than anything else, to be on the road constantly, to risk the collapse of his own family life, the shelter of his own privacy, and even—after the rock 'n' roll deaths of the last years I don't feel very romantic saying this—his sanity and his life.

"If I couldn't perform I'd give up," said Rod Stewart. "It's not a question of the money side of it. I don't have to work for the rest of my life. I don't want to. But not having that ninety minutes up there anymore. Phew. I don't like to think about it. It frightens me." And he went on: "I'm not willing to get married, because I think there are some people who just shouldn't get married. Elvis Presley should never have been married." He's not talking about the fall-off in a movie star's mail when he takes the sacred vows, but about the freedom to act in the midst of an audience. To be the kind of rock 'n' roll star Stewart is is to be like a politician who campaigns every moment of his life.

"In America," Newman sings, "every man is free / To take care of his home, and his family." But no more than that, is the bitter, unsung line. And that may not be enough, even if it is all most of us see.

The constriction of vision produced by that kind of life points to why Newman is right when he feels it is risky to get up on stage and sing from inside the soul of a rapist. It's not just a matter of what people will think of Newman; what if someone heard the song and went looking for a woman to rape? Oh, ridiculous, we might say. That's like pretending someone could listen to the Beatles sing a good old rock 'n' roll fuck song like "Helter Skelter" and take it as a sign to go out and murder seven people.

Good art is always dangerous, always open-ended. Once you put it out in the world you lose control of it; people will fit it into their lives in all sorts of different ways. If so much of the rock 'n' roll of the post-Beatle era is closed off and one-dimensional, like the politics it serenades and reinforces, if the aesthetic of solipsism is freezing the imagination and our ability to respond openly, it is Newman's risk taking that makes him so valuable. As a rather lazy Southern Californian who just wants a good life with his wife and his kids, his sense of risk makes him shrink from his audience; but as an artist, that sense makes him reach for bigger risks.

NEWMAN'S AMERICA, II

To introduce his greatest song, Randy will tell a little story about a movie he almost made, with all the big stars: "'Van,' that's Van Morrison, Elton, you know Elton . . ." The joke of this small-time rock 'n' roller up there with the big guns is more than obvious, but still funny. It would be even better if Newman made the whole thing up; it would somehow add to the charm of a song he will do later, "Lonely at the Top." It was written for Frank Sinatra, who, most likely thinking it was a slur on his need for a toupee, turned it down.

Up on stage Newman is still entranced by his tale of the silver screen stardom he might have had. Each singer will be given fifteen minutes to prepare and perform any kind of scenario he wants—do it all. And Newman has a wonderful idea. He will dress himself in a pure white planter's suit, white shoes, white hat—perhaps a red string tie, for color. As the camera zooms in for its opening shot, Newman is poised on the quarterdeck of a great clipper ship, testing his profile against the wind. What's he doing there? He's a recruiter for the slave trade.

His profile suitably established, Newman steps ashore. He is met by a hushed crowd of Africans, who hang on his every word. (Finally, Newman is a star.) He begins to sing, in a voice that combines the lazy drawl of the black man (something his audience will invent in their new land) with the gentle assurance of the holiest rabbi. The music, as Newman ultimately recorded it, comes in on the soundtrack (in the theater, Newman begins the song on his piano), and it is beautiful. And the slaver sings:

> *In America*
> *You'll get food to eat*
> *Won't have to run through the jungle*
> *And scuff up your feet*
> *You'll just sing about Jesus and drink wine all day*
> *It's great to be an American*

We are back in Harmonica Frank's medicine show, and it is the softest sell of all. "By the second verse," Randy confides, "they're already running for the boat."

> *Climb aboard little wog*
> *Sail away with me*

And if they are caught up in Newman's vision, the pure feel of it, so am I. "Sail away," he sings, "Sail away," and the grace of his singing conquers the last resistance. It is majestic. You can see the glassy waters, the birds hovering over the ship as the last glimpse of Africa drops over the horizon.

*We will cross the mighty ocean into Charleston Bay**

You can dredge through all the antebellum fantasies kicked up to defend the peculiar institution and you will never find an image of slavery as lovely as this one.

This peaceful, quiet song is more outrageous than anything the Rolling Stones have ever done—or would be, if the nation heard Newman do it on the radio every day. Scary, astonishing, Newman has presented an American temptation—tempting not only the Africans, who became Negroes, and went on to create the music that finally tossed up Elvis Presley, rock 'n' roll, Newman, and his audience, but tempting America to believe that this image of itself just might be true.

"Sail Away" moves on one of the most seductive melodies ever to grace a popular song. It is just out of reach, with a fabulous edge of déjà vu, calling up the classic Ray Charles records of the early sixties—"Born to Lose," "You Don't Know Me," "That Lucky Old Sun"—calling up a thousand songs and a thousand happy endings.

The power of the song is in the simple, perfectly accomplished idea that something so horrible and charged with guilt as slavery could take on such real beauty. The focus is not on those who are to be enslaved, but on the singer, the confidence man. Of course he is lying. He has seen babies thrown into the sea, smelled the death and excrement in the hold, watched the brand burn into the flesh. He has looked without flinching into the bewildered eyes that are perhaps the most terrible of all. But for the moment, he believes himself. A secret ambivalence of four hundred years of American life finds a voice in this song. It is not particularly liberating; too strange for that, it is like a vision of heaven superimposed on hell.

Y'all gonna be an American

Rock 'n' roll has always specialized in racial paradoxes, but none as queer as this. It has virtually nothing to do with "rock 'n' roll" as a mu-

* Words and Music by Randy Newman. © 1972 WB Music Corp. & Randy Newman. All rights reserved. Used by permission of Warner Bros. Music.

sical form (save that Newman's singing owes so much to the blues) and everything to do with the rock 'n' roll audience. Newman offers it a vision its members have spent years driving from their minds, bringing them back to a home that was never there.

The song transcends its irony. It is, in the end, what America would like to believe about itself, and what ten years of a war across the ocean and ten years of bitter black faces will never let it believe, even in secret: that everything America did was for the good. Better than good: that God's work really was our own and meant to be. That we brought something new and precious into the world, a land even the most miserable slaves would recognize as Eden.

For if they did not, how could we believe it?

Sailing across the ocean, the slaver and his slaves are in love.

NEWMAN'S FAILURE

"Every great artist must create for a great audience," Bob Christgau pronounced one night when we were delving into The Great Randy Newman Mystery (Why isn't this genius as big as he deserves to be?). Christgau meant an aggressive, critical audience, with a conscious sense of itself as an audience, but he also meant a big, broad audience, one whose complexity and diverse needs can push an artist beyond comfortable limits.

When a single like the O'Jays' "Back Stabbers" rams home the result of years of shifting black consciousness and takes over the charts, it creates a cultural moment shared by a good part of the country, shoving a particular sensibility through all sorts of ordinary barriers that grow up between audiences. The passion and clarity of the song can connect a black pimp, whose life it was virtually meant to define, to a middle-class white kid, who just digs the beat and will find his or her place in the lyrics soon enough. When a movie like *The Godfather* becomes the national pastime, you can feel, as you sit for perhaps the first time in a theater half black and half white, that for better or for worse America's fantasies are at last becoming common property; that artists and audiences have come to a verge, that the stakes of American life have been raised.

If *The Godfather* had succeeded merely as a genre classic, it would have been a very different movie—the response it provokes changes how we see and understand it. Like "Back Stabbers," it matters, has its particular meanings, partly *because* it is a hit. Without massive public response, we would not even get close to two crucial democratic questions, questions worth asking about any interesting work of popular culture: How far can this work take its audience? How far can its audience go with it? Only works that can't be ignored—liking them is hardly the point—raise such questions and bring them to life. In one way or another we are all affected by hits, and are forced to define ourselves in terms of our response to them, just as we are all, for good or ill, affected by the romantic heroism of the Westerns, and not necessarily by, say, the chaotic heroism that is the subject of Orson Welles's movies. Certainly we are caught up in those things that impelled Welles, but his version of them, the shape of his vision, has not inevitably become part of us; we don't have to live in the world as he tried to define it, as we helplessly live out and respond to the nostalgia of John Ford or Howard Hawks. The life of a whole generation is authentically quickened and brightened by the Beatles, but it is not disturbed and sharpened by Randy Newman. The point is not that it would be "good for people" if the radio were playing "Sail Away" all day long, but that such exposure might be the only way to find out how strong the song really is. But Newman is quite different from Orson Welles, who lost a great fight with Hollywood in his attempt to get his movies made, because Newman is barely on the battlefield.

His quandary is not unlike the one the Kinks fell into in the late sixties. After a string of post-Beatle Invasion hits based on a chopped and channeled version of "Louie Louie," the sensibility of Ray Davies, their resident ex-art-student genius (every British band had one in those days), began to take over the group. The Kinks became less of a band, less a bundle of ambition and lust for money, fame, and fun, and more of a means to Davies's fantasies. He became a social critic, or more appropriate for rock 'n' roll, a social complainer. He squeezed a few hits out of this stance, but the last chart success he got in the sixties crystallized his new view of the world and dropped the commercial bottom out of the group. "Sunny Afternoon" (1966) could have been another put-down of the English middle class, but instead the hunter was captured by the game. This was an ode to upper-class boredom. The Kinks became a classy little outfit, neurotic, long on intelligence and short on raunch, and their album sales dropped into the low thousands. They were idolized by the critics and ignored by everybody else.

You couldn't call Davies's world dark, exactly; it was dimmed. Like Newman's, it was completely idiosyncratic, if generally a lot less compelling. An anthem Davies wrote to himself defined it best: a fearsome, ferocious piece of hard rock he slipped onto the flip side of "Sunny

Afternoon," and which didn't surface on an American album until seven years later—"I'm Not Like Everybody Else."

Davies opened the song as a sickly kid pushed up against the wall by a gang of thugs (that is, everybody else), and then broke wide open with a rage that negated the whole world he wouldn't serve, that he wouldn't and couldn't change into. By the last fiery choruses he was free, as free to ignore his listeners as they had always been to ignore him. It was a great record.*

Davies commenced to delineate the subtleties of nostalgia, the quirks of inadequacy, the aesthetics of oddball. For a time his insulation produced appropriate fantasies, and also his best songs (such as "Waterloo Sunset," an unbearably lovely tune about an old man who watches lovers from his window). Artistic privacy also produced terrible self-indulgence and embarrassing cuteness. The critics cheered the good and the bad, as they do with Newman, but finally even they began to weary in their proselytizing. Paul Williams, an original Kinks booster, reviewed their last bomb "for those who love the Kinks," formally ending the great struggle to spread the word.

But not quite. Davies had written *Arthur*, an "opera" about a post-Victorian lost in a twentieth-century world; some of it was brilliant and some of it wasn't, as with all Kinks albums, which shouldn't have made any difference one way or the other. But an extraordinary push by two *Rolling Stone* reviewers (one of whom, I confess, was me), and its release at the same time as the Who's *Tommy* (suddenly nothing was as salable as the concept of Opera, which is to say, Art), made *Arthur* a decent success. The Kinks stumbled back to America for their first tour in years, and eventually got another hit, a big one, with "Lola," the tender tale of a shy country boy meeting up with a big-city transvestite—superb rock 'n' roll and a pop masterpiece.

The Top 40 audience, which had grabbed for the record, not "the Kinks," settled back, but as happens whenever a group gets a hit, the band picked up enough new fans to make them successful, seventies-style. Instead of a little cult, they had a big cult. Davies's insulation was gone, and the sharp edge of his feel for being different collapsed into gross parody of the big bad world. His songs became either hysterically unfunny (the next album was called *Lola v. the Power-Mad Money Men*, or something like that) or merely dull. An uncritical audience—a cult—was even worse for the band than uncritical critics. Davies's outsider

---

* And I swear I hear a hint of the closet Davies later came out of; doesn't he scream, "I won't go to bed like everybody else?"

stance, which had given his work what strength and vitality it had, was vitiated by the presence of an automatic audience.

And yet the echo of that wonderful statement, "I'm Not Like Everybody Else," is still there—not in Davies's work, but in Newman's: the idea that communication is failure, because if you get what you have to say across to a mass audience, that means what you have to say is not deep enough, or strong enough, to really matter. Newman has said he feels his songs are disturbing; that his lack of success is due to the weight of his material and the discomfort of his version of the truth. He is not surprised by his small audience, just frustrated by it, because if he cannot get his work across he is failing his work. That is, he can't win.

Newman's most accessible songs (as he performs them, which is all that concerns me, and all I think really concerns Newman) are generally his sledge-hammer ironies like "Political Science" (Let's drop the bomb on all our snotty so-called allies) or "Burn On." The genre only parodies the depth of Newman's talent, and it is impossible that he doesn't know it. If his thinnest, weakest work gets the most applause, what's he to think? That his audience isn't good enough for him? That he panders to his audience? This genre may expand anyway, because one part of Newman wants the great audience because he knows his work deserves it. And what often happens to the American popular artist, who feels he must grab the country itself and fails to even scratch it, is that he tries so desperately and honestly to alter his work in order to make it matter (not even compromising to make it palatable, though the line is hard to draw, especially for the artist), that he loses all sense of what impelled him in the first place. Either his career declines, and he is forgotten, or he hits, and decides that he has betrayed himself— and his audience. Someday this may happen to Newman; his music will lose its subtleties, even his humor will fall flat. Then he will be easier to accept, and useless as an artist.

Well, he knows all this, puttering around the house watching *Secret Storm* and vaginal deodorant commercials just like I do when I'm trying to avoid doing some *serious work* like writing this book, but in one sense none of it matters—in *his* case—because the deepest thing keeping Randy Newman from the American audience is his own sensibility.

There is something to Newman's idea that his marginal status in the rock 'n' roll world is a matter of the darkness and perversity of his vision, but I think it has more to do with the ambivalence that underlies that vision. Pop careers are not gifts of the muse, they are won, and Newman, finally, is all doubt as to whether or not the fight is worth it. There is one song he has written that captures his ambivalence so perfectly I can hardly believe he ever cranked himself up to write another one; it's called "My Old Kentucky Home." Imagine one of those automatic L.A. country backing tracks, straw on the studio floor, anything that helps set the scene, and then Randy (not Jewish or black this time, just drunk), warbling a timeless tribute to nothingness, negating the ambition rock 'n' roll demands just as Davies wiped out his audience:

Turpentine and dandelion wine
I've turned the corner and I'm doin fine
Shooting at the birds on the telephone line
Pickin' em off with this gun a mine

Brother Gene he's big and mean
And he don't have much to say
He had a little woman who he whupped each day
But now she's gone away
He got drunk last night
Kicked mama down the stair
But I'm alright so I don't care

You can't get any farther into ambivalence than that. The connection between Newman's sense of himself, and the way the world looks to him, could hardly be more exact. He might turn into a homosexual someday, he told Susan Lydon, get religion, find a God. Maybe his entire generation would. Maybe the whole world will turn upside down and Newman will say Yes to all of it. Or something.

He's not particularly ambiguous; his meanings, though they expand if you keep his songs in your head, are clear enough—even if some singers have willfully deluded themselves into recording "Sail Away" as if it were a rewrite of "Born Free" (changing that disagreeable line about "Climb aboard, little wog" to "little child," which I suppose means they know quite well what the song is about after all).

But if his meanings are clear, their value is something else. We know what the slavemaster has in mind and what will happen to his audience as soon as he gets it on the ship, but who knows how to take it? You can't get out from under, that music just washes over you and makes you feel clean. When beauty and evil are so perfectly intertwined, what choices are really possible?

There are no cheap thrills in "Davy the Fat Boy," because Newman's performance is strong enough to force the listener into all its roles: purveyor, victim, and drooling carny audience. His best songs implicate the listener. He goes far enough to wonder if everything might not be worth doing, which means he is far enough gone to wonder if anything *is* worth doing—such as pursuing an audience. If God, as Newman likes to see Him, is something worse than ambivalent in His heaven, how could *man* be any better? Since man is cursed anyway ("I recoil in horror," says Newman's God, "from the foulness of thee ... / How we laugh up here in heaven at the prayers you offer Me / That's why I love mankind"), wouldn't any act of will lead straight to that realm of folly and sin that is Newman's garden—so far limited to his art, not yet taking over his life? Isn't it almost true by Newman's definition of how the world works that desire and action produce disaster at worst and failure at best? If Newman is necessarily ambivalent about the ambitions of his characters, how could he regard his own ambitions any differently?

The answer is that he could be filled with such rage at the world for being the way it is that nothing could stop him from conniving against it. Herman Melville's view of the world was not so different, and when he finally understood the trap God had set for man (and he was no older than Newman), he had the time of his life trying to write his way out of it. Even though he saw clearly enough to know he would never make it, he was caught up in a vision of what a remarkable fight it would be.

But if such a perception of the nature of things was enough to set an American's teeth on edge more than a hundred years ago, it may not be anymore. America is tired; Newman is not a driven artist like Melville, or for that matter a sixties Bob Dylan (hero of another young America, itself grown weary by the time Newman arrived to stake a claim to it)—perhaps he cannot afford to be. Newman is ambivalent even about his own talent; as a factual matter of daily life, he cannot decide if it is worth writing a song, let alone recording it once it is written. He lacks what Chandler called "the hard core of selfishness necessary to exploit talent to the full"—the aggression and insanity that lie beneath the pop version of the Alger dream. Newman is very distant from that, and close enough to see it for what it is; he is a Bartleby, the man who would prefer not to.

Newman skirts the rock 'n' roll audience, but he and a few others keep the margins of possibility open. Aesthetically a figure of real genius and culturally a born cult hero, his America does not come across quite as readily as that of Chuck Berry, the Rolling Stones, or the Band. In his own peculiar way, Randy Newman is much closer to the Sly Stone of *Riot*.

Newman's rock 'n' roll is short on musical force, vocal exuberance, and the promise of good times no matter what (everything Sly willfully removed from *Riot)*; his work lacks the undeniable satisfaction we get from Mick Jagger roaring he can't get none. *That* kind of satisfaction is what we ask from rock 'n' roll; but if Norman Mailer is right when he says that the worst American promise is the promise of an unearned freedom from dread, Randy Newman's songs may give us some of what we need.

Laconic, funny, grim, and solitary, Randy Newman is a typical figure in the American imagination: the man who does not like what he sees but is wildly attracted to it anyway, a man who keeps his sanity by rendering contradictions other people struggle to avoid. For the moment, he carries the weight of one version of America on his shoulders—not that anyone has asked him to, as audiences have asked Bob Dylan, Elvis Presley, and Sly Stone—but his real task is to make his burden ours.

CODA: NEWMAN'S SUCCESS

Newman's cult status was deceptive. Over the years, he had won more and more fans and more and more rave reviews; as a sort of antipop pop star, he had become more and more hip. His work had grown stronger; the more listeners he attracted, it seemed, the more ambitious he became. In 1974, two years after "Sail Away," he brought out *Good Old Boys*: nothing less than a portrait of the South from the 1920s to the present, as seen through the eyes of a redneck. Newman's cult was, sort of, ready to explode into the pop mainstream. *Good Old Boys* was a small hit—for Newman, it was a big hit—and it hung onto the charts for almost half a year. Newman toured seriously for the first time; at a few concerts, he performed with a full orchestra conducted by his Uncle Lionel. Then, three years later, came the shock. Newman had a national smash—and a national scandal.

"Short People," six-foot-plus Randy tried to convince his interviewers, was a joke: a satire on, you know, bigotry. With its unforgettable tag line—"Short people got no reason to live"—the song went to number two on the *Billboard* charts. It was number one on others, and banned from numerous radio stations: program directors claimed the song was "disturbing to little children," but one suspected little disc jockeys were more to the point. *Little Criminals*, the album that contained "Short People," hit the top ten. Suddenly, Newman was, well, not a star, exactly, but something other than he had been. The effect of all this on his music was very odd.

In pop terms, Newman had already been received as a star on the *Good Old Boys* tour. His fans had given him absolution; he could do no wrong. Applauding wildly for every number, the crowds weren't responding to the songs, but cheering Newman himself. He was "a genius"; he knew.

Newman was being celebrated as someone who was more than, other than, an entertainer; this made him want to entertain, to please, to flatter his audience. The number that made this indelibly clear was "A Wedding in Cherokee County," the most affecting cut on *Good Old Boys*: an almost impossible song about a backwoods farmer, his wedding day, and his impotence.

The man has always been laughed at; no one has considered the woman he is marrying worth laughing at. On record, Newman took a listener to the edge of laughter, but never allowed the listener to cross it; singing as the farmer, his touch was never more delicate. "Lord, help me if you will," he pleaded, anticipating failure; you shared a bit of the man's suffering, knowing there was no help.

It may have been that, in a concert hall, there was nothing Newman could have done to keep an audience from laughing at the people in this song. Newman's audience may have been too smug, and Newman at his best too subtle—and performance, after all, requires a certain level of dramatization. But on stage, Newman made it impossible for a crowd not to laugh at the people in his song. Introducing "A Wedding in Cherokee County" as the surviving remnant of a discarded "rock opera about Albania"—thus distancing himself and his audience from the tune to the most extreme extent—Newman did not merely fail to put the song across, he destroyed it. He promised that the song was a joke, that its characters were jokes, and that their predicament was something those smart enough to buy tickets to a Randy Newman concert could take as a freak show staged for their personal amusement. The farmer and his bride truly became "morons," as one reviewer approvingly called them. On *Good Old Boys*, Newman made a listener respect his characters; in concert, he had the crowd in the aisles before the first verse was over. He turned his audience into the people who paid to see Davy do his famous fat-boy dance, and himself into the carny barker who egged them on. Face to face with the Northern, white, liberal, well-educated audience whose preconceptions about the redneck South *Good Old Boys* was meant to change, Newman—himself a childhood Southerner—stepped back from the complexity of his song, and offered instead a postcard of an old Kentucky moonshiner with flies buzzing around his head.

If Newman's trashing of the man and woman in "Cherokee County" indicated a lack of trust in the ability of his audience to catch the subtleties of his music, it also made the rest of *Good Old Boys*—the autobiography of a Birmingham steelworker and, perhaps, of one of his forebears—seem anything but subtle. It made the disc sound like a liberal fantasy about the goodness of the white South, a fantasy generated more by fears that Richard Nixon and Spiro Agnew were right about the "Silent Majority" than by anything else. The statements Newman made about himself in concerts across the country indicated a more serious insecurity—and allowed his audience a deeper smugness.

Sold-out halls notwithstanding, Newman was appearing as a cult figure; his fans were thus defined as those in the know. So on stage, in the midst of his first full-scale national tour, Newman made much of the fact that—with his album rising to the lower reaches of the top of the charts—he was "selling out" to the mass audience. "I want Shea Stadium!" he cried—the ironic point being that the audience was not to take Newman's rising mass popularity all that seriously. Deep down, Newman was assuring the crowd, he would remain theirs, unsullied by the mob. The audience liked this, and they got the joke.

What the fans missed was the truth—Newman did want Shea Stadium. He thought his work deserved it, and, maybe, needed it. But playing cult hero on the verge of success, Newman found it necessary to speak coyly: to pretend he didn't want the mass audience, and that his fans weren't part of it. His use of the Shea Stadium line at every concert he gave in 1974 made it seem as if he were always selling out *tomorrow* night; his talk allowed even arriviste ticket-buyers admission to his cult. The implicit idea was that Newman's cult could grow bigger and bigger, until it really did become something like a mass, national audience—at which point, still maintaining the cult cachet that was its reason for being, it would have to feel superior to itself. But Randy Newman had not sold out to the mass audience; he had only sold out to his cult.

These contradictions were buried at the time, but they surfaced in 1977 with "Short People" and *Little Criminals*. Released concurrently with the stunning debut of Elvis Costello, whose songwriting showed that he had learned much from Newman, the record was bland; Newman's edge was off, as if he were afraid he might lose his new fans if he challenged them. "Short People" was not that far from such earlier headbangers as "Political Science" or "Burn On," but it had a better melody, a better hook, and a catchier idea—and so it became a hit.

Newman's burgeoning cult had nothing to do with the song's chart success; in terms of his career, it was clearly a fluke. What counted was the emptiness of *Little Criminals*, a record that did not connect.

Newman had, far more perfectly than anyone could have expected, fallen into the trap of acclaim: the audience he had won with *Good Old Boys* disarmed him. But the fury over "Short People" made him think; he understood that he, like the Monotones with "Book of Love," was likely destined for one ride on the charts, and one only. And so, as he told the reporters who flocked to him in the wake of the protests against "Short People," he went back to work on "a broader insult."

And he got it. Released in 1979, the prescient *Born Again* opened with a ditty called "It's Money that I Love." Digging in with a rumble of New Orleans piano, Newman tossed off a mad inversion of the Moral Majority's new American agenda: he performed as a good liberal, born-again as a saint dedicated to greed. "I used to worry about the black man / Now I don't worry about the black man," Randy sang. "Used to worry about the starving children of India / You know what I say now about the starving children of India?"

What did Randy Newman say now?

He said, "Oh, mama."

He was back at the margin, scheming.

ELVIS
Presliad

FANFARE

Elvis Presley is a supreme figure in American life, one whose presence, no matter how banal or predictable, brooks no real comparisons. He is honored equally by long-haired rock critics, middle-aged women, the City of Memphis (they finally found something to name after him: a highway), and even a president.* Beside Elvis, the other heroes of this book seem a little small-time. If they define different versions of America, Presley's career almost has the scope to take America in. The cultural range of his music has expanded to the point where it includes not only the hits of the day, but also patriotic recitals, pure country gospel, and really dirty blues; reviews of his concerts, by usually credible writers, sometimes resemble Biblical accounts of heavenly miracles. Elvis has emerged as a great *artist*, a great *rocker*, a great *purveyor of shlock*, a great *heart throb*, a great *bore*, a great *symbol of potency*, a great *ham*, a great *nice person*, and, yes, a great American.

In 1954 Elvis made his first records with Sam Phillips, on the little Sun

---

* Richard Nixon had Elvis over to the White House once, and made him an honorary narcotics agent. Nixon got his picture taken with the King. An odd story, though, from rock critic Stu Werbin: "It seems that the good German who arranges the White House concerts for the President and his guests managed to travel the many channels that lead only in rare instances to Col. Tom Parker's phone line. Once connected, he delivered what he considered the most privileged invitation. The President requests Mr. Presley to perform. The Colonel did a little quick figuring and then told the man that Elvis would consider it an honor. For the President, Elvis's fee, beyond traveling expenses and accommodations for his back-up group, would be $25,000. The good German gasped.

"'Col. Parker, nobody gets paid for playing for the President!'

"'Well, I don't know about that, son,' the Colonel responded abruptly, 'but there's one thing I do know. Nobody asks Elvis Presley to play for nothing.'" (*Creem*, March 1972) label in Memphis, Tennessee; then a pact was signed with Col. Tom Parker, shrewd country hustler. Elvis took off for RCA Victor, New York, and Hollywood. America has not been the same since. Elvis disappeared into an oblivion of respectability and security in the sixties, lost in interchangeable movies and dull music; he staged a remarkable comeback as that decade ended, and now performs as the transcendental Sun King that Ralph Waldo Emerson only dreamed about—and as a giant contradiction. His audience expands every year, but Elvis transcends his talent to the point of dispensing with it altogether. Performing a kind of enormous victory rather than winning it, Elvis strides the boards with such glamour, such magnetism, that he allows his audience to transcend their desire for his talent. Action is irrelevant when one can simply delight in the presence of a man who has made history, and who has triumphed over it.

Mark now, the supreme Elvis gesture. He takes the stage with a retinue of bodyguards, servants, singers, a band, an orchestra; he applies himself vaguely to the hits of his past, prostrates himself before songs of awesome ickiness; he acknowledges the applause and the gasps that greet his every movement (applause that comes thundering with such force you might think the audience merely suffers the music as an excuse for its ovations); he closes with an act of show-biz love that still warms the heart; but above all, he throws away the entire performance.

How could he take it seriously? How could anyone create when all one has to do is appear? "He *looks* like Elvis Presley!" cried a friend, when the Big E stormed forth in an explosion of flashbulbs and cheers. "What a burden to live up to!" It is as if there is nothing Elvis could do to overshadow a performance of his myth. And so he performs from a distance, laughing at his myth, throwing it away only to see it roar back and trap him once again.

He will sing, as if suffering to his very soul, a song called "This Time, You [God, that is] Gave Me a Mountain," which sums up his divorce and his separation from his little girl. Having confessed his sins, he will stand aside, head bowed, as the Special Elvis Presley Gospel Group sings "Sweet, Sweet Feeling (In this Place)." Apparently cleansed of his sins, he will rock straight into the rhythm and blues of "Lawdy, Miss Clawdy" and celebrate his new-found freedom with a lazy grin. But this little melodrama of casual triumph will itself be a throwaway. As with the well-planned sets, the first-class musicians, the brilliant costumes, there will be little life behind the orchestration; the whole performance will be flaccid, the timing careless, all emotions finally shallow, the distance from his myth necessitating an even greater distance from the musical power on which that myth is based.

Elvis gives us a massive road-show musical of opulent American mastery; his version of the winner-take-all fantasies that have kept the world lined up outside the theaters that show American movies ever since the movies began. And of course we respond: a self-made man is rather boring, but a self-made king is something else. Dressed in blue, red, white, ultimately gold, with a Superman cape and covered with jewels no one can be sure are fake, Elvis might epitomize the worst of our culture—he is bragging, selfish, narcissistic, condescending, materialistic to the point of insanity. But there is no need to take that seriously, no need to take anything seriously. "Aw, shucks," says the country boy; it is all a joke to him; his distance is in his humor, and he can exit from this America unmarked, unimpressed, and uninteresting.

"From the moment he comes out of the wings," writes Nik Cohn, "all the pop that has followed him is made to seem as nothing, to be blown away like chaff." That is exactly what that first moment feels like, but from that point on, Elvis will go with the rest of it, singing as if there are no dangers or delights in the world grand enough to challenge him. There is great satisfaction in his performance, and great emptiness.

It is an ending. It is a sure sign that a culture has reached a dead end when it is no longer intrigued by its myths (when they lose their power to excite, amuse, and renew all who are a part of those myths—when those myths just bore the hell out of everyone); but Elvis has dissolved into a presentation of his myth, and so has his music. The emotion of the best music is open, liberating in its commitment and intangibility; Elvis's presentation is fixed. The glorious oppression of that presentation parallels the all-but-complete assimilation of a revolutionary musical style into the mainstream of American culture, where no one is challenged and no one is threatened.

History without myth is surely a wasteland; but myths are compelling only when they are at odds with history. When they replace the need to make history, they too are a dead end, and merely smug. Elvis's performance of his myth is so satisfying to his audience that he is left with no musical identity whatsoever, and thus he has no way to define himself, or his audience—except to expand himself, and his audience. Elvis is a man whose task it is to dramatize the fact of his existence; he does not have to create something new (or try, and fail), and thus test the worth of his existence, or the worth of his audience.

Complete assimilation really means complete acceptance. The immigrant who is completely assimilated into America has lost the faculty of adding whatever is special about himself to his country; for any artist, complete assimilation means the adoption of an aesthetic where no lines are drawn and no choices are made. That quality of selection, which is what is at stake when an artist comes across with his or her version of anything, is missing. When an artist gives an all-encompassing Yes to his audience (and Elvis's Yes implicitly includes everyone, not just those who say Yes to *him)*, there is nothing more he can tell his audience, nothing he can really do for them, except maybe throw them a kiss.

Only the man who says No is free, Melville once wrote. We don't expect such a stance in popular culture, and those who do might best be advised to take their trade somewhere else. But the refusal that lurks on the margins of the affirmation of American popular culture—the margins where Sly Stone and Randy Newman have done their best work—is what gives the Yes of our culture its vitality and its kick. Elvis's Yes is the grandest of all, his presentation of mastery the grandest fantasy of freedom, but it is finally a counterfeit of freedom: it takes place in a world that for all its openness (Everybody Welcome!) is aesthetically closed, where nothing is left to be mastered, where there is only more to accept. For all its irresistible excitement and enthusiasm, this freedom is complacent, and so the music that it produces is empty of real emotion—there is nothing this freedom could be for, nothing to be won or lost.

At best, when the fans gather around—old men and women who might see their own struggles and failures ennobled in the splendor of one who came from the bottom; middle-aged couples attending to the most glamorous nightclub act there is; those in their twenties and thirties who have grown with Elvis ever since he and they created each other years ago (and who might have a feeling he and they will make their trip through history together, reading their history in each other)—at best, Elvis will confirm all who are there *as* an audience. Such an event, repeated over and over all across the land, implies an America that is as nearly complete as any can be. But what is it worth?

When Elvis sings "American Trilogy" (a combination of "Dixie," "The Battle Hymn of the Republic," and "All My Trials," a slave song), he signifies that his persona, and the culture he has made out of blues, Las Vegas, gospel music, Hollywood, schmaltz, Mississippi, and rock 'n' roll, can contain any America you might want to conjure up. It is rather Lincolnesque; Elvis recognizes that the Civil War has never ended, and so he will perform the Union.

Well, for a moment, staring at that man on the stage, you can almost believe it. For if Elvis were to bring it off—and it is easy to think that only he could—one would leave the hall with a new feeling for the country; whatever that feeling might be, one's sense of place would be broadened, and enriched.

But it is an illusion. A man or woman equal to the song's pretension would have to present each part of the song as if it were the whole story, setting one against each other, proving that one American really could make the South live, the Union hold, and slavery real. But on the surface and beneath it, Elvis transcends any real America by evading it. There is no John Brown in his "Battle Hymn," no romance in his "Dixie," no blood in his slave song. He sings with such a complete absence of musical personality that none of the old songs matter at all, because he has not committed himself to them; it could be anyone singing, or no one. It is in this sense, finally, that an audience is confirmed, that an America comes into being; lacking any real fear or joy, it is a throwaway America where nothing is at stake. The divisions America shares are simply smoothed away.

But there is no chance anyone who wants to join will be excluded. Elvis's fantasy of freedom, the audience's fantasy, takes on such reality that there is nothing left in the real world that can inspire the fantasy, or threaten it. What *is* left is for the fantasy to replace the world; and that, night after night, is what Elvis and his audience make happen. The version of the American dream that is Elvis's performance is blown up again and again, to contain more history, more people, more music, more hopes; the air gets thin but the bubble does not burst, nor will it ever. This is America when it has outstripped itself, in all of its extravagance, and its emptiness is Elvis's ultimate throwaway.

There is a way in which virtually his whole career has been a throwaway, straight from that time when he knew he had it made and that the future was his. You can hear that distance, that refusal to really commit himself, in his best music and his worst; if the throwaway is the source of most of what is pointless about Elvis, it is also at the heart of much of what is exciting and charismatic. It may be that he never took *any* of it seriously, just did his job and did it well, trying to enjoy himself and stay sane—save for those first Tennessee records, and that night, late in 1968, when his comeback was uncertain and he put a searing, desperate kind of life into a few songs that cannot be found in any of his other music.

It was a staggering moment. A Christmas TV special had been decided on; a final dispute between Colonel Parker (he wanted twenty Christmas songs and a tuxedo) and producer Steve Binder (he wanted a tough, fast, sexy show) had been settled; with Elvis's help, Binder won. So there Elvis was, standing in an auditorium, facing television cameras and a live audience for the first time in nearly a decade, finally stepping out from behind the wall of retainers and sycophants he had paid to hide him. And everyone was watching.

In the months preceding Elvis had begun to turn away from the seamless boredom of the movies and the hackneyed music of the soundtrack albums, staking out a style on a few half-successful singles, presenting the new persona of a man whose natural toughness was tempered by experience. The records—"Big Boss Man," "Guitar Man," "U.S. Male"—had been careful, respectable efforts, but now he was putting everything on the line, risking his comforts and his ease for the chance to start over. He had been a bad joke for a long time; if this show died, little more would be heard from Elvis Presley. Did he still have an audience? Did he still have anything to offer them? He had raised the stakes himself, but he probably had no idea.

Sitting on the stage in black leather, surrounded by friends and a rough little combo, the crowd buzzing, he sang and talked and joked, and all the resentments he had hidden over the years began to pour out. He had always said yes, but this time, he was saying no—not without humor, but almost with a wry bit of guilt, as if he had betrayed his talent and himself. "Been a long time, baby." He told the audience about a time back in 1955, when cops in Florida had forced him to sing without moving; the story was hilarious, but there was something in his voice that made very clear how much it had hurt. He jibed at the Beatles, denying that the heroes who had replaced him had produced anything he could not match, and then he proved it. After all this time he wanted more than safety; he and the men around him were nervous, full of adventure.

"I'd like to do my favorite Christmas song," Elvis drawls—squeals of familiarity from the crowd, the girls in the front rows doing their job, imitating themselves or their images of the past, fading into an undertone of giggles as the music begins. Elvis sings "Blue Christmas," a classically styled rhythm and blues, very even, all its tension implied: a good choice. He sings it low and throaty, snapping the strings on his guitar until one of his pals cries, "Play it dirty! Play it dirty!"—on a Christmas song! All right! But this is re-creation, the past in the present, an attempt to see if Elvis can go as far as he once did. Within those limits it works, it is beautiful. The song ends with appropriate, and calculated, screams.

"Ah think Ah'll put a strap around this and stand up," Presley says. AHAHAHAHAHAHAHAAHAHA! God, what's that? Nervous laughter from a friend. Slow and steady, still looking around for the strap no one has bothered to hook onto the guitar, Elvis rocks into "One Night." In Smiley Lewis's original, it was about an orgy, called "One Night of Sin" (with the great lines, "The things I did and I saw / Would make the earth stand still"); Elvis cleaned it up into a love story in 1958. But he has forgotten—or remembered. He is singing Lewis's version, as he must have always wanted to. He has slipped his role, and laughing, grinning, something is happening.

> . . . *The things I did and I saw, could make* . . .
> *these dreams— Where's the strap?*

Where's the strap, indeed. He falls in and out of the two songs, and suddenly the band rams hard at the music and Elvis lunges and eats it alive. No one has ever heard him sing like this; not even his best records suggest the depth of passion in this music. One line from Howlin' Wolf tells the tale: "When you see me runnin', you know my life is at stake." That's what it sounds like.

Shouting, crying, growling, lusting, Elvis takes his stand and the crowd takes theirs with him, no longer reaching for the past they had been brought to the studio to reenact, but responding to something completely new. The crowd is cheering for what they had only hoped for: Elvis has gone beyond all their expectations, and his, and they don't believe it. The guitar cuts in high and slams down and Elvis is roaring. Every line is a thunderbolt. *AW, YEAH!*, screams a pal— he has waited years for this moment.

> *UNNNNNNH! WHEW! When* . . . I ain't nevah did no wrong!

And Elvis floats like the master he is back into "One night, with you," even allowing himself a little "Hot dog!", singing softly to himself.

It was the finest music of his life. If ever there was music that bleeds, this was it. Nothing came easy that night, and he gave everything he had—more than anyone knew was there.

Something of that passion spilled over into the first comeback album, *From Elvis in Memphis;* into "Suspicious Minds," the single that put him back on top of the charts; into his first live shows in Las Vegas; and then his nerves steadied, and Elvis brought it all back home again. You can still hear the intensity, the echo of those moments of doubt, in the first notes of most songs Elvis sings on stage—just before he realizes again that the crowd cares only that he is before them, and that anyway, the music would be his if he wanted it, that his talent is so vast it would be demeaning to apply it. So he will revel in his glory, acting the part of the King it has always been said he is; and if that is a throwaway, it is at least thrown at those who want it. A real glow passes back and forth between Elvis and his audience, as he shares a bit of what it means to transcend the world of weakness, failure, worry, age and fear, shows what it means for a boy who sprung from the poor to be godly, and shares that too.

I suppose it is the finality this performance carries with it that draws me back to Elvis's first records, made when there was nothing to take for granted, let alone throw away. Those sides, like "One Night," catch a world of risk, will, passion, and natural nobility; something worth searching out within the America of mastery and easy splendor that may well be Elvis's last word. The first thing Elvis had to learn to transcend, after all, was the failure and obscurity he was born to; he had to find some way to set himself apart, to escape the limits that could well have given his story a very different ending. The ambition and genius that took him out and brought him back is there in that first music—that, and much more.

HILLBILLY MUSIC

"This is the sacred mystery of democracy," intoned Woodrow Wilson (dedicating the log cabin where Abraham Lincoln was born, in words ponderous enough to suit the mayor of Tupelo, Mississippi, when he dedicated the birthplace of Elvis Presley), "that its richest fruits spring up out of soils which no man had prepared and circumstances amidst which they are least expected . . ."

I like those words. The question of history may have been settled on the side of process, not personality, but it is not a settlement I much appreciate. Historical forces might explain the Civil War, but they don't

---

ELVIS ECHOES: Introducing a series of interruptions of Presley-Presence that, occurring while this chapter was written, are an essential part of its context, but do not fit anywhere else.

*EE #1. Elvis is to perform at the Oakland Coliseum in 1972. Back in the Dark Ages, two San Francisco high school girls win a "Why I Love Elvis" contest and are flown to Hollywood to be kissed. *Their principal expels them:* "We don't need that kind of publicity," he explains. Now, some babies and divorces later (for Elvis, too), the winners return. The word is passed; they are ushered backstage; they are kissed once more. It is a link to the past, but I am willing to bet that most of those in the hall (16,000) are meeting Elvis in the flesh for the first time, as am I. I have a bad seat, and the fortyish woman next to me passes her binoculars. I trade off with her preteen daughter. I notice that the best seats are occupied by couples who look old enough to substitute for El's grandparents. A thought from my friend Mary Clemmey comes to mind: In his present-day audience, Elvis sees the ghost of his mother, and the family life he has had to give up in order to be what he is. Behind me, a hippie pulls furiously on a joint. Is he performing an act of rebellion? Against Elvis? Or affirming that, in a bouffant utopia, he alone keeps the true Presley spirit alive?

account for Lincoln; they might tell us why rock 'n' roll emerged when it did, but they don't explain Elvis any more than they explain Little Peggy March. What a sense of context does give us, when we are looking for someone in particular, is an idea of what that person had to work with; but for myself, it always seems inexplicable in the end anyway. There are always blank spots, and that is where the myths take over. Elvis's story is so classically American (poor country boy makes good in the city) that his press agents never bothered to improve on it. But it is finally elusive too, just like all the good stories. It surrounds its subject, without quite revealing it. But it resonates; it evokes like crazy.

Now, the critical (and least tangible) point in the biography of any great man or woman is just that place where that person's story begins to detach itself from those of countless others like it. Take Lincoln again; was it that famous hike when he brought the borrowed book back? The moment on the stand facing Douglas when he knew he had him licked and loved it? The day he was born? You can't answer such questions, not computer-style, but you have no claim on the story unless you risk a guess.

They called Elvis the Hillbilly Cat in the beginning; he came out of a stepchild culture (in the South, white trash; to the rest of America, a caricature of Bilbo and moonshine) that for all it shared with the rest of America had its own shape and integrity. As a poor white Southern boy, Elvis created a personal culture out of the hillbilly world that was his as a given. Ultimately, he made that personal culture public in such an explosive way that he transformed not only his own culture, but America's.

It was, as Southern chambers of commerce have never tired of saying, A Land of Contrasts. The fundamental contrast, of course, could not have been more obvious: black and white. Always at the root of Southern fantasy, Southern music, and Southern politics, black Americans were poised in the early fifties for an overdue invasion of American life, in fantasy, music, and politics. As the North scurried to deal with the problem, the South would be pushed farther and farther into the weirdness and madness its best artists had been trying to exorcise from the time of Poe on down. Its politics would dissolve into night-riding and hysteria; its fantasies would be dull for all their gaudy paranoia. Only the music got away clean.

The North, powered by the Protestant ethic, had set men free by making them strangers; the poor man's South that Elvis knew took strength from community.

The community was based on a marginal economy that demanded cooperation, loyalty, and obedience for the achievement of anything resembling a good life; it was organized by religion, morals, and music. Music helped hold the community together, and carried the traditions and shared values that dramatized a sense of place. Music gave pleasure, wisdom, and shelter.

"It's the only place in the country I've ever been where you can actually drive down the highway at night, and if you listen, you hear music," Robbie Robertson once said. "I don't know if it's coming from the people or if it's coming from the air. It lives, and it's rooted there." Elegant enough, but I prefer another comment Robbie made. "The South," he said, "is the only place we play where everybody can clap on the off-beat."

Music was also an escape from the community, and music revealed its underside. There were always people who could not join, no matter how they might want to: tramps, whores, rounders, idiots, criminals. The most vital were singers: not the neighbors who brought out their fiddles and guitars for country picnics, as Elvis used to do, or those who sang in church, as he did also, but the professionals. They were men who bridged the gap between the community's sentimentalized idea of itself, and the outside world and the forbidden; artists who could take the community beyond itself because they had the talent and the nerve to transcend it. Often doomed, traveling throughout the South enjoying sins and freedoms the community had surrendered out of necessity or never known at all, they were too ambitious, ornery, or simply different to fit in.

The Carter Family, in the twenties, were the first to record the old songs everyone knew, to make the shared musical culture concrete, and their music drew a circle around the community. They celebrated the landscape (especially the Clinch Mountains that ringed their home), found strength in a feel for death because it was the only certainty, laughed a bit, promised to leave the hillbilly home they helped build only on a gospel ship. Jimmie Rodgers, their contemporary, simply hopped a train. He was every boy who ever ran away from home, hanging out in the railroad yards, bumming around with black minstrels, pushing out the limits of his life. *He* celebrated long tall mamas that rubbed his back and licked his neck just to cure the cough that killed him; he bragged about gunplay on Beale Street; he sang real blues, played jazz with Louis Armstrong, and though there was melancholy in his soul, his smile was a good one. He sounded like a man who could make a home for himself anywhere. There's so much *room* in this country, he seemed to be saying, so many things to do—how could an honest man be satisfied to live within the frontiers he was born to?

Outside of the community because of the way they lived, the singers were tied to it as symbols of its secret hopes, of its fantasies of escape and union with the black man, of its fears of transgressing the moral and social limits that promised peace of mind. Singers could present the extremes of emotion, risk, pleasure, sex, and violence that the community was meant to control; they were often alcoholic or worse, lacking a real family, drifters in a world where roots were life. Sometimes the singer tantalized the community with his outlaw liberty; dying young, he finally justified the community by his inability to survive outside of it. More often than not, the singer's resistance dissolved into sentiment. Reconversion is the central country music comeback strategy, and many have returned to the fold after a brief fling with the devil, singing songs of virtue, fidelity, and God, as if to prove that sin only hid a deeper piety—or that there was no way out.

By the late forties and early fifties, Hank Williams had inherited Jimmie Rodgers's role as the central figure in the music, but he added an enormous reservation: that margin of loneliness in Rodgers's America had grown into a world of utter tragedy. Williams sang for a community to which he could not belong; he sang to a God in whom he could not quite believe; even his many songs of good times and good lovin' seemed to lose their reality. There were plenty of jokes in his repertoire, novelties like "Kaw-Liga" (the tale of unrequited love between two cigar store Indians); he traveled Rodgers's road, but for Williams, that road was a lost highway. Beneath the surface of his forced smiles and his light, easy sound, Hank Williams was kin to Robert Johnson in a way that the new black singers of his day were not. Their music, coming out of New Orleans, out of Sam Phillips's Memphis studio and washing down from Chicago, was loud, fiercely electric, raucous, bleeding with lust and menace and loss. The rhythmic force that was the practical legacy of Robert Johnson had evolved into a music that overwhelmed *his* reservations; the rough spirit of the new blues, city R&B, rolled right over his nihilism. Its message was clear: What life doesn't give me, I'll take.

Hank Williams was a poet of limits, fear, and failure; he went as deeply into one dimension of the country world as anyone could, gave it beauty, gave it dignity. What was missing was that part of the hillbilly soul Rodgers had celebrated, something Williams's music obscured, but which his realism could not express and the community's moralism could not contain: excitement, rage, fantasy, delight—the feeling, summed up in a sentence by W. J. Cash from *The Mind of the South*, that "even the Southern physical world was a kind of cosmic conspiracy against reality in favor of romance"; that even if Elvis's South was filled with Puritans, it was also filled with natural-born hedonists, and the same people were both.

> To lie on his back for days and weeks [Cash wrote of the hillbilly], storing power as the air he breathed stores power under the hot sun of August, and then to explode, as that air explodes in a thunderstorm, in a violent outburst of emotion—in such a fashion would he make life not only tolerable, but infinitely sweet.

In the fifties we can hardly find that moment in white music, before Elvis. Hank Williams was not all there was to fifties country, but his style was so pervasive, so effective, carrying so much weight, that it closed off the possibilities of breaking loose just as the new black music helped open them up. Not his gayest tunes, not "Move It on Over," "Honky Tonkin'," or "Hey Good Lookin'," can match this blazing passage from Cash, even if those songs share its subject:

> To go into the town on Saturday afternoon and night, to stroll with the throng, to gape at the well-dressed and the big automobiles, to bathe in the holiday cacaphony ... maybe to have a drink, maybe to get drunk, to laugh with the passing girls, to pick them up if you had a car, or to go swaggering or hesitating into the hotels with the corridors saturated with the smell of bicloride of mercury, or the secret, steamy bawdy houses; maybe to have a fight, maybe against the cops, maybe to end, whooping and goddamning, in the jailhouse ...

The momentum is missing; that will to throw yourself all the way after something better with no real worry about how you are going to make it home. And it was this spirit, full-blown and bragging, that was to find its voice in Elvis's new blues and the rockabilly fever he kicked off all over the young white South. Once Elvis broke down the door, dozens more would be fighting their way through. Out of nowhere there would be Carl Perkins, looking modest enough and sounding for all the world as if he was having fun for the first time in his life, chopping his guitar with a new kind of urgency and yelling: "Now Dan got happy and he started ravin'—He jerked out his razor but he wasn't shavin'"—

He hollered R-R-RAVE ON *chillen, I'm with ya!*
RAVE ON CATS *he cried*
It's almost dawn and the cops're gone
Let's alllllll get dixie fried!

Country music (like the blues, which was more damned and more honestly hedonistic than country had ever been) was music for a whole community, cutting across lines of age, if not class. This could have meant an openly expressed sense of diversity for each child, man, and woman, as it did with the blues. But country spoke to a community fearful of anything of the sort, withdrawing into itself, using music as a bond that linked all together for better or for worse, with a sense that what was shared was less important than the crucial fact of sharing. How could parents hope to keep their children if their kids' whole sense of what it meant to live—which is what we get from music when we are closest to it—held promises the parents could never keep?

The songs of country music, and most deeply, its even, narrow sound, had to subject the children to the heartbreak of their parents: the father who couldn't feed his family, the wife who lost her husband to a honky-tonk angel or a bottle, the family that lost everything to a suicide or a farm spinning off into one more bad year, the horror of loneliness in a world that was meant to banish that if nothing else. Behind that uneasy grin, this is Hank Williams's America; the romance is only a night call.

Such a musical community is beautiful; but it is not hard to see how it could be intolerable. All that hedonism was dragged down in country music; a deep sense of fear and resignation confined it, as perhaps it almost had to, in a land overshadowed by fundamentalist religion, where original sin was just another name for the facts of life.

RAISED UP

Now, that Saturday night caught by Cash and Perkins would get you through a lot of weekdays. Cash might close it off—"Emptied of their irritations and repressions, left to return to their daily tasks, stolid, unlonely, and tame again"—and he's right, up to a point. This wasn't any revolution, no matter how many cops got hurt keeping the peace on Saturday night. Regardless of what a passport to that Southern energy (detached from the economics and religion that churned it up) might do for generations of restless Northern and British kids, there is no way that energy can be organized. But the fact that Elvis and the rest could trap its spirit and send it out over a thousand radio transmitters is a central fact of more lives than mine; the beginning of most of the stories in this book, if nothing near the end of them.

For we are treading on the key dividing line that made Elvis "King of Western Bop" (they went through a lot of trouble finding a name for this music) instead of just another country crooner or a footnote in someone's history of the blues: the idea (and it was just barely an "idea") that Saturday night could be the whole show. You had to be young and a bit insulated to pull it off, but why not? Why not trade pain and boredom for kicks and style? Why not make an escape from a way of life—the question trails off the last page of *Huckleberry Finn*—into a way of life?

You might not get revered for all time by everyone from baby to grandma, like the Carter Family, but you'd have more fun. Reality would catch up sooner or later—a pregnant girlfriend and a fast marriage, the farm you had to take over when your daddy died, a dull and pointless job that drained your desires until you could barely remember them—but why deal with reality before you had to? And what if there was a chance, just a chance, that you *didn't* have to deal with it? "When I was a boy," said Elvis not so long ago, "I was the hero in comic books and movies. I grew up believing in a dream. Now I've lived it out. That's all a man can ask for."

Elvis is telling us something quite specific: how special he was; how completely he captured and understood what for most of us is only a tired phrase glossing the surfaces of our own failed hopes. It is one thing, after all, to dream of a new job, and quite another to dream of a new world. The risks are greater. Elvis took chances dreaming his dreams; he gambled against the likelihood that their failure would betray him, and make him wish he had never dreamed at all. There are a hundred songs to tell that story, but perhaps Mott the Hoople, chasing

---

*EE #2. May 1972. I read in *Modern Screen* that top GOP politicos are giving *serious consideration* to placing Elvis's name in nomination for the vice-presidency (a plot to get around that $25,000 fee?). The article is illustrated by fifteen-year-old shots of girls waving ELVIS-FOR-PRESIDENT banners. Elvis, the story says, thinks this is a good idea, and has recently addressed a group of Black Panthers in order to test his forensic skills. He told them, and I quote: "Violence is not where it's at. It's a real turn-off, man." I do not know how to take this, especially as I recall it a year later when a TV trailer announces, "Tonight, immediately following the President's speech on Watergate, see Elvis further the cause of rock 'n' roll in *Roustabout*." I am more disoriented by the idea that Elvis could further the cause of *anything* in a movie like *Roustabout* than I am by the missed chance of his involvement in the Watergate scandal. But then, he would have known how to handle it. To Elvis, Watergate would have been something like a cosmic paternity suit.

the rock 'n' roll fantasy Elvis made of the American dream, said it best: "I wish I'd never wanted then / What I want now twice as much."

Always, Elvis felt he was different, if not better, than those around him. He grew his sideburns long, acting out that sense of differentness, and was treated differently: in this case, he got himself kicked off the football team. Hear him recall those days in the midst of a near-hysterical autobiography, delivered at the height of his comeback from the stage at the International Hotel in Las Vegas: ". . . Had pretty long hair for that time and I tell you it got pretty weird. They used to see me comin down the street and they'd say, 'Hot dang, let's get him, he's a squirrel, he's a squirrel, get him, he just come down outta the trees.'"

High school classmates remember his determination to break through as a country singer; with a little luck, they figured, he might even make it.

Out on the road for the first time with small-change country package tours, though, Elvis would plot for something bigger—for everything Hollywood had ever shown him in its movies.

On North Main in Memphis, as Harmonica Frank recalls Elvis, this was nothing to put into words. Talking trash and flicking ash, marking time and trying to hold it off, what did Elvis really have to look forward to? A year or so of Saturday nights, a little local notoriety, then a family he didn't quite decide to have and couldn't support? It would be all over.

Elvis fancied himself a trucker (if there weren't any Memphis boys in the movies, there were plenty on the road), pushing tons of machinery through the endless American night; just his version of the train whistle that called out to Johnny B. Goode and kept Richard Nixon awake as a boy. If it is more than a little odd that what to Elvis served as a symbol of escape and mastery now works—as part of his legend—as a symbol of everything grimy and poor he left behind when he did escape, maybe that only tells us how much his success shuffled the facts of his life—or how much he raised the stakes.

You don't make it in America—Emerson's mousetrap to the contrary—waiting for someone to come along and sign you up. You might be sitting on a corner like a Philly rock 'n' roller and get snatched up for your good looks, but you'll be back a year later and you'll never know what happened. Worst of all, you may not even care. What links the greatest rock 'n' roll careers is a volcanic ambition, a lust for more than anyone has a right to expect; in some cases, a refusal to know when to quit or even rest. It is that bit of Ahab burning beneath the Huck Finn rags of "Freewheelin'" Bob Dylan, the arrogance of a country boy like Elvis sailing into Hollywood, ready for whatever kind of success America had to offer.

So if we treat Elvis's words with as much respect as we can muster—which is how he meant them to be taken—we can see the first point at which his story begins to be his own. He took his dreams far more seriously than most ever dare, and he had the nerve to chase them down.

Cash's wonderful line—"a cosmic conspiracy against reality in favor of romance"—now might have more resonance. Still, if the kind of spirit that romance could produce seems ephemeral within the context of daily life, you would not expect the music it produced to last very long either. Not even Elvis, as a successful young rocker, could have expected his new music to last; he told interviewers rock 'n' roll was here to stay, but he was taking out plenty of insurance, making movies and singing schmaltz. You couldn't blame him; anyway, he liked schmaltz.

Within the realm of country music, the new spirit dried up just like Saturday fades into Monday, but since rock 'n' roll found its own audience and created its own world, that hardly mattered. Rock 'n' roll caught that romantic conspiracy on records and gave it a form. Instead of a possibility within a music, it became the essence; it became, of all things, a tradition. And when that form itself had to deal with reality—which is to say, when its young audience began to grow up—when the

---

*EE #3. Elvis's 1973 TV special, *Aloha from Elvis in Hawaii*, was beamed by satellite to one-third of the world's population. Or so his publicity men announced. Perhaps it was that if the one-third of the world—principally the heathen part—had TV sets, it could have watched. It doesn't matter; the conceit of the concept is what matters.

You can see him now, Col. Thomas Andrew Parker, ex-carny barker, the great medical menagerist, tossing helplessly on his bed, scheming—after all these years, still peddling Elvis pens at press conferences, hustling glossies in the aisles at concerts, Colonel Parker does not rest—and what keeps him awake is that *even now there are people who do not know about Elvis Presley!* There are worlds to be conquered! There is work to be done!

Finally, he drops off to sleep. Yes, there are poor beggars somewhere in the Amazon jungle who have yet to get the word (perhaps the King would succeed where dozens of casseroled missionaries have failed—make a note of that), but the Colonel will deal with that tomorrow . . . wait for tomorrow.

Parker dreams.

It is perhaps 1990. Elvis is in his middle fifties now, still young, still beautiful. His latest single—"Baby Let Me Bang Your Box," backed with "My Yiddishe Mama"—has topped all charts. Parker has had his third heart transplant. The world has received the long-awaited actual communication from intelligent beings beyond the solar system. Earth's greatest scientists have assembled in Japan to decipher the message, and after years of error they have succeeded. It consists of only one word, one question on which the fate of ten billion people may rest:

"ELWIS?"

So Colonel Parker rests easy. Age has mellowed him, and his expectations do not go beyond the Milky Way.

compromise between fantasy and reality that fills most of this book was necessary to preserve the possibility of fantasy, the fantasy had become part of the reality that had to be dealt with; the rules of the game had changed a bit, and it was a better game. "Blue Suede Shoes" had grown directly into something as serious and complex, and yet still offhand, still take-it-or-leave-it-and-pass-the-wine, as the Rolling Stones' "You Can't Always Get What You Want," which asks the musical question, "Why *are you* stepping on my blue suede shoes?"

Echoing through all of rock 'n' roll is the simple demand for peace of mind and a good time. While the demand is easy to make, nothing is more complex than to try to make it real and live it out. It all sounds plain, obvious; but that one young man like Elvis could break through a world as hard as Hank Williams's, and invent a new one to replace it, seems obvious only because we have inherited Elvis's world, and live in it.

Satisfaction is not all there is to it, but it is where it all begins. Finally, the music must provoke as well as delight, disturb as well as comfort, create as well as sustain. If it doesn't, it lies, and there is only so much comfort you can take in a lie before it all falls apart.

The central facts of life in Elvis's South pulled as strongly against the impulses of hedonism and romance as the facts of our own lives do against the fast pleasures of rock 'n' roll. When the poor white was thrown back on himself, as he was in the daytime, when he worked his plot or looked for a job in the city, or at night, when he brooded and Hank Williams's whippoorwill told the truth all too plainly, those facts stood out clearly: powerlessness and vulnerability on all fronts. The humiliation of a class system that gave him his identity and then trivialized it; a community that for all its tradition and warmth was in some indefinable way not enough; economic chaos; the violence of the weather; bad food and maybe not enough of that; diseases that attached themselves to the body like new organs—they all mastered him. And that vulnerability produced—along with that urge to cut loose, along with that lively Southern romance—uncertainty, fatalism, resentment, acceptance, and nostalgia: limits that cut deep as the oldest cotton patch in Dixie.

Vernon Presley was a failed Mississippi sharecropper who moved his family out of the country with the idea of making a go in the city; it's not so far from Tupelo to Memphis, but in some ways, the journey must have been a long one—scores of country songs about boys and girls who lost their souls to the big town attest to that. Listen to Dolly Parton's downtown hooker yearning for her Blue Ridge mountain boy; listen to the loss of an America you may never have known.

They don't make country music better than that anymore, but it's unsatisfying, finally; too classical. This country myth is just one more echo of Jefferson pronouncing that, in America, virtue must be found in the land. I like myths, but this one is too facile, either for the people who still live on the land or for those of us who are merely looking for a way out of our own world, for an Annie Green Springs utopia. The myth is unsatisfying because the truth is richer than the myth.

"King Harvest (Has Surely Come)," the Band's song of blasted country hopes, gives us the South in all of its earthly delight and then snuffs it out. All at once, the song catches the grace and the limbo of the life that must be left behind.

The tune evokes a man's intimacy with the land and the refusal of the land to respond in kind. The music makes real, for the coolest city listener, a sense of place that is not quite a sense of being at home; the land is too full of violence for that. One hears the farmer's fear of separating from the land (and from his own history, which adhering to the land, is not wholly his own); one hears the cold economic necessities that have forced him out. The melody—too beautiful and out of reach for any words I have—spins the chorus into the pastoral with a feel for nature that is *really* hedonistic—

Corn in the field
Listen to the rice as the wind blows cross the water
KING HARVEST HAS SURELY COME*

—and a desperate, ominous rhythm slams the verses back to the slum streets that harbor the refugees of the pastoral disaster: "Just don't judge me by my shoes!" Garth Hudson's organ traces the circle of the song, over and over again.

The earliest picture of Elvis shows a farmer, his wife, and their baby; the faces of the parents are vacant, they are set, as if they cannot afford an unearned smile. Somehow, their faces say, they will be made to pay even for that.

You don't hear this in Elvis's music; but what he left out of his story is as vital to an understanding of his art as what he kept, and made over. If we have no idea of what he left behind, of how much he escaped, we will have no idea what his success was worth, or how intensely he must have wanted it.

*   *   *

Elvis was thirteen when the family left Tupelo for Memphis in 1948, a pampered only child; ordinary in all respects, they say, except that he liked to sing. True to Chuck Berry's legend of the Southern rocker, Elvis's mother bought him his first guitar, and for the same reason Johnny B. Goode's mama had in mind: keep the boy out of trouble. Elvis sang tearful country ballads, spirituals, community music. On the radio, he listened with his family to the old music of the Carter Family and Jimmie Rodgers, to current stars like Roy Acuff, Ernest Tubb, Bob Wills, Hank Williams, and to white gospel groups like the Blackwood Brothers. Elvis touched the soft center of American music when he heard and imitated Dean Martin and the operatics of Mario Lanza; he picked up Southern blues singers like Big Bill Broonzy, Big Boy Crudup, Lonnie Johnson, and the new Memphis music of Rufus Thomas and Johnny Ace, mostly when no one else was around, because that music was naturally frowned upon. His parents called it "sinful music," and they had a point—it was dirty, and there were plenty of blacks who would have agreed with Mr. and Mrs. Presley—but Elvis was really too young to worry. In this he was no different from hundreds of other white country kids who wanted more excitement in their lives than they could get from twangs and laments—wanted a beat, sex, celebration, the stunning nuances of the blues and the roar of horns and electric guitars. Still, Elvis's interest was far more casual than that of Jerry Lee Lewis, a bad boy who was sneaking off to black dives in his spare time, or Carl Perkins, a musician who was consciously working out a synthesis of blues and country.

The Presleys stumbled onto welfare, into public housing. Vernon Presley found a job. It almost led to the family's eviction, because if they still didn't have enough to live on, they were judged to have too much to burden the county with their troubles. Elvis was a loner, but he had an eye for flash. He sold his blood for money, ushered at the movies, drove his famous truck, and divided the proceeds between his mother and his outrageous wardrobe. Looking for space, for a way to set himself apart.

Like many parents with no earthly future, the Presleys, especially Gladys Presley, lived for their son. Her ambition must have been that Elvis would take all that was good in the family and free himself from the life she and her husband endured; she was, Memphian Stanley Booth wrote a few years ago, "the one, perhaps the only one, who had told him throughout his life that even though he came from poor country people, he was just as good as anybody."

On Sundays (Wednesdays too, sometimes) the Presleys went to

their Assembly of God to hear the Pentecostal ministers hand down a similar message: the last shall be first. This was democratic religion with a vengeance, lower class and gritty. For all those who have traced Elvis's music and his hipshake to his religion (accurately enough—Elvis was the first to say so), it has escaped his chroniclers that hillbilly Calvinism was also at the root of his self-respect and his pride: the anchor of his ambition.

His church (and the dozens of other Pentecostal sects scattered throughout the South and small-town America) was one part of what was left of the old American religion after the Great Awakening. Calvinism had been a religion of authority in the beginning; in the middle-class North, filtered through the popular culture of Ben Franklin, it became a system of tight money, tight-mindedness, and gentility; in the hillbilly South, powered by traveling preachers and their endless revivals, the old holiness cult produced a faith of grace, apocalypse, and emotion, where people heaved their deepest feelings into a circle and danced around them. Momentum scattered that old authority; all were sinners, all were saints. Self-consciously outcast, the true faith in a land of Philistines and Pharisees, it was shoved into storefronts and tents and even open fields, and no less sure of itself for that.

Church music caught moments of unearthly peace and desire, and the strength of the religion was in its intensity. The preacher rolled fire down the pulpit and chased it into the aisle, signifying; men and women rocked in their seats, sometimes onto the floor, bloodying their fingernails scratching and clawing in a lust for absolute sanctification. No battle against oppression, this was a leap right through it, with tongues babbling toward real visions, negating stale red earth, warped privvies, men and women staring from their sway-backed porches into nothingness. It was a faith meant to transcend the grimy world that called it up. Like Saturday night, the impulse to dream, the need to escape, the romance and the contradictions of the land, this was a source of energy, tension, and power.

Elvis inherited these tensions, but more than that, gave them his own shape. It is often said that if Elvis had not come along to set off the changes in American music and American life that followed his triumph, someone very much like him would have done the job as well. But there is no reason to think this is true, either in strictly musical terms, or in any broader cultural sense. It is vital to remember that Elvis was the first young Southern white to sing rock 'n' roll, something he copied from no one but made up on the spot; and to know that even though other singers would have come up with a white version of the new black music acceptable to teenage America, of all who did emerge in Elvis's wake, none sang as powerfully, or with more than a touch of his magic.

Even more important is the fact that no singer emerged with anything like Elvis's combination of great talent and conscious ambition, and there is no way a new American hero could have gotten out of the South and to the top—creating a whole new sense of how big the top was, as Elvis did—without that combination. The others—Perkins, Lewis, Charlie Rich—were bewildered by even a taste of fame and unable to handle a success much more limited than Presley's.

If Elvis had the imagination to come up with the dreams that kept him going, he had the music to bring them to life and make them real to huge numbers of other people. It was the genius of his singing, an ease and an intensity that has no parallel in American music, that along with his dreams separated him from his context; and for the rest of this chapter, we can try to discover what that singing was all about.

THE ROCKABILLY MOMENT

There are four of them in the little studio: Bill Black, the bass player; Scotty Moore, the guitarist; in the back, Sam Phillips, the producer; and the sexy young kid thumping his guitar as he sings, Elvis Presley, just nineteen. 1954.

Sam Phillips is doing all right for himself. He has been among the first to record men who will be giants in the world of postwar blues: B. B. King, Junior Parker, and the Howlin' Wolf himself. The names on Phillips's roster show his willingness to try anything: wonderful names like Big Memphis Ma Rainey, the Ripley Cotton Choppers, Dr. Ross, Hardrock Gunter, Rufus "Bear Cat" Thomas, Billy "The Kid" Emerson, the Prisonaires (a vocal group from the state pen), the immortal Hot Shot Love. There are plenty more knocking on the door, and with no more than this, Phillips's place in the history of American music would be assured—not that a place in history is quite what he is looking for.

In the records Phillips makes you can discern something more than taste, something like vision. He has cooked up a sound all his own: hot, fierce, overbearing, full of energy and desire, a sound to jump right out of the jukebox. But Phillips wants money, a lot of it, and he wants something new. Deep down in a place not even he sees clearly, he wants to set the world on its ear.

The kid with the guitar is . . . unusual; but they've been trying to put something on the tape Sam keeps running back—a ballad, a hillbilly song, anything—and so far, well, it just doesn't get it.

The four men cool it for a moment, frustrated. They share a feeling they could pull something off if they hit it right, but it's been a while, and that feeling is slipping away, as it always does. They talk music, blues, Crudup, ever hear that, who you kiddin' man, dig this. The kid pulls his guitar up, clowns a bit. He throws himself at a song. *That's all right, mama, that's all right* . . . eat shit. He doesn't say that, naturally, but that's what he's found in the tune; his voice slides over the lines as the two musicians come in behind him, Scotty picking up the melody and the bassman slapping away at his axe. Phillips hears it, likes it, and makes up his mind.

All right, you got something. Do it again, I'll get it down. Just like that, don't mess with it. Keep it simple.

They cut the song fast, put down their instruments, vaguely embarrassed at how far they went into the music. Sam plays back the tape. Man, they'll run us outta town when they hear it, Scotty says; Elvis sings along with himself, joshing his performance. They all wonder, but not too much.

Get on home, now, Sam says. I gotta figure what to do with this.

They leave, but Sam Phillips is perplexed. Who is gonna play this crazy record? White jocks won't touch it 'cause it's nigger music and colored will pass 'cause it's hillbilly. It sounds good, it sounds sweet, but maybe it's just . . . too weird? The hell with it.

Sam Phillips released the record; what followed was the heyday of Sun Records and rockabilly music, a moment when boys were men and men were boys, when full-blown legends emerged that still walk the land and the lesser folk simply went along for the ride.

Rockabilly was a fast, aggressive music: simple, snappy drumming, sharp guitar licks, wild country boogie piano, the music of kids who came from all over the South to make records for Sam Phillips and his imitators. Rockabilly came and it went; there was never that much of it, and even including Elvis's first Sun singles, all the rockabilly hits put together sold less than Fats Domino's. But rockabilly fixed the crucial image of rock 'n' roll: the sexy, half-crazed fool standing on stage singing his guts out.

Most important, the image was white. Rockabilly was the only style of early rock 'n' roll that proved white boys could do it all—that they could be as strange, as exciting, as scary, and as free as the black men who were suddenly walking America's airwaves as if they owned them. There were two kinds of white counterattack on the black invasion of white popular culture that was rock 'n' roll: the attempt to soften black music or freeze it out, and the rockabilly lust to beat the black man at his own game.

Sam Phillips had the imagination to take in a country folksinger like Johnny Cash and a Stan Kenton fan like Charlie Rich; he was commercial enough to get rock 'n' roll out of both of them. Phillips gave a funny-looking kid named Roy Orbison the chance to growl that no girl had the style to match him, and the music to prove it. Sun tossed up Warren Smith, who claimed he had a girl who looked like a frog; Sonny Burgess, who dyed his hair red to match his red suit and his red Cadillac and told anyone who would listen he wanted to boogie with a redheaded woman; Sun offered us Billy Lee Riley, who blithely argued that rock 'n' roll was so strange it had to come from Mars. The little green men taught him how to do the bop, was the way he put it.

Carl Perkins found greatness here, and nowhere else; Jerry Lee Lewis simply took greatness as his due. ("*I* played on 'em," Jerry Lee told an interviewer who had asked the names of the musicians who had played on his records, "what else do you need to know?") Jerry Lee stormed his way through the whorehouse rock of "Deep Elem Blues" like Elmer Gantry moonlighting from the revival tent (celebrating the Dallas red light district that crawled with sin and blues piano); he tumbled into "Big Legged Woman," leering at an imaginary audience with the arrogance that would bring him down.

Let me tell ya, tell ya, tell ya something
WHAT I'M TALKIN' ABOUT
*I bet my bottom dollar there ain't a cherry in this house**

While it lasted, Sun was a space of freedom, a place to take chances. The music Sun produced was ominous, funny, kicking up rhythm and bursting with exuberance, determination, and urgency, full of self-conscious novelty and experiment. Most of the first rock 'n' roll styles were variations on black forms that had taken shape before the white audience moved in and forced those forms to turn its way; rockabilly was almost self-contained, a world of its own, and as authentically new as any music can be.

Back in those days I knew some country kids who captured the spirit

* Copyright © P. Donald White. Used by permission.

of the music as well as any 45: farm boys, long, lean, tough, and good-humored. They flashed me my first picture of Little Richard, kicked raccoons to death with their bare feet, rustled sheep, chased Indian girls into the bushes, and made it into town on Saturday night to watch the razor fights. They were easy to idolize; one night they got drunk, drove their car to the railroad tracks, and got themselves blown to pieces.

Rockabilly was squeaky Charlie Feathers, a country singer of no special talent or even much drive, trekking up to Cincinnati, after failures at Sun, for the chance to yell, "Aw, turn it *loose!*" and then disappear. He reached once, and he missed, but these lines have stayed with me ever since a scratchy tape of his one great song arrived in the mail:

> *Well, I'm a tip-top daddy an' I'm gonna have my way*
> *Dontcha worry 'bout me baby, dont worry what they say*
> *I got one hand, baby, let it swing by my side*
> *Just gimme one hand loose, and I'll be satisfied*
> *Satisfied!**

"Maybe someday your name will be in lights," Chuck Berry promised the young rockers, and most of them never got past the "maybe." There was a price for all that unexpected vitality and flash. Carl Perkins, still billing himself "The King of Rock 'n' Roll" on the thin line of one hit and a score of failures, sunk into alcohol; Johnny Cash nearly killed himself on pills; Gene Vincent found himself exiled to England, where some still remembered, and died of a bleeding ulcer before he was forty. Johnny Burnette, Eddie Cochran, Buddy Holly, chasing after Elvis's pot of gold, died in accidents, in fast cars and chartered planes. Most simply vanished and were forgotten—if they were lucky enough to have been known at all. They fell back into the predictability of country music or the day-to-day sameness they had meant to escape. All they left behind was rock 'n' roll, and an audience that twenty years later was still acting out their fantasies and seeking novelty and amusement in their ghosts.

It was an explosion, and standing over it all was Elvis. In the single year he recorded for Sam Phillips—July 1954 through July 1955—ten sides were released (four more were used by RCA to fill up Elvis's first album); about half derived from country songs, the rest took off from blues. His music stands to the rest of rockabilly as genius does to talent.

The blues especially have not dated at all. Not a note is false; their excitement comes through the years intact, unburdened by cuteness,

---

* Copyright © 1956 by Fort Knox Music Company.

mannerism, or posturing.* Nothing is stylized. The music is clean, straight, open, and free.

That's what these sides are about: finding space in the crunch of the worn-out and overfamiliar; finding a way to feel free in that space and finding the voice to put that feeling across.

The best evidence of Sam Phillips's spirit is in the sound of the records. Each song is clear, direct, uncluttered, and blended into something coherent. There is that famous echo, slapping back at the listener, and a bubbling tension that is never quite resolved; no comforts of vocal accompaniment, but the risk of one young man on his own. The sound is all presence, as if Black and Moore each took a step straight off the record and Elvis was somehow squeezed right into the mike. "I went into the studio," Sam Phillips recalled years later, "to draw out a person's innate, possibly unknown talents, present them to the public, and let the public be the judge. I had to be a psychologist and know how to handle each artist and how to enable him to be at his best. I went with the idea that an artist should have something not just good, but totally unique. When I found someone like that, I did everything in my power to bring it out."†

The sides Phillips cut with Elvis might have worked in the twenties, and they might do for the eighties; not simply as listenable music— there is no doubt about that—but as music that still sounds new, that still breaks things open.‡

* For most of us, the songs are unburdened by any sort of nostalgia as well. In their time, they were little heard outside of the South, and most turned up on albums only when Elvis was off in the Army and RCA had to scrape its vaults for something to release. None ever made the national pop charts. Today they are rarely played on the radio (though spinning the dial on Elvis's thirty-eighth birthday, I picked up "That's All Right"—on a country station). Until 1976, Colonel Parker, or Elvis himself, deemed it vital that the King be protected from his past, so the songs were not, as with most classic rock, reissued in a package that might attract an audience. Given the publicity that has come with Elvis, these sides remained almost invisible, the result of a prepop moment; but *their* result is as public as rock 'n' roll. From one point of view they are the basis of the whole show. So there is a lot of power packed into these records, and not all of it is musical.
†From an interview with John Pugh, *Country Music*, November 1973.
‡Even the lyrics evade any possibility of camp—unlike so much of fifties rock 'n' roll, including Elvis's RCA material, which was made with a trendy commercial ear. The blues and country motifs of the Sun sides are as lively today as they were old in 1954; if it takes little effort to trace "That's All Right" and "Milkcow Blues Boogie" back to Son House's epic "My Black Mama," cut in 1930, it takes even less to follow the trail forward to the Rolling Stones or the Allman Brothers.
   Not surprisingly, on the album that today features House's masterpiece (*Really! The Country Blues*), there is an ancient, quiet statement of the theme Elvis brought home with such force. Made in 1928, it comes deadpan, spoken over a pretty little guitar line by one William Moore—an old, old mood, there too in Harmonica Frank or the Allmans' "Pony Boy," but to modern ears, *about* what Elvis *was*. This is "Old Country Rock": "Come on, Bill, let's take them for an old country rock. Let's go back down the Rappahanock, down Tappahanock way. Look at Bill while everybody rocks. Get that old rock, Bill. Everybody rock. Old folks rock. Young folks rock. Boys rock. Girls rock. Trot back, man, and let me rock. Rock me, sis, rock me. Rock me till I sweat. Trot back, folks,

Elvis can tell us what was new and distinctive about his time without being trapped by it, and without trapping us. He can do it because to a great degree ELVIS PRESLEY was the distinctive item. For all the writers who have found a neat logic to the development of the music Elvis made, and have lost his genius in a process, that is not what I hear; I hear a whole world of music that by no means had to crystallize as it did. "I heard the news," Elvis would sing in "Good Rockin' Tonight"— but he was the news.

Elvis's Memphis records—"Milkcow Blues Boogie," "You're a Heart-breaker," "Good Rockin' Tonight," "Baby Let's Play House"—might be his best; a choice between the Sun sides and "Hound Dog," "Don't Be Cruel," "All Shook Up," "Reconsider Baby," "Suspicious Minds" and "Long Black Limousine" is not one I ever want to make. Elvis's first music deserves a close and loving attention not simply because it rep-resents all that Elvis and those he has sung for have lost—youthful exuberance, innocence, haven't we tired of that story?—but because this is unquestionably great music, fun to think about, and because this music foreshadows, and contains, the entire aesthetic Elvis has worked out over the twenty years of his career. This is emotionally complex music that can return something new each time you listen to it. What I hear, most of the time, is the affection and respect Elvis felt for the limits and conventions of his family life, of his community, and ulti-mately of American life, captured in his country sides; and his refusal of those limits, of any limits, played out in his blues. This is a rhythm of acceptance and rebellion, lust and quietude, triviality and distinction. It can dramatize the rhythm of our own lives well enough.

ELVIS MOVES OUT

Elvis first went into Sam Phillips's studio to work in June 1954, and it did not take him long to get to the point where he could make his first record. It is impossible to imagine a more natural sound. There's more here than anyone could have guessed, he seems to be saying: more soul, more guts, and more life.

---

let your pappy rock. Pappy knows how. Children rock. Sister Ernestine, show your pappy how you rock. Mighty fine, boys, rock it, rock it till the cows come home. Whip that box, Bill, whip it. Too sad, I mean too sad for the public. Now up the country, back down the country again on that old rock. Rappahanock. Tappahanock. Cross the river, boys, cross the river. Man, it's sporty. Play it, Bill, play it till the sergeant comes." No one could ask for a better summation than that.

"That's All Right" was one of three Arthur Crudup tunes Elvis recorded. Crudup had cut many sides for RCA's Bluebird outlet in the forties and early fifties; he wrote good songs, pointed little messages of loss fitted to bright blues melodies, but he was a minimal guitarist and an erratic singer, a bit one-dimensional. Only on numbers that verged on country or pop styles (as with his lovely "So Glad You're Mine," which Elvis recorded in a disinterested manner soon after reaching RCA) does Crudup seem to hit his stride.

Elvis reduces the blueman's original to a footnote. He takes over the music, changing words and tightening verses to suit himself, hanging onto the ends of lines as Scotty Moore chimes in with pretty high-note riffs. Elvis sounds very young, sure of himself, ready to win; he turns Crudup's lament for a lost love into a satisfied declaration of independence, the personal statement of a boy claiming his manhood. His girl may have left him, but nothing she can do can dent the pleasure that radiates from his heart. It's the blues, but free of all worry, all sin; a simple joy with no price to pay.

Phillips put out the record on July 19, 1954, and it soon earned its place on the Memphis R&B charts, along with new hits by Muddy Waters and Johnny Ace. *Cashbox*, oblivious to Presley's color, reviewed the side as a blues; *Billboard*, prophetically, saw potential in all markets. It was an event, to some a scary one, but if "That's All Right" brought home the racial fears of a lot of people, it touched the secret dreams of others; if it was a threat, it was also another ride on the raft. "It was like a giant wedding ceremony," said Marion Keisker, Sam Phillips's working partner, and the one who first heard in Elvis's voice everything Phillips was after. "It was like two feuding clans who had been brought together by marriage."

> "That's All Right" was a tremendous hit with teenagers, and in Memphis, where the record broke first, the current greeting among the teenagers is still a rhythmical line from the song: "Ta dee dah dee dee dah."
>
> Memphis *Press-Scimitar*, 1954

You can't get that kind of success in *Billboard*; "Sun's Newest Star," as the *Press-Scimitar* called Elvis, wasted no time taking advantage of it. He tried out his material in the local clubs, drew three thousand people to the opening of a shopping center, and busted up a big country review when he sang a song called "Good Rockin' Tonight." Phillips, for his part, wasted no time getting Elvis back into the studio and a new record into the stores.

"That's All Right" was an easy ride. "Good Rockin'" is a cataclysm; it reflects the new confidence of a young man who knows what it means to satisfy an audience, to take them beyond their expectations. The record is charged with an authority that no other country rocker ever approached.

Roy Brown, the most influential blues singer of the forties, wrote the tune, and Wynonie Harris made it a hit in 1948. Harris was a sophisticated uptown R&B vocalist; his "Good Rockin'" is a conventional jump blues, lacking real tension or drama. He seems unable to exploit the stomping promise of the lyrics in rhythm or phrasing; he bumps words into each other and sometimes trips on them. He's too removed from the country revel the song is all about, and too cool.

Elvis opens with a high, wild "WELLLLLLLLL . . ." and pulls fast and hard into the first verse before the echo of his shout has had a chance to fade. His voice is raw, pleading and pushing, full of indescribably sexy asides, the throaty nuances that would flare up into "All Shook Up" and "Burning Love." Elvis slows for a second in the middle of a line, drawling softly, over his shoulder, as if he can't quite bring himself to say out loud how good the party's going to be; and then suddenly he is out of breath, as if he's run for miles to tell his story, but there's good rockin' tonight and everybody *has* to know—how could they live if they miss it? Tonight his girl will get everything *she's* been missing. "We're gonna rock—ALL OUR BLUES AWAY!" He can't tell it fast enough, he can barely keep up with himself. Near to bursting, the song slams home.

"Milkcow Blues Boogie" came out in January 1955, with writer's credit on the label going to Kokomo Arnold, a Georgia-born blues singer who recorded "Milk Cow Blues" in Chicago in 1934. One always reads that Elvis re-created Arnold's song, though apparently no one has bothered to listen to both men—Elvis takes all of one verse from the bluesman. Presley's style might well owe something to Arnold; they share a fast, nervous delivery, full of unpredictable swoops and moans, a flair for crazy-quilt tempo changes of tremendous excitement, and the ability to come down with a great force on a key line. But "Milkcow" was a song held in common long before Elvis was born, recorded by more blues and country singers than anyone has bothered to count. What Elvis did, in fact, was to throw a bit of Arnold—who perhaps Phillips played for him—into Bob Wills's western swing hit, "Brain Cloudy Blues," which was cut in 1946. "Brain Cloudy," highlighted by Wills's fiddle and a tough guitar solo, featured the straight, insulated vocal of Tommy Duncan up against Wills's patented cornball asides, which worked very effectively to bleed the punch out of every line. Elvis started with Wills's second verse, dropping the "brain cloudy" motif; faded to Arnold; and then finished off with Wills's words, changing lyrics when Duncan's crisp, almost effete diction threw him off.

I go into the musicology of this song in some detail because of what it can tell us about how these first records came about. The book on Elvis's early music is that it was "spontaneous," "without any evident forethought," "unself-conscious." In other words, Elvis was the natural (and, the implicit assumption is, likely unthinking) expression of a folk culture. I've tried to present some hints of the culture Elvis came out of as a set of forces that could have held him back and worn him down as easily as they gave him life; to build a context that puts us in touch with will and desire, not just smug sociology. Researching his biography of Elvis, Jerry Hopkins dug back into the world Elvis left behind in Memphis, and he found that nearly every record Elvis made with Sam Phillips was carefully and laboriously constructed out of hits and misses, riffs and bits of phrasing held through dozens of bad takes. The songs grew slowly, over hours and hours, into a music that paradoxically sounded much fresher than all the poor tries that had come before; until Presley, Bill Black, and Scotty Moore had the attack in their blood, and yes, didn't have to think about it. That's not exactly my idea of "spontaneity" or "unselfconsciousness."

Elvis had the nuance of cool down pat—the pink pants-and-shirt outfit he wore to his audition, the carelessness of his swagger, or the sneer around the edges of his smile—because the will to create himself, to matter, was so intense and so clear. He strolled into the studio and didn't leave until every note was perfect. Even later at RCA, still on the way up and wavering between complete self-confidence and a lingering doubt, he would demand thirty takes on "Hound Dog," pleading for one more try long after everyone else was satisfied.

---

*EE #4. At a DJ convention early in 1973, I sit drinking with Bobby Vee and Brian Hyland, veterans of the Now-That-Elvis-Is-in-the-Army-We-Can-Cash-in-on-the-Vacuum Era. I am interviewing Bob (he has changed his name back to Veline and is a folksinger now) in order to pen six thousand words of liner notes to a greatest hits package, an essay that will no doubt be the only extended critical discussion of his *oeuvre*. Bob tells me that, yes, for him it all began with Elvis— and suddenly the whole tone of the conversation is different. Professional cool drops away and we are shameless fans, awed by our subject. Vee and Hyland have met Elvis: he got drunk with Hyland (so Brian says) and was surly to Vee (I believe that). Well, they are outcasts in the rock 'n' roll world now, two very ordinary looking men; for all their triviality as rock singers, they once did their best to live up to Elvis and keep the faith. You can almost feel them gazing at Elvis as he is today, as if in his comeback they still see a glimmer of a future for themselves, just as they did when he started out years ago.

Try to wash the images of success from your mind and picture a twenty-year-old in a tacky studio on perhaps his fifteenth take of a song that is coming together out of fragments of memory, old 78's, and pure instinct. Everything was riding on each new release: whether Elvis could really take his career beyond the commonplace expectations of those around him; whether he could top that last record; whether he could find a sound that would give him room to breathe and yet hold the fans he had won and spread the word. The little success he had achieved was fragile; each new record risked it. He had to take that energy of desire and distance himself from it, throw it into the song so that it would be coherent and powerful *as* a song; so that when he sang, "Tonight she'll know I'm a mighty mighty man," it would sound like an obvious, thrilling statement of the facts. Whatever strain there might have been in his voice or his hopes—that unpleasant hint of the small time that you can hear so plainly in Bill Haley and so many of Elvis's imitators—it had to go. The talent was there, and it was extraordinary, but it was complex, and it needed a form. They were in the studio a long, tiresome time to catch the spirit of a boy who, on record, sounded as if he flew in, stopped long enough to blow the walls back, and exited through the unhinged back door with a grin.

With "Milkcow Blues Boogie" we are back to the image Cash chose as the essence of the soul of the back country South: hot heavy air bursting all over the sky in lightning and rain. No music of any kind captures it better than this record.

Wills and Arnold move right into the song; Elvis lingers over the first lines, and his voice drips an erotic tension that must have melted the mike. "Oh well, Ah woke up . . . this moanin'—An' Ah looked out . . . the doah—." He has you; you're hungering for whatever comes next, but he cuts you off. "Hold it fellas!" he shouts. "That don't *move* me!" Soft and sultry again: "Let's get real . . . *real* gone, for a change." It's too perfect; you think he must be reading lines, as if this is a scene from one of his movies; and it is, I guess, even if at this point the dreams were only in his head.

Elvis charges the song, shooting that boundless *Wellllllllll* out ahead of himself, and the three of them are off. Elvis spurs the changes with his guitar, flying all over the story he is telling—his woman is gone and he wants her back but she's got about five minutes to make up her mind—singing with the crazy shifts from high to low that with Buddy Holly sounded funny and with Elvis sound frightening. In two and a half minutes he carries his listener through anger, loss, bemusement, melancholy, violence, defiance, fatalism, menace, delight, freedom, and regret. The song is as sure and tough a tale of breaking loose as any there is.

Yodeling, roaring his anger, yelling out to Scotty Moore—"Let's *milk* it!"—he comes off the guitar solo in a new mood, almost reflective now, meditating, this is all moving very fast but his guitar has somehow settled the music, and if his girl is gone, if that milkcow is never coming home, he still has time to step back and bring us into the song with a little blues philosophy:

Wellll, good evenin'
Don' that sun look good goin' down
Wee-eee-ell, good evenin'
Don' that sun look good goin' down
Well, dont that old moon look lonesome
When your bay-ay-ayby's not around?

And then rage pours back over his acceptance. He calls back his woman and faces her down, the song picking up momentum, his voice shimmering and shaking through night air:

Well I tried everything
To git along with you
Now I'm gonna tell you what I'm gonna do
I'm gonna quit my crying
I'm gonna leave you alone

and suddenly driving even harder, cursing with two of the most perfect lines in blues:

If you don't believe I'm leavin'
YOU CAN COUNT THE DAYS I'M GONE

Again, it is his authority that is so astounding. Scores of singers, black and white, have sung those lines, but few if any have ever made them seem so real, *so final*. The fatalism that is written right into the song, in that lovely image of the setting sun and the rising moon, will not do for Elvis, and he sings those last hard lines with an intensity that wipes out everything that has come before. A blues singer would use this verse as balance, to dramatize the rise and fall of his spirit, translating the circle the natural world draws around him into a metaphor for his inability to master his life. For Elvis, young and on his way, feeling his growing power over audiences, the growing space between himself and everything he should have taken for granted, there comes a point where he cannot settle for what others have made of this song, and the balance tips to fury. Our boy will get what he deserves; everyone else can get out of the way.

THE BOY WHO STOLE THE BLUES

I slicked myself up,
Till I looked like a guinea!

CARL PERKINS, "Put Your Cat Clothes On"

For Carl Perkins and the rest of the rockabilly heroes, the liberation of the new music must have been a bit like a white foray into darktown, a combination of a blackface minstrel show and night riding—romantic as hell, a little dangerous, a little ridiculous. At the start, Elvis sounded black to those who heard him; when they called him the Hillbilly Cat, they meant the white Negro. "The guy put out the record," Elvis said onstage almost fifteen years to the day after "That's All Right" was first played on the radio. "Just overnight my hometown people were saying, 'Is he, is he?' and I'm going, 'Am I, am I?'"

Well, I can't hear that anymore. I hear a young man, white as the whale, who was special because in his best music he was so much his *own* man, one who took the musical and emotional strengths of the blues as a natural and necessary part of the world he was building for himself—one part of that world, no more, but clearly the finest stuff around at the time.

True as it is in an historical or commercial sense, too much has been made of Elvis as "a white man who sang black music credibly," as a singer who made black music acceptable to whites. This and too many whites trying to do the same thing have corrupted any sense of what Elvis did do, of what was at stake in his personal culture. Most white blues singing is singing at the blues; what comes out is either entirely fake, or has behind it the white impulse to become black: to ask for too much without offering anything in return.

Real white blues singers make something new out of the blues, as Jimmie Rodgers, Dock Boggs, Elvis, and Bob Dylan have; or, they sing out of a deep feeling for the blues, but in a musical style that is not blues—not formally, anyway. But we can trace their strength to the blues; what links their music to the blues is an absolute commitment to the material, an expressive force open to some whites because they have been attracted to another man's culture in a way that could not be denied. This is the music of whites not so much singing the blues as living up to them.

Van Morrison's "Listen to the Lion" would have to be my best example, but Rod Stewart and Charlie Rich have done their work here too, singing as if the fate of the whole world rested on their ability to reach deeply enough into their souls to get all the way into ours. I saw Rich do it not so long ago, in a setting so anachronistic he came near to leaving his audience behind him, because they were in a mood to be confirmed, not moved.

It was in August 1973, at a country music affair sponsored by Columbia Records, attended mostly by record industry heavies and hangers-on. Singer after singer took the stage, offering songs that made pain trivial and good times bland; music as sterile as it was predictable as it was (within a tight, well-regulated country market) commercially effective. The producers and song publishers and publicists sat near the stage, waiting for the singers to humble themselves before them, and as each did, I thought the humility might be worth a lot more if it were cynical than if it were real. It was that kind of day; I yearned for some rock 'n' roll arrogance, no matter how fake *that* might be.

Charlie Rich, who has always had too much of the blues in his style to fit easily into the country music market, was riding a number one country single that had, because it was more than country, crossed over into the upper reaches of the pop charts. He closed the show. Forty years old, a big man with white hair and lines deep in his face, he took his seat behind the piano and sang a harmless tune from his current album. After almost twenty years in the music business he had only three hits to show for it; even as "Behind Closed Doors" was climbing, the clerk in the record store marked up my Charlie Rich album under "nostalgia." A song Rich's wife Margaret Ann wrote about him, a haunting ballad of failure called "Life's Little Ups and Downs," tells the truth of Rich's career, but that day at the convention the crowd's truth was that Rich was on top and would stay there. Right as they may have been, I could not believe it was more than a public moment in an invisible career, and that made each song more precious and each missed chance that much more depressing.

Rich sang his hit, and it had grown for him. It meant more now than it had when it was just another throw of the dice, and it was a triumph. Because Rich was the star of the day, the men running the show gave him an encore. Staring into the keys, trying to balance the moment,

Rich introduced his song. "I wrote this for Peter Guralnick," he said, "who wrote the book *Feel Like Going Home*." Named for the most ter- rifyingly lonely of all Muddy Waters's songs, it is probably the most loving book ever written about American music; Charlie Rich is the subject of its finest chapter.

"Today," Rich said, "I would like to dedicate this song to the Presi- dent of the United States." And so for Nixon, just then slipping over the line to the point where his whole existence would become a na- tional joke, Rich sang,

> *I tried and I failed*
> *And I feel like going home.*

The words stayed in my mind throughout the strange, difficult song; they didn't change the president, or the country, or the world, but they changed how a few of us who were there to listen understood those things. They cut through everything I believe to uncover a compassion that I never, never wanted to feel.

We won't find Elvis here. The idea that the blues is a feeling and not a form can bring us closer to what Rich did that afternoon—but for Elvis, the blues was a style of freedom, something he couldn't get in his own home, full of roles to play and rules to break. In the beginning the blues was more than anything else a fantasy, an epic of struggle and pleasure, that he lived out as he sang. Not a fantasy that went beneath the surface of his life, but one that soared right over it.

Singing in the fifties, before blacks began to guard their culture with the jealousy it deserved, Elvis had no guilty dues to pay. Arthur Crudup complained his songs made a white man famous, and he had a right to complain, but mostly because he never got his royalties. Elvis sang "That's All Right" and "My Baby Left Me" (one of his first sides for RCA, and the only one in the Sun rockabilly style) with more power, verve, and skill than Crudup did; his early records were more than popular with blacks; but still the implication, always there when Crudup or Willie Mae Thornton (who made the first version of "Hound Dog") looked out at the white world that gave them only obscurity in ex- change for their music and penned them off from getting anything for themselves, is that Elvis would have been nothing without them, that he climbed to fame on their backs. It is probably time to say that this is nonsense; the mysteries of black and white in American music are just not that simple. Consider the tale of "Hound Dog."

Jerry Leiber and Mike Stoller were Jewish boys from the East Coast who fell in love with black music. Hustling in Los Angeles in the early fifties, they wrote "Hound Dog," and promoted the song to Johnny Otis, a ruling R&B bandleader who was actually a dark-skinned white man from Berkeley who many thought was black. Otis gave the song to Thornton, who made it a number one R&B hit in 1953; Otis also took part of the composer's credit, which Leiber and Stoller had to fight to get back. Elvis heard the record, changed the song completely, from the tempo to the words, and cut Thornton's version to shreds.

Whites wrote it; a white made it a hit. And yet there is no denying that "Hound Dog" is a "black" song, unthinkable outside the impulses of black music, and probably a rewrite of an old piece of juke joint fury that dated back far beyond the birth of any of these people. Can you pull justice out of *that* maze? What *does* Huck owe Jim, especially when Jim is really Huck in blackface and everyone smells loot? All you can say is this was Elvis's music because he made it his own.

Here's a better story. In 1955 the Robins (a black vocal group that had passed through seven labels with no real success) and Richard Berry (a black singer with two duds to his name) were brought together by Leiber and Stoller. Together they made the classic "Riot in Cell Block #9," which helped change the Robins into the Coasters and brought Berry his first notoriety. Leiber and Stoller went on to fame and fortune and the Coasters at least to fame; Berry, after losing out with "The Big Break," an outrageous follow-up to "Riot," made "Louie Louie" in 1956, but though it was his biggest hit, it never made the pop charts.

In 1962 a white Portland group called the Kingsmen unearthed "Louie Louie," and their version hit number two in the country. Paul Revere and the Raiders, another Portland band, rode the tune into a gold mine on the West Coast. As rock records, these discs were virtually definitive: hard rhythm, harder lead guitar, and a vocal that made no sense whatsoever. Within months every high school band in the country was playing "Louie Louie," and every other person you met had a copy of the *real* lyrics, which were reputedly obscene. Some highlights I recall from locker room days: "Gonna make her again," "Gotta rag on," "Fuck that girl across the sea." (Not much, I admit, but those were thin years for rock 'n' roll.) Soon even Congressmen got into the act; they investigated the tune, duly played it (at 45, 33, 78, and 16 rpm), and charmingly pronounced the song "indecipherable at any speed." By this time, everyone but the man who owned the copyright—and likely he too—had forgotten all about Richard Berry, whose original lyrics would have been beside the point anyway.

Ten years later a white New York group called Stories released a single called "Brother Louie," and the record went to number one. "Louie, Louie, Loo-aye," went the chorus—familiar, to say the least. Obviously, the chorus was what caught your attention; it always had been. Since rock 'n' roll had been around long enough for its fans to develop a sense of history, a few people remembered Richard Berry. And what was this new "Louie Louie" about? A black girl and her white boyfriend—Louie—and his mean racist parents. "Ain't no difference if you're black or white," Stories sang. "Brothers, you know what I mean." But this time, the "brother" was white; and finally the old song contained the racial contradictions that had sustained it.

If Elvis drew power from black culture, he was not exactly imitating blacks; when he told Sam Phillips he didn't sing like nobody, he told the truth. No white man had so deeply absorbed black music, and transformed it, since Jimmie Rodgers; instead of following Rodgers's musical style, as so many good white singers had—Lefty Frizzell, Ernest Tubb, Tommy Duncan, and, in his more personal way, Hank Williams, following that style until it simply wore out—Elvis followed Rodgers's musical strategy and began the story all over again.

Elvis didn't have to exile himself from his own community in order to justify and make real his use of an outsider's culture (like the Jewish jazzman Mezz Mezzrow, who would claim that his years on the streets of Harlem had actually darkened his skin and thickened his lips; like Johnny Otis and so many real white Negroes); as a Southerner and white trash to boot, Elvis was already outside. In 1955 he had at least as much in common with Bobby Bland as he did with Perry Como. Which is to say that Elvis was also hellbent on the mainstream, and sure enough of himself to ignore the irony that it would be his version of the backdoor freedoms of black music that would attract the mainstream to him, giving him the chance to exchange his hillbilly strangeness for acceptability.

Elvis's blues were a set of sexual adventures, and as a blues-singing swashbuckler, his style owed as much to Errol Flynn as it did to Arthur Crudup. It made sense to make movies out of it.

THE PINK CADILLAC

By the time "Baby, Let's Play House" came out in April 1955, the rockabilly singers were coming out of the swamps. Phillips was shifting his company from black to white, setting up an outbreak of rock 'n' roll that would follow hard on Presley's already discussed and taken-for-granted move up to a national label. Phillips had Malcolm Yelvington (a Memphis country singer endowed with false teeth and the best rockabilly name outside of Elvis's) cut the first of many country rock versions of Stick McGhee's 1949 R&B classic, "Drinkin' Wine Spo-Dee-O-Dee," and its message summed up the new mood: drinkin' and fightin' are what life is all about, and if anybody argues, give 'em a drink or lay 'em out.

Elvis had finished his early tours, ranging from Texas to Florida; he was set for Cleveland—alien territory, crucial to proving himself outside the South—and he was booked with acts as disparate as Roy Acuff and Pat Boone. The Colonel had made his initial connections. In Lubbock, Texas, a kid named Charles "Buddy" Holley bowed to the East every night and began getting a band together. There was, to put it mildly, excitement in the air.

Elvis's dive into "Baby, Let's Play House"—a wild crash of hiccups, gulps, and baby-baby-babys—measured perfectly the distance he had traveled since he broke into tears at the sight of his first record. There is a new spirit here, a lightness and a sense of fun, as if his whole little career has suddenly hit him as a wonderful joke. The dreams are coming true; that drive and secret ambition can afford to open up. He knows now that his mother was right, and he is safe. That throwaway superiority for which he has worked so hard can blossom out into arrogance, humor, and pure good times.

What was it his mother told him? That he was just as good as anybody? Or did she whisper, late at night when no one else was there to hear, that her boy could never lose?

Arthur Gunter, a black singer working for the Excello label in Nashville, wrote and recorded "Baby, Let's Play House," and got a hit with the black market in early 1955. He used a tight acoustic band and walked right through, vaguely interested in telling his girl that she might think she's hot stuff, but she'd better come on back and get down to it, or there'd be, you know, trouble. It was all very low-key (that splendid intro was all Elvis); Gunter's lack of concern was his charm. Still, he didn't sound very convincing.

Elvis wailed. He turned the song into a correspondence course in rock 'n' roll, and it was by far the most imitated of his first records. For pure excitement, he may never have matched it.

The rhythm was heavy, the syncopation astonishing—a fast, ominous bass tromping over a cottonmouth guitar—the band drove hard into every chorus and cut out for all the best lines. "Aw, let's play house," Elvis shouted, and Scotty punched out a few riffs; "HIT IT!" Elvis cried, and Moore and Black rammed home music so tough it wasn't touched until Elvis pushed them into the earthquake that was "Hound Dog."

Elvis made one crucial change in the lyrics. The girl he's after in this song is high-class stuff: she might go to college, he sings, she might go to school, but she'll never really get away, never be so sure of herself she can get along without the loving only he can give her. She might even get religion, Gunter had added, which won't help her either; but Elvis threw in a faster, flashier image that was more to his own point: "You may have a pink Cadillac / But dontcha be nobody's fool!" Elvis had just bought one for himself.

Now, the obvious thing to say here is that the Pink Cadillac and All that it Implied proved Elvis's undoing: out there in mass culture America, Elvis would lose his talent in its reward. Dontcha be nobody's fool? The poor boy should have taken his own advice.

Well, we should be careful about this sort of thing. There is a deep need to believe that Elvis (or any exemplar of American culture one cares about) began in a context of purity, unsullied by greed or ambition or vulgarity, somehow outside of and in opposition to American life as most of us know it and live it. Even RCA first presented Elvis as "a folksinger" (claiming, in the notes to his second album, that the simple-country-boy-with-guitar stance pictured on the cover was "most appropriate" for him). A writer as tough and sensitive as Stanley Booth can write (in a piece that seems to miss the point of its own title, "A Hound Dog, to the Manor Born"): "All that was really necessary was that [Elvis] stop doing his thing and start doing theirs. His thing was 'Mystery Train,' 'Milkcow Blues Boogie.' Theirs was 'Love Me Tender,' 'Loving You,' 'Jailhouse Rock,' 'King Creole.'" Charlie Gillett, author of *The Sound of the City*, as definitive a history of rock 'n' roll as we are likely to get, complains that Elvis sold out his true culture when he let RCA put *drums* on his records. It is virtually a critical canon that Elvis's folk purity, and therefore his talent, was ruined by (a) his transmogrification from naïve country boy into corrupt pop star (he sold his soul to Colonel Tom, or Parker just stole it), (b) Hollywood, (c) the Army, (d) money and soft living, (e) all of the above.*

This approach may contain some figures, but not Elvis. "Milkcow Blues" was not "his thing"—it was one of many—so much as it was Sam

---

* This Faustian scenario is an absolutely vital part of Elvis's legend, especially for all those who took part in Elvis's event and felt bewildered and betrayed by his stagnation and decline. We could hardly believe that a figure of such natural strength could dissolve into such a harmless nonentity; it had to be some kind of trick. Even a decade after the fact, Phil Spector was convinced that Colonel Parker hypnotized Elvis.

Phillips's. Phillips loved money and he loved the blues, the basic pop combination; pairing a blues and a country tune on Elvis's first record gave him a successful commercial formula, and he stuck to it on every subsequent Presley release and on most of the records he cut by other rockabilly singers. But when Elvis left Memphis to confront a national audience as mysterious to him as he was to it, he had to define himself fully, and he did so by presenting his authentic multiplicity in music. I am, he announced, a house rocker, a boy steeped in mother-love, a true son of the church, a matinee idol who's only kidding, a man with too many rough edges for anyone ever to smooth away. Something in me yearns for a settling of affairs, he said with his pale music and his tired movies; on the other hand, he answered with his rock 'n' roll and an occasional blues, I may break away at any time. You never know. At RCA, where the commercial horizons were much broader than they were down at Sun, Elvis worked with far more "artistic freedom" than he ever did with Sam Phillips.

Two things did happen that led to the collapse of Elvis's music. His multiplicity opened up the possibility that he could be all things to all people, but his eagerness to prove it, with records like *Something for Everybody*, destroyed his ability to focus his talent. He wound up without a commitment to any musical style; his music lost that dramatic shape Sam Phillips helped give it. And his ambition, the source of so much of the intensity and emotion he put into his early music, plainly outstripped itself. Two years after making his first record he had won more than anyone knew was there; he had achieved a status that trivialized struggle and made will obsolescent. His success turned his life upside down; from this point on, he would have in his hands what he set out to get, but he would have to reach for the energy and desire that had made his triumph possible.

The Pink Cadillac was at the heart of the contradiction that powered Elvis's early music; a perfect symbol of the glamour of his ambition and the resentments that drove it on. When he faced his girl in "Baby, Let's Play House" (like Dylan railing at the heroine of "Like a Rolling Stone," or Jagger surveying the upper-class women who star in "19th Nervous Breakdown," "Play With Fire," and "You Can't Always Get What You Want"), Elvis sang with contempt for a world that had always excluded him; he sang with a wish for its pleasures and status. Most of all he sang with delight at the power that fame and musical force gave him: power to escape the humiliating obscurity of the life he knew, and power to sneer at the classy world that was now ready to flatter him. Not the real upper class, of course; it would be years before socialites set out in pursuit of the Rolling Stones and academics began to fawn over the Beatles. Still, the jump Elvis made from the woods and welfare to simple respectability was far more epic. Girls who had turned up their noses in high school were now waiting in line, just as today men and women who are barely hanging on to the edge of the middle class wait in line to see a man who has achieved an eminence class can never bring.

Elvis sang out his song with a monumental disdain for all those folk who moved easily through a world that had never been easy for him (anyone who had ever shown the Presleys *exactly who they were*); he grinned at the big car he had dreamed about, because finally it was within reach, and he could take it, on his terms.

A bit farther into the image of the Pink Cadillac, something more interesting was going on. If Elvis was looking down on his smart girl's Caddy from the vantage point of his own, he was implicitly presenting his new successful self as a target for his own resentments, and singing with more than enough emotion to hit the bullseye. He was the Star; not asserting, in the conventional Uriah Heep country style, that all his wealth don't buy him happiness (it does, it does), but burlesquing and damning the complacency of the rich and powerful by flaunting *his* power and riches, and getting away with it. Somehow taking both sides, Elvis could show his listeners just how much, and how little, that Pink Cadillac was worth: more and less than anyone would have guessed.*

This is a kind of rock 'n' roll drive—the vitality that endows the artifacts of materialism with life—that is captured perfectly in *The Harder They Come*, a movie about the Jamaican version of the American pop dream, when Jimmy Cliff steals a white Cadillac and spins it over a golf course with an unbeatable smile on his face. He's a refugee from the most terrifying poverty, a reggae-singing people's outlaw with reflexes instead of politics. "You can get it if you really want," he sings. "The harder they come, the harder they fall, one and all." He wants the car and the whole world it stands for; he doesn't want it, he wants to smash it all up. He hasn't made the connections; he hasn't worked it all out any

---

* In America, after all, the final proof of grace is *economic* sanctification; which is to say, Elvis can have the piety of the poor along with the ease of the rich and know that since he never lost the first, he deserves the last. Still full of the energy of his comeback in early 1969, Elvis went back to Memphis and sang a song called "Long Black Limousine"—the tale of a hometown girl punished for her sins and her fancy city ways, mourned and damned by the poor country boy who has waited all these years for a better ending than the car crash that did his sweetheart in. The tension as the song opens is almost unbearable, and Elvis never lets go of the song. He is completely convincing. And yet of course he is the country boy captured by the city if there ever was one; he's that girl, riding in her long black limousine on her way to the graveyard, as surely as he is King Elvis, speeding away from the studio in his own black limousine. When he smashes through the contradictions of his career with such music, we have Elvis at his greatest.

more than a twenty-year-old Elvis did. But he knows that car belongs to him because he can take more pleasure from it than anyone else.

What is most remarkable is that Elvis was able to laugh at the persona he drew from "Baby, Let's Play House" as convincingly as he acted it out—as if a combination of the freedom to realize his desires and a freedom to ignore them was what freedom really meant. He was less into the music than on top if it, feigning toughness, feigning anger, finding it, for the famous lines

I'd rather see you dead little girl
Than to be with another man

and then all fun again, as if the venom he'd put into those words struck him at once as ludicrous, and maybe a little frightening. He put even more of himself into the song, and still parodied his menace, lowering his voice to a rumble, getting out of the tune with a chuckle that gave it all away: deep down he was just a good boy, out for a real good time.

Put it together and you may have the quintessential performance of Elvis's career: an overwhelming outburst of real emotion and power, combined with a fine refusal to take himself with any seriousness at all. Finding that power within himself, and making it real, was part of the liberation he was working out in this music; standing off from that power, with a broad sense of humor and amusement, was another.

This was the saving grace of Elvis's ambition, and a necessary counter to it. It allowed him to transcend his success and his public image just as his ambition allowed him to achieve and enjoy his success; that casual élan would let him see at least part of the way through the unprecedented adulation he received, just as his ambition would ultimately make it impossible for him to be satisfied with anything less. And if that lack of seriousness today distances Elvis not only from the absurdity of his reward but from his talent too, gives us a throwaway and a man virtually unable to take anything seriously, this side of Elvis has also brought a marvelous warmth to his best music, no matter if it's in the records he made back in Memphis, or the show he's sure to be putting on tonight.

ELVIS AT HOME: THE COUNTRY SIDES

Elvis's blues are music of drama, humor, and risk; the country tunes are very different. At their most vital, they capture the kind of beauty and peace of mind that can be found only within limits, when a lot has been given up, and you know exactly how far you can go.

Elvis gives us respect—for the musical form, for the established country music audience these songs were aimed at, for his mother, who was sure to be listening to *this* music—in place of resentment and personal authority. The music flows with the kind of grace the Allman Brothers found in their incandescent "Blue Sky": a sense of value that seems to come not from a feel for the open possibilities of life, but from a pretty deep understanding of its fragility.

There is a modesty of spirit. In this world you will hope for what you deserve, but not demand it; you may celebrate your life, but not with the kind of liberation that might threaten the life of someone else. The public impulse of the music is not to break things open, but to confirm what is already there, to add to its reality and its value.

This is the kind of freedom D. H. Lawrence had in mind when he wrote about America in an essay called "The Spirit of Place."

Men are free when they are in a living homeland, not when they are straying and breaking away. Men are free when they are obeying some deep, inward voice of religious belief. Obeying from within. Men are free when they belong to a living, organic, *believing* community, active in fulfilling some unfulfilled, perhaps unrealized purpose. Not when they are escaping to some wild west. The most unfree souls go west, and shout of freedom. Men are freest when they are most unconscious of freedom. The shout is a rattling of chains, always was.

Men are not free when they are doing just what they like. The moment you can do just what you like, there is nothing you care about doing.*

So speaks the stern English father to his rowdy American children; it's not a message America has ever had much time for. We much prefer Elvis's shout of freedom, sure that what chains there are in our world must be applied by other men. Something close to Lawrence's idea, though, that sense of staying at home in a place where one belongs, is part of what Elvis has always offered America—on the flipside, as it were.

Elvis's country sides, like his later gospel records for RCA, reveal how deeply he felt a pull at odds with the explosions of his new rock 'n'

* From *Studio in Classic American Literature* (New York: Viking, 1964, originally published 1923).

roll and the frenzy of his first stage shows. They let us in on the secret that his little drama of breaking loose could take on the extremes that gave it power because he knew he had a home to which he could always return; even as he set out to win his independence, he prepared his accommodation. The America that Elvis brings to life in this music grew out of his willingness to accept the limits of a community, and his desire for the pleasures of familiarity. It's a place of gentleness, and restraint.

In the least of this music, though—"I Forgot to Remember to Forget," "I Don't Care If the Sun Don't Shine," "Just Because," "I Love You Because," "I'll Never Let You Go (Little Darlin')"—it is the sound of a young man confined by his community that is most striking. Elvis is faceless, indistinguishable from a hundred others; he sounds less like a man who has been defeated than like one who has never wondered what it might mean to try to win. There's no real warmth in the music, only an imitation of it; if on the blues sides he took on the originals and outclassed them, here he defers. The emotional tone seems contrived, almost secondhand; this is the music of someone doing what he has always been told to do.

"I Don't Care If the Sun Don't Shine" has energy, but not soul; "Just Because" has a little bounce, but no passion. "I Love You Because" (actually the very first song Elvis recorded professionally) is truly painful to hear; he's so polite to the material he can't even sing it. There is certainly nothing that could give that "believing community" any strength.

Here Elvis embodies exactly that world his blues fantasy let him escape. If murder—the face of Charley Starkweather imposed on Elvis's, the edge of sadism in Presley's music that made one producer tag him as just right for *In Cold Blood*—was the dark side of rockabilly flash and the flight from limits, then a death of possibility and a stupefying ordinariness was the dark side of this music, the first version of Elvis's empty Yes.

You can't have a community that grows and renews all who are a part of it without the tension that comes from the need to break away, without the resentment produced by the tendency of any community to grow in on itself and shut out the rest of the world. Tom Sawyer's fooling around won't give us that tension; you need Huck's nerve and his suffering, perhaps an edge of Ahab's obsessions, and, in America, you probably need Nigger Jim too.

Elvis was a rebel in the music that made him famous. But he knew, and has always told anyone willing to listen, how hard it is to break away, and how much you have to give up to make it—more than he has been willing to part with. So Elvis lives out his story by contradicting himself, and we join in when we take sides, or when we respond to the tension that contradiction creates. The liveliness of that tension is as evident in the best of Elvis's country sides as it is in his blues.

When Elvis sings Bill Monroe's "Blue Moon of Kentucky" as if he's going to jump right over it, he isn't, as has always been said, singing the blues on a country song, any more than he was really singing hillbilly on a blues with "That's All Right." What Elvis is doing is both more complex and more coherent.

When I listened to an early take of "Blue Moon of Kentucky" (on a rockabilly bootleg that includes studio dialogue as well as music), I heard Elvis lost in the song, touching each line gently, playfully, bringing every word to life. The singing is rough, even though Elvis is clearly a long way past the first tries; Scotty Moore has trouble following the vocal. He drops back, and then there is just Elvis, drawing out an unbelievably sensual portrait of his Southern landscape.

It sounds so primitive to me; music out of the Mississippi woods, a hundred years gone. Sam Phillips hears something else.

PHILLIPS: *Fine, fine,* man, hell, that's different! That's a *pop song* now, nearly 'bout! That's good!
SCOTTY MOORE: Too much vaseline!
Elvis laughs, nervously, proudly.
MOORE: I had it too!
ELVIS: Y'aint just *a-woofin'!*
MOORE: (imitating an eye-rolling black falsetto): Please, *please,* please—
ELVIS: What?
MOORE: *Damn,* nigger!

By the time Elvis reached the fast, confident version that appeared on the flip of his first record, most of the primitive feeling had disappeared, but not the vaseline; Elvis was celebrating a classic piece of white country music, but more than that he was celebrating himself. He was keeping the old song alive by bringing something new to it, putting some life back into his community by telling an old story in a way that no one had heard before—and he was reaching beyond his community, with the "pop song" Sam Phillips knew he had to make.

There is a delight in adventure and novelty here that we can't touch with pure musicology: Elvis's affection for a song he's heard for years, combined with the exuberance and satisfaction of a kid who's dreamed for years of making a record, and who is now actually pulling it off. And there are the new rhythms of "That's All Right," cut a few nights before—not "blues" now, but Elvis's music, Scotty Moore's music—Southern energy that blacks had trapped and put into the air where anyone could get it.

Elvis could not have sung "Blue Moon of Kentucky" as he did without the discoveries of "That's All Right"—but what he discovered was not his ability to imitate a black blues singer, but the nerve to cross the borders he had been raised to respect. Once that was done, musically those borders dissolved as if they had never existed—for Elvis. He moved back and forth in a phrase. But Scotty Moore might well have been speaking for the audience waiting outside the studio when he called Elvis a nigger—for many, it was the *fact* of a white boy singing a black man's song without clothing it in fiddles and steel guitar that they heard, not the strange ambiguities of the music. Perhaps if Phillips had put out the "country" side without the "blues," it would have warmed the community; the combination thrilled some and threatened others. There were country stations that refused to play any Elvis records, no matter how white they seemed to be. He was too complicated, this Presley boy; you couldn't tell what he might be slipping over, could you?

Yet "You're a Heartbreaker," another country side, is a masterpiece of reassurance. It is one of the most affecting records Elvis ever made; it gives us a young man who takes comfort, and pleasure, from a sure sense of all that he has to fall back on when something goes wrong: his

---

*EE #5. I know a woman, black and about sixty, who loves old country blues. The albums I have given her are mostly unheard, though, because she lives with her mother, a devout woman in her eighties, who forbids her to play them. The mother, who is blind, spends much of her time listening to the TV set, and once I found her attending to a kind of blues she apparently considered innocuous enough to tolerate: Elvis's film *G.I. Blues*.

I didn't know what to make of that. It seemed to represent a double dead end of American cross-culture, but there was something I liked about it. Partly, it was the movie itself. Elvis, as usual, plays a good-natured stud who breaks into song about every ten minutes and makes all the women snap their fingers (though curiously, none of them can keep time). The Sergeant Bilko-reject plot has to do with El's attempt to raise a stake for the nightclub he and his two Army accompanists want to open when they get back in mufti. It comes down to rival platoons placing bets on which can field a man to seduce Juliet Prowse, the biggest glacier in Germany. Elvis, naturally . . .

He walks through the flick with the same air of What-Am-I-Doing-Here bemusement he employs in most of his other movies. When he strums his acoustic guitar, an electric solo comes out. When bass and guitar back him, you hear horns and electric piano. When he sings, the soundtrack is at least half a verse out of sync. These films are the throwaways of a man—perhaps I ought to say an industry—who doesn't even need to title his product as long as he can put his name on it, much like Elvis's post-comeback albums (randomly constructed out of leftover recordings, unmixed live tapes, plastered with shoddy composite promo photos and ads for old LP's), all of which seem to be called simply "E L V I S," in fact. The movies are so tacky no one else could possibly get away with them—and still make money.

self-respect (the rounded edge of the new superiority of the blues-boy); the steady, ongoing patterns of life that never range too far in one direction or the other. If the impulses of community were at odds with the extremes of Southern life, here Elvis captures the soul of the one just as he acted out the other side. It is a tribute to his range and his honesty that he can do this without making you feel he is offering less than the whole story.

How would you act if you lived in a community that *did* enclose extremes without making life banal and dull? You might act as Elvis sounds on this song, with a delicate grace and a modest affection. Flip the record over to "Milkcow Blues Boogie," and the same story— Elvis's girl has left him—is a matter of life and death. And yet, despite the apparent lack of struggle, of intensity, a certain truth is being told here; a balance is being worked out; and the song is satisfying, leaving any listener richer than before.

With "Tryin' to Get to You," the boy who always seemed bent on escape in the blues now has his eyes turned toward home. I got your letter and I came a-runnin' is the plot—"I've been traveling over mountains," Elvis sings, and you believe him. The passion is there (also humility—Elvis remembers to thank the Lord for helping him along), but what is interesting is how controlled the feeling is. This is an elegant record. The arrangement is very professional, very strict; Elvis sings

---

Someday, French film critics will discover these pictures and hail them as a unique example of *cinéma discrépant;* there will be retrospectives at the *Cinémathèque,* and five years after that Harvard students will cultivate a lopsided grin and Elvis movies will be shown on U.S. public TV, complete with learned commentary deferring to the French discovery and bemoaning America's inability to appreciate its own culture. Elvis will be touring the People's Republic of China and during an audience with Chairman Mao will be drawn into a discussion of the conflicting aesthetics of "Milkcow Blues Boogie" and "No Room to Rhumba in a Sportscar." The Chairman, being a staunch advocate of "The Folk," will cite James Agee's famous essay on the corruption of folk art by the nature of reality; Elvis will reply that while he has never read the piece, he once saw some pictures from *Let Us Now Praise Famous Men* in a copy of *Life* he picked up on an airplane, and thought they were all right. "My 'folk' can be summed up very easily," he will tell Mao with a knowing smile. "'The short and simple annals of the poor.'"

All right, then—where does all this fit in with an old woman hardening her heart against Skip James and passing her time with Elvis? Only in that at its blandest, the American mainstream has no limits at all; even Mao could get his hand caught in this tar-baby. It contains everyone from moment to moment, covering over and melting down and seducing the best along with the worst, until the toughest, wisest pessimist is defeated by his secret yearning for a happy ending and the cheap tears it brings to his eyes. And that mainstream—which could turn "Bartleby" into a musical as easily as it allowed Elvis to turn himself into *Tickle Me*— provides such a perfect antithesis to the realities of American life that inevitable discrepancies come out of the woodwork, come with enormous force—a surprise, again—and with them come the resentment and the humor that keep the soul of the place hanging onto life.

Big words? Heavy stakes? Too much to drop on a vitiated country boy and an old lady who in all probability was just too bored to change the channel? Well, if that's not America, I'll never recognize it.

beautifully, but he submits to the music. He never really takes it over. Some emotions, he might be saying, are authentic only when they are restrained—just as some emotions are authentic only when they are utterly free.

"I'm Left, You're Right, She's Gone" is cut from the same mold. It brings together a superb vocal, an unforgettably clean guitar solo, and a good rhythm—no rave-up, but just over the line into rock 'n' roll. There is a happy ending—Elvis finds a new girl—and maybe that's the real clue to these sides. Everything works out, in the lyrics, in the music (even the guitar parts are neatly resolved, while those in the blues tempt chaos), in the commercial and cultural context the singer can take as close to a given. What is missing is the suspense of a man creating himself, by the pure force of his will and desire, that one can hear in Elvis's blues.

There is an alternate version of "I'm Left," usually called "My Baby Is Gone," that shows how naturally Elvis's flair for this kind of material evolved into his later—and present-day—ballad style. All the mannerisms are there.* The performance is stunning: every line is measured out as if it costs the singer his soul to confess his loss. Elvis drops down so low on the scale he can barely get the words out; he blows up the subtleties of his phrasing into shameless melodrama, and it works. The song tells us what Elvis was after and where he was going as well as anything. The tune was written as a conventional country tear-jerker, but in this version Elvis stepped gently away from his community even as he gave that community something it could accept: a Hollywood movie, a Valentino love scene complete with heavy breathing. "Blue Moon" takes this blending of cultures even farther; it's more like "pre-Elvis" pop music than any of these sides, and queerer, too. "Blue Moon" comes with clippity-clop hoofbeats worthy of Gene Autry, and with a bit of Elvis's acoustic guitar; he sings like a swamp-spirit, making his way through the fog to that lamp post Frank Sinatra used to cart out for all his album covers. Whining and wailing between the lyrics—which, as Elvis sings them, sound quite surreal—he turns this old standard into a combination of a supper club ballad and an Appalachian moan.

This music is good enough, committed enough, to make you almost forget Elvis's Wild West. He played both ends against the middle; in the good moments, he escaped the deadening artistic compromise the

---

* The mannerisms of his great ballads, like "I Was the One," "Is It So Strange," "Don't," "Fame and Fortune," "Anyway You Want Me," "If I Can Dream," or "Suspicious Minds," and the awful ones, like "Tonight's All Right For Love," "Fool," and a couple of hundred others.

middle demands. This seems to have worked because both sides of his character, at this point in his career, were pulling so hard.

Jerry Lee Lewis, second in the hierarchy of white Southern rockers, had talent and drive that stopped just short of Presley's, but he gained only a fraction of Presley's success, perhaps because he lacked the broad scope of Elvis's ambition and Elvis's sure sense of where he meant to go—not to mention Elvis's understanding of how to act once he got there. If Elvis had a bit of grace to him, Jerry Lee seemed possessed; and Jerry Lee, far more than Elvis, came to represent all the mythical strangeness of the redneck South: lynch-mob blood lust, populist frenzies, even incest. When Jerry Lee made it onto national TV, Steve Allen didn't bother squeezing him into white tie or chaining him to the floor: in a vain attempt to parody the excess that made Jerry Lee Lewis great, tables and chairs were thrown across the stage while Jerry Lee pounded out "Whole Lotta Shakin'." Elvis's early music has drama because as he sang he was escaping limits, testing them, working out their value; unlike Jerry Lee, he at least knew the limits were there. With Southern power in his music, Elvis had mainstream savvy in his soul.

The problem was that the shallowness of the poorest of the music that captured Elvis's restraint, and the inoffensiveness of the best of it, opened up the I-Walked-Like-a-Zombie saga that Elvis would act out in the long years before his comeback in 1968—a saga that, in a much more extravagant way, he acts out today.

Elvis was very comfortable with his country music, and with the romantic ballads that were its mainstream equivalent; so were his first teenage fans. This was mother's milk; the responses the music elicited

---

*EE #6. One night in 1973 we went out to catch El's latest movie; the theater was almost empty. There were a few couples in their late twenties, an elderly pair who left almost immediately, an old black man sitting alone, maybe just looking for a roof in the rain. The film was *Elvis on Tour*, a documentary of his post-comeback apotheosis—with gestures toward History.

There are kinescopes of the first triumph: Elvis rocking out on *The Ed Sullivan Show* with "Ready Teddy." The performance is astounding, otherworldly, and it is hard to believe anyone now living was really around to see such a sight (though, of course, *we* were). "That's All Right" plays under a shot of a train running on down the line, as Elvis talks about his childhood. "Never saw a git-tar player was worth a damn," he remembers his Daddy telling him. "I was born about ten thousand years ago," Elvis sings in one of his recent songs, and that seems to say it all, to sum up the jumbled sense of time that governs the movie, and us; the beginning of it all seems at least that distant, and brings home just how long Elvis and we have been caught up with each other.

Somewhere near the end of the flick is a wonderful sequence of Elvis-movie kisses, a perfect critical attack on the aggressive meaninglessness of the movie years: like dominoes, one starlet after another falls into Elvis-arms. Ah, Elvis says to us here, this is what I *became*, but this is not the *real me*. Well, what is? That pudgy flyer up on the screen, filmed live in concert after concert, mechanically grinding out the same songs and choreographed karate chops (the seventies equivalent of swiveling hips?) as if his life were a tape loop? The kiss sequence is meant to parody the past, but it only parallels the present.

were virtually automatic. Elvis's ability to sing this music and to like it—to put it across without lying to himself or to anyone else—would never have brought him fame or burst any limits. But that ability was crucial to his power to hold onto his success, and to keep at least that part of his original audience (and to attract so many more) who didn't grow with the musical culture Elvis founded: those who, all through the sixties, lived in an America that was ignored or damned by the Rolling Stones and the counterculture; those who put the endless movies into the black; who made the soundtrack to *Blue Hawaii* the best-selling Elvis album of all (over 5 million copies at last count); those who bought reassurance tinged with a memory of excitement and independence. When all this proved too dull and predictable even for Elvis— when he came roaring out in the explosion of vitality and commitment that was his comeback (returning, then, as a King of Rock 'n' Roll who was also a definitive Middle American)—there were plenty from every sort of white rock 'n' roll audience who were glad to leave whatever they had made of the sixties behind and join him in his pageant. Elvis's accommodations, all larger than life, and brilliantly orchestrated on stage to preserve the thrills that were once discovered in his blues, make a very glamourous home for our own retreats.

The country sides, the later music that derived from them, the shining acceptance of the great stage show, give us the contradictions that have kept pace with rock 'n' roll from the beginning (contradictions that are, of course, much bigger than the music): the desire of the rebel to conform; the wish for quiet despite allegiance to an ideology of noise; the need for rest after excitement; the retreat that replaces ambition, be that ambition personal, cultural, or political. But this aesthetic—of rest, of quiet, of retreat—so convincing in those first country records, grows easily into a riskless aesthetic of smooth-it-away. This is really the last word of our mainstream; its last, most seductive trap: the illusion that the American dream has fulfilled itself, that utopia is complete in an America that replaces emotion with sentiment and novelty with expectation. Elvis contained this aesthetic within himself— Tocqueville's bad dream, the aesthetics of playing it safe. When he is ready to play it safe, that aesthetic contains him, just as it usually contains most of us. Breaking loose and starting over cost more every time, and in the America that Elvis has come to symbolize so powerfully, in an America that only wants to applaud, to say Yes and mean it, the risks are hard to find.

MYSTERY TRAIN

It was the last record Elvis made at Sun; to me, it tells the best tale of all.

Junior Parker and Sam Phillips wrote "Mystery Train" together in 1953; the original, a slow, dark blues released under the name of Little Junior's Blue Flames, was exquisite. An odd, chopping beat carried the threat of the title; a sax brought out the inevitable train sound with an unusually ominous flair. And Parker sang halfway from the grave, chasing his lover through the gloom, giving just the slightest suggestion that she had been kidnapped by a ghost. There was a feeling of being in the wrong place at the wrong time, a hint of a curse.

This was the blues realism of Robert Johnson: one of those tunes that says, this is the way the world is, and there's nothing you or anyone can do about it.

> *Train I riiide,*
> *Sixteen*
> *Coaches long*
> *Train I riiide,*
> *Sixteen*
> *Coaches long*
> *Well, that long black train*
> *Carry my baby and gone*

They may ride the same train—somehow, it runs away from itself.

To understand the strangeness of those lines, we have to go back to the place where Parker and Phillips found them: back to the Carter Family's "Worried Man Blues" of some twenty years before. It was a folk song, passed back and forth between the races, that in truth was older than anyone's memory.

"Worried Man" is the story of a man who lays down to sleep by a river and wakes up in chains. The Carters don't tell you if the man is black or white; if he killed someone, stole a horse, or did anything at all, and the man doesn't know either. You would have to go a long way to match that as an image of the devil in the dream, or as the plain symbol of a land whose profound optimism insures that disaster must be incomprehensible.

There is no protest in the song, no revolt, only an absolute, almost supernatural loneliness: a bewilderment that is all the more terrifying because it is so self-effacing and matter-of-fact. The emotion is there in the steady roll of the beat, in the resignation of Mother Maybelle's guitar, and in Sara Carter's squeaky, toneless singing; the sound of a man who has told his story more times than he can remember, and who hopes that one more telling will finally let him rest. He rides a train to nowhere.

> *The train I ride is sixteen coaches long*
> *The train I ride is sixteen coaches long*
> *The girl I love is on that train and gone**

Like the rest of the song, it makes no sense; it simply defines the singer's world, and there is no way out, save for the death the man promises will someday save him from his song.

Even without these details—the mystery behind their train song—and even with a tacked-on happy ending that gives the singer back his girl, Parker and Phillips re-created this mood, or submitted to it. So, when Parker sings that his baby will come home, that the train will surely bring her back, you don't really believe him. He sounds as if he has already lost more than anyone can return.

The Carter Family was completely real to Elvis; the white gospel culture they represented was implicitly *his* in a way that no other culture, be it Hollywood or the blues, could ever quite be. This was his inheritance and his birthright; the blues and the movies were something he made real for himself. On the earlier Sun records, Elvis had left home with the blues and come back on the flipside; "Mystery Train" gave him a blues that was rooted in his own community, and the context was not so open.

There was the purely musical side; most of the material Elvis had used at Sun was weak or undeveloped in its original form, giving him plenty of freedom to exploit possibilities others had missed. With "Mystery Train," both originals were brilliant. They took the train as far as it could go—in one direction—and the hard meaning Junior

---

*EE#7. I had a dream one night, 4/25/73. In the dream, I am looking into a carny peepshow machine, wherein tiny shots of Elvis, Scotty Moore, and Bill Black, circa 1954, flicker in and out of view. Naked, they are rehearsing their live act, kicking their legs in tandem like the Rockettes. Slowly, the camera moves in on Elvis's penis. It is an accurate dream: I look to see if Elvis is circumcised, and of course he is not. In close-up his member fills the screen. A message has been carved on his penis in block letters. "ELVIS LIVE AT THE INTERNATIONAL HOTEL LAS VEGAS," it reads.

Parker and the Carter Family gave to the song was also part of Elvis's inheritance. If that meaning was forcefully obscure, that uncertainty was the song's point: the uselessness of action, the helplessness of a man who cannot understand his world, let alone master it. The singer was to enter this world, suffer it, make that world real, and thus redeem it. Elvis had his job cut out for him if he was to make the song his own.

One more time, he found an opening and made it through. His attack on "Mystery Train" is as strong as Sly Stone's transformation of "Que Sera, Sera" from a little hymn to the benevolence of fate into a massive ode to dread. If the two performances go in different directions, maybe that tells us how far we have come; tells us that rock 'n' roll had to begin with an honest refusal of doubt and fatalism, and grow, along with its audience, to the point where it would have to absorb such things to survive.

Inspired by the feeling of going up against the old meaning of the tune, or determined to beat out Junior Parker, the black man, or simply thrilled by the music, Elvis sings this song with shock: he rebels against it. There is so much fire in his singing, so much personality and soul, that he changes the meaning of the song without smoothing it over. There is a tremendous violence to the record: "Train I ride," Elvis sings, but he sounds as if he's going to run it down. "It took my baby," Parker had moaned (riding us back to the days when a black locomotive was the symbol of a force no one could resist, of fate on wheels): "It's gone do it again." "Well," Elvis declares, "it took my baby—BUT IT NEVER WILL AGAIN—no, not again." His rhythm guitar seizes the music, forcing the changes; Scotty Moore, as he always did, lives up to Elvis's passion. Moore gives us one hard solo, which seems to hang the song between what it has always been and what Elvis is making of it, and then Elvis is back, and he turns the train around. As he speeds off into the night with the girl he has stolen off that mystery train, he cuts loose one more time. "Woo, woo—WOOOO!" he shouts, full of delight; he laughs out loud; and he's gone.

Elvis escaped the guilt of the blues—the guilt that is at the heart of the world the blues and country music give us—because he was able to replace the sense that men and women were trapped by fate and by their sins with a complex of emotions that was equally strong and distinctive. As he sang, Elvis changed the personae his songs originally offered his listeners. When the persona was one of anger, or delight, he outdistanced it. He didn't have to tell us that the blues is about displacement, about not being at home, about a brooding fear the music was meant to ease, but not resist. And if at its deepest the blues is hellfire music, worth the trouble of the black preachers who have damned it, that Elvis escaped this truth and still made his music ring true was precisely his genius.

FINALE

These days, Elvis is always singing. In his stage-show documentary, *Elvis on Tour*, we see him singing to himself, in limousines, backstage, running, walking, standing still, as his servant fits his cape to his shoulders, as he waits for his cue. He sings gospel music, mostly; in his private musical world, there is no distance at all from his deepest roots. Just as that personal culture of the Sun records was long ago blown up into something too big for Elvis to keep as his own, so the shared culture of country religion is now his private space within the greater America of which he has become a part.

And on stage? Well, there are those moments when Elvis Presley breaks through the public world he has made for himself, and only a fool or a liar would deny their power. Something entirely his, driven by two decades of history and myth, all live-in-person, is transformed into an energy that is ecstatic—that is, to use the word in its old sense, illuminating. The overstated grandeur is suddenly authentic, and Elvis brings a thrill different from and far beyond anything else in our culture; like an old Phil Spector record, he matches, for an instant, the bigness, the intensity, and the unpredictability of America itself.

It might be that time when he sings "How Great Thou Art" with all the faith of a backwoods Jonathan Edwards; it might be at the very end of the night, when he closes his show with "Can't Help Falling in Love," and his song takes on a glow that might make you feel his capacity for affection is all but superhuman. Whatever it is, it will be music that excludes no one, and still passes on something valuable to everyone who is there. It is as if the America that Elvis throws away for most of his performance can be given life again at will.

At his best Elvis not only embodies but personalizes so much of what is good about this place: a delight in sex that is sometimes simple, sometimes complex, but always open; a love of roots and a respect for the past; a rejection of the past and a demand for novelty; the kind of racial harmony that for Elvis, a white man, means a profound affinity with the most subtle nuances of black culture combined with an equally profound understanding of his own whiteness; a burning desire to get rich, and to have fun; a natural affection for big cars, flashy clothes, for the symbols of status that give pleasure both as symbols, and on their own terms. Elvis has long since become one of those symbols himself.

Elvis has survived the contradictions of his career, perhaps because there is so much room and so much mystery in Herman Melville's most telling comment on this country: "The Declaration of Independence makes a difference." Elvis takes his strength from the liberating arrogance, pride, and the claim to be unique that grow out of a rich and commonplace understanding of what "democracy" and "equality" are all about: No man is better than I am. He takes his strength as well from the humility, the piety, and the open, self-effacing good humor that spring from the same source: I am better than no man. And so Elvis Presley's career defines success in a democracy that can perhaps recognize itself best in its popular culture: no limits, success so grand and complete it is nearly impossible for him to perceive anything more worth striving for. But there is a horror to this utopia—and one might think that the great moments Elvis still finds are his refusal of all that he can have without struggling. Elvis proves then that the myth of supremacy for which his audience will settle cannot contain him; he is, these moments show, far greater than that.

So perhaps that old rhythm of the Sun records does play itself out, even now. Along with Robert Johnson, Elvis is the grandest figure in the story I have tried to tell, because he has gone to the greatest extremes: he has given us an America that is dead, and an unmatched version of an America that is full of life.

All in all, there is only one remaining moment I want to see; one epiphany that would somehow bring his story home. Elvis would take the stage, as he always has; the roar of the audience would surround him, as it always will. After a time, he would begin a song by Bob Dylan. Singing slowly, Elvis would give it everything he has. "I must have been mad," he would cry, "I didn't know what I had—Until I threw it all away."

And then, with love in his heart, he would laugh.

EPILOGUE

ITINERANT SINGER REVEALS NAME ON TAIL OF SHIRT
'Disgusting,' Witnesses Claim

REPORT HUGE STONES BLOCK ALL ROADS

MAN WITH BLACK WHIP SEEN AGAIN IN CEMETERY—
ONLY COMES OUT AT NIGHT
Gravediggers Threaten Walkout

ALTERCATION OVER STETSON HAT ENDS IN DEATH

AFRICANS EAGER TO 'SEE THE USA' ASSERTS TRAVEL AGENT—
'BIG BUCKS IN NEW TOURIST MARKET'

MAN FOUND IN CHAINS HELD, DENIES ALL WRONGDOING
'Only Wanted Nap,' Claims Prisoner

FIANCEE DISAPPEARS ON TRAIN, REPORTS ASTONISHED PASSENGER
'Old Story,' Says Stationmaster

MAN AND WOMAN ESCAPE TRAIN WRECK UNHARMED
'Line Hasn't Run For Thirty Years,' Maintains Rail Exec

Walt Whitman once wrote that he didn't want an art that could decide presidential elections; he wanted an art to make them irrelevant. He was interested in an artist's ability to determine the feel of American experience; to become a part of the instinctive response of the people to events; to affect the quality and the costs of daily life. Whitman cared less that he would be remembered (though he certainly cared about that) than that his beliefs in the promises of American life would be lived out by other Americans—those of his time, and those far beyond his time. He thought that his work might affect whether or not his country would grow, and die, and start over again; whether his country would, at the margins of change, maintain a soul and a vitality that could be recognized, loved, and feared far more easily than it could be defined.

I think few artists have come closer to these dreams than those whose stories make up this book. Harmonica Frank, known to no one; Elvis, known to all; and the others: each catch an America that has shape within an America that is seamless—and that, most likely, is the best one can really hope for.

But Whitman, like Elvis or the Beatles or any true pop original, wanted it all, a grand battle between art and politics pitched right here. "Did you too," he wrote in *Democratic Vistas*, "suppose democracy was only for elections, for politics, for a party name?" Whitman thought limits were undemocratic. As good democrats, we fight it out within the borders of his ambition.

Notes and Discographies

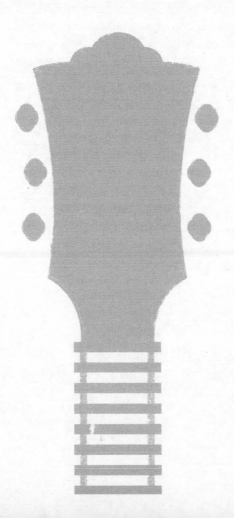

HARMONICA FRANK

Frank Floyd's parents, Stella Miles and Bruce Floyd, did not give their son a name (after years as "Shank," he chose "Frank" for himself as a teenager). They separated soon after his birth; Frank grew up in Arkansas under the care of his paternal grandparents. After the death of his grandmother, Frank, with his grandfather Bud Floyd, a fiddler, took to the road. Bud died of a heart attack in 1922, after he and Frank caught a ride with a trucker; the trucker ran, leaving Frank with the body. "I'd sleep in ditches," Frank said years later, "and know that if I died that night, no one would know who I was or where I come from."

Frank got his first regular job in the late '20s, with the Cole Brothers Carnival, and for the next two decades trekked over the country ("He told me that for thirty-five years of his life he never spent two nights in the same place," the late all-knowing Memphis music man Dickinson, who recorded Frank in 1979, said in 2002), spending most of his time with such legendary outfits as Happy Phillipson's Medicine Show and the Dr. Hood Medicine Show. He ate fire, pulled up tents and pulled them down; he performed in blackface. That milieu, plus many of the commonplace lines and breakdowns that would find their way into Frank's own songs, is conjured up with startling immediacy in the forty-eight numbers on *Good for What Ails You: Music of the Medicine Shows 1926–1937* (Old Hat). Throughout the '20s, up to 1934, the bank robber and killer Pretty Boy Floyd was running wild in Missouri, Ohio, and Oklahoma: a cousin, Frank liked to say, somewhere down the line. In 1930 Frank married one Gladys Dunigan, who died in 1937; their daughter Laura Jane was born in 1931, and raised by her mother's family. In 1966 she presented her father with his first birthday cake. Frank taught himself to read and write; in 1963, though he had given up performing, working instead as an ice cream vendor in Dallas and as a farmer near Memphis, he took a course and learned to read music.

In 1951, after nearly thirty years of living off his music and his wits, Frank cut his first records with Sam Phillips (1923–2003); in 1954 they recorded "Rockin' Chair Daddy" and "The Great Medical Menagerist" (Sun 205). "Now, here was a musician I was very much into," Phillips told Martin Hawkins in 1985, for notes to the Bear Family box set *The Sun Country Years, 1950–1959.* "He was what I call a modern-day hobo. He didn't stay *anywhere* for very long. He was unique, and he fascinated me . . . You have to keep in mind along that time, music was getting somewhat less pure than it had been—had I been able to spend the money on Frank Floyd, I think, because of the sheer fact that he was so different, he could have become an institution here."

If Frank was indeed Phillips's first attempt to find "a white man who had the Negro sound and the Negro feel," as the late Marion Keisker, Sun's comanager in the 1950s, remembers Phillips saying about no one in particular, Frank was never identified as such by Phillips himself, partly because for many years Phillips denied saying any such thing, about anyone. It was only in 1997, on Terry Gross's NPR show *Fresh Air*, that Phillips finally changed his story—after, it must be said, any number of Northern writers, convinced that all white Southerners must be racists, shamelessly followed the happily late Elvis Presley biographer Albert Goldman's twisting of Phillips's words into "If I could find a white boy who sang like a nigger . . ." "'If I could find a white man . . .'" Gross quoted the original phrase back to Phillips. "Did you really say that?" "In essence I did," Phillips said in a reflective tone. "There is nothing like the *feel* of black music . . . I still feel that is a *true* statement." He went on to talk about how hard it was to get any airplay for black musicians in the 1950s; if he could find a white singer to sing convincingly in a black idiom, he remembered thinking, and if people knew that the singer was white, Phillips thought he "might broaden the base of the music for both black and white."

Of the many numbers Frank put down in 1951, five were released as blues on the Chess label in Chicago (the rest, including "Christmas Time Again," were erased; tape was expensive). Frank's early recordings were once very hard to come by, and I thank the late Greg Shaw for providing the bootlegged tapes that sparked my interest in the first place.

All of the 1951 and '54 sides, plus a dazzling 1958 single, "Rock a

Little Baby" (issued by Frank himself on his own F&L label; the forgotten Memphis singer Larry Kennon took the B-side with "Monkey Love"), were included on *The Great Original Recordings of Harmonica Frank* (Puritan LP, 1974; reissued in 2010 as a 10-inch LP on Hog Maw as *Mouthin' Blood Blues*—not terribly useful information, but the title is too good to leave out). Along with the music came photos of Frank in 1920 (a ringer for any drawing of Huckleberry Finn), the late '40s, (as a cowboy singer), and 1972—one of the latter showing how Frank played two harmonicas simultaneously, one with his mouth, the other with his nose. For that trick, he balanced the instruments with his hands; he also played harmonica no-hands, while he sang and played guitar, the device held in his mouth like a cigar.

Frank's music does not lend itself to classification. As he told blues researcher Steve LaVere, who located him in 1972: "I spent a lot of time listening to the darkies in days gone by singing in the cottonfield down south, and I picked up their songs and speech. That is the reason people think I am a colored man, but I really am white." That seemed to matter. "I never played with no blacks," Frank wrote me in response to a query, "but I was a fan of Blind Lemon Jefferson, Lonnie Johnson, and Fats Domino." And, he might have added, a contemporary of all three, though he far more closely resembles the great blackface singer Emmett Miller (1900–62), whose indispensable collection of late '20s recordings, *The Minstrel Man from Georgia* (Columbia Legacy), conjures up a lost world of trickster race changelings—chronicled in a trance of mystical pedanticism in Nick Tosches's lovely *Where Dead Voices Gather* (Boston: Little, Brown, 2001). In the mid-'70s, Frank finally did play with black musicians, notably the Beale Street bluesman Furry Lewis, with whom he re-created routines from their medicine-show days from the '20s and '30s.

Frank learned many styles so he could play for many audiences—which by the seventies included college students at folk and blues festivals across the U.S., most prestigiously the Smithsonian Institution's Festival of American Folklife in 1972. His music can be heard as country on the above-mentioned *The Sun Country Years* and on the anthology *Memphis Ramble* (Rhino); in the context of early rock on *The Best of Sun Rockabilly Vol. 1* (Charly), an unmatched collection of Sun rarities; and as part of Sam Phillips's pan-American sensibility on *The Sun Records Collection* (Rhino box set). His masterpiece, "Goin' Away Walkin'," can be heard in the setting of Memphis blues on *Memphis and the Delta: The 1950s* (Blues Classics). Beyond the Sun material, "Train Whistle Boogie," written by Frank and recorded by Charles Dean and the Rondells in 1959 for the Benton label, can be found on the anthology *West Tennessee and Arkansas Rockin'* (Collector); Frank never recorded it himself. The anthology *Step It Up and Go* (Redita LP) includes three Frank tunes purportedly recorded in the late sixties; all are available in more accessible versions.

Frank began performing again almost immediately upon his involvement with LaVere. Along with Sam Chatmon ("The Mississippi Sheik") with "Forgive Me Too Blues," Sleepy John Estes's "President Kennedy Stayed Away Too Long" and "Yellow Yam Blues," Bukka White's "Bed Spring Blues," and Furry Lewis's "Mary Tell Blues," the anthology *Memphis Blues Caravan, Vol. 1* (Mimosa) includes a stunning harmonica extravaganza and a mud-to-his-armpits vocal on "Goin' Away Happy"—Frank at his highest, it would seem—recorded in Memphis in 1972. The performance, unparalleled in blues recording for the sound of a sly, gnarled drifter gazing from a roadside as the traffic speeds by, begs only one question: where's the rest of the night? Frank's first album was no answer: though he recorded in 1972 and after, nothing was released, and when *Harmonica Frank Floyd* (Adelphi) finally did appear in 1976, it was a severe disappointment, with almost every cut lacking flair and spark. (The much rougher, more playful *The Great Medical Menagerist*, a collection of 1972 outtakes notable for "Movement Like an Elgin," which shares motifs with Robert Johnson's "Walking Blues," appeared in 1997 on Adelphi/Genes.) In the meantime, though, Frank cut a magnificent album for a different company: *Blues That Made the Roosters Dance* (Barrelhouse, an adventurous, even arty blues label) fully equaled his Sun sides. The man was close to seventy; not even an old carny like Frank himself could have guessed his age by listening. Numbers included the Mississippi Sheiks' "Sittin' on Top of the World," a fine tribute to Jimmie Rodgers, "Ring Tail Tomcat" (featuring numerous animal imitations), "Shanghai Rooster Breakdown," and "Shampoo (The Whorehouse Special)," a talking blues that's filthy, not dirty. "Fuckin' for *free*," the singer cries in disbelief at the song's wayward daughter. The performances on the anthology *The Missing Link* (Memphis International), the 1979 recordings coproduced by Jim Dickinson and cut in Bluff City at Ardent Studios and live at Bartlett High School and Farmington Elementary School, were not released until 2002. They are warm, open, and satisfied, from "Deep Elum Blues" to "You Don't Know My Mind."

Frank Floyd died in 1984. He once asked me to mention that of all those who reissued his music, only Chris Strachwitz, who runs the Blues Classics label, ever paid him any money for it.

ROBERT JOHNSON

Before Columbia Records began its release of Johnson's music in 1961, his tunes traveled as rare 78 originals, an occasional foreign blues bootleg, cover versions by Chicago bluesmen, deteriorating reel-to-reel tapes passing from hand to hand. Some of his most important compositions—"If I Had Possession Over Judgment Day" and "Traveling Riverside Blues"—had never been released before. While Johnson's music has appeared in different formats since then, with the release, fifty years later, of the definitively remastered—in engineering terms, all but reimagined—*The Centennial Collection* (Columbia, 2011), all twenty-nine of Johnson's master recordings, thirteen alternates, and a tiny snatch of Johnson speaking, it was as if his songs had never quite been heard at all. The music was so full, its shadings so subtly vivid, that whatever one's familiarity it felt completely new. The sound called up a room: you were in it with the singer, breathing the same close air, and the singer was looking you in the face; when he asked you if you could hear the wind blow, he put you on the spot.

The sixteen original tracks of *King of the Delta Blues Singers* (reissued in 1998 by Columbia Legacy, retaining Frank Driggs's liner notes, Burt Goldblatt's dramatic cover painting,* adding an otherwise unavailable outtake of "Traveling Riverside Blues," and imprinting the CD with a facsimile of the obscure Romeo label, one of several on which Johnson's 78s were issued in the thirties) offer nearly all of Johnson's greatest songs: "Cross Road Blues" and "Come on in My Kitchen" (with producer Frank Driggs in both cases omitting versions released in the thirties in favor of alternate takes where Johnson completely recast the pieces), "Terraplane Blues" (named for the bank robbers' favorite—"In the air it's aeroplaning, on the sea it's aquaplaning, but on the land it's Terraplaning"—and Johnson's only release even approximating a blues hit: Johnny Otis claims to have heard it on the radio in Berkeley in

---

* In 1961, Bob Dylan writes in *Chronicles, Volume One* (New York: Simon & Schuster, 2004), John Hammond, the legendary record man who signed him to Columbia, gave him a test pressing of *King of the Delta Blues Singers*. (Hammond had tried to recruit Johnson for his 1938 "Spirituals to Swing" concerts in New York City; as Johnson was already dead when Hammond began looking for him, Hammond, after hearing the news, played Johnson records at the concert, the only instance in which recorded music was used in place of a performer.) Like so many, Dylan had never heard of Johnson, but the cover pulled him in: "He showed me the artwork, an unusual picture where the painter with the eye stares down from the ceiling into the room and sees this fiercely intense singer and guitar player, looks no more than medium height but with shoulders like an acrobat. What an electrifying cover. I stared at the illustration. Whoever the singer was in the picture, he already had me possessed."

1936), "Traveling Riverside Blues," "Walking Blues," "Rambling on My Mind," "Me and the Devil Blues," "Stones in My Passway," "Hellhound on My Trail." With that last, the great English musicologist Wilfrid Mellers wrote in 1964 in his landmark *Music in a New Found Land* (rev. ed., New York: Oxford, 1987), "we have reached the ultimate, and scarifying, disintegration of the country blues. The howls and falsetto yells are now not only savage and grotesque, they are also broken, lost, centreless. The almost lunatic emotional excitement is reinforced by the harsh dissonances of the guitar, its piercing vibrato scraped with knifeblade or bottle-neck on reiterated single-notes; voice and instrument no longer comfort one another in dialogue, but stimulate one another to further frenzy. On the words 'gotta keep moving,' the blues-form is literally disrupted, the harmony displaced, the modulations weirdly awry. Sometimes Johnson has no need of the conventional harmonic sequences, but makes do with a quavering drone, as in the most primitive folk style; sometimes he relinquishes song altogether and mutters to himself. The expression of lonesomeness—the singer speaking with and through his guitar—could be carried no further." Such an affirmation of Johnson as a modernist—an artist responding to the dislocations of the twentieth century no less than Picasso or Satie, and with the same Cubist impulses—was anything but common, and is still denied in a nearly Stalinist manner by blues writers seemingly afraid of art.

"The best record of all time," the Fluxus violinist and guitarist Henry Flynt said of *King of the Delta Blues Singers* in 2004, but nearly forty years before, he was making a harder, even desperate case. "The only significant 'modern' non–European Serious Culture so far is Afroamerican Serious Music," Flynt wrote in 1965 or 1966 in "European-U.S. Cultural Imperialism," at a time when he was leading demonstrations calling for a boycott of concerts by Karlheinz Stockhausen because of his dismissal of American black music, not to mention the Everly Brothers. "At first, the only Black music in the U.S. was the music of Afroamerican toiling people, because the enslaved Afroamerican national minority had no ruling layer. Of the earlier Afroamerican toilers' musicians, let me mention *Robert Johnson*, who was unique, who stands alone." Flynt ranted, making errors of fact (placing Johnson's recording sessions in his native Mississippi rather than in San Antonio and Dallas) without opening holes in his ideas: "Communists who are aware of *Afroamerican Serious Music* have equated it with imperialist Modern Art and then attacked it as reactionary, decadent, anti-humanist, against the masses, and diversionary. Remember, these same Communists consider it obligatory to venerate Bach, the Serious Music of the *white* imperialist American. During the period when Robert Johnson was recording in Mississippi, American Communism's top 'social musician' was the composer Marc Blitzstein. Just how revolutionary this Communist Music was can be judged from the fact that in 1964, Blitzstein was honored with a memorial concert in Philharmonic Hall, produced by Leonard Bernstein (remember, the champion of 'intellectually high-level jazz'), and favorably reviewed by imperialist critics. U.S. imperialists absolutely cannot give Robert Johnson comparable honors . . . What is this Communist stance? Are the Communists saying, 'Get that filthy n——r music out of here'?! Are they saying that 'it might n——r up the pure revolution'?! How dare they imply such vile contempt for a Robert Johnson!" (Flynt's manifesto courtesy Branden Joseph; see also Henry Flynt and the Insurrections, "*I Don't Wanna*," blazing 1966 neo-primitive rock 'n' roll issued in 2004 by Locust.) Writing in the *Oxford American* in 1999, Roy Blount, Jr., made the same argument; only the names were changed. "Arthur Schwartz—the eminent composer of 'Dancing in the Dark' and many another standard—is quoted in *Our Huckleberry Friend* as declaring that 'Blues in the Night' is 'the greatest blues song ever written, and that includes "St. Louis Blues."' Hooey. He must have thought 'Love in Vain' and 'Trouble in Mind' were cave paintings. No wonder Elvis blew those old guys away. It's a miracle of American disassociation that Robert Johnson didn't twenty years earlier."

Sales throughout the sixties for *King of the Delta Blues Singers* probably did not exceed ten thousand copies, but only a handful of records released in that decade were so influential. Cream's "Crossroads" and the Rolling Stones' "Love in Vain" (Johnson's original was still unavailable on LP when the Stones' cover version appeared in 1969) prompted *King of the Delta Blues Singers, Vol. II* (Columbia Legacy). It collected the remainder of Johnson's recorded compositions, and included "Love in Vain," "Stop Breakin' Down Blues," "Phonograph Blues," "I Believe I'll Dust My Broom," "Sweet Home Chicago" (a long-time South Side standard), and others, plus some alternate takes, and was graced by evocative paintings of Johnson's first recording session by Tom Wilson of Daily Planet—part Edward Hopper, part Thomas Hart Benton. The anthology *Mississippi Blues: Complete Recorded Works (1935–1951)* (Wolf, Austria) contains searing 1941 electric performances by Robert Jr. Lockwood (1915–2006), Johnson's stepson, of two tunes attributed to Johnson, "Little Boy Blue" and "Take a Little Walk with Me." No less fiery is Johnson's road buddy Johnny Shines's version of Johnson's unrecorded "Tell Me Mama," on his 1972 *Traditional Delta Blues* (Biograph). The anthology *The Roots of Robert Johnson* (Yazoo) and the more extensive *Back to the Crossroads: The Roots of Robert Johnson* (Yazoo, issued to complement Elijah Wald's *Escaping the Delta: Robert Johnson and the Invention of the Blues*; see below) assemble blues that may have directly influenced Johnson's composition of specific songs, connecting, say, Skip James's "Devil Got My Woman" with "Hellhound on My Trail." The presentation is interesting, but the dogmatic, reductive claims of the liner notes dissolve as soon as you click your CD player and replace "the roots" with the result. A better version of a similar idea is the anthology *Robert Johnson Classics* (Jasrac, Japan). Here, surrounded by blues, jazz, and country songs from either before his time or after it, as musical influences and effects, as context and conversation, Johnson may lie down on someone else's bed (Leroy Carr's "When the Sun Goes Down"), but he always wakes up as his own man, in his own dream. What remains unheard, save for "They're Red Hot" (covered in 1991 by the Red Hot Chili Peppers on *Blood Sugar Sex Magik*, Warner Bros.), is the non-blues side of Johnson's repertoire. As a street singer, Johnson no less than Harmonica Frank had to be ready to sing anything, and he did: Jimmie Rodgers blue yodels, Bing Crosby hits (there is Bing Crosby in the "I was lonesome, I felt so lonesome" in "Love in Vain"), show tunes (Johnny Shines: "Any kind. Polka. Irish. Jewish. Well, like 'Stardust,' 'Danny Boy,' 'Willow Weep for Me.' You play and put the hat down")—maybe even commercial jingles. Imagine: "I got stones in my passway / And my road seems dark as night / But you know that Ex-Lax / Makes everything all right . . ."

In 1975 Columbia announced the imminent release of "The Complete Robert Johnson: The Man and His Music," a promised three-LP set. As a trusting person, I mentioned it in the first edition of this book; one reader braved a Minnesota blizzard to find it, hitting every record store in the Twin Cities. The occasion for the set was the discovery of the facts of Johnson's life, along with the Grail of the blues: photographs of the man himself. Eleven years would pass before even one saw the light of day—and *Robert Johnson: The Complete Recordings* (Columbia) did not appear until 1990. What happened?

Working independently, two researchers—Steve LaVere, Harmonica Frank's rediscoverer, and Mack McCormick, a blues researcher associated with the Smithsonian—had after years of work made contact with Johnson's surviving sister in Baltimore. By means of keepsakes unpacked and clues left behind, this led to a reconstruction of Johnson's life, including the details of his murder—but for those who had spent years living with Johnson's music, the pictures spoke more clearly than any facts.

The first to surface appeared in a special issue of *Rolling Stone* (February 13, 1986) celebrating the induction of the first members of the Rock & Roll Hall of Fame; Johnson was honored as an "Early Influence." Originally made in a coin-operated photo booth in the early '30s, the shot shows Johnson in a white shirt and suspenders, with a cigarette in his mouth and a guitar in his hands. The face is smooth and serious, and you can read any of Johnson's songs into his flat, silent gaze, but it is the fingers that are riveting: long, almost prehensile fingers that snake over the neck of the guitar like hoodoo bone charms. Three years went by before a second photograph appeared, in *78 Quarterly*, volume 1, number 4, 1989 (the issue included a debunking essay by Stephen Calt and Gayle Dean Wardlow—interviews with various knew-him-whens insisting that Johnson was nothing special either as a guitarist or a singer, you should have heard my cousin Ira—and a useful guide to local, archaic, or misleading terms in Johnson's lyrics, by Calt). The photo (like the first, provided by LaVere, who went on to market both as posters and T-shirts), made at the Hooks Brothers studio in Memphis, showed a grinning, handsome man superbly dressed in fedora, double-breasted pin-striped suit, and shiny black shoes; only the fingers on the guitar Johnson held like a trophy matched the power of the first shot. In 2005, the guitarist Steven Schein found a photo identified as "Old Snapshot Blues Guitar BB King?" on eBay and ordered it. When it arrived, showing a dark-skinned man with a white Stetson and long fingers, and a lighter-skinned man in a black hat, Schein identified it as a portrait of Johnson and Johnny Shines. Publication in *Vanity Fair* set off years of dispute; the Houston forensic analyst Lois Johnson, working with the Robert Johnson estate, authenticated the photo in 2013. Johnson's right eye is bright, his left eye half-closed; in a dark suit and a striped tie, he has a young man's grin.

Both the photo-booth and the studio photos were included, along with photos of Johnson's mother, stepfather, sister, wife, and contemporaneous blues players, as illustrations for Steve LaVere's extensive notes to *The Complete Recordings*, the double-CD box set that finally kept, or broke, the fifteen-year-old promise of "The Complete Robert Johnson." Produced by LaVere and Frank Driggs (who had produced *King of the Delta Blues Singers* twenty-nine years earlier), to my mind the package was a botch from beginning to end. Both photos of Johnson were badly cropped; the forty-one then-extant Johnson recordings (minus a later-discovered take of "Traveling Riverside Blues" included on the 1998 reissue of *King of the Delta Blues Singers*) were programmed with alternate takes following master takes, which meant that listening to the set was like reading a discography. LaVere's extensive historical and interpretive essays were an embarrassment, at times verging on surely unintentional racism, and his comments on his own sometimes incomplete transcriptions of Johnson's lyrics were occasionally stupefying. LaVere described Johnson's "I can study rain" and "I been studyin' the rain" (in "Preaching Blues") as "phonetically correct, although meaningless"; presumably he meant "syntactically" or "grammatically" correct, but it's the second claim that's meaningless. "Studying rain" is symbolism, carried forward from many older blues songs to Bob Dylan songs, echoing back to Shakespeare: it means to contemplate dread. In 2011, along with *The Centennial Collection*, Columbia issued a grossly irrelevant, extraordinarily expensive box set, comprised of the double CD of Johnson's recordings, 45 rpm 10-inch replicas of the Johnson 78s released in 1936 and 1937, a collection of 1928–32 blues recordings issued by Victor (which, as RCA Victor, was now part of Sony/Columbia), recordings made by other performers at the sessions for which Johnson was present ("folk and hillbilly, cowboy and Mexican"), and a DVD of the Peter Meyer documentary discussed below. Not included in the box but available separately, the one great result of this white elephant, which may actually have sold in the dozens, was "Robert Johnson's Hellhound on My Ale" (Columbia Legacy/Dogfish Head Craft Brewery). The twenty-five-ounce bottle looked to be all concept, no beer: "With lemons," the label read, "as a shout-out to Robert Johnson's mentor Blind Lemon Jefferson." It was rich, with a huge head. Flavors swam through the glass. It was so smooth it was like drinking a sunset. When I reached again for the bottle it was empty.

The most effective critical attack on LaVere's work—which was followed by his licensing of countless redundant Johnson collections, often with Johnson's recordings programmed alongside second-rate cover versions—was Gene Santoro's "Robert Johnson" in the *Nation*, October 8, 1990, collected in his *Dancing in Your Head* (New York: Oxford, 1994). The most comprehensive—and alarming—examination of LaVere's business practices was Robert Gordon's "The Devil's Work: The Plundering of Robert Johnson" in *LA Weekly*, July 5–11, 1991. By far the most gratifying spawn of the set was Tony Scherman's "The Hellhound's Trail: Following Robert Johnson" in *Musician*, January 1991. Scherman drew out Eric Clapton, Keith Richards, Billy Gibbons, Vernon Reid, Robert Plant, Ry Cooder, Robbie Robertson, and more on Johnson; as shameless fans or resentful competitors they talked about genes, madness, Faust, and rhythm, in almost every case adding something new to music most of them had been listening to at least since Bob Dylan included *King of the Delta Blues Singers* as one of the talismans scattered across the cover of his 1965 *Bringing It All Back Home*. Dollars, in a way, confirmed the story. *The Complete Recordings* made the *Billboard* charts; it went gold; it won a Grammy. Johnson was no longer an invisible pop star; he was simply not present. The Columbia publicity department got used to journalists and disc jockeys calling to inquire whether Mr. Johnson might be available for interviews. That he was not allowed the U.S. Postal Service, which does not recognize the living, to bring out a lovely Robert Johnson stamp in 1994: the photo-booth image, absent the cigarette.

But that was later. In the early 1970s, both McCormick and LaVere came up with much of the same material; releases were obtained from Johnson's apparent heirs, but they cancelled each other out; a struggle over copyrighting, possession of documents, invasion of privacy, and licensing provoked a legal battle that, despite LaVere's successful marginalization of McCormick, was not settled until July 15, 2000, when the Mississippi Supreme Court affirmed a 1998 decision by the Leflore County Chancery Judge Jon Barwell that Claude Johnson, of Crystal Springs, Mississippi, was Johnson's son and sole legal heir. His mother, Virgie Jane Smith, had had intercourse with Johnson in 1931; Claude Johnson was born nine months later. In 1937, Claude Johnson remembered, his father came to visit; his grandparents, with whom he was living, would not allow the boy to meet him. "They told my daddy they didn't want no part of him," Johnson told Rick Bragg of the *New York Times* ("Mississippian Is Son of Father of the Blues," June 17, 2000). "They said he was working for the devil, and they wouldn't even let me go out and touch him. I stood in the door, and he stood on the ground, and that is as close as I ever got to him." The court's decision was based on the videotaped deposition of Eula Mae Williams, a friend of Virgie Jane Smith's, who described witnessing Smith having sex with Johnson—as she herself was nearby, in "the lush piney woods of Copiah County," as Claude Johnson's attorney, Jim Kitchens, put it, making love with her own boyfriend. With the site of Johnson's burial a matter of fierce contention, DNA evidence was unavailable. "As far as we know," Judge Mike Mills wrote for the court, "Johnson is buried 'down by the highway, so his old evil spirit can get a Greyhound bus and ride.'" Claude Johnson did not have to take the bus to Los Angeles when, in 2006, he was present at the Grammy Awards to accept a Lifetime Achievement Award on behalf of his father: his first royalty payments, made in 1999, amounted to close to two million dollars. "Make some noise for RJ," LL Cool J said at the Grammys, as the camera panned to pick up Claude Johnson. "I found it incredibly powerful to learn and see that Robert Johnson's son is alive and well," wrote David Marchese, at the time a journalism student at NYU. "It makes RJ seem real in a way that had never occurred to me before. As if John Henry or Paul Bunyan's kid showed up somewhere."

McCormick's once-promised book on Johnson, *Biography of a Phantom*, has never appeared, and over time McCormick has come to doubt many of his own discoveries, not to mention those of others, but works partly based on his research are worth seeking out. The late Robert Palmer's *Deep Blues* (New York: Viking, 1981; see also Robert Mugge's documentary version of the same name, Winstar Video) included a good summary; Peter Guralnick's short book *Searching for Robert Johnson* (New York: Dutton, 1989) combines biography with a close musical analysis. There are other ways of listening. "When You Walk in the Room" (*Village Voice*, 1986; collected in my *The Dustbin of History*, Cambridge, MA: Harvard, 1995) is an argument for the uniqueness of Johnson's work. "Instrumental Break," in my *The History of Rock 'n' Roll in Ten Songs* (New Haven, CT: Yale, 2014), draws on my notes to the admittedly completely redundant *Martin Scorsese Presents the Blues: Robert Johnson* (Columbia Legacy, 2003) with a story of the life Robert Johnson might have lived if he hadn't died when he did; by the end, in 2012, he's trying to squeeze royalties out of the White House. Charles Shaar Murray's discussion of Johnson in *Crosstown Traffic*, a study of Jimi Hendrix (London: Faber and Faber; New York: St. Martin's, 1989), erases the mystification that often accompanies comment on the blues and brings Johnson to life as an ordinary historical actor—not that such a conception will ever rule, because of a story so appealing to the imagination it has become a floating, even automatic signifier, its own frame of reference: "There's the Bob Dylan lyric, about staging the apocalypse for our entertainment, which is what I do," the screenwriter and director Paul Haggis, best known for the 2005 film *Crash*, said in 2014, promoting a new project, not to say himself. "The real Highway 61 actually divided the country, and my movies are kind of divisive. But the real reason was because it was at the crossroads of Highway 61 where the bluesman Robert Johnson sold his soul to the Devil for his talent. And I think, in some ways, I've sold my soul for my talent."

Enough! Or not. Researching his *Delta Blues* (New York: Norton, 2008), Ted Gioia asked McCormick "if the time had come to put" the story of Johnson selling his soul "to rest," Gioia wrote in 2012 in the journal *Radio Silence*. "When I went to New Orleans in the late 1940s to visit some record collectors," McCormick said to Gioia, "they told me the same story. You need to remember that almost nothing had been published on Robert Johnson at that time . . . Yet these record collectors had heard about Robert Johnson selling his soul to the devil. I subsequently heard the same story within the black community. The fact that the same story circulated among these two groups—groups that had very little to do with each other—impressed me. It suggested that the story had deep roots, probably going back to Johnson himself." Still, the artist Kevin Bradley may have had if not the last word, the best. In his *Robert Johnson*, one of a series of letterpress posters he placed on the walls of the meandering corridors of the Chelsea Market in New York in 2009, Johnson appeared with backlit eyes and filed teeth, surrounded by a testament: "THEY SAY HE SOLD HIS SOUL BUT HE TRICKED SATEN BY PUTTING HIS SOUL IN HIS MUSIC." Maybe the late Tony Wilson had the best last word on the matter, in his punk-record-man autobiography, *24 Hour Party People* (London: FAC/Channel, 2002), recalling the first Sex Pistols show in Manchester, England, on June 4, 1976, with, by his count, forty-two people present: "God, what is this? Bloody hell, it's 'Stepping Stone.' And in the next sixty seconds, hearing the Pistols violently murder and then resurrect this simple pop classic, all was made clear as all was destroyed. Only in hearing the old was the new revealed. I will destroy the temple and in three minutes I will rebuild it, sayeth the Lord, sayeth Johnny Rotten . . . In its complete indifference to the niceties of technique and respect, they restored to the popular song the spirit that is the only fucking reason it exists in the first place. Robert Johnson sold his soul at the crossroads. He sold it for this. Good deal."

The dream of the great Robert Johnson film remains unrealized, though not for lack of trying—and despite the suggestiveness of Andre Braugher, who throughout most of the nineties played Detective Frank Pembleton on the great Baltimore cop show *Homicide* as if he were Robert Johnson's nephew, in terms of both Braugher's dead-ringer looks and the hellhound at Pembleton's back. Alan Greenberg's blazingly readable, semi-fictional screenplay *Love in Vain*, first published in 1983 (New York: Da Capo, 2001), has bounced back and forth between different producers, directors, and actors (Prince as Robert Johnson? No? Why not Sean Combs?) ever since. Shot instead, by Walter Hill in 1986, was John Fusco's moronic script for *Crossroads*, in which smarmy white Juilliard guitarist Ralph Macchio decides that the discovery of an unrecorded Johnson song will make him rich and famous—and, in a cutting contest with a white blues guitarist standing in for Old Scratch, triumphs by playing Mozart. The first legitimate project to make it to the screen—or video—was Chris Hunt's 1992 *The Search for Robert Johnson* (Sony Music Video); starring John Hammond, Jr., the son of Columbia's John Hammond, as compère, it was notable mainly for dazzling footage of Willie Mae Powell, the "Willie Mae" of "Love in Vain," beautiful in the '30s and beautiful half a century later. Peter Meyer's 1997 *Can't You Hear the Wind Howl: The Life & Music of Robert Johnson* (WinStar Video), included in Columbia's 2011 box set, was better. With narration by Danny Glover, interviews with contemporaneous bluesmen and friends, and reenactments featuring the blues singer Keb' Mo' as Johnson (with as much charisma on-screen as he displays on record, which is to say none, Mo' is effective in ensemble situations when the camera keeps its distance), the picture begins in magic. A credit sequence is built around "Come On in My Kitchen": As Johnson enters a photo booth, each note stands out, tells its own story, then seems to abstract itself from the song, flying off like a bird, then circling back over the singer, as if trying to decide whether to light. The film moves on with a young Johnson making a diddley bow, a new husband dancing in tall grass with his new wife, Johnson and Johnny Shines busking on Highway 61 outside of Memphis after their hotel has burned down. Shines talks about playing an all-white town in Illinois where he and Johnson were "exhibited as niggers." "He say he done that, went to the crossroads," the blues singer Honeyboy Edwards says. "No, he never told me that line," Shines replies. "If he would have, I'da called him a liar right to his face. 'Cause I know it's a lie. You have no control over your soul. You don't know what you're going to do ten minutes from now. You think you do . . . How you going to do anything with your soul? You *are* a soul." "That word 'devil,'" says the bluesman Henry Townsend, taking a more businesslike view of the matter. "You'd be surprised how *effective* it is."

Aside from documentaries, the most interesting cinematic references to Johnson appear in Ian Softley's 2005 *The Skeleton Key*, a twisted, not to say tied-in-knots, tale of hoodoo in Louisiana just before Hurricane Katrina destroyed New Orleans, which ends with Elvis's "If I Can Dream" sounding behind the credits, and begins with a dying man listening to "Come On in My Kitchen" on a phonograph (the recording "not treated as an honored [read: moribund] part of our heritage, but as something strange and singular, both enticing and forbidden," Charles Taylor wrote at the time; see "They Were Expendable," *New Jersey Star-Ledger*, September 25, 2005), and in *Phoenix*, a cops-as-robbers bloodbath made in 1997 for HBO by Danny Cannon. In the

Arizona bar she runs, Anjelica Huston leans over a jukebox playing Johnson's "Terraplane Blues," a cigarette dangling from her lower lip as if it's glued there. Cop Ray Liotta walks in, catches the tune: "My grandfather used to have one of those," he says. "Good car." "It's not about a car," Huston says mordantly. They banter back and forth, tossing lines from the tune at each other like Humphrey Bogart and Lauren Bacall running their horse-racing double entendres in *The Big Sleep*, as if familiarity with Robert Johnson songs on the part of even vaguely cool middle-aged white people can be taken for granted. Later, Liotta, holding his guts inside his body with one hand, desperately flags down a truck; the trucker has Johnson's "From Four Until Late" on her radio. Liotta smiles, but for him it's already too late. "Robert Johnson, there's fear there, yeah," Keith Richards said years later. "A fear of what? If you've faced fear yourself, you want to tell other people it's faceable. There's no point in ignoring it. That's an element of the expression in what we've done, in, say, 'Gimme Shelter.' Fear is just a viable element, an emotion to use in a song as any other emotion" (from Mikal Gilmore, "Love and War Inside the Rolling Stones," *Rolling Stone*, May 23, 2013).

It's in literary fiction and poetry, more than in film or critical analysis, that Johnson seems to have found a true second home. Though sophomoric fictional riffs on Johnson have been common coin for decades (T. Coraghessan Boyle's breathless "Stones in My Passway, Hellhound on My Trail" is an early example), the first work of lasting value was probably Stanley Booth's "Standing at the Crossroads," a nine-page playlet (meant to let some of the air out of Alan Greenberg's *Love in Vain* screenplay, where Johnson first meets the devil in a movie theater) collected in Booth's landmark *Rythm Oil: A Journey Through the Music of the American South* (London: Cape, 1991; New York: Da Capo, 2000, which like the 1992 Pantheon edition omits a portfolio of William Eggleston photos from the original edition). Here, with all of the supernatural and none of the magic stripped from the tale, Robert Johnson sells his soul to the devil, or rather he trades his shoes to an old tramp in exchange for a guitar lesson—you be the judge. It's a story to make you nervous, just as Lewis Shiner's "Steam Engine Time," collected in Joe R. Lansdale's Western anthology *The New Frontier* (New York: Doubleday, 1989), is a heartbreaker: the small, blocked adventure of a kid showing up in the world with something he calls "blue music," but too early, even before the storied evening in 1903, in a depot in Tutwiler, Mississippi, where W. C. Handy encountered a guitarist singing a song about "Where the Southern cross the Dog": "The weirdest music I ever heard," Handy wrote. "Was that supposed to be some kind of minstrel song?" a woman asks the young guitarist in Shiner's story. "No," he says, "it wasn't no minstrel song." "Ain't heard nothin' like it before," she says. "Not supposed to have," he says. "Things everybody heard before is for shit. 'The Little Old Cabin in the Lane.' Songs like that make people the way they are."

In 1995 two novels with Johnson as a shadow character appeared: Sherman Alexie's *Reservation Blues* (New York: Atlantic Monthly Press), about a Spokane Indian band possessed of Johnson's guitar (still alive in 1992, he's taken up residence on their reservation) and Walter Mosley's *RL's Dream* (New York: Norton). *Reservation Blues* regressed too quickly into a rock-band novel, but *RL's Dream*, set in the present in New York City, bringing together a wounded young white woman and a dying bluesman, blazed its own trail. It was a huge step for Mosley, justly celebrated for his continuing series of Easy Rawlins detective novels, tense, masked accounts of a black man picking his way through postwar Los Angeles (held up to a doo-wop mirror in my "In a Secret Country," *Los Angeles*, August 2002, collected in *Best Music Writing 2003*, edited by Matt Groening, New York: Da Capo, and with his exacting *Little Scarlet* played against what was on the radio in the summer of 1965 in my *Like a Rolling Stone*, New York: PublicAffairs, 2005). *RL's Dream* revealed the limits of the Rawlins books; freed from the constraints of genre, just as the constraints of genre had originally freed him as a writer, Mosley began to imagine his characters past their own limits. The bluesman, thinking back to the short times he'd shared with Johnson in the 1930s—times that left him at once rich and poor, wealthy with a glimpse of possibility, impoverished with the knowledge of all that would forever lie beyond his grasp—now remembers "decades between the notes," and so passionately a reader can fill in all that isn't said. "Christopher Marlowe and other white geniuses changed in my eyes once I saw them in the contrast to Johnson," Mosley wrote in his literary memoir "Me and Satan" (*Conjunctions* 16, Bard College/Random House, 1991). "They were no longer figures against whom I compared black genius. Marlowe, in his way, introduced me to Robert Johnson. I was allowed to see this black master of blues in the light of history. In turn Johnson introduced me to myself."

In the Alabama-born poet Diann Blakely's as yet uncollected "Duets with Robert Johnson," appearing in *BOMB* and other literary journals since 2002, she weaves a very few lines from Johnson's songs into her own reveries, and the result is that Johnson joins a broader territory than the ethnographic patch of ground to which, in the same years, blues writers have more and more insistently consigned him. He becomes a citizen of the whole country, traveling through its entire history, as if his art can make any past present. In Blakely's "Crossroad Blues," the only person named is Ashley Wilkes; in her "Little Boy Blue," a Johnson mentor "sings, but history shakes with louder sounds," and the sound of country blues is suddenly the overwhelming sound of the Battle of Vicksburg, and the little blue boys are dead Union soldiers. In her "Ramblin' on My Mind," Blakely truly does let her mind wander. One of her own ancestors appears as a haunt, her wounds still open, "the first woman killed by Nat Turner's gang"; she fades into a slave owner, and then into a modern world that Blakely nails shut with her last line. It's a world that, as she hears it, Johnson "claimed for songs / Which foretold more bad news: factory stockyard closings / King shot in Memphis, schoolkids selling crack / By fallen tractor sheds. All great migrations done." In "Dead Shrimp Blues," from the July 15, 2011, number of *The Chronicle of Higher Education*, she has Tennessee Williams and Maggie from *Cat on a Hot Tin Roof* cross paths with Johnson in Clarksdale, so she can address him directly, circling around the imagery in at least one of two Johnson songs built around a metaphor for impotence. She writes like a window-peeper in reverse: "I'll undress / Down to my humid white-girl slip." In lines you can imagine Johnson writing, Kevin Young, in "Flash Flood Blues," from his collection *Dear Darkness* (New York: Knopf, 2008), is at once more down-to-earth, final, and Greyhound-bus funnier: "Even my wages of sin / Been garnished." In 2007, in *The Yiddish Policeman's Union* (New York: HarperCollins), Michael Chabon put a detective on a stakeout: "Landsman waits out the funeral in his car, studying it through the good Zeiss lenses and running down the car battery with a CBC radio documentary about the blues singer Robert Johnson, whose singing voice sounds as broken and reedy as a Jew saying Kaddish in the rain . . . Landsman weighs the sholem in his hand now—a cute little Beretta .22 with a plastic grip—poisons himself on nicotine, and tries to understand the lamentations of this black Delta yid."

I like Ace Atkins's *Crossroads Blues: A Nick Travers Mystery* (New York: Thomas Dunne/St. Martin's, 1998). Travers is a white musicology professor at Tulane in New Orleans; there's a story going around about a 1938 Robert Johnson recording session and nine sides no one has ever heard, and after another professor disappears looking for them, it's a story no one can quite disbelieve. Travers soon encounters an albino black man who was present at Johnson's death, and a cretinous teenage hit man and Elvis lookalike named Jesse Garon, who threatens out of sheer stupidity to destroy the treasure everyone is after—just as, it's hinted, the heedless culture Elvis created all but destroyed the culture Johnson crafted with such worry and care. "Shut his ass up, Willie," an old black man who holds court in Three Forks, Mississippi, named as the place where Johnson was killed, says of the facts Travers has at his command. "Just made me fifty bucks yesterday from some Japanese. They thought I was Robert Johnson's son." The book folds in on itself when Atkins sees through his own tale, realizing that the story will resist even one clever enough to make a detective novel out of it. Travers dreams: "Black-and-white images of searching for Robert Johnson— his music grinding beneath a huge needle. Johnson gagging on his own blood. Johnson smiling up at him and telling him, *You're not welcome . . . You're not part of this, he said. You're not welcome.*"

Johnson was born in Hazelhurst, Mississippi; as a baby he traveled with his mother and sister through migrant labor camps, and then to Memphis; he grew up in nearby Robinsonville, Mississippi. (Tom Freeland's "Where the Blues Was Born," *Oxford American*, Summer 1999, is a good sketch of Johnson's Hazelhurst; Bob Herbert's "Haunted by Segregation," *New York Times*, May 16, 1999, is a harsh portrait of a place fundamentally unchanged despite decades of New South propaganda.) Almost every great early bluesman was said to have a shadowy teacher who provided instruction in both musical technique and the black arts, and Johnson, it seems, came close enough. After being chased off as an incompetent by the ruling Delta players, Johnson returned to Hazelhurst and, for a year or more, worked with an Alabama-born guitarist named Ike Zimmerman (in some accounts referred to as Zinneman or Zinnerman). In 2011, for Alabama Arts Radio, Zimmerman's daughter Loretha Zimmerman Smith described her father taking Johnson to a cemetery (owned by white people, she said gleefully) to play, sitting on gravestones—a Johnson-lore ghost story here presented as plain family fact. "He learned Robert so *good*, how to play the guitar, that he was telling him he was ready to leave and go back, to where he came from. And my understanding, now, he came from Tennessee, where he was trying to play the guitar, but when he went back he could play better, than any of them. And so they named my daddy the *devil*, because they felt like no human being could teach a person to play like that. But my dad, he wasn't the devil. He was a good man." Zimmerman never recorded, so one can only guess at the sounds he made—but Johnson came back from Hazelhurst transformed. "He had a chance to make some records, and he did," the Chicago blues guitarist Michael Bloomfield (1943–81) said just before his death from a heroin overdose, "and some people say they're the greatest country blues records of all time. I don't know if I agree with that, but I do know that in them you can hear a young man, a young man with an amazing amount of young man's energy, the kind of thing that you would find in the early Pete Townshend, or early Elvis, or in any young man who's just burning up his energy . . . it just leaps out at you from the turntable." (From an interview with Tom Yates; see Ed Ward, *Michael Bloomfield: The Rise and Fall of an American Guitar Hero*, New York: Cherry Lane Books, 1983.)

Johnson attracted international attention in his lifetime: in 1937 the British music weekly *Melody Maker* reprinted a John Hammond item from the June 8, 1937, issue of the *New Masses*. (Hammond, likely the writer who, in an earlier *New Masses* piece, credited to one Henry Johnson, referred to Robert Johnson as "the greatest Negro blues singer to have cropped up in recent years . . . Johnson makes Lead Belly sound like an accomplished poseur," called Johnson the "star" of Hot Springs, Arkansas—while complaining that his primary label, Vocalion, "records no work songs or songs of protest by Negro artists.") Shortly before his death, Johnson reportedly formed a band, with piano and drums ("ROB-ERT JOHNSON" emblazoned on the bass drum); there are even claims that he was using an electric pickup on his guitar. These developments by themselves would not have been unknown (Howlin' Wolf may have been playing an electric guitar in Mississippi about the same time; Son House was working on propulsive rhythms with harmonica and fiddle accompaniment in 1941). But the rhythmic structures of Johnson's songs suggest that any band of his might have been making music recognizable as rock 'n' roll—full-blown, not protean rock 'n' roll, where rhythms are defined most of all by a feeling of contingency, the feeling that the music can break into a new direction at any moment, the sense that everything is up for grabs—at least by 1938, the year he was murdered.

Poisoned by a jealous husband at a juke-joint show near Green-wood, Mississippi (more than thirty years after the fact, McCormick identified a still-living man as the killer and reported him to the local police; they were not interested), Johnson lingered for several days before passing away on a date that now marks the death of Elvis Presley: August 16. A death certificate, which may have been prepared decades after the fact, is included in Gayle Dean Wardlow's *Chasin' That Devil Music* (San Francisco: Miller Freeman, 1998): "The plantation owner said it was his opinion the negro died of syphilis," it reads. According to LaVere, Johnson used what strength he had left to set down a final testament, a document pictured in the opening montage of the *Can't You Hear the Wind Howl* documentary: "Jesus of Nazareth, King of Jerusalem, I know that my Redeemer liveth and that He will call me from the grave"—and you never know. In the words of "Moonshiner," the Appalachian ballad best done by Bob Dylan (see his 1963 demo, collected on *the bootleg series, volumes 1–3 [rare & unreleased], 1961–1991*, Columbia): "Let me eat when I'm hungry / Let me drink when I'm dry / Give me dollars when I'm hard up / Religion when I die." Proprietors of different grave sites still vie for primacy. In 1991 a monument was placed in the cemetery of the Mount Zion Missionary Baptist Church near Morgan City, Mississippi, where Johnson had supposedly been buried in an unmarked grave. "Isn't it wonderful," said Pastor James Ratliff, "that somebody that sold his soul to the devil can do so much good for the church?" In 2000 the A&E channel went with Greenwood, with Paul Winfield providing a sonorous *Is this land cursed?* narration for a *City Confidential* documentary on the town, which used Johnson's death as a precursor to tales of modern-day adultery and murder. Four years later, some members of the Little Zion Missionary Baptist Church in Greenwood objected to the inclusion of its cemetery, another supposed Johnson burial ground, on a $75 Robert Johnson bus tour; LaVere had put his money down on the site as Johnson's true resting place and erected a headstone. "The blues and the church are separate, and they should not be mixed," congregant Kimberley Jones-Gatewood wrote in a letter to the *Greenwood Commonwealth*. "It's not like the man is going to get out of his grave and come in the church," said the Rev. McArthur McKinley, the church head. "If he does that, then I'll be the first one out there." In 2003 David Lynch released *Blue-Bob* (Solitude), a collection of songs he wrote and recorded with the singer and guitarist John Neff in 1998–2000. "A dog, a dog," Neff sang in "Pink Western Range," "barking like Robert Johnson."

There will be more to say about Bobby Bland in the Band discography, but I should mention that "Lead Me On," recorded in 1959 and quoted at the beginning of the Johnson chapter, comes from Bland's finest album, *Two Steps from the Blues* (MCA; also on Bland's *I Pity the Fool/The Duke Recordings, Vol. 1*, MCA, a superb double CD). The *Two Steps from the Blues* cover shows Bland posed in front of a blue building, which does indeed have two steps. Performances included a harrowing "St. James Infirmary" (collected on *Turn on Your Love Light/The Duke Recordings, Vol. 2*, MCA), "I Pity the Fool," and the ghostly "I'll Take Care of You" (both on *I Pity the Fool*), which opens with these lines: "I know you've been hurt / By somebody else / I can tell by the way / You carry yourself." Bobby Bland and Robert Johnson would have had a lot to talk about.

JOHNSON AND ROCK 'N' ROLL

From the midsixties on down, Johnson's music was recorded by more and more rock 'n' roll groups. Someone calling himself "Woody Payne" took to putting his name on Johnson's songs: "Love in Vain" on the Rolling Stones' *Let It Bleed*, for one. Payne wasn't the first and likely he won't be the last, but such piracy merely illustrated how wasteful some found it that such valuable material was in the public domain (on *The Complete Robert Johnson*, all of Johnson's compositions were protected by LaVere's new copyrights). At any rate, I offer a rock 'n' roll top ten plus one of Johnson's tunes—although there is perhaps a better version of the pop Robert Johnson than can be found on any record. In 1989, reacting to published reports that the Who were considering a one-shot re-formation for a concert where tickets would sell for up to $2000, Gina Arnold of the Berkeley *Express* invited readers of her weekly "Fools Rush In" column to contribute suggestions as to what concert might possibly be worth such a price. The winning entry, from Marc Buonocristiani: "A lineup consisting of the Clash, circa 1977, the Rolling Stones (before they got bored, say around '68, '69), and Bob Dylan (before he got born, say 1966 before the accident), all on the same bill and all opening for Robert Johnson." "Why?" Arnold asked. "Because," Buonocristiani said, "it would be worth two grand just to yell for Robert while Mick was singing. Oh yeah, I'd make one other condition: you can't get a ticket if you don't know why the first three should be opening for the other guy. That way I won't have to hear some moron yell something stupid while he's playing."

To the chart:

1. Rolling Stones, "Stop Breaking Down," from *Exile on Main Street* (Rolling Stones, 1972). This was the fifth straight album on which the Stones included a country blues, but the first on which they approached country blues as rock 'n' roll, likely because in sound and spirit the rest of the album approached rock 'n' roll as country blues. *Exile* was a nice tour of morgues, courthouses, sinking ships, claustrophobic rooms, deserted highways. The whole record was a breakdown, one long night of fear. Johnson's hottest bragging song ("In the words of the immortal Robert Johnson," Bob Dylan said as he accepted the Album of the Year

award for his *Time Out of Mind* at the 1998 Grammys, "'the stuff we got will bust your brains out'") gave the Stones a chance to blow the fear away. With Mick squeaking his harp, calling for chorus after chorus, this stands as one of the Stones' best.

2. Taj Mahal, "The Celebrated Walking Blues," from *Taj Mahal* (Columbia Legacy, 1967). From his first album, and still *his* best. The long, long piece—with the feeling of a man stretching his arms and legs until the joints crack—is not completely Johnson, and Johnson's song was based on Son House's 1930 "Walking Blues." Taj refashions the song with bits from Willie Brown's 1930 "Future Blues" ("Minutes seem like hours / Hours seem / Just like days"), Muddy Waters's variant, and many other sources. The music is driven by Gary Gilmore's deep bass and Taj's high harp; the vocals are outrageously blacked up, until after a few minutes the slow pace of the performance brings forth a deeper singer—more tired—and a deeper blackness shows through the mask.

3. Cream, "Crossroads," from *Wheels of Fire* (PolyGram, 1968). "Eric Clapton, vocals!" said Cream bassist Jack Bruce after he, the guitarist, and drummer Ginger Baker finished the song onstage at the Fillmore Auditorium in San Francisco; though the album title is description enough, this is the only performance on the album that lives up to the title.

The Cream number was a cover of not only Johnson but almost of itself: in early 1966, a few months before Cream formed, as Eric Clapton and the Powerhouse (Clapton, Bruce, singer Steve Winwood, with Paul Jones on harp, Ben Palmer on piano, and Pete York on drums) had recorded a spirited but very small "Crossroads" (see the anthology *What's Shakin'*, Collectors' Choice Music, 1966). The Cream version was itself covered; in 1995, Anheuser-Busch briefly marketed "Cross Roads Beer" (not where you sell your soul to the devil and end up as a drunk living on the street, but "Where Substantial Flavor and Easy Drinking Meet"). TV commercials showed white people in urban frolic as a Cream-style version of what in the '60s was known as the absent Johnson's signature piece pounded the theme right out of the frame. In 2000 came "Crossroads of American Values": a Toyota commercial that blanketed the airwaves for months. "*Down* to the crossroads / Tryin' to flag a ride," someone sang in a horribly hyped-up white blues voice to kick it off: cars are streaming, people are engaging in transactions, it's just full of busyness. "Goin' *down* to the crossroads," the voice finishes up: "I believe I'm goin' down," which means *down* to the Toyota dealer's. Blues may be prosaic, but not this prosaic. Toyota paid; who collected? As Dion put it in a 2005 interview with Dave Marsh, going back over Johnson's version: "This guy has a bunch of mixed emotions, going down to the crossroads. In a way we're all there every day, with decisions, and choices—which make our lives. You make the right choices, you prepare for the future with a little *grace*. You make the wrong kind of choices, they take away your *freedom*. And put you in jail. But this is a great song. He's worried about a lot of things. His girl, the environment—'cause, you get caught on a road there, hitchhiking, after the sun goes down, you get hung from a *tree*. That's in there too."

A little grace was what Clapton finally tried to take from the song. As a man who had gone through alcohol and heroin addiction, in 1998 he opened a rehabilitation facility in Antigua, in the West Indies: Cross-roads Centre. "Standing at the Crossroads / trying to read the signs / to tell me which way I should go / to find the answer," its motto reads; despite the homage, the music in the descriptive video on the Cross-roads Web site (narrated by Clapton, picturing black and white thera-pists, black and white clientele, the sun setting as waves kissed the beach at sunset) is light piano and strings.

Cream's "Crossroads" was included on Clapton's *Crossroads* (Poly-Gram), a 1988 four-CD career retrospective that left behind a sense of confusion and disregard; the monument seemed to add up to noth-ing. The same feeling of irreversible torpor suffused Clapton's 2004 tribute album *Me and Mr. Johnson* (Duck/Reprise). Long an MOR stal-wart, he no longer had anything to give the songs, and he could take nothing from them. Were "Layla" and "Any Day" (from Derek and the Dominos' 1970 *Layla and Other Assorted Love Songs*, Polydor) illusions? They weren't. At its most distinctive, there was something heroic and something tragic in Clapton's playing. You don't feel self-expression ("I felt that he was being really truthful to himself, that he was writing poetry about himself," Clapton said in an interview promoting *Me and Mr. Johnson* of first hearing the man; see Dan Neer, "Me and the Devil," *Tracks*, June 2005) so much as struggle: the resistance of the music in the guitarist's mind to his will to realize that music, his resis-tance to abandoning himself to the sound he can make. It's a kind of neurotic distance, the fear that by embracing what one most loves, one might cease to be; the result, for Clapton, was focus, elegance, balance. It's there in 1966 in his solo in Cream's "Spoonful" (on Cream's first album, *Fresh Cream*, Polydor), especially in the three final notes. And yet it might have been that elegance and balance of that solo that opened the door to "Tears in Heaven" and "Wonderful Tonight," the huge Adult Contemporary hits that closed the door to Clapton's first music. As Michael Tolkin writes of the movie producer who storms his way through *The Return of the Player* (New York: Grove Press, 2006), he had learned "to give up his own taste . . . and to surrender to the audience. He consoled himself with the example of Eric Clapton, a brilliant musician who might have been as difficult for the masses as Bob Dylan, or Hendrix if he had lived, but Clapton pursued the middle way."

4. Barack Obama, "Sweet Home Chicago," closing "Red White and Blues," the White House, February 21, 2012 (whitehouse.gov). In what would have been his 101st year, Johnson's song was sung by the president of the United States. As if he'd heard it all his life.

5. Rolling Stones, "Love in Vain," (from *Get Yer Ya-Yas Out!* (Abkco, 1970). The studio version on *Let It Bleed* is stiff; onstage, Mick Taylor's guitar and Charles Watts's drums said whatever it might have been that Mick Jagger left out. (Writer's credit went to "Trad."—you remember him—this time around.)

6. Gov't Mule, "If I Had Possession Over Judgment Day," from *Hellhounds on My Trail: The Afterlife of Robert Johnson*, directed by Robert Mugge (WinStar Video, 1998). Drawn from the Robert Johnson conference sponsored by the Rock & Roll Hall of Fame, Mugge's film included excerpts from various panels and speeches, field interviews conducted by Steve LaVere (Johnson's childhood friend William Coffee: "When Robert walked in, they'd jump up. It was like the president walked in"), and performances of Johnson songs by everyone from Irma Thomas to the sadly emptied Peter Green, whose two collections of Johnson songs, from 2000 and 2003, are like a coffin for the man who, with Fleetwood Mac, made such deep blues as "Love That Burns" (see *Mr. Wonderful*, Essential, 1968, or numerous collections). There were a lot of fat-white-guy talking heads, so it was perhaps appropriate that Gov't Mule, a power trio of fat white guys, stole the show. They did more than that; they took one of Johnson's most obviously profound songs and hammered it like vulcans.

7. Captain Beefheart and His Magic Band, "Tarotplane," from *The Mirror Man Sessions* (Buddha, 1965). A visionary nineteen-minute exploration of the idea of picking up someone in a Terraplane.

8. Chris Whitley, "Hellhound on My Trail," from *Hellhound on My Trail: The Afterlife of Robert Johnson*, directed by Robert Mugge (WinStar Video, 1998). With seven years to live, he looked dead-man skinny in a white T-shirt; a black bowler made him look like Malcolm McDowell

in *A Clockwork Orange*. He shook the strings of his National Steel guitar into an odd, atonal, broken account of Johnson's most resistant composition, and made you believe he understood it from the inside out. "What then are the situations, from the representation of which, though accurate, no poetical enjoyment can be derived?" Matthew Arnold wrote in 1853. "They are those in which the suffering finds no vent in action; in which a continuous state of mental distress is prolonged, unrelieved by incident, hope, or resistance; in which there is everything to be endured, nothing to be done." Whitley seemed to take the song as close to that abyss as he could with disappearing into it.

9. Cat Power, "Come On in My Kitchen," from *All Tomorrow's Parties 1.1*, an anthology curated by Sonic Youth (ATP, 1998). The most delicate of Johnson's songs, and others take it up at their peril. Cat Power sucks the piece into her own drifting, solipsistic notion of the blues, and the tune emerges stripped of any association with the past, sounding more like a young white woman embellishing her troubles in a writers'-workshop story than a story written by an itinerant young black man before the mother of the woman singing was born. You can hear that as a travesty, or you can just get lost. "He played the old ballads and standards with a long series of caresses that led nowhere and subsided into nothing," Geoff Dyer wrote in his portrait of Chet Baker in *But Beautiful* (New York: North Point, 1996). "Every time he played a note he waved it goodbye. Sometimes he didn't even wave." That's what happens here.

10. Dion, "Travelin' Riverside Blues," from *Bronx in Blue* (DMR, 2006). The old rocker solo, playing guitar as he did on his hits, railing through "Crossroads," kicking up the traces with "Walkin' Blues," and, on a syncopated beat that lets him sling the words more than sing them, slipping into this song as if it were a suit he only wears on his birthday. There was also his 2011 "Ride's Blues (For Robert Johnson)," from *Tank Full of Blues* (Blue Horizon). Coming after the three cool, expert, casual-love-and-trouble numbers that open the album, this is immediately elsewhere, calling up a place that's all menace, and a deadpan sense of fatalism settles over the trees. "He told me on the way there / That he was born in sin," the man recounting the story mutters. "Huh. So what else is new?"

Plus one: Rolling Stones, "Love in Vain," from *LIVER Than You'll Ever Be* (OMS). Recorded November 9, 1969, at the Oakland Coliseum Arena, at a keyed-up and contentious three-hours-late two a.m. show, and just about the only moment of calm—even if, in the first bars, the music rises with a majesty only a fool would deny. No writer's credit at all, because it's a bootleg. So *that's* the answer.*

JOHNSON AND POSTWAR BLUES

Johnson's impact as a stylist cut all across the board, but on the Mississippi-to-Chicago arc, Muddy Waters (1915–83), Elmore James (1918–63), and Johnny Shines (1915–92) were his most direct inheritors. Waters's first, Mississippi recordings, cut in 1941–42 by Alan Lomax for the Library of Congress (see *The Complete Plantation Recordings*, MCA), were uncertain imitations; by 1948, with "Feel Like Going Home," and 1950, with the extraordinary "Rollin' Stone" (see *The Best of Muddy Waters*, or the great *Chess Box*, both MCA), Waters had taken what he wanted from Johnson; when his music came out of his mouth and his fingers it was his alone. The spidery lines of his guitar-playing on "Rollin' Stone" are unparalleled in their tension; the singing is hard, unassuming, and terrifying. The book to read is Robert Gordon's *Can't Be Satisfied: The Life and Times of Muddy Waters* (Boston: Little, Brown, 2002).

As Peter Guralnick once wrote, Elmore James took Johnson's "Dust My Broom" and made a career out of it. Waters reached for the distant margins of Johnson's music; James went for his sound, his volume, and his flash. A near contemporary of Johnson's, and later the idol of the Rolling Stones, the early Fleetwood Mac, the Yardbirds, and numerous other British bands, James did not record until 1951, when he cut "Dust My Broom" as "Elmo James," with Sonny Boy Williamson (Rice Miller) on harp; he stepped out with a wild, trebly electric guitar style and a slashing vocal attack that traded subtlety for excitement. His many recordings of the same songs on many labels are collected on many retrospectives, single CDs, and box sets; the best introduction is *The Sky Is Crying: The History of Elmore James* (Rhino), which begins with James's

* After changing the *Let It Bleed* "Love in Vain" credit from "Woody Payne" to "Trad., arranged Jagger/Richards" on *Get Yer Ya-Yas Out!*, a strategy followed in 1972 for the *Exile on Main Street* "Stop Breaking Down," the Rolling Stones went with "adapted with new words © 1970" for the version of "Love in Vain" included on their 1995 live-and-rehearsals album *Stripped* (the new words consisted of the substitution, in one line, of "baby" for "blues"). In 2000, in a suit brought by Steve LaVere and his company Delta Haze against ABKCO Music, which had copyrighted the arrangements, Judge Pamela Ann Rymer of the Ninth Federal Circuit Court of Appeals ruled that neither song was in the public domain. Advancing an argument that would be made again by Elijah Wald and others in Johnson-debunking books, ABKCO attorney Donald Zakarin claimed that no one really knew who wrote Johnson's songs, and that, by implication, the Rolling Stones were carrying on a noble tradition: "Virtually none of the blues music then was copyrighted by anyone. [Musicians] viewed it as available to anyone." On the 2002 reissue of *Let It Bleed*, the credit for "Love in Vain" read "Robert Johnson."

first session and continues to 1961, along the way picking up superb versions of "The Sun Is Shining," "Done Somebody Wrong" (Eric Clapton's first moment of greatness, with the 1965 Yardbirds), "I Need You," "The Sky Is Crying," "Something Inside Me," "Standing at the Crossroads," "I Can't Hold Out," and the wonderfully syncopated "Madison Blues" (the last two highlights of Fleetwood Mac's famous 1969 session at the Chess studios—see *Fleetwood Mac in Chicago*, Rhino).

Johnny Shines often traveled with Johnson in the thirties. Shines moved to Chicago in 1941, but recorded only occasionally until the blues revival of the mid-'60s; with James dead and Muddy Waters committed to the Chicago band style, Shines emerged as the true master of Johnson's legacy. In his best moments, he didn't merely add to Johnson's story, he told his own. There is a horror in his 1966 "Mr. Tom Green's Farm" (see *The Johnny Shines Band*, Testament) that fully equals anything Johnson conjured up, but speaks a different language. Shines finds evil in the white man's rule while Johnson found it in himself no less than in the world, but it is Shines's ambiguous acceptance of the horror—I mean the peculiar strength he assumes when he speaks *for* it—that makes the performance so disquieting.

Shines's first recordings, made in 1946, can be found on the anthology *Chicago Blues: The Beginning* (Testament LP); his scorching "Joliet Blues," cut in 1950, which Chess left unissued for almost twenty years, is on the anthology *Drop Down Mama* (Chess/MCA); *Sweet Home Chicago: The JOB Sessions*, credited to Shines and Robert Jr. Lockwood, collects "Fish Tail," a reworking of "Terraplane Blues"; Shines's six numbers on *Chicago/The Blues/Today!* (Vanguard), among them "Dynaflow" ("Terraplane" again), amounted to his putative rediscovery, but his best work was still to come. Of the numerous albums Shines put out over the next years, strongest are the 1968 *Last Night's Dream* (WEA; the original LP on Blue Horizon is worth seeking out for the cover art, a photo collage of a woman who has awakened to find that her hair has turned into a nest of snakes) and the incomparable *Too Wet to Plow* (Tomato). This set, cut in 1975, is the record Shines lived his life to make: all acoustic, utterly controlled and passionate singing, a touch on the guitar strings so light you can feel the rain clinging to leaves on the trees.

JOHNSON AND MISSISSIPPI COUNTRY BLUES

A perfectly good case can be made that the Mississippi blues was worked out from about 1900 in and around the Dockery Farms plantation—but it is not clear such a case would mean anything at all. The date is inadequate. Blacks and whites began to notice a faraway, unexpected form of discourse emerging among Southern African-Americans from at least the early 1890s: a discourse of moans, wordless songs, suppressed wails, notes coming off a guitar like a shiver and hanging in the air like smoke, a vast family of wishful phrases and philosophical couplets that migrated from person to person, state to state, road to road, dust to dust. The phrase "worked out" suggests an intentional, collaborative effort—as opposed to "came to be," say, which would open the door to a folk process in which the needs and desires of a people crystallized into a cultural form—but why not "discovered," or made up?

First recorded in the twenties and thirties, the music makes up an aesthetic world that today can seem complete in itself—but while the blues scholar Sam Charters once wrote that only a black man, living in the Mississippi Delta in the 1930s, could possibly understand what Son House meant when he sang "My black mama's face shines like the sun," to say that the world of Mississippi blues is complete is not to say that it is exclusive. There is a uniquely American language in the shared body of riffs and lyric fragments that change in function and meaning from singer to singer: an attempt to confront a landscape and a way of life that, as a language, evades the limits of both. There is something very old about this music, something that has little to do with dates, or words like archaic or primitive. The music is old in the way that some of Faulkner's characters, black and white, seem to have been old before they were born. Questions of the musicological origins of the music remain unsettled, even as questions. While such anthologies as Alan Lomax's *The Roots of the Blues* (New World) or *Blues Roots* (Rhino) are intriguing—both include African tribal recordings, field hollers, work chants, and notably crude gospel or blues-like rag performances—they are also misleading. They give the impression that blues coalesced more or less naturally, as a result of the inevitable intermingling of extant forms and traditions. As even the least accomplished '20s or '30s delta recording can often suggest, or as Arthur Flowers makes plain in his lovely novel *Another Good Loving Blues* (New York: Viking, 1993), blues can also be seen as self-conscious, romantic, and absolutely individualistic: as a modernist art music that defines itself to the degree that it is *not* traditional.

In 2002, the historian Luc Sante argued in "The Birth of the Blues" (collected more brazenly as "The Invention of the Blues" in Sante's *Kill All Your Darlings: Pieces 1990–2005*, Portland, Oregon: Verse Chorus

Press, 2007) that just as geneticists now believe that all living people are descended from a single woman who lived perhaps 140,000 years ago, the blues—defined strictly as "a particular song form made up of 12 measures of three-line verse, with a line length of five stressed syllables and an AAB rhyme scheme" (Charley Patton, 1929: "Hitch up my pony, saddle up my black mare / Hitch up my pony, saddle up my black mare / I'm gonna find a rider, baby, in the world somewhere")—did not emerge, evolve, or develop in any folk sense at all. The blues "could only have been invented," by a "particular person or persons," just as "the x-ray and the zipper and the diesel engine were invented in the same decade" by particular persons, Sante wrote. We know their names, though: if the blues was invented, why by 1910 at the latest did nobody know by whom, when, where? Illiteracy, poverty, racism, Sante suggests—but also because the blues was so portable that once the first blues singer sang the first blues to the first blues listener, "it is easy to imagine that within 24 hours a dozen people had taken up the style, a hundred inside of a week, a thousand in the first month. By then only ten people would have remembered who came up with it, and nine of them weren't talking."

It seems like a veil lifting—but as Nathan Zuckerman says in Philip Roth's *The Human Stain* of finally solving the mystery of his dead friend Coleman Silk, "Now that I knew everything, it was as if I knew nothing." The Mississippi blues is a kaleidoscope of invention, discovery, trading, borrowing, theft, gathering, ambush, escape. Sante's revelation will take you to Son House, but it won't get you within miles of Geeshie Wiley. "I started playing when I was about eleven years old," L. V. Thomas (1891–1979), aka Elvie Thomas, who along with Wiley in 1930 recorded some of the most idiosyncratic blues ever heard, told Mack McCormick in 1961, when she was almost seventy. "There were blues even back then . . . I can't hardly name them—I don't know that the songs had a name. One song was, 'Oh, My Babe Take Me Back,' and another was 'Jack O' Diamonds.'" Their music was both archaic and Futurist. As the blues scholar Don Kent has written of Wiley, "If she did not exist, it would not be possible to invent her." So did she invent herself? And, long after the fact, as if for the first time, the blues?

Though I will never surrender my affection for *Really! The Country Blues*, an old Origin Jazz Library LP that brought together the supreme performances of Skip James ("Devil Got My Woman"), Garfield Akers (the dynamic and mystical "Cottonfield Blues"), Tommy Johnson ("Maggie Campbell Blues"), and Son House ("My Black Mama"), the collection that now best provides an entry into the music is *Masters of* the *Delta Blues—The Friends of Charlie Patton* (Yazoo), which includes Willie Brown's "Future Blues," Bukka White's "I Am in the Heavenly Way," and a slew of trump cards from House and Tommy Johnson. It is a powerful academic document. In a set programmed in the late '50s but not issued until 2000, one can hear the pack-rat anthropologist Harry Smith (1923–91) integrate Texas and Mississippi blues of the '30s with old-time country, incipient bluegrass, Cajun airs, and gospel on *Harry Smith's Anthology of American Folk Music, Volume* 4 (Revenant)— and just as striking is the way Smith integrates Robert Johnson's 1936 "Last Fair Deal Gone Down" with Lead Belly's 1935 "Packin' Trunk Blues," Joe Williams's Washboard Blues Singers' 1935 "Baby Please Don't Go," and Bukka White's 1940 "Parchman Farm Blues." Johnson's opening guitar figure signals a formal mastery that makes the masterpieces surrounding his recording seem generic by comparison. Still, Smith's compilation is an argument about style, and style doesn't tell the story. Dating to the early '60s, issued in Berkeley as a bootleg, *Really! The Country Blues* is now even more of a relic than were the then unspeakably rare, otherwise unhearable sounds it presented to the public: a relic left behind by a small group of white people—record collectors— who set out to discover an America created decades earlier by small groups of black people—set out to discover a *real* America, free of shame and lies, a place of passion, danger, and splendor, and found it: "The first time in history," as the punk bandleader and blues archivist Jack White put it in 2013, "that a single person was writing a song about themselves." Today, of course, no right-thinking person believes there ever was such a place.

"And it was there, in the Williamsburg YMCA, in a single room sometime in the mid-1940s," Marybeth Hamilton writes in her questing, querulous *In Search of the Blues: Black Voices, White Visions* (London: Cape, 2007; New York: Basic Books, 2008) about the Brooklyn record collector James McKune, who kept his Charley Patton and Son House 78s in a box under his bed, "that the Delta blues was born." Invention, even after the fact and a thousand miles away? This is part of what fascinates Patricia R. Schroeder in *Robert Johnson: Mythmaking and Contemporary American Culture*, an intellectually generous, morally acute study of Johnson in the common imagination (Urbana and Chicago: Illinois, 2004), and it is what infuriates Elijah Wald in *Escaping the Delta: Robert Johnson and the Invention of the Blues* (New York: Amistad, 2004) and Barry Lee Pearson and Bill McCulloch in *Robert Johnson: Lost and Found* (Urbana and Chicago: Illinois, 2003). They argue that the delta blues is a fiction, a fantasy spawned by generations of white mythomaniacs; they mean to replace mystification with scholarship and history. The result is a kind of hysterical philistinism—far more evident with Pearson and McCulloch, but at the heart of both books. If the "Delta Blues" is a white fantasy—or an oppressive, socially and aesthetically imprisoning white dogma forced on black Southern musicians for whom it could have had no meaning at all—then the delta blues could not have existed, and if it did not, then neither, as the figure he has become, did Robert Johnson. If Robert Johnson is the perfect embodiment of a romantic white fantasy of the black man—a black version, so to speak, of Norman Mailer's white Negro: a noble savage, a martyr, a phantom, a reprobate, scorning all codes of behavior, the very embodiment of freedom—then he cannot have been anything so congruent with the fantasy as a great artist. He must be ordinary, derivative, obvious, and finally insignificant. "As far as the evolution of black music goes," Wald writes, "Robert Johnson was an extremely minor figure, and very little that happened in the decades following his death would have been affected if he had never played a note."

Pearson and McCulloch have done careful and valuable work detailing the historical, scholarly, and musical errors of earlier writers, myself included, but they are blind, or deaf, to anything that cannot be reduced to a fact. They see white collectors and record producers conspiring to invent a world of doom and profundity: for his sequencing of *King of the Delta Blues Singers*, they argue, Frank Driggs did not merely replace an inferior but originally released version of "Cross Road Blues" with a far stronger alternate take—he replaced a version of "Cross Road Blues" that "contains six references indicating the song is addressed to a woman" with a version that has only one. "This is the version that set the tone for the way Johnson and his songs would be heard on the reissue album, a clear case of spin doctoring," Pearson and McCulloch write—as if it was not Johnson but Driggs who had created the work in the first place. "Driggs recast Johnson as a mystery man and loner, at odds with the supernatural rather than with the natural woman his traditional audiences would have recognized."* For Wald, Johnson

* In 2003, John Gibbens, author of *The Nightingale's Code*, argued in "Steady Rollin' Man: A Revolutionary Critique of Robert Johnson" that ("if I'm not completely crazy") Johnson's 78s were intentionally speeded up, possibly "to make them more exciting in an age in which the Delta tradition he came out of was already a thing of the past." The result, Gibbens found when he slowed the recordings down "to 80 percent of the speed at which they normally play," was the disappearance of Johnson's "fleeting, harried or fragmented" sound, his "half-swallowed, garbled, or strangled" vocal delivery, and, especially, "his wraith-like persona" as "the Rimbaud of the blues." *Steady Rollin' Man*, a set Gibbens produced of twenty-four slowed-down Johnson recordings, can be found, with his essay, at www.touched.co.uk/press/rjnote.html.

is most of all a dogged compiler of other people's work, a brilliant student. As a student, he was also a fool, because in Wald's book the school of the delta blues—with its masters and pupils, insiders and outsiders, with every stylistic innovation quickly absorbed or cast aside, with its codes of hazing and initiation, all rooted in a common language of chords, melodies, and words that functioned to the degree to which the individual man or woman could escape the anonymity to which white America had consigned the black American and, if only for a moment, be heard as someone no history could have predicted and no social system could silence—was a commercial falsity. Mississippi blues singers, like any other pseudo-folk, semi-commercial musicians, were really pop musicians (Wald does not like the word artist), who, as Johnny Shines says of himself and Robert Johnson, sang anything people wanted to hear; delta blues was not *their* music, because it didn't exist. It was just one pop style among countless others; as a music it was created by white producers who demanded from their happily multicultural black singers a particular kind of song they thought they could sell to a particular kind of audience. And it was the commercial failure of that strategy that for Wald proves the point. His review of records of juke-joint jukeboxes shows that the music popular among black delta Mississippians in the 1930s was pretty much what was popular anywhere else: "Delta Blues" 78s were conspicuous by their absence, and Johnson's were barely there at all. Wald's challenge to Johnson is simple: *If you're so smart, why weren't you rich?*

"This is crazy," wrote the critic Chris Walters. "The revisionist thesis only works if you overlook Johnson's music."* In 2004, in *Chronicles, Volume One*, Bob Dylan answered Wald, Pearson, and McCulloch before the fact. It's 1961; John Hammond has just given him a test press-

---

* The most hysterical revisionism, in both senses of hysterical, comes with the attempt, in both *Robert Johnson: Lost and Found* and *Escaping the Delta*, to prove the negative that Johnson did not, could not have, would not have sold his soul to the devil—as if by puncturing Johnson's myth (itself presented as a white fantasy, though, like Mack McCormick in New Orleans, Michael Bloomfield spoke of "Johnny Shines, Sunnyland Slim, Muddy Waters, and Elmore James—all of them told me that story"), the authors could extinguish any spark of transcendence in his music. "Many have wondered whether Johnson really sold his soul to the Devil at the crossroads," Cameron Siewert wrote in 2003. "The real question lies in who—or what—Johnson's Devil was" ("Down the Dirt Road: The Quest for America in the Mississippi Delta Blues," senior thesis in anthropology, Princeton University). "I was already aware of the 'myth' of Robert Johnson, of selling his soul to the devil at the crossroads," Jack White wrote in 2007 of coming across *The Complete Robert Johnson* years before. "After finally listening to it, I could believe it. It was so unearthly. I can't fathom it was actually recorded by human beings—that the guy who recorded it on the acetate cutter might have shouted, 'That's a great take, Robert, let's try another.' It doesn't seem possible that someone would sing like that—and, on top of that, that people would think it was interesting enough to record and sell on to other people. It comes down to record companies wanting to sell record players to black families" (*Mojo*, June 2007).

ing of *King of the Delta Blues Singers*. Thrilled by the cover, he rushes to the home of his mentor, the Greenwich Village singer Dave Van Ronk, to play the record. Van Ronk has never heard of Johnson; they put it on. Dylan is thrown back: "The stabbing sounds from the guitar could almost break a window . . . I immediately differentiated between him and anyone else I had ever heard." Van Ronk isn't impressed: "He kept pointing out that this song comes from another song and that one song was an exact replica of a different song." Van Ronk plays Leroy Carr, Skip James, Henry Thomas: " 'See what I mean?' I did see what he meant," Dylan says, speaking of what Woody Guthrie had taken from the Carter Family, "so I didn't think much of whatever it meant." After one of the most precise and detailed analyses written about how Johnson's music not only spoke but spoke in its own language, Dylan takes a step back. "I thought about Johnson a lot, wondered who his audience could have been. It's hard to imagine sharecroppers or plantation field hands at hop joints, relating to songs like these. You have to wonder if Johnson was playing for an audience that only he could see, one off in the future."

For a map of a place that was, *Blues in the Mississippi Night* (Rykodisc) is indispensable, both as a document and as an experience in time travel. Recorded in 1946 by Alan Lomax, falling somewhere between New Deal–era WPA interviews with former slaves and Theodore Rosengarten's *All God's Dangers: The Life of Nate Shaw* (New York: Knopf, 1974), this is bedrock American history: a long talk between Lomax (1915–2002), Memphis Slim (Peter Chatman, 1915–88), Big Bill Broonzy (1893–1958), and John Lee "Sonny Boy" Williamson (1914–48)—talk sometimes sung and played—about peonage, white supremacy, labor, professionalism, violence, death, and the blues tradition. There is a stunning conversation and performance on "Stagger Lee," which is presented as ordinary, everyday life; slavery is not distant here, and there is no new world waiting. The language spoken summons up an ancient world still promising most of all that it will never change: referring to a holster, Memphis Slim speaks of a scabbard. He and his fellow bluesmen were certain they and their families would be killed if their talk was made public, so Lomax locked the tapes away; when he finally released them, in the late '50s, the names of the speakers were changed. Now along with the recorded conversation is a complete, word-for-word transcript: a brutal and poetic prehistory of the civil rights movement, one that can be read alongside Adam Gussow's *Seems Like Murder Here: Southern Violence and the Blues Tradition* (Chicago: Uni-

versity of Chicago, 2002), an academic study of the relationship between blues and the lynching mania that from the 1890s through the
1920s had as great an effect on American social life as the First World
War.

Charley Patton (1887–1934), a rough, fierce singer who may have
had as much influence on Captain Beefheart as he had on Howlin'
Wolf, was the first focal point of the music. He was famous as a wild
entertainer; when the guitarist John Fahey, in his groundbreaking 1970
study *Charley Patton* (London: Studio Vista) wrote that what distinguished delta blues from other styles was that it was "more individual
(perhaps more personal), irregular, and textually incoherent or ambivalent," he could have been writing about Patton alone, because Patton
took the latter qualities to greater extremes than anyone else. Son
House once recalled how shocked he was to hear Patton on record,
where his pieces were shapely, dramatic, and emotionally readable,
since in person, before a crowd, they were often fragments flying
through the air like bats. (See David Hinkley and Debra Rodman's
superb text for *The Rolling Stones: Black and White Blues, 1963*, a collection of photography by Gus Coral, Atlanta: Turner Publishing, 1995.)
Patton's highly popular and consistently promoted recordings, made
between 1929 and 1934, are collected in many forms, most thrillingly
on the ultra–box set *"Screamin; and Hollerin' the Blues": The Worlds of
Charley Patton* (Revenant, 2001), which brings together Patton's recordings (all on the Paramount label of Grafton, Wisconsin, and issued
under his own name, as Elder J. J. Hadley, and as "The Masked Marvel") with work by contemporaries and inheritors, historical and critical
essays by Fahey, Dick Spottswood, David Evans, and others, a reprint
of Fahey's book, a collection of lurid Paramount Records ads for individual titles, and more, all packaged in the form of an album of 78s—
with each of the seven CDs presented on cardboard discs *as* 78s. There
were many photographs, including the single known Patton photo, a
head shot, which had circulated since the early '60s; it was only in 2002
that the entire portrait was discovered. It showed a handsome man with
wavy hair and great authority, dressed in a suit with wide lapels, a bow
tie, a striped shirt, and a pair of gleaming spats. (See John Teftteller,
"Gold in Grafton! Unknown Patton Photo, Paramount Artwork Surface After 70 Years!" *78 Quarterly*, number 12, 2003.) Also worth seeking out are Stephen Calt and Gayle Dean Wardlow's *King of the Delta
Blues Singers: The Life and Music of Charlie Patton* (Newton, New Jersey:
Rock Chapel Press, 1988) and R. Crumb's biography "Patton," in *R.
Crumb Draws the Blues* (London: Knockabout Comics, 1992; it also

includes "That's Life," about the disease of record collecting), where one can find a graceful panel of a "high-strung teenager named Robert Johnson" peeking out from under his cap as two older bluesmen work out a new song.

The music of Son House (1902?–88), either as recorded for Paramount in 1930 or by Columbia and other labels from 1965 on, has enormous presence. House played a heavy, rough guitar; he sang in a deep, muddy voice that nevertheless made space for lyricism, a sort of reverie in the midst of action—what in blues language is called a second mind. Listening to his original recordings, the most distinctive of them fully six minutes long, spread over both sides of a 78 ("My Black Mama," "Preachin' the Blues," "Dry Spell Blues"), you can hear how he might have been a mentor to Robert Johnson, and you can hear how readily Johnson would have taken everything he needed to know from House and gone elsewhere. *Son House and the Great Blues Singers (1928–1930)* (Document) collects the above-mentioned numbers from House, along with his "Walking Blues," and also Willie Brown's 1930 "Future Blues," Kid Bailey's ineffable 1929 "Rowdy Blues" (covered in 2003 with quiet conviction by the Be Good Tanyas on *Chinatown*, Nettwerk America), Garfield Akers's six-minute "Cottonfield Blues," and more. House's *The Complete Library of Congress Sessions, 1941–1942* (Travelin' Man), with Willie Brown and others, are loose and dynamic. Of House's later work, *Father of the Delta Blues: The Complete 1965 Sessions* (Columbia Legacy) is basic; more lively is *The 1970 London Sessions: John the Revelator* (Sequel), recorded at the 100 Club, where six years later the Sex Pistols would take the stage. The "death letter" theme runs all through House's music, from "My Black Mama" on down; no House song has been so insistently taken up by others, and I've tried to trace that line in "Death Letters," included in *Listen Again: A Momentary History of Pop Music*, edited by Eric Weisbard (Durham, NC: Duke, 2007).

Skip James's high voice gives the sense of a bird looking down at human follies it's seen many times before. He was the most individualistic of the Mississippi singers (and guitarists, and pianists); along with Johnson he was most consciously an artist (he gets deeply into theory, practice, and art-market strategy in my "Skip James on Art," in the December 2010 issue of *Oxford American*), and some rank him higher. *Complete 1931 Recordings in Chronological Order* (Document) collects his eighteen original Paramount performances, including the indelible "Devil Got My Woman," the almost mystically reflective "If You Haven't Any Hay Get on Down the Road," and "Special Rider Blues."

James (1902–69) did not record again until his 1964 rediscovery;* of the many recordings he made from that point on, *Skip James/Today!* and *Devil Got My Woman* (Vanguard, 1966, 1968 respectively) are standard, but the best might be the 1964 sessions produced by Fahey, Ed Denson, and Bill Barth, rereleased in 1993 as *She Lyin'* (Genes). A new audience met James in 2001 in *Ghost World*, directed by Terry Zwigoff, in earlier days a collecting buddy of R. Crumb's. Thora Birch's miserable eighteen-year-old punk Enid buys a blues sampler LP from Steve Buscemi's miserable record collector at a yard sale, takes it home, closes the door to her room, drops the needle on a phonograph she probably got for her fifth birthday, and "Devil Got My Woman" fills the room—and it fills her. She goes back the next day, asking Buscemi for "more records like that." "There aren't any more records like that," he says. ("A big fantasy for Terry," Crumb says. "The 18-year-old thinks the cranky, alienated old record-collector nerd is a cool guy and they end up having sex!")

Tommy Johnson (ca. 1896–1956) made fewer than twenty recordings for Victor in Memphis in 1928 and Paramount in Wisconsin in 1929, but they were at once unique and enormously influential; his songs, including "Cool Drink of Water Blues," "Canned Heat Blues," "Slidin' Delta," "Big Mare Blues," and "Big Road Blues" (so freely and powerfully adapted by Canned Heat for Alan Wilson's long, dark daydream "On the Road Again" in 1968; see *Uncanned*, EMI, or Al Wilson, *The Blind Owl*, a painful, rich collection issued by Severn in 2013, forty-three years after Wilson's death) are among the most delicate in the blues, and his slurred, fading moans are a secret language in and of themselves. His *Canned Heat (1928–1929)* (Document) is a displacing production, partly for the inclusion of "Alcohol and Jake Blues," a 78 discovered only in 1989; a test pressing of the crooning but still extreme "I Want Someone to Love Me" was discovered in 2001 and included on the CD sampler that accompanied the 2004 Blues Images calendar. As dramatized in Ethan and Joel Coen's 2000 *O Brother, Where Art Thou?* it was Tommy Johnson who bragged that he had sold his soul to the devil for musical prowess. Hitching a ride with three white fugitives from a chain gang, dressed like a professional bluesman in suit and tie, Chris Thomas King's quietly underplayed Johnson (confused by

---

* "I had to go," John Fahey, then a fanatical record collector, wrote of his part in the quest, "so I could stop playing those accursed records. Answer the questions and destroy my obsessions with them." See "Skip James," a raging, seductive portrait of both James and the sixties blues revival, in *How Bluegrass Music Destroyed My Life*, a book that contains the most sardonically dramatic music writing ever committed to the page (Chicago: Drag City, 2000).

most reviewers with Robert Johnson) relates the transaction he's just pulled off as if he'd talked a storekeeper down a penny for a Coke. Johnson adds startling guitar to a fast version of "Man of Constant Sorrow" and offers a chilling account of Skip James's "Hard Time Killing Floor Blues"; when he's all too quickly seized by the Ku Klux Klan for ritual sacrifice, he figures it's simply the bill coming due sooner than he bargained for.

Paul Oliver's well-illustrated *The Story of the Blues* (Baltimore: Penguin, 1972) tells the story from Africa to Chuck Berry; Peter Guralnick's *Feel Like Going Home* (1971; New York: Back Bay Books, 1999) combines a short country blues history with wonderful portraits of Skip James, Johnny Shines, Howlin' Wolf, and Muddy Waters; Guralnick's *Nighthawk Blues* (1980; New York: Thunder's Mouth, 1988) is a fine novel about the strange process by which forgotten black artists were found in the '60s by white admirers they could hardly have imagined existed; Stephen Calt's *I'd Rather Be the Devil: Skip James and the Blues* (New York: Da Capo, 1994) is an always caustic, occasionally almost demented cautionary tale for anyone who takes blues too casually.

More speculative, and just as essential, are the late Albert Murray's *The Omni-Americans: Some Alternatives to the Folklore of White Supremacy* (1971; New York: Da Capo, 2001) and Michael Ventura's essay on hoodoo, "Hear That Long Snake Moan," from his *Shadow Dancing in the USA* (Los Angeles/New York: Tarcher/St. Martin's, 1985). In very different ways, Murray, a black Harlem novelist and jazz critic, and Ventura, a white Los Angeles movie critic and novelist, argue for blues as the site of the most complete, and the most heroic, version of the American story. And there is Stanley Booth's "Even the Birds Were Blue," an April 16, 1970, *Rolling Stone* piece collected in *The Rolling Stone Rock & Roll Reader*, edited by Ben Fong-Torres (New York: Bantam, 1974), from which I drew in the Johnson chapter; it stands as a moving, depressing account of black bluesmen suffering the good intentions of their white fans, and the finest example of neo–Raymond Chandler prose I know. There is Howard Hampton's summation of Robt. Williams's paintings (*Bookforum*, Winter 1998) as "a Tijuana bible of the American inferno," with "This Sunday's sermon: A TIGER IN EVERY TANK AND A HELLHOUND ON EVERY TRAIL." Which fades into "King of the Delta Blues Singers," a project Rhino Films had in development in 2000, based on a screenplay not only about Robert Johnson but by Robert Johnson. One of those things: it's a common name. There are seventeen in my telephone book, probably as many or more in yours, and one in none.

THE BAND

Music from Big Pink (Capitol) came out late in the summer of 1968, and while it never rose higher than #30 on the charts, it stayed on the charts for nearly a year, and a lot of people thought it was number one anyway. In a review in *Rolling Stone*, Al Kooper called the Band's debut an event, and in youthful communities around the country it was that and more.* The day after the record hit the stores you could hear people on the street singing the chorus to "The Weight"; before long, the music became part of the fabric of daily life. As they had with Dylan songs, people used *Music from Big Pink* as a new way of talking—if not a new way of walking.

The first line of "The Weight" may have come when Robbie Robertson chanced to look into the sound hole of his guitar and saw "C. F. Martin & Co. Nazareth, Pennsylvania"—but only because as a metaphor *Nazareth* is nearly bottomless. The song, Robbie has always said, came out of an immersion in Luis Buñuel—"I was fascinated by a theme in his movies about people trying to do good for others but something would happen and it got turned around"—but it's as well a dramatization of a deeply American instinct for separation, distance, suspicion, the mistrust of community, America as a foreign country with every citizen a stranger, "Don't Tread on Me" as the national motto, unless it's the sign NO TRUST that Melville hangs up in *The Confidence Man*. "Hey Mister can you tell me / Where a man might find a bed / He just grinned and shook my hand / No was all he said," Levon sang in "The Weight"; "In 1679, two Dutch missionaries, Jasper Dankers and Peter Sluyter, rowed over from Brooklyn," Andy Newman wrote in the *New York Times* in 2006. "They found Staten Island aswarm with wildlife but otherwise fairly inhospitable. After getting lost, they came upon an Englishwoman's farmstead. They asked 'for something to drink, and also for someone to show us the road, but she refused the last, although we were willing to pay for it,' they wrote." The piece was called "Trekking Around Staten Island, and Glimpsing the Unknown New York"; even if no one in the Band had ever been to Staten Island, with "The Weight" they had been there and gone.

The leitmotif of the album, I think, was obligation; "The Weight" was obligation in reverse. It was a kind of secret theme, at the heart of

---

* As with many pieces published in English on the Band, Kooper's review can be found on the superb Web site theband.hiof.no.

both words and music: What do men and women owe each other? How do they keep faith? How far can that faith be pushed before it breaks? These are questions community and friendship share, and they arose naturally from men who were preparing to present their partnership to the public, and who, after all their years together out of the light, had to find out what the essence of their particular group identity was.

Certainly "Long Black Veil," the only song on *Music from Big Pink* written by neither the Band nor Bob Dylan, takes obligation as far as it can go. A murder has been committed; a man is singled out from the crowd as the culprit, but he will not give up his alibi, because he's "been in the arms of my best friend's wife."* She keeps silent as well. The singer, the man accused, owes something to her, something to his friend, and something to his community, to justice; the woman won't injure her husband by revealing the secret, and she keeps faith with her lover as he goes to the gallows—allowing him to die with his friendship intact, and then forever after haunting his grave. The song took the shape of an ancient Southern murder ballad, on the order of "Omie Wise" or "Poor Ellen Smith"; it was written in 1959 by Danny Dill and Marijohn Wilkin, and was a country hit for Lefty Frizzell that same year. It was "an instant folk song," Dill told the country music historian Dorothy Horstman—inspired by "The Lady in Black," who appeared annually at the grave of Rudolph Valentino, Red Foley's "God Walks These Hills with Me," and an old news story. "There was a Catholic priest killed in New Jersey many years ago," said Dill, "under a town hall light [a key image in 'Long Black Veil']. There were no less than fifty witnesses. They never found a motive. They never found the man."

Before making *Big Pink*, and after Manuel, Danko, and Hudson had moved into their big pink Woodstock house, the Band, without a name, was fooling around. With Levon still absent in Arkansas, along with Bob Dylan the rest had been recording old songs of all sorts at Dylan's nearby house—the beginnings of the sessions, lasting from the spring of 1967 into early 1968, that became known as the Basement Tapes. When the confabulations moved into the Big Pink basement, the Band tested recording equipment they'd scrounged with two nights of tape they ended up calling "Even If It's a Pig, Parts I and II"—a series of parodies of everything from Liberace to "Stagger Lee," from stumble-bum horn playing by Rick Danko to *Twilight Zone* monologues by

* The same alibi, William A. Adler established in 2011 in *The Man Who Never Died* (New York: Bloomsbury), that the IWW songwriter Joe Hill refused when he was arrested for murder in Utah in 1914—and even as he was executed a year later.

Garth Hudson—that opened a pathway to the absurdist nonsense of so many Basement Tapes performances, and the freedom of language, the trust in gaps and holes, of the songs on *Music from Big Pink*. Most of the results from the Pig nights remain locked away; there is detailed description in my *The Old, Weird America: The World of Bob Dylan's Basement Tapes* (New York: Picador USA, 2011, originally published 1997 as *Invisible Republic*; in the UK, *Invisible Republic*, London: Faber and Faber, 1997). The group backed Tiny Tim on "Be My Baby" and "I Got You Babe" for the hippie film *You Are What You Eat*, a 1968 exploitation number described by Pauline Kael as "the kind of movie about youth one might expect Spiro Agnew or George Wallace to make"; the appalling results can be found on the soundtrack album (Sony) and, for the outtakes "Memphis, Tennessee" and "Sonny Boy," on various bootlegs. More to the point, or a point, with Levon back in the fold, the group began sketching their own songs and recording demos. The old country tunes "I Want to Be a Single Girl Again" (thank you, Levon) and "Little Birdie," the latter a highlight of the Band's early tours that featured Levon on mandolin, have yet to surface. Such stabs in the dark as "Ruben Remus," "Orange Juice Blues," "Bacon Fat," and more were included on the 2005 five-CD (plus DVD) box set *The Band: A Musical History* (Capitol; hereafter *History*), along with the fully realized "Katie's Been Gone," the 1975 demo "Bessie Smith," and "Ain't No More Cane" (a Texas chain gang song popularized by Lead Belly that ranks with the Band's best work), plus "Long Distance Operator" (Manuel singing lead) and the fabulously ribald "Don't Ya Tell Henry" (Levon), both written by Dylan. There is as well perhaps the hottest version known of the often-recorded "Yazoo Street Scandal"; a take with Robbie singing in a conspiratorial whisper can be found on the lovingly made three-CD Band bootleg *Crossing the Great Divide: Genuine Bootleg Series, Vol. 4* (Genuine Bootleg Series; hereafter *Crossing* bootleg).

Capitol's rerelease of all of the Band's albums, other than *The Last Waltz* soundtrack, began in 2000, combining comprehensive remixing and remastering with mostly unnecessary additional tracks on each record—demos and alternate takes that, whatever their merit, disfigured the beginning-to-end shape of the original titles. The augmented *Music from Big Pink* was notable for a more open sound—more room for horns and organ—and, among nine extra tracks, a perfect cover of Charlie Poole and the North Carolina Ramblers' signature number, the 1927 "If I Lose, I Don't Care," a version of "Yazoo Street Scandal," and the early Band tune "Ferdinand the Imposter." Richard Manuel sang in the voice of the last friend of Ferdinand Demara, telling the tale of how the romantic con artist who in the fifties found success as doctor, lawyer, and Indian chief solely on the strength of his charm finally went down; today you can hear Manuel's own story in the song. "Yazoo," first released in 1975 on Bob Dylan and the Band's *The Basement Tapes* (Columbia), is good-humored menace in the vein of Bo Diddley's (and the Hawks') "Who Do You Love," with Levon turning cartwheels in an attempt to keep up with the story. The off-the-wall characters ("The Cotton King," "The Widow," "Breezy," "Sweet William," "Liza"—or is it "Elijah"?) and the sort of Biblical imagery that would sail through *Big Pink* push the tale of a man seduced by the local mystery woman—apparently at the urging of his girlfriend. What's he to make of that? "She rocked me kinda slow, and kinda easy," is all he can tell us.

"It is inconsequential to me who wrote the songs," Harold Bloom wrote in 2002 ("Sound and Vision," *Film Comment*, May–June). "Helm disputes Robertson's assertions as to sole credit, and Manuel evidently made considerable contributions. What matters is that the songs at their best seem always to have been there, until refined by the Band . . . They express the North American loneliness, with its related malaise that no American feels free if she or he is not alone . . . A nihilistic and anarchic quasi-mysticism is endemic in their music. There is, as I have argued elsewhere, a post-Protestant gnosis in North America, which could be called 'the American religion.' The Band's performances, at their most intense, can seem to emanate directly from that gnosis, as the Dylan of 1965–1975 seemed to also. If our freedom is our solitude, it is also our wavering sense that what is best and oldest in us is no part of that creation. A spirituality that unsponsored has its sorrows, some of which the Band caught and rendered permanently." Most of the songs that mapped this territory appeared in the fall of 1969 on *The Band*.

The Band (Capitol, #9) was the group's most popular album, as it deserved to be. "Films about America should be composed entirely of long and wide-shots, as music about America already is," Wim Wenders wrote in 1969; you can figure he'd just heard "Across the Great Divide." The sound of *The Band* was clean and immediate; in every way, the record was easier to hear than *Big Pink*. The 2000 release includes seven alternate takes, most memorably Manuel's "Whispering Pines." The single "Up on Cripple Creek" even got some airplay, rising to #25. In American folklore, Cripple Creek is a place where all fears vanish beyond memory; you can hear the Band's song begin to take shape forty years before in Harry McClintock's 1928 "Big Rock Candy Mountain," where the singer sounds both entranced by the hobo's paradise of the song and as if he's trying to sell you swampland in Florida (included on the soundtrack to the 2000 film *O Brother, Where Art Thou?* Mercury).*

A perfect complement is the video *Classic Albums: "The Band"* (Rhino Video). Directed by Bob Smeaton, this remarkable documentary on the making of the album features Robertson, Helm, Hudson, Danko, and John Simon, producer for both *Big Pink* and *The Band* (not to mention *You Are What You Eat*), sitting at mixing boards, cutting up the original tapes of the songs, deconstructing them piece by piece, instrument by instrument, sometimes note by note, and then putting them back together, re-creating them as you watch, as you take part—an approach I tried to follow in my rejected notes for *History* (see "The Lost Waltz," collected in my *Bob Dylan by Greil Marcus, Writings 1968–2010* [New York: PublicAffairs, 2010; London: Faber and Faber], hereafter *BD by GM*). Levon communicates a bottomless joy as "Rockin' Chair" takes shape as if for the first time; Robbie sits at a piano to play and sing "The Night They Drove Old Dixie Down" like a folk tune, handed down (when he says "It's a time I remember oh so well," you believe he does);† when he breaks down "King Harvest" to show the motor of the music in the bass and drums, explaining that it is in the fall, not the spring, when life is truly renewed, the music explodes like a summer downpour. The video includes some commentary by me, but I added little or nothing to what the filmmakers had already mapped out.

When they first took the likes of "Across the Great Divide" public, the Band encored with Little Richard's 1956 "Slippin' and Slidin'." With Richard Manuel pouncing on the opening notes like a cat, Rick Danko shouting his head off, and Garth Hudson looking like Dostoyevsky, it's best heard in a version from the 1970 Festival Express tour included on *History*, and seen in the documentary *Festival Express* (New Line Home Video)—an otherwise tedious picture, except for a single, blasted singalong on "Ain't No More Cane," with Danko, his face

---

* The Band never had much impact on Top 40 radio; the closest a Band song came to a hit was via Joan Baez's abominable cover of "The Night They Drove Old Dixie Down," #9 in 1971, in which she turned Robert E. Lee, in the Band's version the general, into a boat.

†"A week or two ago," the musician Oliver Hall wrote in 2006, "[we] passed through Greenville, North Carolina, and a wonderful space of appearances called Spazzatorium gallery. Afterwards I sat around with some locals and we sang loud, drunken harmony together: Woody Guthrie, Carter Family, some Civil War ballads I didn't know (one in which 'Jeff Davis rides a dappled gray mare, Abe Lincoln rides a mule'). When we were well in our cups, I began to sing 'The Night They Drove Old Dixie Down,' but after the first chorus, the Southerners begged me to stop. They had tears in their eyes and said the song was too painful for them to sing."

spreading with happiness, leading Janis Joplin, Jerry Garcia and Bob Weir of the Grateful Dead, and Marmaduke of the New Riders of the Purple Sage, who in his Peninsula School days was merely John Dawson.

Stage Fright (Capitol), out in the summer of 1970, climbed a bit higher on the charts than *The Band*—#5—but it was not truly as popular, probably because, as a collection of songs rather than a town or a country, it depicted so accurately the confusion and fragmentation that were its subject. A certain vibrancy was missing; the music was too worked out, too careful—something you can hear in reverse in the wandering freedom of Levon's vocal on the early version of "All La Glory" included on *History*, something that would be completely gone by the time of the master take. "The Rumor," potentially the most compelling of the tunes, was at once over-arranged and unfinished. "*Stage Fright* needs one cut to really shake things up," Dave Marsh wrote; "The Shape I'm In" came close, but it wasn't the one. "Don't Do It," recorded as a studio tryout in Bearsville, planned as a single but left unissued, was.

Collected in full force on the 2000 release of *Cahoots* (and with a thin, don't-shake-things-up sound on *History*), this was hard rock beyond the reach of any band you'd care to name, including, as far as official releases went, the Band itself. Onstage they sometimes risked going out of control to make music that can't be reached any other way; on their albums, never. Here, with a cover of "Baby Don't You Do It," a 1964 Marvin Gaye number they had worked into their act some time before, along with Rick Danko's version of the Four Tops' "Loving You Is Sweeter Than Ever," the Band acknowledged their enormous debt to Motown—the Temptations in their vocals, James Jamerson behind Danko's bass, the essential Motown aesthetic of control and craftsmanship in the music as a whole. But on this one song, the Band outdid Motown as well. They made most rock 'n' roll sound fragile.

What the Band did with Gaye's performance was what white groups usually do with black material: they held to the original arrangement, amplified the beat, turned up the volume, and yelled. They delighted in the technology of two or three electric guitars, an electric organ, super-miked drums. They didn't worry about worrying a line into an elusive rendering of soul; they simply sang as hard as they could.

They hit everything hard. Robertson defines the beat; Levon sounds as if he has four hands, two on each stick. Danko's bass works like fuel injection on a '63 Corvette. Hudson lets loose a screech that stays constant throughout the number, while Manuel hangs on to the edge of the noise, hitting one key on his piano over and over again. "My biggest mistake was loving you too much"—*blam blam*—"and letting you know—"

Gaye's "Baby Don't You Do It" is perfectly adequate. It's narrow in its arrangement, careful in its production. It feels like "Ain't That Peculiar," to which it was the follow-up: immediate genre music, a play on the expectations of an audience that had already bought a similar sound. Motown's strategy of change was always incremental. The Band's version is every man at extremes. Gaye sings against a polite female chorus, and you get the idea his girl won't really do it—break his heart—because, after all, her sisters are right there pleading alongside of him. The Band enlist their full arsenal of voices, each man coming in at his own pace to declaim, "Oh, baby, don't you do it, don't break my heart, *please*, don't do it," marching across the battlefield of broken dreams like an army of men ready to give it all for love. They wail on until they reach the point where the song ought to end, and suddenly Robbie seizes the music and drives straight out of the song. His pals catch up, cut him off, and slam the tune to a close. There were moments like this in the Band's concerts, but there were never enough.

Nineteen seventy-one saw the first Band side project: Robbie produced the debut album of Louisiana-born rockabilly singer Jesse Winchester (1944–2014), whose opposition to the Vietnam war had led him to exile in Canada. *Jesse Winchester* (Ampex),* featuring Robbie on guitar and Levon on drums and mandolin, had a brittle sound and a bitter edge; longing and doubt were all over the music, with small-band punch and a smoky sense of fate. Such projects were relatively infrequent, given the Band's high profile, and rarely as memorable. In 1972 Rick Danko coproduced *Bobby Charles* for the New Orleans singer best known as the composer of "See You Later, Alligator" (Bearsville); in 1975 Levon coproduced and played drums on *The Muddy Waters Woodstock Album* (Chess/MCA), a passable session notable mainly for Cajun accordion by Garth. In 1976 Robbie produced Hirth Martinez's *Hirth from Earth* (Warner Bros.), the suggestion being that the UFO-oriented singer-philosopher Martinez was so strange he was probably from somewhere else, and Neil Diamond's *Beautiful Noise* (Sony), a #4 hit that left the composer of *Jonathan Livingston Seagull* as earthbound as ever.

The Band's own *Cahoots* (Capitol) appeared late in 1971 and peaked

---

* In most cases in the Notes section, both for context and because reissues go in and out of print so rapidly, original labels are cited.

at #21; it was literal where the other records were tantalizing, strained where they moved. There was a flatness in the music, good ideas forced through a banal, didactic mesh. The idea of cahoots was the soul of the group, but nothing about the disc captured it, except perhaps the photograph originally meant for the sleeve. Robbie had chosen an Irving Penn portrait of two Peruvian children (see the anthology *Photographing Children*, New York: Time-Life, 1971): brother and sister, dressed in work clothes and posing formally. They weren't cute. The way they looked at the camera and held their small bodies told you they would stick to each other as long as they could. Capitol vetoed it because someone, no doubt remembering the old story of the Peruvian child who gave birth at the age of eight, thought the little girl looked pregnant.

Rock of Ages (Capitol), a two-record set recorded at the Academy of Music in New York City, mainly on New Year's Eve 1971, and released in the fall of 1972, hit #6. The sound was deep and full, the Band was blazing, and the horn men—New York jazzmen on a busman's holiday with the strong, witty charts of Allen Toussaint, the premier rock 'n' roll producer of New Orleans—added a new dimension to mostly familiar material. On almost every song, the Band and their horn section outran studio versions. They fought over "Chest Fever"; it took on a strident urgency as the horn men slapped back at Levon's hammering drums near the end. "Rag Mama Rag" was the knockout; Rick Danko's opening slices on his fiddle just before the song kicked off were inexplicably spooky, and Howard Johnson's unhinged tuba solo ranks with anything King Curtis played with the Coasters—or Ronnie Hawkins. The performance of "Loving You Is Sweeter Than Ever" on the 2001 rerelease, also included on *History*, combines Danko's impassioned lead with a hard, chopping beat and Levon's back-country shouts; here as elsewhere on the many added tracks one can hear the Band's crossing vocals and the camaraderie they signified return with a vengeance. That quality stands out at its fullest on "The Soundboard Mix" discs on the 4-CD plus DVD package titled *Live at the Academy of Music 1971* (Capitol, 2013), all surprise, chance, luck, shooting blind without targets and hitting them anyway.

Toussaint dug down into New Orleans traditions for his charts—into Dixieland, blues, Zydeco accordion riffs, '50s and '60s rock. There had always been a lot of New Orleans in the Band, especially the wild piano and general hilarity of Huey "Piano" Smith, and Toussaint brought it to the surface. The riff he used to open up the encore, Chuck

Willis's 1958 "(I Don't Want To) Hang Up My Rock and Roll Shoes," runs "Dat *DAH* (boomp boomp) / Dat *DAH* (boomp boomp)," and it teases the memory—because it's one of those timeless fragments that can pop up anywhere, like a country blues line in a Top 40 hit, for a moment seemingly tying all of American music together. That little rhythmic signature linked the Band to the first bars of Shirley and Lee's 1956 Crescent City classic, "Let the Good Times Roll"; to the pre-jazz, second line funeral marches of the 1890s; and to the unique New Orleans singer Richard "Rabbit" Brown, who probably got more feeling out of the notes than anyone else when he used them to open his 1927 "James Alley Blues," which I sometimes think is the greatest record ever made. "I seen better days," Brown sang. "But I'm puttin' up with these." The performance is best heard on the *Anthology of American Folk Music*, compiled by Harry Smith for Folkways in 1952, reissued by Smithsonian Folkways in 1997; along with Brown's four other recordings, it can be found on the anthology *The Greatest Songsters: Complete Recorded Works (1927–1929)* (Document).

Rock of Ages also showcased Garth Hudson's crazy concert piano on "The Weight"; his long organ fantasia, which from the Band's first tours grew out of the fanfare that begins "Chest Fever" (the lead-in here titled "The Genetic Method," a walk through nineteenth-century popular music, from stovepipes to bandboxes to parlor music to merry-go-rounds, with a pause for "Auld Lang Syne," though the *Academy of Music* reissue includes a version that leans more to Porky Pig and Betty Boop); a staggering "Don't Do It"; and a tune written years earlier but not released, "Get Up Jake." This last—about a man so lazy the whole town turns out to watch him get out of bed—was in some ways the best of all. "Me and Jake worked out on the river, on a ferry called the *Baltimore*," it began: one of those commonplace evocations of a hazy frontier the Band had made their own. It's a very modest performance; Garth never played more prettily. The original 1968 studio recording, dating to the sessions for *The Band*, first turned up as the misidentified flipside of the Band's 1973 single "Ain't Got No Home"; it's now collected on *History*, with an alternate take on the 2000 release of *The Band*.

Other mid-career live recordings include the five numbers with Bob Dylan on the 2001 *Rock of Ages*, most notably "Like a Rolling Stone," where Jimi Hendrix, as he sang the song at the Monterey Pop Festival in 1967, seems to be coming out of Dylan's mouth ("We haven't played this in six years—sixteen years," you can hear someone say on the *Academy of Music* set); four 1971 London performances on *History*; on *Across the Great Divide*, a botched three-CD box set Capitol issued in 1994,

"Ain't No More Cane" from the 1969 Woodstock festival, a 1970 "Slippin' and Slidin'," and, credited to the 1975 Watkins Glen Festival, which took place in 1973, Chuck Berry's "Back to Memphis," "Don't Ya Tell Henry," and Hudson's instrumental "Too Wet to Work," an attempt at stop-the-rain magic augmented by what sound like dubbed-in thunderclaps. More Woodstock numbers—"Long Black Veil," "The Weight," "Loving You Is Sweeter Than Ever"—appeared in 1994 on the four-CD set *Woodstock: Three Days of Peace and Music: Twenty-fifth Anniversary Collection* (Atlantic).

Moondog Matinee came out late in 1973. The title was a tip of the hat to Alan Freed's founding 1951 Cleveland rock 'n' roll radio show (the "Moondog Rock 'n' Roll Party" on WJW, which featured black rock 'n' roll exclusively), to which all of the future Band members listened at the time ("That's when I realized there were people over there having more fun than I was," Garth once said). Edward Kasper's detailed sleeve painting pictured Danko, Manuel, Helm, Hudson, and Robertson as they were in 1973, haunting the Cabbagetown Café, a Toronto dive that once knew them as the Hawks. Made up of rock classics they often played in those days, the album sold poorly, topping out at #28, even though it coincided with the Band's 1974 tour with Bob Dylan, up to that time likely the most publicized outing in rock history.

Moondog Matinee held some of the Band's best music—flop or not. (Robbie had the idea that the instrumental "Third Man Theme" was going to be the Top 40 hit the Band never had—hey, in 1950 it was a number one hit *twice*—but while a single was released, it went nowhere.) The six throwaway additional numbers on the 2001 version of the album were highlighted by "Shakin'," a primitive sketch with a Levon Helm vocal that sounds less like the Band than Levon and the Hawks sneaking into a studio in 1964, somewhere in Texas, then running out with a demo they had no time to get right.

The album went places the Band hadn't reached before. "Share Your Love" outclassed Bobby Bland's original; Manuel had more to give the song, and Garth's knack of making his Lowrey organ sound like a complete string section added great warmth. "Mystery Train" was almost completely retooled by Robertson; he kept the first verse, added two of his own, and made up the chords from scratch. After a haint-ridden false start, the Band climbed onto the train like bindle stiffs, the music dark and funny; when Robbie's new lyrics emerged, they sounded as if they'd been in the song since it was first sung, seventy years or twice as long before. Levon cried,

Come down to the station meet my baby at the gate
Ask the station master if the train's running late
He said If you're a-waitin' on that 4:44
I hate to tell you son that train don't stop here anymore

"I tried to get to that old Robert Johnson-Arthur Crudup mood," Robbie said. He did; those were the best lines he'd written since *The Band.*

Northern Lights—Southern Cross (Capitol) appeared in 1975. As the Band's first album of new material since 1971, it proved disappointingly quiet, and reached only #26 on the charts. The action took place between the lines; if *Moondog Matinee* was Richard Manuel's album, this one, despite the fact that Robbie wrote all the songs, was Garth Hudson's. He played with deceptive anonymity; his music worked as a presence, tapestries hung in back rooms. No nuance escaped him—no shade of emotion, no matter how elusive, seemed beyond him. The set's big piece, "Acadian Driftwood," the story of French Canadians forced to migrate to Louisiana, where they turned into Cajuns, aimed for the level of *The Band,* and missed.

Nineteen seventy-six saw the release of *The Best of the Band* (Capitol), which included one previously unissued cut, "Twilight," here so prettified it evaporates as it's played, though the song took other forms. A cracked and soulful demo, with a vocal by Robbie, appears on *History*; Danko recorded a free, passionate version in 1988 (included on his *Cryin' Heart Blues,* Other People's Music, 2005). There was a new single in the fall, a remake of Ray Charles's "Georgia on My Mind," nicely sung by Manuel and meant as the Band's endorsement of Jimmy Carter for the presidency. The flip, appropriately enough, was "The Night They Drove Old Dixie Down." The disc missed the charts, but Jimmy was said to be pleased.

Shortly after Carter's election, on Thanksgiving night, the Band formally ended their years together on the road with "The Last Waltz," a long, star-laden concert at Winterland in San Francisco, where they had made their formal debut seven and a half years before. On hand to perform (with the Band backing them up) were Paul Butterfield, Ronnie Hawkins, Muddy Waters, Dr. John, Bobby Charles, Van Morrison, Joni Mitchell, Neil Young, Neil Diamond, Eric Clapton, and Bob Dylan, plus a *Rock of Ages*-style horn section (my "The Band's Last Waltz," from *Rolling Stone,* included in *BD by GM* as "That Train Don't Stop Here Anymore," is a walk through the night). Robbie promised the farewell did not mean the Band was breaking up—"The Band will never break up," he said, echoing Otis Redding's "I've Been Loving You Too Long (To Stop Now)," "it's too late to break up"—but that was what it meant.

It was a year and a half after Thanksgiving 1976 before the film and album of the concert appeared; in between, in 1977, came *Islands* (Capitol), the Band's weakest and weakest-selling album (#64), which was notable for "Georgia on My Mind," a dead-horse cover of Sam and Dave's "Ain't That a Lotta Love," and two small gems: "Knockin' Lost John," a tune about the Great Depression (sung by Robertson) and "Livin' in a Dream," a lovely Levon Helm reverie based on "Row Row Row Your Boat."

The Last Waltz, directed by Martin Scorsese, was released in the spring of 1978; it was an immediate hit (the 2002 MGM DVD release includes commentary by Scorsese, Robertson, many other participants, and me; my "Save the Last Waltz for Me," from *New West*, collected in *BD by GM*, recounts a conversation with Robertson and Scorsese on the night of the film's premiere). The strongest moments came with Muddy Waters's performance of "Mannish Boy": for seven minutes, the camera kept Waters in tight focus, his face lit by a single ghostly spot, and he held the screen like no singer before him. The *Last Waltz* album, a three-LP set (superseded in 2002 by a vastly expanded four-CD Rhino/Warner Bros. box set that includes ferocious rehearsal versions of Van Morrison's "Tura Lura Lural" and "Caravan," and which reduces "Chest Fever" to an appallingly few seconds of Hudson's introduction and an elephantine horn finale—like the chopped-up Top 40 version of the Doors' "Light My Fire," only without Jim Morrison) was not nearly as popular as the film, though it reached #16, and lacked the rough clatter of the in-theater soundtrack. Highlights are a ripping "Who Do You Love," sung by Ronnie Hawkins and powered by Garth; "Mystery Train" (the Junior Parker/Elvis Presley version), with a hurricane vocal by Levon and perhaps the strongest harp work of Paul Butterfield's career;* "The Night They Drove Old Dixie Down," which Levon sang with an anger he'd never before given the song; a stunning "Caravan"; and the two takes of "Baby Let Me Follow You Down" with which Bob Dylan opened and closed his set—ragged, fleshy shouts that cut through the professionalism everyone else brought to their perfor-

---

* He had sung the song himself in 1965, on his own band's first album (see *The Paul Butterfield Blues Band—An Anthology—The Elektra Years*, Elektra); his night with the Band was perhaps the last great moment of a life that came to a wasted end with Butterfield's death from a heroin overdose in 1987, an event that closes "Paul Butterfield: The Final Note," Tom Ellis III's account of Butterfield's Woodstock years and his work with Levon Helm and others (*Blues Access* number 31, Fall 1997).

mances, shots in the dark that revealed the unsettled nation everyone else thought they were singing about.

The last section of *The Last Waltz* set was made up of studio material; there was the new "Out of the Blue," with a careful but lovely vocal from Robertson, and a new recording of "The Weight," with Levon, Rick, and the rhythm 'n' gospel singers Pop Staples and his daughter Mavis Staples trading the verses back and forth. Exactly what Elvis was presumably aiming for in "An American Trilogy," the performance quite intentionally took in the whole of the country: blacks and whites, men and women, Northerners and Southerners, immigrants and the native-born, the old and the young. It was also a dirge, dark and pietistically apocalyptic. It seemed to end the Band's story right where it had begun.

Endings are never so simple, or so shapely. Over the next years, Danko, Helm, Hudson, and Manuel would again take up the name of the group. Manuel would die in 1986, Danko in 1999, and Helm in 2012. There were decades of mediocrity, and moments when the present must have seemed at least half as real as the past.

After the demise of the group, the various members contributed star turns to albums by various other people, none of the contributions particularly memorable—Levon and Danko had been there and gone in 1974 with Neil Young's *On the Beach* (Reprise), especially with "Revolution Blues," where you could feel the Manson Family coming right out of the ground.

In 1977 Rick Danko, whose singing had become impossibly mannered after *Stage Fright*, made a desultory solo album, *Rick Danko* (Arista, number 119), and an instructional video, *Rick Danko's Electric Bass Techniques* (Homespun Tapes). Dating from the late 1980s are live radio performances featuring has-beens and never-weres from the Woodstock folkie crowd as assembled on Arnie and Happy Traum's WAMC-FM show; collected on two *Bring It on Home* anthologies are Danko's "Blue Tail Fly" (Garth on piano), a tough "Mystery Train," a long, satisfying version of Buddy Holly's "Raining in My Heart," and a late-night (i.e., drunk) group massacre of "The Weight." Danko was much the best voice on the *Danko/Fjeld/Anderson* collaboration with the sixties folk singer Eric Anderson and the Norwegian singer-songwriter Jonas Fjeld (Rykodisc, 1991), especially for a version of Chris Kenner's "Sick and Tired." A follow-up recorded in 1994, *Ridin' the Blinds* (Rykodisc), lacking any distinguished original songs, was much stronger: a combination, in its sound, of muscle and resignation. *One More Shot* (Appleseed, 2002) collected the first album along with a 1991 concert from Norway.

* * *

Levon Helm became a good movie actor, debuting as Loretta Lynn's father in *Coal Miner's Daughter* (1980—he looked great in a coffin) and, for the soundtrack (MCA), cutting a version of "Blue Moon of Kentucky." ("I had to swallow hard," Helm once said, "and ask the producer how he'd like to follow the Blue Grass Boys and Elvis Presley.") In 1983 he played Chuck Yeager's sidekick in *The Right Stuff* as a white Stepin Fetchit; the 1986 *The Man Outside* (an anthropologist goes looking for a lawyer hiding out in the Arkansas hills) made room for Danko, Manuel, and Hudson; in the 1989 Lee Grant film *Staying Together*, Helm sang "Hotel Buick," a tune about living in your car ("The room service is terrible") by Stan Szelest, the Hawks pianist Richard Manuel replaced in 1962. One of Helm's odder movies was the 1997 *Fire Down Below*, where the left-wing action star Steven Segal, operating in a correctly pronounced Appalachia, played perhaps the first non-wimp EPA agent in film history, kicking major toxic-waste butt, taking on the coal companies, and finally busting Kris Kristofferson's Mr. Big ("I own this state, so what's the problem?"). Helm was Reverend Goodall, a compromised but decent man who's burned to death in his church when he goes over to Segal's side, though next to him Helm looked like an elf (filmed in Hazard, Kentucky, with most of the songs by Segal). In 2004, in *The Three Burials of Melquiades Estrada*, hero Tommy Lee Jones comes across the "Old Man with Radio"— Helm as a blind desert rat, clutching a bottle and railing against his faithless progeny. "Shoot me," he says. In 2007 he played the ghost of Confederate General John Bell Hood in *In the Electric Mist*, Bernard Tavernier's adaptation of James Lee Burke's Dave Robicheaux mystery.

Helm made a flat album with Paul Butterfield, Dr. John, and Booker T & the MG's, *Levon Helm and the RCO All-Stars* (ABC, 1977, #142); a vaporous one with Muscle Shoals backup, *Levon Helm* (ABC, 1978); running out of titles, another *Levon Helm* in 1982 (Capitol); and in between, in 1980, drawing on tracks spun off from soundtrack sessions for *Coal Miner's Daughter* and cut with many of the Nashville musicians who worked on Bob Dylan's *Blonde on Blonde*, an album worthy of his name, *American Son* (MCA). That same year he teamed with the country singer Johnny Paycheck for the double-billed *Live from the Lone Star Cafe* (LSC) and signed up with Johnny Cash, Charlie Daniels, Eric Clapton, Rosanne Cash, and others less notable for Paul Kennerley's soundtrack to a would-be movie that featured Helm on numerous sub-Band Americana numbers ("Quantrill's Guerillas," "Northfield: The Plan"), later available under Kennerley's name as *White Mansions/The*

Legend of Jesse James (A&M). In 1989 Helm and Rick Danko joined Ringo Starr and His All-Starr Band both for Starr's hit studio albums and for star turns of their own on "The Weight" and "Raining in My Heart" (captured at the Hollywood Bowl on the appropriately titled 1990 Rykodisc album). Helm's *RCO All-Stars Live at the Palladium NYC New Year's Eve* 1977 (Levon Helm Studios) did not appear until 2002; the unusually punctuated Helm retrospective *The Ties That Bind: The Best of . . . 1975–1996* (Raven), drawn from late and post-Robertson Band material as well as from Helm's solo records, included an awful duet on "Rock Salt & Nails" from John Martyn's 1993 *No Little Boy*; it did not include Levon's 1986 Lone Star Cafe duet with Bob Dylan on "The Weight," with Dylan taking Helm's original parts and Helm taking Rick Danko's—a priceless mess followed by a sizzling Dylan lead on Chuck Berry's "Nadine," with Levon wailing in the background (on the *Crossing* bootleg). Helm's own Homespun instructional video, *Levon Helm on Drums and Drumming*, was highlighted by his insistence that his primary formative percussive influences were Peck Curtis of Sonny Boy Williamson's *King Biscuit Flower Hour* band (no surprise) and the Grambling State Marching Band (the nation reeled, then sat up and said, "Yeah, why didn't I think of that?").

Watching *The Last Waltz*, many people thought Scorsese was positioning Robbie as a movie star (see Stephen E. Severn's "Robbie Robertson's Big Break," *Film Quarterly*, Winter 2002–03); it was no surprise when he too went into movie work. In 1981 he coproduced, cowrote, and with Jodi Foster and Gary Busey starred in *Carny*, an atmospheric film about a grifter's world he knew from the inside; the soundtrack (Warner Bros.) featured his version of Fats Domino's first record, "The Fat Man." He scored or produced source music for Scorsese's *Raging Bull* (1981—the augmented soundtrack on Capitol is a marvelous collection of forties pop songs, swing, Italian airs and laments, from Frankie Laine's "That's My Desire" to Patricio Teixeira's "Nao Tenho Lagrimas"), *The King of Comedy* (1983, Warner Bros., #162, featuring a Robertson vocal on "Between Trains"), *The Color of Money*, a film where the soundtrack music, or rampant noise, had more life than anything on the screen (1986, MCA, #81), and *Casino*, where again the soundtrack, a storm of songs from the Velvetones' 1957 "The Glory of Love" to a harrowing, previously unheard alternate take of the Rolling Stones' "Gimmie Shelter," blew the flimsy movie off the screen (1995, MCA). He contributed tunes to the 1993 nowhere film *Jimmy Hollywood* (Atlas), and "Canon (Part 2) (includes 'Playing Chess with Bobby Fischer at Bellevue Reverie')," a cool, backstreet reading from Charles Mingus's autobiography, *Beneath the Underdog*, for producer Hal Willner's tribute album *Weird Nightmares—Meditations on Mingus* (Columbia, 1992). For years Robertson produced the performance segments of the Rock & Roll Hall of Fame inductions, which in 1994 included the Band itself.

Aside from a contribution to "Between Trains" for the *King of Comedy* soundtrack, plus occasional wispy backups here and there, Richard Manuel went missing on record; the heartbreaker "She Knows," recorded in 1986 with Danko and Hudson, did not surface until 1994, on the *Across the Great Divide* set.

Garth Hudson was like a mole in the ground, under his own name appearing when he could be least expected, disappearing as soon as your head turned. In 1980 he worked with the sculptor Tom Duquette at the Armory of the California Museum of Science and Industry in Los Angeles on the "celebratory environment" *Our Lady Queen of the Angels*, a vast exposition of gigantic religious figures in a setting that glowed with suggestions of miracles and spells; Aimee Semple McPherson would have been right at home. With Garth's shifting, dream-like textures, folding Walt Disney's *Fantasia* into half-speed tapes of wrens chirping, "Amazing Grace" into ragtime, you heard an old man remembering not faces, words, or deeds, but weather. Hudson's *Music for Our Lady Queen of the Angels* (originally released in 1980 as a cassette on his own Buscador label, issued on CD in 2005 by Other People's Music) used synthesizers, vocoders, organ, accordion, and saxophone, the voices of Hudson's wife, Maud Hudson, Richard Manuel, his wife Arlie Starr, and more, not to mention a poem by Ray Bradbury read by Charlton Heston, to create a Los Angeles that, called into being by the Virgin Mary, might be reclaimed by the desert. In 1981, with Manuel, he composed instrumental music for the soundtrack to *Kent State* (RCA); through much of the decade Hudson worked with the Santa Cruz post-punk band the Call ("I liked their seriousness about social issues," he said), and gigged regularly with the wonderfully named Shutouts, a Southern California country combo. In 1985, again with Manuel, he contributed to "Best of Everything" on Tom Petty and the Heartbreakers' *Southern Accents* (MCA); in 1999, with Rick Danko, he was part of "Gone Again" on the Indigo Girls' *Come on Now Social* (Epic). In 1989 Hal Willner recruited Hudson for a Marianne Faithfull concert at St. Anne's Church in Brooklyn, released the next year as *Blazing Away* (Island), and for his Disney-music tribute album *Stay Awake* (A&M—Garth offered "Feed the

Birds"); the next year Willner talked Hudson into a solo concert of his own at St. Anne's, with the music ranging from Ontario to Alabama to Romania. In 1998 Hudson offered the lay-back-in-your-daddy's-arms reverie "Garth Largo" to Rob Hyman's project *Largo* (Mercury), playing organ, synthesizer, accordion, and gorgeous soprano and tenor saxophones, with Maud Hudson adding old-west harmonies. The set is somewhat corny—along with David Forman, Levon came up with a front-porch number called "Gimmie a Stone"—but worth seeking out for the Hudsons alone. That same year, along with Levon and his daughter Amy Helm, Garth took part in Mercury Rev's impenetrably pretentious sessions for *Deserter's Songs* (V2), playing alto and tenor saxophones on "Hudson Lane." The album title borrowed a skeptical writer's description of Dylan and the Hawks' 1967 basement-tapes recordings: the boys hiding out in the Catskills while the war raged outside. For all I know this was recorded in the same basement, but someone forgot to let the air in.

Absent Robertson, the Band re-formed in 1984 as an oldies act, with a fill-in guitarist and occasionally other musicians. It was the ultimate indignity, the final rock 'n' roll self-humiliation, the earthly version of the Great Car Wash in the Sky, but they needed the money and, no doubt, the audiences. They went back to where they'd been twenty years before, mixing their own tunes with R&B classics and whatever was on the jukebox, be it J. J. Cale or Lionel Richie; on May 4, 1986, after a show at the Cheek to Cheek Lounge in Winter Park, Florida, Richard Manuel went next door to his motel room, wrapped his belt around the shower curtain rod, and hung himself. He was forty-two. The two-CD Manuel bootleg *The Last Moving Shadows* (Massive Attack), drawn from scattershot 1980s shows in various combinations, made it clear what Manuel had left behind: nightclubs full of clinking glasses, boorish audiences, the shame of reaching for one's own soul even there. There is a fine "You Don't Know Me" from Tokyo, a horribly self-parodying "Unfaithful Servant" with Rick Danko, then an entire set from the Lone Star Cafe on February 8, 1986, Manuel's last performance in New York. Levon briefly fights off the crowd with a harp solo on "Milk Cow Blues" ("Heee-HAH!" someone shouts, in tribute to the Southerner, as others bark and howl like dogs); Manuel gives in on "Ain't Got No Home." "I'm a lonely boy," he sings. "But I feel lower than a junkie." He gets back everything he threw away with a deep, slow "Share Your Love" (mistitled "Ill Wind Blowin'"), then waits for the night to end. There is the less compelling Manuel set *Whispering Pines: Live at the Getaway*

1985 (Other People's Music, 2005); it begins well, with the warm "Grow Too Old," written by Bobby Charles, Fats Domino, and David Bartholomew (as "Silver and Gold," the song was heartbreakingly covered on Joe Strummer's posthumously released *Streetcore*, Hellcat, 2003), and then slips. In some ways, Manuel wrote his own epitaph fifteen years before the fact, with a performance of "I Shall Be Released" from the New Year's Eve show that produced *Rock of Ages*, and which can now be found on *Live at the Academy of Music 1971*. He sings very slowly; his voice is terribly high, scratching, damaged, the sound of a man at the end of his rope. "I shall be released"—that night, his only intention could have been to give the line the lie.

Robertson included a song about Manuel, "Fallen Angel," on *Robbie Robertson* (Geffen, 1987, #38), his first solo album. Save for a song here and there on the Scorsese soundtracks, this was his first significant music since *The Last Waltz*: a concept album about the complexities of North American identity, with Robertson himself as "The Half-Breed" (Robertson's mother was Mohawk, his father Jewish) at the center. With small contributions from Danko and Hudson and more prominent offerings from members of U2, Peter Gabriel, Gil Evans, and Maria McKee, the record was vastly overproduced and labored; it received enormous publicity and celebratory, fawning reviews, but all I heard was grandiosity without detail, stories without wit, ambition without goals.

The 1991 *Storyville* (Geffen, #69) was different. It had a clean sound and a sly demeanor; such New Orleans stalwarts as the Meters, Aaron Neville, the Rebirth Jazz Band, and Chief Bo Dollis of the Wild Magnolias (not to mention Garth Hudson) did not get in the way. Robertson's voice, draped with damask curtains on the previous album, was smoked, airy, pinched, ranging from a whisper to a rasp, but most of all it was unprotected, which it to say believable. The story in *Storyville*—the legendary New Orleans red-light district—was spectral, outside of any references to gumbo or second line; the music began with a "Night Parade" and followed it.

In 1994, Robbie released *Music from "The Native Americans"* (Capitol), the soundtrack to a television documentary; credited to Robertson and the Red Road Ensemble, the work brought together compositions and performances by numerous writers and musicians, but a sensibility of loss—sentimental, bitter, expansive—was present throughout. The strongest number was perhaps "Akuta Tuta," an Innu chant about home ground by the Northwest Quebec group Kashtin, with Robertson on guitar; Daniel Jean's violin took to the skies and, in harmonies, the other musicians pursued, swirled, and caught up with him. The ambitious and fully realized *Contact from the Underworld of Redboy* (Capitol) came four years later. It was an intricate but flowing collaboration on Indian identity with, among others, Leah Hicks-Manning, Laura Sutterfield, DJ Premier, the Six Nations Women Singers, Verdell Primeaux, Johnny Mike, and the imprisoned Native American activist Leonard Peltier; the result was at once traditional and personal. Where all of this came from was traced in Findlay Bunting's 1995 documentary *Robbie Robertson: Coming Home* (Cherry Lane/Brilliant Media), which included stills of a very geeky teenage would-be guitar hero. In a sense Robbie produced his own version with the 2011 *How to Become Clairvoyant* (Macrobiotic/429). It opened with a young Robertson meeting Sonny Boy Williamson ("He wore a striped suit and used someone else's name") and moved on to the end of the Band with "This Is Where I Get Off." The song's title caught the hipster reserve that was the engine of the music, regardless of the uninspired contributions by Eric Clapton and Tom Morello: the feeling was that of a man watching a movie from the shadows of his own life, like the woman in the Hopper painting. In lieu of a long-promised autobiography, in 2013 Robbie—along with his son Sebastian Robertson and others—published a children's history lesson, *Legends, Icons & Rebels: Music That Changed the World* (Toronto: Tundra). That same year he dropped the likes of Elmore James's "Dust My Broom" and Howlin' Wolf's "Smokestack Lightning" into Scorsese's *The Wolf of Wall Street*, with the harsh, alluring music all but calling for the characters in the hollow, hysterical film to step out of the movie and address the audience, or James and Wolf, directly: "I'm not worthy." A hint of the stories Robertson has yet to tell can be found in a long interview he did with Tony Scherman, published as "Youngblood: The Wild Youth of Robbie Robertson" (*Musician*, December 1991).

After Richard Manuel's death, the Band took a third form with three new, putatively full-time members: drummer Randy Ciarlante, keyboard player Richard Bell, and guitarist Jim Weider. In 1990 the group appeared as part of Roger Waters's egomaniacal production *The Wall: Live in Berlin* (Mercury—Garth's synthesizer all but provided a sound-and-light show for Van Morrison on "Comfortably Numb," in 2006 a soundtrack highlight of Martin Scorsese's *The Departed*) and in 1992 as part of the endless retinue of Bob Dylan's *30th Anniversary Concert Celebration* (Columbia Legacy), essaying a feeble performance of their always inferior version of Dylan's "When I Paint My Masterpiece." In 1993 the Band added their voices to Bill Clinton's inaugural celebrations—at the Arkansas ball, with both Ronnie Hawkins and Bob

Dylan joining in. In 1994 they were present for the twenty-fifth-anniversary reprise of the Woodstock Festival in Saugerties, New York, joined by Bob Weir of the Grateful Dead, Bruce Hornsby, and others.

In 1993 the band released *Jericho* (Pyramid, #166), a long-delayed return to recording: so long delayed that its highlight was "Country Boy," a tune Richard Manuel had cut in 1985; the set also included piano by Stan Szelest, who had died in 1991. Unpromisingly, the cover art featured a painting of the long-abandoned Big Pink, a caption to a tribute photo misspelled Richard Manuel's name, and it was all down-hill from there.* Though the opening cut, "Remedy," had lift to it, the disc revealed a dispirited poverty of material, with pointless covers of Bruce Springsteen's "Atlantic City," Bob Dylan's radioactive "Blind Willie McTell," Muddy Waters's pro forma "Stuff You Gotta Watch," and a long, dull rendition of the born-dull "Blues Stay Away from Me," not to mention one true atrocity, "Amazon (River of Dreams)," an environmentalist protest song by Artie Traum. For three men whose grasp of roots music should have been without limits, the album made no sense. Oddly, on the *Crossing* bootleg, one can find a demo of "Blind Willie McTell" where Levon sounds as if he knew the man (he could have), and an "Atlantic City" demo where he sounds ready to cut his wrists. That such spirits were gone by the time the master takes were committed to tape only spoke again for the fear of going too far, of letting the music sing the singer rather than the other way around, that had dogged the Band since 1968.

In 1995, on *Till the Night Is Gone—A Tribute to Doc Pomus* (Forward/ Rhino), a vibrant collection of covers of songs cocomposed by the great New York tunesmith the Hawks met in the early '60s (a photo of Pomus, 1925–91, attending one of the concerts that produced *Rock of Ages*, was among the liner illustrations for the LP release of the set), there was a dirty-old-men's version of the Leiber-Stoller-Pomus "Young Blood," first done by the Coasters in 1957. With Levon leading in his creaking-porch voice, the Band may not have matched the contributions of Rosanne Cash ("I Count the Tears") or Bob Dylan ("Boogie Woogie Country Boy"), but the cut did mark Garth's legitimate vocal debut, closing out the spoken choruses. "Lookee there," said Helm, the rail-thin ancient stud ogling girls passing on the corner. "Lookee there,"

---

* The Pyramid label's other big release of the time was *Nothing Good Comes Easy* by Roger Clinton, Bill Clinton's black-sheep younger brother; my "The Roger Clinton Experience," about a Clinton-for-President show that Roger Clinton and his band played in San Francisco in 1992, is in my *Double Trouble: Bill Clinton and Elvis Presley in a Land of No Alternatives* (New York: Picador USA, 2001).

agreed Danko, portly now, but with a huge grin. "Lookee *thaaaar*," said the man with the long white beard.

In 1996 the Band worked with the Crickets for a sharp version of the title tune of *Not Fade Away (Remembering Buddy Holly)* (Decca), and then released their own *High on the Hog* (Pyramid). It was a long leap past *Jericho*; this Band would never make rock 'n' roll history, but it was, it seemed, a band again. The key was "Crazy Mama"—if the Band could get nearly five sensuous minutes out of J. J. Cale's dragging circle dance, they could turn En Vogue's 1992 hit "Free Your Mind" into a country manifesto. Rick Danko rarely sounded more bereft, or more convincing, than he did on "Where I Should Always Be," which unmasked a pathos the Band had seemingly buried with Richard Manuel, whose "She Knows" was present as well. On the road in 1996, the group was part icon, part honky-tonk, looser than they had ever been in their glory days, and in moments more emotional. "Blind Willie McTell" was slowed down into a séance that seemed almost to bring its namesake onto the stage; "Where I Should Always Be" climbed past its recorded version; Band standards were dropped without protest. The shame of failure lifted off.

Nineteen ninety-seven saw the Band joining with Keith Richards for "A Deuce and a Quarter," a contribution to Scotty Moore and D. J. Fontana's *All the King's Men* (Sweetfish—keyed to the publication of Moore's memoir, *That's All Right, Elvis*, itself keyed to the twentieth anniversary of Elvis's death); later in the year Weider, Bell, and Ciarlante worked with original Rock 'n' Roll Trio guitarist Paul Burlison on *Train Kept A-Rollin'* (Sweetfish), with Levon taking the lead on "Hound Dog." As winter turned the group began recording again, writing songs, tossing ideas back and forth in Levon's Woodstock studio. The result was *Jubilation* (River North/Platinum Entertainment), which in its best moments turned the Band into a small-time outfit that could trip you up, offering more than you had any reason to expect in the middle of a newly written tune you could swear you'd heard before. The Band became an old-timey combo, not that far from the New Lost City Ramblers of the '50s or the Skillet Lickers of the '20s, moving with the sound of a car held together with rubber bands and chicken-coop wire—with the feeling, as Danko put it on the first track, of a "Book Faded Brown." Highlights included "Last Train to Memphis," written by Bobby Charles, "White Cadillac" (Ronnie Hawkins's car in the early '60s), and Allen Toussaint's "You See Me," but the record mapped unknown ground with its last track, a solo Hudson improvisation on synthesizer and saxophones called "French Girls." Garth allowed himself only two minutes; you could hear decades, past, present, and future. All sense of renewal collapsed back in on itself with the Band's why-are-we-here version of "One Too Many Mornings" on the 1999 *Tangled Up in Blues: Songs of Bob Dylan—This Ain't No Tribute* (House of Blues). Richard Manuel took the first verse for a basement tapes version; here Danko had to lead, and he sounded as if he was looking for the door.

Outside of ever-less-frequent Band dates, Danko's working life faded into a miasma of haphazard tours and a shrinking milieu of Woodstock musicians and drug dealers. Grossly overweight, he played embarrassing solo shows in upstate towns—a long slide chronicled in Marianna Fikes's tortured and unflinching "Nature's Way: Rick Danko's Later Years" (*Perfect Sound Forever*, September/October 2003, www.furious .com). Syracuse, New York, 1997: "The crowd seemed full of aging hippies and oversexed trashy harridans. Rick had become a veritable stand-up comedian, but the humor's jadedness was overwhelming and inescapable. When the line 'I just spent sixty days in the jailhouse' (in reality six weeks) from 'The Shape I'm In' met with an explosion of screams and whoops—making plain the audience's smirking knowledge of Rick's recent bust in Japan for heroin possession—I wished only for a gun . . . The worst had to be when he altered [a line] from 'The Blue-Tail Fly' (that *kids'* song immortalized by *Burl Ives*) to 'Jimmy smoke crack and he'll die!' . . . Rick's encore that night was 'I Shall Be Released'—I wrote 'Egads!' either before or after a die-hard party gal at one of the tables went 'Wooooo!' Prison! Suicide! Wooooo!" On December 10, 1999, just after the release of *"Live on Breeze Hill"* (Breeze Hill), a friends-and-neighbors gather-round credited to the Rick Danko Band, Danko died in his sleep. He was fifty-six. Garth Hudson and Levon Helm let the working name of the Band die with him.* "I don't want to sit here with a bunch of guilty-ass people who had their hands in Rick's pockets," Levon raged to an interviewer be-

---

* Posthumous Rick Danko albums included *"Times Like These"* (Breeze Hill), a mix of studio and live performances notable for a strong new reading of "All Our Past Times," a tune written with Eric Clapton that first appeared in 1976, as a Danko-Clapton duet, on Clapton's *No Reason to Cry* (PolyGram; Robertson and Manuel also contributed to the album, with Manuel dueting with Clapton on the blues "Last Night"). The spookiest moment came not from Danko but from his accompanist Jim Eppard, who, playing his way into "This Wheel's on Fire" on a National steel-bodied guitar, rewrote the song from the inside out. *In Concert* (Breeze Hill) caught Danko with drummer Randy Ciarlante and pianist Aaron Hurwitz on a good night. More compelling is *Cryin' Heart Blues* (Other People's Music), a 2005 release that combined often soulful studio recordings from 1977 through 1988 with a coolly troubled 1990 "Mystery Train," Danko playing acoustic guitar, his voice full, the pace slow, the crowd at Ella Guru's in Knoxville, Tennessee, waiting on every word. My *Rolling Stone* obituary for Danko, "The Man on the Left," is included in *BD by GM*.

fore a memorial service in Bearsville. "You want to know what killed Rick Danko? He worked himself to death. That's what happens when people steal your money."

For Levon, there were continuing guest spots here and there—most memorably, in 2003, with Hudson, for the gospel perennials the Dixie Hummingbirds' *Diamond Jubilation* (Treasure), and, one would hope more lucratively, in 2004, again with Hudson, for Nora Jones's *Feels Like Home* (Blue Note). Helm had retreated to Woodstock long before, with such results as a 1998 release with the unpromisingly titled *Souvenir Vol. I*, credited to Levon Helm and Crowmatix (Woodstock), a mostly live set featuring Helm (terrific on "Don't Ya Tell Henry" and Danko's "Java Blues") along with the hapless soul belter Marie Spinosa.

That same year he opened Levon Helm's Classic American Café on Decatur Street in New Orleans. When I passed by, two weeks before Danko's death, the place, defunct since the spring, already looked as if it had been closed for years. The marketing of nostalgia made even the word "American" communicate like a lapsed trademark. A "Live at Levon's" poster had an insert of a Ronnie Hawkins & the Hawks flyer and a design spelling out "BAND" to remind you; the last schedule listed Levon and Amy Helm with the Barn Burners, Levon Helm's Classic Blues Band, Levon Helm with Allen Toussaint, Levon Helm with James Cotton, Levon Helm with Cork, Levon Helm with the Dirty Dozen Blues Band. He was a working musician; the smell of death was in the way you could read a now-impoverished musician reaching back to the days when limousines met private jets—the way you could read that in the menu. In the "I'm a Lonely Boy . . . I Ain't Got No Home" po'boys; the "Up on Cripple Creek" seafood; the "King Harvest Has Surely Come" salads; the "Last Waltz" desserts.

But that wasn't the end, Levon said in 2000: just one more case of getting conned by a promoter. "Levon and Amy Helm with the Barn Burners," from the American Café poster, noting the presence of Levon's daughter, turned out to be the next chapter. In 1999 Levon was diagnosed with throat cancer, and radiation treatments burned his voice down to a scratch; still, it was the beginning of a turnaround. In 2000 he appeared in the otherwise forgettable A&E documentary *Bob Dylan: American Troubador*; for "Don't Ya Tell Henry" his voice struggled out of his throat like a gopher. He clutched his mandolin to his chest as tightly as he held to the song, as if it were the last one he remembered, calling up a simple music that would outlive its singers. In 2001 he and the saxophonist Bobby Keyes of Lubbock, Texas, who had played with Buddy Holly and soloed on the Rolling Stones' 1970 "Brown Sugar," went on the road with the Barn Burners, a white blues band whose four members, including Amy Helm and singer Chris O'Leary, were a good thirty years younger than they were. A show in San Francisco was spirited—"They're using that in Viagra commercials now," Maria Muldaur said at a show in San Francisco when the group tore into Muddy Waters's "I'm Ready"—but also strange. From Howlin' Wolf's "Wang Dang Doodle" to Faye Adams's "Shake a Hand," the combo was attacking material Levon and the Hawks were playing well before the younger Barn Burners were born; the group was good, but also a copy, not of the Hawks but of the kind of second-class '60s white blues outfit—the Siegel-Schwall Band, say—the Hawks would have trashed in any battle of the bands.

Levon sounded a hundred years old, but he looked like Porter Wagoner, pleased to be right where he was. A few years later he inaugurated the Midnight Ramble shows at his Woodstock barn, loose jams with a local crew and big-name guests (Sheryl Crow, Elvis Costello, Emmylou Harris) playing for upstate denizens and fans able to score the increasingly prized tickets. *Ramble Sessions* CDs and DVDs were sold on Helm's website; Vanguard released a 2008 performance from the original home of the Grand Ole Opry as *Ramble at the Ryman* in 2011, and in 2014 *The Midnight Ramble Sessions Vol. 3*, which, though it included only three Helm vocals, closed with his storming version of "Take Me to the River," a performance so convincing it made it hard to believe he wasn't still there to hear it. But musically, all the *Ramble* discs, which often featured such mediocrities as one Little Sammy Davis, were back-page news compared to *Dirt Farmer* (Vanguard), an ambitious, old-timey set released in 2007. The album kicked off with a seductive version of the Stanley Brothers' "False Hearted Lover's Blues" (like Dock Boggs's "Country Blues," one of countless remakings of "Darlin' Corey," a wail for a wasted life); despite a cover of Steve Earle's paint-by-numbers protest song "The Mountain," and a few tracks where the spirit seemed to depart, the record was a true statement of purpose and faith: an almost a cappella duet with Amy Helm on the traditional "Anna Lee," accompanied only by coproducer Larry Campbell's eighteenth-century fiddle, along with "The Girl He Left Behind" and "Little Birds," made it seem as if Helm were opening a door to a secret room.

Brought in to make a video for a *Dirt Farmer* song, Jacob Hatley walked right in and came out with the documentary *Ain't in It for My Health: A Film About Levon Helm* (Kino Lorber, first shown in 2010, though went into general release only in 2013, following Helm's death).

Though in small part retracing Helm's career—with startlingly down-to-earth testimony from Elizabeth Danko, living in a senior center ("This hell-hole") and Libby Titus Fagen, Helm's first wife ("Heroin?" she says of the Band's 1974 tour with Bob Dylan. "Yes. I sensed a difference")—the film took place mostly inside Helm's Woodstock house. As Helm works with Larry Campbell on another album, life goes on all around him. *Dirt Farmer* is nominated for a Grammy (for Best Traditional Folk Album), not to mention a Lifetime Achievement Award, which Helm all but rejects out of hand: where were these people when Richard Manuel and Rick Danko were still alive? "I got my doubts about how sincere it all is anyway," he says, "which is fine, 'cause I ain't too sincere about it myself. Bastards." Amy gets pregnant. Again, Levon's voice disappears; again cancer is crawling toward his vocal cords. A vocal therapist asks Levon if he knows "Amazing Grace," which is akin to asking him if he knows his own name, though we've seen him barely able to say that; he scratches out the song. Amy Helm gives birth to a son, Lavon, Levon's given name. *Dirt Farmer* wins. Most fascinatingly, throughout the film Levon and Larry Campbell try to find their way through an unfinished Hank Williams song, part of a newly discovered cache of sketches. "You'll Never Again Be Mine," it must be called—that's the refrain—but they're stuck on the bridge, which opens with "My heart holds no hatred or pain," and then stops. Campbell pushes out new lines; Helm tests them against the melody they've found. With Helm's voice only a memory, Campbell is still shifting words, though Helm can only nod or look stone-faced, as if realizing that the song, which may never be born, will nevertheless outlive him. It feels like a miracle—not medical, not God-given, just hard to believe—when finally he and Campbell are ready to call the song done, and Helm is ready to sing it, to give it everything it wants, proud to reach back more than five decades to shake hands, to write a song with Hank Williams: "My heart holds no hatred or pain / Though sometimes I feel it may die / But it always beats stronger / When I hear your name / And it won't let me say goodbye." A formal recording appeared on *The Lost Notebooks of Hank Williams* (Columbia, 2011), which also included Patty Loveless with "You're Through Fooling Me," Bob Dylan with "The Love That Faded," and the highlight of the set, Jakob Dylan with "Oh Mama, Come Home," which felt as if it was written and sung on the spot.

Electric Dirt (Vanguard, 2009) was taking shape inside *Ain't in It for My Health*. It too won a Grammy, for the newly devised Americana category, but that was merely noise. With fuller orchestration, it made *Dirt Farmer* sound like a concept album: this was fun. Before he was fifteen Helm saw the Rabbit Foot Minstrels and he saw Elvis Presley; you could hear both events in the music, especially in the call-and-response in Campbell's "When I Go Away" and Allen Toussaint and Steve Bernstein's sliding New Orleans horn arrangements, most subtly on Helm's version of Randy Newman's "Kingfish," though it's a cackling rehearsal of the song in *Ain't in It for My Health* that brings Huey P. Long back on the campaign trail. You could believe Levon's best music since the Band was ahead of him, and when he died in 2012, the reaction seemed to come from every corner of the nation. It was as if the whole country had lost a common treasure, a fated voice.

In the aftermath, a whole crew of tribute album regulars, with Garth Hudson performing "Little Birds" and accompanying John Prine, gathered for an endless memorial concert, released in 2013 as *Love for Levon* (Time Life Entertainment), a misbegotten, not to say insincere project that reached its lowest of low points with a version of "Don't Do It" by David Bromberg and Joan Osborne that was like someone breaking into your house and holding you hostage so they could sing for you, and touched an actual believable emotion—everyone else was just *so proud* to be there—only with Marc Cohn's "Listening to Levon." But the best tribute had come in advance, with Tracy K. Smith's "Alternate Take (for Levon Helm)," collected in her 2011 *Life on Mars* (Minneapolis: Graywolf). It's a slowly building poem in which the writer ("I've been beating my head all day long on the same six lines") wants nothing more than to feel like the singer must have felt when he sang—what song would it have been? "Chest Fever"? "The Weight"? "You know how, shoulders hiked nice and high, chin tipped back," Smith wrote. "So the song has to climb its way out like a man from a mine."

Garth Hudson had bided his time. After *Our Lady Queen of the Angels*, he waited twenty-one years before putting out another record with his name on it. *The Sea to the North* (Breeze Hill, 2001) was made of what used to be called fantasias—a romantic, deliriously experimental music that drifted from era to era, style to style, without quite touching down. "Film music," Hudson said in 2007. "Just imagine two people in a canoe, in the first cut," he wrote in his liner notes about "The Saga of Cyrus and Mulgrew," named for the pianists Cyrus Chestnut and Mulgrew Miller, "two French-Canadian explorers, two minimalist explorers, two pianists who were really cool—and then they go right over the rapids." The music took shape with an almost unrecognizably open version of the Grateful Dead's "Dark Star." When Garth went into a monologue at the end ("Shall we go?" he murmured. "The transitive night full of diamonds . . . A lady in velvet walks out, walks out") he was back in his soliloquies for "Even If It's a Pig" in 1967, declaiming like a gnarly-voiced beat poet, up all night: "Our truant members' fondest pagings, reach for the brim, but catch only the offerings."

Garth and Maud Hudson's *Live at the Wolf*, recorded in Garth's old hometown of London, Ontario, in 2002 (Make It Real, 2005), was paltry; Maud Hudson's deep voice and her slow cadence, more that of a preacher or a fortune-teller than a singer, was exposed against Garth's solo piano. But there was another live recording that told a story you could imagine the Band always reached for, and never quite found.

The occasion was Hal Willner's continuing adventure in inhabiting the specters of old songs with new bodies—unless in the shows he staged to recast the four volumes of Harry Smith's *Anthology of American Folk Music* the songs were the bodies and the new performers the specters. At UCLA on April 25, 2001, as documented on *The Harry Smith Project: Anthology of American Folk Music Revisited* (Shout box set, two concert CDs, a concert DVD, and Rani Singh's documentary film *The Old, Weird America*), acolytes from Marianne Faithfull to Wilco to David Thomas took up the likes of "James Alley Blues" and "Way Down the Old Plank Road." With a severe accordion solo, Garth set the stage for his wife's performance of the Carter Family's "No Depression in Heaven," a number Levon too occasionally performed.

I attended a similar event Willner staged at the Getty Center in Los Angeles a few days before. There were fourteen people on the stage; the sixties Cambridge blues singer Geoff Muldaur led off the night. He looked like the kindly town pharmacist; when he opened his mouth Noah Lewis's 1928 "Minglewood Blues" came out like a tiger. "You're going to be killing a lot of people tonight, aren't you?" the fiddler Richard Greene asked Rennie Sparks of the Handsome Family, who was one of only four or five people under forty, or fifty, on the stage. "That's what I do best," she said sweetly. She introduced the Blue Sky Boys' 1936 "Down on the Banks of the Ohio" as a song in which "a woman is slaughtered to ensure that the river remains full." "This record sounds like it came from Mars," Greene said, kicking off Floyd Ming and His Pep Steppers' 1928 "Indian War Whoop" (a parade band plays the tune in *O Brother, Where Art Thou?* to celebrate the arrest of Baby Face Nelson); at the Getty it sounded just like Slim Whitman's "Indian Love Call," which in *Mars Attacks!* makes all the Martians' heads explode. The band was heading toward cuteness when Garth began to play. Boxed in by three sets of keyboards, hoisting his accordion, he was everywhere at once. As soon as you thought he caught a tune—"Home

Sweet Home," "Shenandoah"—it vanished. He was an avant-garde pianist in a silent-movie palace, forgotten girlie flicks and In-a-Castle-Dark costume epics turning profound under his fingers. And then, like a funeral oration, came Maud Hudson's voice, now so thick, so unbending, you ceased to hear the music Garth was playing around her. She sang from her wheelchair, her whole body in every word, insisting on the Great Depression as God's will, punishment for sins unknown, even uncommitted, and pronouncing the only solution, which was suicide, or parents killing their children before they kill themselves. "I'm going where there's no Depression," she sang, with the Carter Family hovering behind her, as they were in 1936, their cracked hands reaching out to the nation like Pied Pipers in rags, leading the way to heaven: "There'll be no hunger, no orphan children crying for bread / No weeping widows, toil or struggle." When, with absolute dignity, Maud Hudson grasped the lines "No shrouds, no coffins / And no death," you realized the song was calling for nothing so small as the end of a life, but for the end of the natural order: the end of the world. The end of the singer, and the end of you.

The first book on the Band, Barney Hoskyns's *Across the Great Divide: The Band and America*, did not appear until 1993 (rev. ed. New York: Hal Leonard, 2006). Though decorated with maps in the original edition, it failed to say much about "America"; as the tale of a group caught up in and finally exiled from its times, the book was, absent much cooperation from its principals, readable and thorough from start to finish. Craig Harris published *The Band: Pioneers of Americana* in 2014 (Lanham MD: Rowman & Littlefield): formally up-to-date, and with original interview material with Danko and Robertson, it was also literal-minded, grossly padded (when a minor figure like John Hammond, Jr., comes up, Harris is off to the races), and so frequently inaccurate its most notable claims couldn't stand on their own, not to mention being one more example of touting something interesting on the basis of its supposed influence on something less interesting. Levon Helm's *This Wheel's on Fire: Levon Helm and the Story of the Band*, written with Stephen Davis (1993; rev. ed. Chicago: A Cappella, 2000), was an uneven chronicle. When Levon went back to the '40s for tales of a boyhood shaped by music, in the days before there was anything called rock 'n' roll, you could see his grin and feel his ache; through many periods in the Band's career, you could almost physically sense Davis taking over the authorial voice. Year by year, Helm's story became one of resentment and loathing for Robbie Robertson, for his supposed theft of the Band's soul, not to mention the rights to its songs; as the first-person narrative moved on, "Robbie" became "Robertson." Oddly, when Helm went out on a promotional tour, he disavowed his own book. His trouble with Robertson, he said, was just phony controversy the publisher demanded to pump up sales; off the tour, he went back to a loathing he maintained for the rest of his life. By 2008, as chronicled in *Ain't in It for My Health*, he would barely say "the Band" out loud. "He's choosing to ignore that legacy," Larry Campbell says, shaking his head over Helm's bitterness—or his fortitude.

Other commentary worth seeking out includes the late Ralph J. Gleason's work for *Rolling Stone*, particularly his May 17, 1969, "The Band at Winterland," an account of the Band's disastrous/triumphant first nights in San Francisco (in *The Rolling Stone Rock & Roll Reader*, ed. Ben Fong-Torres, New York: Bantam, 1974; my piece on the same shows, "We Can Talk About It Now," from the *San Francisco Express-Times*, is included in *The Sound and the Fury: A Rock's Backpages Reader*, ed. Barney Hoskyns, London: Bloomsbury, 2003), and his October 18, 1969, review of *The Band*, collected in *The Rolling Stone Record Review* (New York: Pocket Books, 1971). One of the most straightforward and detailed (and least redundant) of Robertson's many interviews is the transcript of a talk with Roelof Kiers, recorded for VPRO-TV, the Netherlands, in 1970, and published that year in the Dutch music paper *Aloha*; Robbie's "once said" quotes in my chapter on the Band come from this source. In 1985 Ruth Albert Spencer conceived a remarkable project—she would actually interview *all* the members of the Band—and the results appeared in the *Woodstock Times*, March 21, March 28, April 4, and April 11, 1985. Her account of Richard Manuel's funeral (Garth Hudson, who began public performance in 1952 as Sunday-school pianist at St. Luke's Anglican Church in London, Ontario, and in 1954 moved up to evening services organist, provided all the music) appeared in the *Woodstock Times*, March 13, 1986. Certainly the finest piece of uncollected writing on the Band is Ron Horning's "The Moving Shadow of Richard Manuel" ("Rock & Roll Quarterly, Summer 1988," in the *Village Voice*, July 5, 1988), a two-part meditation on Manuel's suicide. Horning begins in Manuel's voice, recounting in all-too-naturalistic detail what it meant for onetime stars to go back onto a narrow road as "The Band," to be thrown back not just on themselves but on their own past, a past that did not comfort but mocked; then Horning shifts, and begins to invent stories about Manuel's death, turning it into an accident, various sorts of murder, each tale more scandalous and unacceptable than the last, until all that remains is waste and squalor. As honest, if not as acute, were Counting Crows' "If I Could Give All My Love (Richard Manuel Is Dead)," from *Hard Candy* (Geffen, 2002) and Drive-By Truckers' "Danko/Manuel," from *The Dirty South* (New West, 2004), an elegy fighting against its own attempt at kindness: "Richard Manuel is dead / God forbid you call their bluff."

John Niven took Horning's work several steps further, and many steps back. His novella *Music from Big Pink* (New York and London: Continuum, 2005) is written in the voice of a former Woodstock dope dealer, now in his forties, a junkie, every day like every other: it's 1986. But nearly twenty years before, when the guys who were making some sort of record didn't even have a name for themselves, every day was different. There's nothing but drugs, flattery, dissipation, pettiness, jealousy, envy, paranoia, and solipsism, another hit, another dollar missing that was there the last time you looked, as in this passage, set on a night in 1968 when the narrator is gearing up for the set the Band were to perform with Bob Dylan at a Woody Guthrie tribute concert, a hippie horror story, presented as a distillation of the world the members of the Band stepped around, stepped into, stepped on:

"YOU WANNA BEER?"

"Yeah, thanks." A neighbor started pounding on a ceiling or a wall somewhere.

"How you been?" he asked me as we walked into the kitchen. There was a girl unconscious on the floor.

"I've been back home. My mom died."

"Shit, man," said Dave, opening the fridge and sounding like I'd just told him I was double-parked. "Ah, fuck!" he said, suddenly furious. "Mallory! MALLORY, YOU FUCKING CUNT!" he was screaming at the girl. She was out cold, man. A fucking corpse. Dave picked her head up by the hair, a thin, clear rope of drool connecting her mouth to the dirty linoleum, and screamed in her ear, "WHO DRANK ALL MY HEINEKENS? WHO DRANK ALL MY FUCKING HEINEKENS YOU FUCKED-UP JUNKIE BITCH?"

Reading the book is like sinking into a swamp. The story it tells seems undeniable—the focus is mostly on Manuel and Danko, who couldn't sue—and its only flaw is that it can't make sense of how the songs on the album the book is named for came out of the milieu it creates. The narrator knows it doesn't: that's what he's still struggling with. He was there. He knows what he did, what he saw, what others did—and yet there was somewhere else in the place where he was, and he wasn't there at all. The weight of the book is that it almost convinces you that no one else was, either.

That wasn't how Levon saw it in *The Band: The Authorized Biography* (ABC Video, 1995). Directed by Mark Hall and narrated by Harry Dean Stanton, for memories and commentary the documentary relied on Helm almost exclusively (Robbie did not take part at all). Helm was monastically intense analyzing Elvis's three-piece backing band; he was country eloquent—been there and gone—on Manuel's suicide. "Richard wasn't afraid to go early, or leave late," he said. "And that was one time he decided to go early. And it's a decision that's strictly between him and his higher power, and I've never tried to second-guess it, or have too strong an opinion of my own about it."

RONNIE HAWKINS & THE HAWKS

Born in Huntsville, Alabama, in 1935, Ronnie Hawkins sometimes claimed to have assembled his first group of Hawks in 1952, when he was a student at the University of Arkansas in Fayetteville. For that matter, he has claimed he made his first record about the same time, a version of "Bo Diddley" that would have predated Bo Diddley's own—a story that might even be true. ("Mention [Hawkins's] name and Bo's face lights up," George R. White reported in *Bo Diddley: Living Legend*, Chessington, Surrey, UK: Castle Communications, 1995. "That's my partner, one *great* dude! He's closer to me than anyone else, and I know the cat better than I know most guys. We go back to the fifties, right back to Arkansas when he was with Conway Twitty and we played the same clubs.") Roy Orbison remembered a Hawkins combo opening a Fayetteville show for him where, to upstage him, they played only Orbison's songs. Still, what sounds like the real story of the original Hawks is better.

Hawkins dropped out of the university in 1956, avoiding the two-year draft by enlisting in the army for a six-month hitch; in 1957 he found himself stationed at Fort Sill in Oklahoma, where the best times going were in nearby Lawton, in the Amvets Club. There, as Ian Wallis recounts the story in *The Hawk: The Story of Ronnie Hawkins and the Hawks* (Kingston, Ontario: Quarry Press, 1996), Hawkins was invited to sit in with and eventually join the Black Hawks, a hammering all-black band featuring Pretty Boy Leroy Moody on guitar and A. C. Reed, Jimmy Reed's half brother, on saxophone; history took a small turn. Later in 1957, Hawkins auditioned for Sun Records in Memphis, but nothing came of it, and he joined with former Conway Twitty guitarist Jimmy Ray "Luke" Paulman to form a new band.* Not long after, on Twitty's advice, Hawkins was working the Golden Rail in Hamilton, Ontario.

As leader of the Ron Hawkins Quartet, Hawkins made his first documented recording in 1958, in a Toronto garage: "Hey Bo Diddley" b/w "Love Me Like You Can," which was issued on the tiny Canadian label Quality (reissued both as Ozark single 9001 and on Hawkins's *rrracket time*, Oxford/Charly LP). The Quartet included Paulman, Will "Pop" Jones on piano, and Levon Helm, eighteen, on drums. The disc went nowhere, but Hawkins persevered with "Forty Days" (Apex 76499). Someone must have heard him, because in the spring of 1959 Hawkins got his first break.

Working with the New York Fury label and producer Bobby Robinson, longtime one-man band Wilbert Harrison redid an old Jerry Leiber–Mike Stoller tune, "K. C. Loving," changing the title to "Kansas City." The record took off like a shot, but lacking cash Robinson was unable to keep up with demand and the single soon disappeared from the stores; the record hung between oblivion and a gold mine as people all over the country tried to find the hit they were hearing on the radio. Quick to take advantage, label after label rushed out cover versions (the best, and most successful, was Little Richard's; it was his performance that Paul McCartney used as the basis for the Beatles' 1964 cover). One producer on the case was the legendary New York record man George Goldner; he put Hawkins in the studio posthaste. Credited to Rockin' Ronald and the Rebels, Hawkins's "Kansas City"—issued on Goldner's End label, and included on Ronnie Hawkins & the Hawks' *The Roulette Years*, a 57-cut double CD (Sequel, 1995)—stands as perhaps the least potent of all attempts to steal Wilbert Harrison's thunder. That may be why Hawkins occasionally denied he ever recorded the tune; in the end, it was Harrison and no one else who took the song to the top of the charts (see Harrison's *Kansas City*, Relic).

End, as it happened, was under the umbrella of Roulette, run by Morris Levy, owner of the nightclub Birdland, killer, gangster, and

* "Luke," Levon has said of the characters in "The Weight," "was Jimmy Ray Paulman. Young Anna Lee was Anna Lee Williams from Turkey Scratch. Crazy Chester was a guy we all knew from Fayetteville who came into town on Saturdays wearing a full set of cap guns and walked around town to help keep the peace. He was like Hopalong Cassidy—two big cap guns he wore, plus a toupee!" (Johnny Black, "Stirrings Down in the Basement," *Mojo*, July 1998.) At a Midnight Rambles show Levon put on with preteen musicians in Woodstock on July 8, 2007, Williams, now Anna Lee Amsden, was in the audience; songs included Chuck Berry's "Around and Around," the Velvet Underground's "What Goes On," and Robert Johnson's "Ramblin' on My Mind."

front man for the Genovese crime family. He was also a charmer, and if Hawkins ever regretted signing a long-term contract he never said so, not even after Levy's death in 1990. Still working out of Toronto, Hawkins and the Hawks cut the Roulette LPs *Ronnie Hawkins* in 1959 and, with Fred Carter, Jr., replacing Paulman on lead guitar, *Mr. Dynamo* the following year.

By this time the Hawks were a rough combination of rockabilly and Clyde McPhatter's mid-'50s Drifters in their up-tempo, "Let the Boogie Woogie Roll" mode, bent on speed and flash. There was an openness and bounce—a swing—in their sound that separated them from most other white rockers, not to mention a certain streak of perversity. A stunning YouTube clip shows the Hawks in 1959, with Paulman and Helm, on the Canadian TV show *After School*, playing "Need Your Lovin,'" a slow, lugubrious number about sex and blackberry wine (hey, it's *after* school). Hawkins is big, burly, slick, smooth—on Yonge Street, Toronto's nightclub district, he'd look more like a pimp than a singer. With a scary grin on his face, he sways to the music—and then he does the moonwalk. Perfectly.

The endless rehearsals Hawkins demanded put the Hawks well beyond most journeyman backup bands of the time, and while Paulman and Carter sounded like Carl Perkins and Jones like Jerry Lee Lewis, Helm already sounded like himself. (Paulman never went as far as he might have; his demo "C-Riff Rock," collected on *The Roulette Years*, follows James Burton on Dale Hawkins's 1957 "Susie Q" and anticipates Jorgen Ingman's 1961 "Apache.") Helm was faster than most rock drummers, and he used a heavier beat; at his best he dominated the music. The Hawks played brash and dirty; Hawkins sang like a lunatic when he could pull it off, which put him squarely in the company of the heroic Southern rockers he longed to emulate.

Ronnie Hawkins contained two chart entries: "Mary Lou," a remake of Young Jessie's 1955 R&B ballad (used to startlingly ominous and undimmed effect in the 1987 slasher film *Hello Mary Lou: Prom Night II*, with Lisa Shrage as an unbearably sexy Mary Lou Mahoney, back from thirty years in the grave to get her revenge), and "Forty Days," another remake of Chuck Berry's 1955 "Thirty Days." (Uproarious "Forty Days" footage from *American Bandstand*, with Hawkins and the Hawks dressed as a barbershop quartet, can be found on YouTube.) The discs reached #26 and #45, respectively; "Mary Lou" went top ten on the R&B charts. *Mr. Dynamo* was highlighted by the spooky "Southern Love," Hawkins's most distinctive number from the period; it included as well "Hey Boba Lu" and "Someone Like You," with Robertson in both cases sharing composer credit, and his first recordings as a guitarist, though he was not credited, having joined Hawkins as a roadie and occasional bass player.* He was soon very much more, appearing with Hawkins at Alan Freed's last Brooklyn Paramount shows ("How old are you, kid?" said Freed, then under assault from bluenose district attorneys and federal prosecutors on charges ranging from payola to criminal anarchy. "You want them to get me on a child-labor rap, too?"), meeting Buddy Holly ("His guitar blasted out of his amp," Craig Harris quotes Robertson: "There was something about it beyond the normal"), scouting songs in New York from the likes of Doc Pomus and Mort Shuman, Otis Blackwell, Jerry Leiber and Mike Stoller, learning the music business from the inside. "He's a good-looking kid," Morris Levy told Hawkins, as Robbie recalled in 2006. "I bet you don't know whether to have sex with him or hire him"—though the term "have sex with" was likely not in Levy's vocabulary.

Robbie took over as lead guitarist later in 1960 (his first recording credit came that year, his first lead credit in 1961), and Rick Danko (first credited in 1961), Richard Manuel (1962), and Garth Hudson (1962), plus saxophonist Jerry Penfound (1961), were recruited in turn out of local bands over the next year or so. Hudson was the catalyst moving the young musicians in their own direction; the rest have all testified that the nearly silent, always poker-faced organist, whose musical knowledge was as vast as it was concrete, and whose instincts, whether on polkas or Bach, tended toward experiment and abstraction, brought the most to the group, though given the disapproval of Hudson's parents for pop music as a career, at first he was officially brought into the Hawks as a music teacher. Staving off a planned future in agricultural research, Hudson had spent the fifties as the organist at a funeral home, in numerous big bands, as pianist in a "musical vaudeville" act called the Three Blisters, accordionist in a pop combo called the Four Quarters, and, before the Philadelphia doo-wop group the Silhouettes made "Get a Job" a number one hit in 1958, in a rock 'n' roll combo of the same name. As early as 1955 he accompanied an entire day of the Simcoe Fair in Simcoe, Ontario, backing everything from the livestock parade to the Fire-Baton-Twirling Young Ladies to Nolan Strong and the Diablos, the great doo-wop quintet from Detroit; in 1959, in New York, he accompanied the Canadian country

* As to claims that Robertson's first recording was as the guitarist on Toronto jazz singer Dianne Brooks's 1960 "The Orbiteer Twist," apparently a promotional device for a toy, his comment forty-seven years later: "I draw a complete blank on this incident. I usually remember all this stuff, but it is beyond vague."

singer Don Crawford on "Sleeping Beauty" b/w "Beauty and the Beast" (REO 8391X).

That same year Garth joined Paul London (born Paul Hutchins, in London, Ontario) and the Capers, a local band that, not withstanding the views of the elder Hudsons, soon began working bars in Detroit, backing up the likes of Bill Haley and Johnny Cash. On their own they played Larry Williams and Little Richard numbers; as a pianist, Hudson concentrated on the daredevil runs of Chuck Berry's pianist Johnny Johnson. The Capers left behind two 1961 singles: "Rosie Lee" (a cover of the 1957 hit by the Mello-Tones with a white-bread vocal and a plinking Hudson piano solo) b/w "Real Gone Lover" (Fascination F1007) and, as Paul London and the Kapers (another band had claimed rights to their "C"), "Sugar Baby" b/w "Big Bad Twist," cut in Chicago at the Chess studios (Checkmate 1006). Additional material was recorded in Chicago for Columbia about the same time but never issued; Hutchins remembered the sessions with pride. "Rosie Lee" and "Real Gone Lover" can be heard on YouTube, and on the anthology *Gang's House* (Buffalo Bop), where, on the cover, by far the best part of the production, three dissolute teenage boys flop in a bare apartment, with only booze and cigarettes on the floor, while a teenage girl whose modest hair and clothes are clearly a day-job disguise looks you in the eye.

Paying at least as much attention to each other as to Hawkins as they worked through southern Ontario, then across Arkansas, Oklahoma, Texas, and places in between, the Hawks began to play blues, or try to—Hawkins insistently cut them back—and two albums they treasured most were by Howlin Wolf (1910–76). *Moanin' in the Moonlight* (Chess, 1959) collected Wolf's early sides, and featured Willie Johnson's fiery guitar on "How Many More Years" (cut by Sam Phillips in Memphis in 1951), plus "Smokestack Lightning," "I Asked for Water" (Wolf's remake of Tommy Johnson's 1928 "Cool Drink of Water Blues"), and other classics. *Howlin' Wolf* (Chess, 1962, with the famous rocking-chair sleeve) was all Chicago, and guitarist Hubert Sumlin's album as much as Wolf's. ("No one knew what he was on about half the time," the great British blues guitarist Peter Green said in 1996, "but it made sense on another level.") Sumlin contributed a crazed solo on "Wang Dang Doodle" (the model for Robbie's solo on "Who Do You Love"), plus stunning efforts on "Down in the Bottom," "Spoonful" (a Charley Patton standard), "You'll Be Mine," and "Going Down Slow." The music, which was to have such an impact in Britain, was at once rougher and more sophisticated ("primitive-modernist," in the words of Memphis veteran Jim Dickinson) than the rockers and ballads the Hawks played nightly as a living jukebox; it was music of drive and nuance, stomp and style.

Just as important to the Hawks was an album split between Junior Parker (1927–71) and Bobby "Blue" Bland (1930–2013): *Blues Consolidated* (Duke, 1958), which collected '50s singles by the two men. Both started out in the late '40s in Memphis, singing with the Beale Streeters, a seminal group that also included Johnny Ace (1929–54) on piano (see the anthology *Blues for Mr Crump*, Polydor LP). Recording in Memphis for Sam Phillips, and later in Houston for Don Robey's Duke label, the three, as soloists (see the anthology *The Original Memphis Blues Brothers*, Ace), came to define a whole new kind of rhythm and blues, stressing a sort of tragic sentimentality expressed through delicate, carefully arranged ballads. *Blues Consolidated* showcased Bland's first big hit, "Farther Up the Road" (1957), and "It's My Life, Baby" (1956). The latter shot miles past "Farther Up the Road"—which may be why, with studio time to themselves in 1961, the Hawks didn't attempt it. They would pass Bland with their version of "Farther Up the Road" (and fall short of themselves with the Robertson/Clapton guitar duet on the tune at the Last Waltz), but there was no way on earth they were going to catch him—or Roy Gaines, his guitar player—on "It's My Life, Baby."

At first one of many Roy Brown imitators, Bland found his style and began a series of superb recordings that continued into the 1980s, which is to say not only predating but outlasting the Band; kin to Charlie Rich, whose songs he covered (and vice versa), he remains the most sensitive and original postwar blues singer. The deceptively quiet, despairing moods of his most distinctive tunes shaped Richard Manuel's singing in particular, not merely in terms of phrasing, but as a matter of sensibility—the morals one can discover as one sings. See, for Bland, *Two Steps from the Blues* (Duke, 1961), *I Pity the Fool/The Duke Recordings, Vol. 1* (MCA—"Farther Up the Road," "It's My Life, Baby," "I'll Take Care of You," "Lead Me On"), and *Turn on Your Love Light/The Duke Recordings, Vol. 2* (MCA—"St. James Infirmary," "Stormy Monday Blues," "Who Will the Next Fool Be," "Share Your Love with Me"). For Junior Parker, see the anthology *Mystery Train* (Rounder—Parker's Sun material, plus the major Sun recordings by James Cotton, "Cotton Crop Blues," and Pat Hare, "I'm Gonna Murder My Baby"; as with *The Original Memphis Blues Brothers*, the cover shows Elvis, Bland, and Parker posing together) and *Junior's Blues: The Duke Recordings, Vol. 1* (MCA). The most notable recordings of Johnny Ace's short career are on his *Memorial Album* (Duke, 1955). The official story is that Ace shot himself backstage during a game of Russian roulette; it was whispered around Houston for years that Don Robey shot him, which doesn't make it true.

While the Hawks were listening to Bland and Wolf—and to Ray Charles ("I don't sound like Ray Charles," Richard Manuel told Ruth Albert Spencer in 1985. "I imply, I make the same implications, I infer the same kind of things. You know what I mean?"), early Motown, the "5" Royales (to hear the sound Robbie was reaching for in his wildest dreams, listen to guitarist Lowman Pauling's never-matched solos on the 1959 "The Slummer the Slum," on *Monkey Hips and Rice: The "5" Royales Anthology*, Rhino), a lot of gospel music, the Staple Singers, and everything else (Manuel: "Ricky Nelson was probably an influence")— they and Hawkins went from night to night. A tape of Hawkins and the full complement of Band-to-be Hawks, plus Jerry Penfound, from December 25, 1962, offers a group egging on a raucous crowd with precision control. There is very good guitar and a piercing organ on "Stormy Monday," parlor organ on "Georgia on My Mind," a little doo-wop, a tease on "What'd I Say" that went back to the minstrel shows of the 1840s ("See the boy with the red dress on / He ain't funny but his hair is long"), and, on a "Bo Diddley"–"Who Do You Love" combo just five songs into the set, the night's first explosion, with Hawkins shouting on Robbie's solo as if it were a cockfight: "Hah! Hah! Hah!" Pieces of sound seem to hurl themselves at an audience you can picture stumbling from table to table and lurching against the walls; there isn't a moment of doubt anywhere in the performance. Still, Hawkins had plenty of doubt; as a recording artist he was going nowhere. In 1960 he'd tried the *Folk Ballads of Ronnie Hawkins* route, with its hilariously lugubrious "Ballad of Caryl Chessman" ("Let him live! Let him live!"), and the dutiful *Ronnie Hawkins Sings Hank Williams* (both Roulette). He cut two more albums with the Hawks, both released in 1963. *The Best of Ronnie Hawkins* (Roulette) featured the Hawks chasing Hawkins through "Who Do You Love," "Come Love" (with backup singing by Dionne Warwick, Dee Dee Warwick, and Cissie Houston), and "Arkansas," a detailed paean both to Hawkins's career and his home state— written by New Yorkers Doc Pomus and Mort Schuman, produced by big-city hipsters Jerry Leiber and Mike Stoller, and featuring the North Carolina blues harmonica player Sonny Terry. *Mojo Man* (Canadian Roulette) contained the Hawks' 1961 versions of "Further on Up the Road" and Muddy Waters's "Nineteen Years Old," mistitled "Have a Party." All of Hawkins's and the Hawks' Roulette production, minus nearly all of the folk and Hank Williams material, plus various oddities and the Hawks' cool "What a Party," a previously unreleased all-the-stars-are-here-tonight roundelay (source of the "Have a Party" confusion), is on Hawkins & the Hawks' *The Roulette Years*. The Band's *History* includes "Who Do You Love," nearly pornographic guitar from Robbie on Hawkins's "Come Love," "Further on Up the Road" and "Nineteen Years Old."

Hawkins gained new fame after the success of the Band, and went on to make two smooth, expert albums for the Cotillion label, *Ronnie Hawkins* (1970) and *The Hawk* (1971)—and even brushed the charts again with a good cover of the Clovers' 1953 "Down in the Alley," #75 in 1970. Among the many halfhearted, small-label albums that followed, there was one definitive, drooling mess-around, *Rock & Roll Resurrection* (Monument, 1973), which finally told Hawkins's story as it was meant to be: "Willie and the Hand Job," more or less. It was swiftly followed by *The Giant of Rock & Roll* (Monument, 1974), a set of ballads ("Dream Lover," "Lonely Hours," "Pledging My Love") dripping with a really touching insincerity. In 1980, in *Heaven's Gate*, Michael Cimino's passionate epic on the 1892 Johnson County War in Wyoming, Hawkins took the role of Maj. Frank Wolcott, leader of the invading Cattleman's Association army ("the bloodthirsty little rooster," Helena Huntington Smith wrote in *The War on Powder River*): Hawkins played the man as a whore, sour, wise, a student of the great Roman generals, all his dreams of glory, even decency, behind him. In 1989, with the writer Peter Goddard, he published the undistinguished *Ronnie Hawkins—Last of the Good Old Boys* (Toronto: Stoddard). In 1995, for his sixtieth birthday, Hawkins set up with the Band in Toronto's Massey Hall for a celebration released as *Let It Rock! The Rock 'n' Roll Album of the Decade* (Quality); also contributing were such lesser lights as Carl Perkins and Jerry Lee Lewis. Hawkins himself thrashed out Chuck Berry's title song, "Mary Lou," and, as if to close the circle, "Bo Diddley." Back in the studio with the Band, he got all weepy and sweet for "Days Gone By." The circle wasn't closed, of course: In 2001 there was the retrospective *Can't Stop Rockin'* (Sony Canada), with three new songs, including the depressed ballad "Blue Moon in My Sign," with Levon on mandolin and drums and Robbie on guitar—the two of them, not speaking, overdubbing their contributions in different studios without being informed that they still did, as Hawkins put it, "play fine together." In 2007 there was the documentary *Still Alive and Kickin'* (Casablanca International DVD), directed by Anne Pick, narrated by Dan Aykroyd, a tribute song by Canadian Paul Anka, and appearances by Bill and Hillary Clinton: with many looks over his shoulder, a year in Hawkins's life, from a diagnosis of pancreatic cancer to a big bounce back.

*   *   *

Helm, Robertson, Danko, Manuel, and Hudson left Hawkins in 1963, along with Jerry Penfound; for a time they were occasionally joined by sometime Hawks utility singer Bruce Bruno. They drifted from border to border, to a club in Texas once owned by Jack Ruby to the Peppermint Lounge in New York City. At first they went out as the Levon Helm Sextet, then as Levon and the Hawks. From a 1964 show in Port Dover, Ontario, comes the version of "Do the Honky Tonk" that appears on the *Across the Great Divide* set; the bootleg *Old Shoes*, credited to Levon & Hawks/The Band, includes "Not Fade Away," "Sweeter Girl Than You," and "Lucille" from the Port Dover show, plus, from a 1964 show in London, Ontario, an eight-minute "Who Do You Love" that would have had the Grateful Dead fleeing the stage of the Fillmore had the Hawks been present in San Francisco a year later to blow them off it; a "Share Your Love" that has girls swooning from the first notes; and the Mashed-Potatoes special "That's What I Know." With screams from the girls and laughter from the boys in the crowd, there's an untitled instrumental, led by Garth, that for the moment turns the place into a strip joint: "I'd like to introduce the future leaders of Canada," one of the Hawks announces. *History* collects Levon and the Hawks demos for Robbie and Garth's "Bacon Fat" (1965), "Do the Honky Tonk," and the instrumental "Robbie's Blues" (both 1964).

In 1965 the Hawks made three singles, all included on *History*: as the Canadian Squires, "Leave Me Alone" (a rewrite of Chuck Berry's "Almost Grown") b/w "Uh-Uh-Uh" (Ware 6002), and, as Levon and the Hawks, "Go Go Liza Jane" b/w "He Don't Love You" (Atco 6625, not released until 1968), and "The Stones I Throw (Will Free All Men)" b/w "He Don't Love You" (Atco 6383). All of the reach and none of the poetry of *Music from Big Pink* and *The Band* are present in "The Stones I Throw": "Something makes me want to stand up and do what's right . . . and take my brother's hand," Richard sang. "I will show them by the stones that I throw." Anything this explicit would have sunk *Big Pink*, a drama of morals, not moralism.

In 1964 Levon, Garth, and Robbie worked with John Hammond, Jr., previously a purist white blues singer, for his *So Many Roads* (Vanguard, 1965). Material included Howlin' Wolf's "Down in the Bottom," Robert Johnson's "If I Had Possession Over Judgment Day," not to mention "Who Do You Love," but despite the jagged, off-beat ricochets of Robbie's solos—as distinctive a sound as anyone had at the time—the music flags, because Hammond has no sense of rhythm. The 1965 sessions for Hammond's *I Can Tell* (Atlantic, 1967), which featured Robbie and Rick, were better; anyone with the stomach to sit through Hammond's blackface vocals can hear what Robbie has always considered some of his best playing: all rough edges, bits of metal piercing the spare rhythm section. There was more session work: Robbie played on the Charles Lloyd Quartet's *Of Love, of Love* (Columbia, 1965), and the whole crew was present, anonymously, to back up the drummer for the Barbarians on his notoriously bathetic autobiographical monologue "Moulty," in which he explained that even though his left hand was a hook, and he used to hate it, he never gave up, and he was just as good as anyone (Laurie 3326, 1966, collected on *Nuggets— Original Artyfacts from the First Psychedelic Era, 1965–68*, Rhino). It was a hit, too.

WITH BOB DYLAN

Stories of how the Hawks hooked up with Bob Dylan abound: through John Hammond, Jr.; through Mary Martin, a Canadian working in the music business in New York; through pure serendipity. However it happened, Robbie and Levon, with Harvey Brooks on bass and Al Kooper on electric piano, backed Dylan at his chaotic August 28, 1965, concert at Forest Hills, New York—Dylan's first show following the infamous Newport Folk Festival performance where, with Kooper, pianist Barry Goldberg, guitarist Mike Bloomfield, bassist Jerome Arnold, and drummer Sam Lay of the Paul Butterfield Blues Band, he scandalized much of the audience by subjecting his folk poetry to commercial electric accompaniment, thus demonstrating that he'd sold out to the almighty dollar. ("Cocksucker!" shouted one offended fan at Forest Hills. "Aw, it's not that bad," Dylan replied.) An audience tape of the Forest Hills show (not exactly full of presence in the music, startlingly immediate in its capture of what sounds like a continuing riot in the crowd) is included on *Bob Dylan Chronicles: 1965 Revisited* (Great Dane), a weirdly completist fourteen-CD bootleg apparently comprised of every 1965 Bob Dylan recorded moment not officially released. To Levon and Robbie, to whom rock was as commercial as living off peanut butter and an Arkansas credit card (a rubber hose used to siphon someone else's car) and nevertheless the staff of life, the response could only have seemed absurd.

Dylan's Forest Hills combo played one more show, at the Hollywood Bowl on September 3 (see *We Had Known a Lion*, Vigatone bootleg). The band falls helplessly into the sound of then-current Top 40; only Levon and Robbie have any idea of where to take the music. Except on "Maggie's Farm" and "From a Buick 6," where Levon gets a big

beat and Robbie snakes solos down the spines of the tunes, the performance is held back by Kooper, Brooks, and Dylan himself. There were
walkouts and booing in Los Angeles; with dates in Texas looming,
Kooper and Brooks jumped ship ("Look what they did to JFK down
there," Kooper remembers thinking), and Levon and Robbie convinced
Dylan that the Hawks were a better band than he could find anywhere
else. They played their first show together on September 24, in Austin,
Texas; discouraged by the catcalls that rained down on the troupe at
almost every stop, Levon quit the group in late November, to be replaced by Bobby Gregg, in early 1966 by Sandy Konikoff (who had
once replaced Levon Helm in the Hawks when Helm briefly turned to
the guitar), and then by Mickey Jones, at the time Trini Lopez's drummer, and after that Kenny Rogers's. Abuse from disillusioned folkies
followed the Hawks all the way to Berkeley and San Francisco in
December—where, for a change, crowds fidgeted during the first half
of the shows, when Dylan appeared alone with his acoustic guitar, and
welcomed the electric noise with standing ovations. The boos returned
with a vengeance in the spring of 1966, when Dylan kept the tour going
through Australia, Scandinavia, France, Ireland, and the UK.

From October 1965 through January 1966 Dylan and the Hawks as
a whole or in part were in and out of Columbia's Studio A in New York,
cutting singles, one number that would turn up on Dylan's 1966 *Blonde
on Blonde* (Columbia), and a collection of discarded tracks that today
shine with a glamorous experimentalism altogether unique in the work
of either Dylan or the Band. The best of it is on the Dylan bootleg *Thin
Wild Mercury Music* (Spank); it's Dylan's phrase, and no one has ever
named the sound so well.

With Levon still present, Dylan and the Hawks cut two takes of
"Can *You* Please Crawl Out Your Window?" one of which was released
as a single in December 1965 (Columbia 43477), and in 1989 included
on Dylan's retrospective *Biograph* (Columbia). This was a carnival version of a song Dylan had earlier recorded (and which Columbia accidentally released as a B-side, and then pulled) with the musicians from
his *Highway 61 Revisited* sessions. I don't think he and the Hawks ever
sounded as if they were having more fun. There was a dangerous, hip-
ster-criminal threat around the edges of the music. "You got a lotta
nerve to say you are my friend," Dylan croaked, parodying "Positively
4th Street," his hit of some months before, which had briefly carried
the first "Crawl Out" on its flip, "if you won't crawl out your window!"
At the same session he and the Hawks taped "Jet Pilot" (lively, but at
this point in Dylan's rock 'n' roll career already generic) and "I Wanna

Be Your Lover" (vehement, funny, completely directionless), both included on *Biograph*, and the unfocused "Medicine Sunday," also known as "Midnight Train."

Despite the runaway train Dylan was riding in the fall of 1965, "Can *You* Please Crawl Out Your Window?" missed the Top 40. "One of Us Must Know (Sooner or Later)" (Columbia 4341), the next single—cut in late January 1966, with Danko on bass, Bobby Gregg on drums, Al Kooper on organ, and Paul Griffin, who had given Dylan's "Like a Rolling Stone" a hidden engine, playing the piano of his or almost anyone's life—didn't make the charts at all. The record was frenzied yet stately; Robbie closed out the tune with a few stinging notes worth more than the solos Dylan's songs had no room for. (The single was an edited version of the track that appeared at full length on *Blonde on Blonde*, an album mostly recorded later in the year with Nashville sidemen, though Robbie was also present, notably on "Obviously Five Believers.") A few days later, the same musicians recorded "Number One," an instrumental track for lyrics that were never written—a soaring, visionary piece that stands on its own.

In between came the most startling results of Dylan's and the Hawks' early collaborations. One was a slow, ruminating version of an older song, "I'll Keep It With Mine," later recorded indelibly by Fairport Convention on their 1969 *What We Did on Our Holidays* (Island) and, with fierce conviction, by Bettie Serveert for the closing credits of Mary Harron's 1996 *I Shot Andy Warhol* (see the soundtrack on Atlantic). There are very different versions of "Seems Like a Freeze-Out" (the original title for "Visions of Johanna," the stark, Nashville version of which highlighted *Blonde on Blonde*), a song Dylan began performing in concert in December, always in the solo parts of his shows. One take, from late November 1966, probably with Bobby Gregg on drums, moves on a loose, jaggedly syncopated rhythm; the piece is irresistible, but the beat doesn't give Dylan the room he needs to find the rhythm in the lyrics, and the performance falls far short of the song, one of Dylan's greatest. Another take is gorgeous—perhaps too gorgeous for the doomed, absolutely fated mood Dylan is trying to build. Garth's organ instantly seems to lift the song, if not the whole studio, about twelve feet off the ground; with Manuel's piano on one side and Robbie's quiet, unobtrusive guitar on the other, the music swirls, round and round, until, like someone waking from a dream of wonders in terror, Dylan ends it with a long, low moan. None of this was any warning for the version that first surfaced on the soundtrack album that accompanied Martin Scorsese's 2005 PBS documentary *Bob Dylan: No Direction Home* (hereafter Scorsese), much of which was made up of alternate takes that, while not featured in the film, had somehow escaped bootleggers for forty years or more. *On The Bootleg Series Vol. 7: No Direction Home* (Columbia) the song, titled "Visions of Johanna," again from late November, is a slashing cacophony of cruel fury, building on itself, threatening to shatter anyone who gets too close, while inside the music a few people nod off in a dank, half-lit room. The singer builds a curse around them; the guitar lines Robbie found for "Who Do You Love" here unravel, sparking a desperate commitment to the sound on the part of the other musicians, each of whom seems to be trying most of all to keep up with everyone else. My God, what is happening here? Who's already dead, and who's next? And who can't wait to find out?

Almost as powerful, again from January 1966, is "She's Your Lover Now," in two versions: the first, just Dylan alone on piano, singing very slowly, darkly; the second, with the Hawks, brutal, devastated, the emotion building on itself to an unbearable pitch of self-loathing and a wish for revenge. Included on Dylan's *the bootleg series, volumes 1–3 [rare & unreleased], 1961–1991* (Columbia), the performance is a black whirlpool. "You just sit around and ask for ashtrays," Dylan sings. "Can't you reach?"*

Many of the concerts Dylan and the Hawks played were recorded. Across three decades, only two numbers were released: "I Don't Believe You (She Acts Like We Never Have Met)," a poor, vague performance taped in Belfast and included on *Biograph*, and "Just Like Tom Thumb's Blues," the flipside of Dylan's 1966 single "I Want You" (Columbia 43683), taped in Liverpool, collected on *History*, and likely the richest and most extreme example of Dylan-Hawks music there is—five and a half minutes of pure hoodoo. It's Garth Hudson's most powerful performance; when Dylan sings his lines about Angel, "who just arrived here from the coast / Who looked so fine at first / But left looking just like a ghost," the sounds Hudson makes make it clear Angel got off lucky.

"He didn't know anything about *music*," Robbie said in 1973 about the Hawks' partnership with Dylan. "He was all folk songs, Big Bill, and we were Jerry Lee. So it'd be, 'Down the streets the dogs are barking— WHAM!' A huge noise. And Bob would say, 'Hey, that's great. Do it again that way.' We had no help; everyone who wasn't telling him the combination was wrong for him was telling us it was wrong for us."

What Dylan didn't know about music was how to work with a group.

---

* The most complete account one is likely to get of the *Blonde on Blonde* sessions, from New York to Nashville, is in Sean Wilentz's *Bob Dylan in America* (New York: Doubleday, 2010).

The marriage of his linguistic instincts, his hipster savvy, and his unmatched feel for the mysteries of American song to the Hawks' training and flair took them both to places they never could have reached alone. The music they made in 1965 and 1966 was the hardest rock 'n' roll anyone had heard, lifted by a lyricism that could turn contemplative in the middle of a storm—surrealistic dandy's blues subsumed by moments of forgiving gentleness and unforgiving confrontation. Onstage, they moved. Dylan and Robertston charged across the boards, stopped dead to play head to head, so close it seemed their hands would tangle in each other's strings; Rick Danko rocked back and forth on his heels as if, in Ralph J. Gleason's words, "he could swing Coit Tower." The group reveled in provcation. In Paris, to face a crowd of French students who understood Bob Dylan as the definitive anti-American ("Il est un *Vietnik*," said a student in Jean-Luc Godard's 1966 *Masculin-Féminin*), Dylan wangled an enormous Stars and Stripes (from the American embassy, it's said), hung it up behind the amps, and almost caused a riot (footage can be seen in *The Band: The Authorized Biography* and in Scorsese). They reveled in melodrama. To open a number, Dylan, Robertson, and Danko would turn from the audience toward drummer Mickey Jones, who would raise his sticks high, hold the pose, and then suddenly bring the sticks down with a crash as the three guitarists leaped into the air, kicking off the song as they whirled to face the crowd and hit the ground.

Out of this period came one official but officially unreleased movie, one shadow film, many bootleg albums, and finally a legitimate release. A bootleg comparison of *Long Distance Operator* (Wanted Man), a strong audience tape from the December 4, 1965, show at the Berkeley Community Theatre, with *A Week in the Life* (Razo) or, still better, *Bob Dylan & the Hawks Play Fucking Loud!* (no label), both superbly recorded and programmed and both drawn from May 1966 shows from across the UK, makes it plain how profoundly the music developed over the months. The Berkeley show, with the arrangements still bound to blues structures, is strong, at times sparkling with invention, but never quite free; the UK performances explode in all directions and reverse themselves in an instant, a dance of will and chance, risk and pleasure, a physical liberation based in the inner control of perfect timing. The supreme document, from 1970 on endlessly bootlegged as "The Royal Albert Hall Concert" but in fact recorded at the Manchester Free Trade Hall on May 17, 1966, was issued in 1998 as the waggishly titled *Bob Dylan Live 1966: "The Royal Albert Hall Concert": the bootleg series, vol. 4*

(Columbia): the entire concert, acoustic and electric, powerfully remastered, a false calm and then the hurricane. This is the famous night when an outraged fan rose to his feet to denounce the rock 'n' roll Dylan as "Judas!"—a moment that in Scorsese can be seen as well as heard (and followed, in riveting detail, in CP Lee's *Like the Night (Revisited): Bob Dylan and the Road to the Manchester Free Trade Hall*, London: Helter Skelter, 2004). The electric half of the show features eight songs, beginning with the unreleased "Tell Me, Momma" and ending with the notorious verbal battle between Dylan and the crowd ("I don't believe you," Dylan says; "C'mon, c'mon," Robbie says, trying to get the music going, the oldest trick in the world when a fight breaks out in front of the bandstand; "Play fucking loud," Dylan commands, and they tumble into "Like a Rolling Stone"). The musicians' timing in "Tell Me, Momma"—the way Robbie's careening solo falls into Jones's thump, the way Danko's bass flips the whole song into a cymbal smash, a dozen other moments—is unlike anything else in pop music, unless you count the rhythmic patterns Phil Spector contrived for Curtis Lee's 1961 "Pretty Little Angel Eyes." "If I told you what our music is really about we'd probably all get arrested," Dylan told an interviewer in Detroit in 1965. Listening to the Manchester "Ballad of a Thin Man," to the earth-cracking blues chord Robbie uses to open it, to Dylan's brutal pressure on every line, to the otherworldly tentacles of Hudson's organ, that boast still seems credible.

D. A. Pennebaker, who had filmed Dylan in England the previous year for the cinema-verité documentary *Don't Look Back*, shot the 1966 tour as well: mostly in the UK, with some filming in Scandinavia and Paris. With Howard Alk, Dylan edited the footage into *Eat the Document*, intended for ABC, rejected by the network, and seen only occasionally since (extended 1998 showings at the Museum of Television and Radio in New York and Los Angeles intercut the film with the sort of commercials it would have carried in 1967). At first *Eat the Document* is a jumble of cutaways, a travelogue with endless shots of crowds gathering outside the Albert Hall, much hotel-room composing and playing between Dylan and Robertson, with the fundamental text a variation on the theme of the betrayed fan ("Rubbish" says one English student after another of Dylan's electric music) and the artist-who-to-himself-must-be-true. *You Know Something Is Happening*, Pennebaker's version, which he has never been permitted to screen publically, remains unfinished. Along with several cute segments of Dylan and company attempting to put people on, the merit of Pennebaker's film is that it goes for long takes, most notably of Dylan and a very thin, scarred Johnny Cash harmonizing backstage on Cash's "I Still Miss Someone"; of Dylan facing the crowd, singing a long and ragged "Like a Rolling Stone," so unyielding it seems like a crime, the singer shouting into the microphone through cupped hands; a cut between pushing and shoving on the street into "Ballad of a Thin Man," the shift coming just as the song's chords change from narrative to warning. Finally, though, Dylan's film is only hard to see immediately: the onstage footage it uses, sometimes constructing a whole song out of bits taken from many performances, sometimes allowing only a kinetic moment, generates a sense of danger and adventure that Pennebaker's movie never hints at. *You Know Something Is Happening* has no theme; it's simply a set of performances circling a void. *Eat the Document* is the story of a cultural war, fought with guile and good humor, and no less powerful for coming at a viewer in pieces. The same can be said of Dana Spiotta's perfect-pitch novel of the same name. As a phrase that had come down the years more as the title of a rumor than a movie, *Eat the Document* (New York: Scribner) caught the sense of waste and disappearance that shot through the tale of a late-1990s fifteen-year-old obsessed with sixties music discovering that his mother is not who she seems—that, in some threatening sense, she has built her whole life to conceal the possibility that she is more like the records he loves than she will ever admit.

In July 1966, just after the release of *Blonde on Blonde*, Dylan's tours with the Hawks came to an end when he was injured in a motorcycle accident near his home in Woodstock. The next year, Dylan, Danko, Manuel, Hudson, and Robertson—the former Hawks now calling themselves the Crackers, or the Honkies, or nothing—regrouped in the Catskills, worked on *Eat the Document*, and began playing together on an almost daily basis, a practice that continued through the fall and winter, when Levon Helm joined the sessions. They ran through old songs from a vast medley of folk and pop genres, and sketched new ones. Mostly in the summer of 1967 they made what came to be known as the Basement Tape, so named because it was recorded in the basement of Big Pink. Never intended for release (fourteen new tunes were registered as publishing demos, and sent off to various performers—Peter, Paul & Mary, the Byrds, Manfred Mann, the Rolling Stones—who, save for the latter, immediately began recording their own versions), but soon bootlegged all over the world, the music the combo made was of greater emotional depth and subtlety than any either Dylan or the Hawks had recorded before, and it was more of a collaboration. (The patchwork documentary *Bob Dylan, the Band, and the Basement Tapes: Down in the Flood*, Sexy Intellectual, 2012, can be ignored.)

As noted above, much of the more finished material (some of it overdubbed) was finally issued in 1975 on *The Basement Tapes* (Columbia), a set that included sixteen of Dylan's vocals, plus eight early and new demos by the Band. Of Dylan's songs, "I Shall Be Released" (unbearable in its seventies incarnation as a pious, "Will the Circle Be Unbroken" mass-concert closer, but still as unearthly as it was first sung—"Aretha Franklin!" said a friend on first hearing the Basement Tape in 1968) was left off the album, but included on *the bootleg series, volumes 1–3 [rare & unreleased], 1961–1991*, along with "Santa Fe." The chilling, lovely, half-incomprehensible "I'm Not There"—stunningly translated by Howard Fishman on his *"The Basement Tapes"* (Monkey Farm, 2006), and, long bootlegged, forming a turning point in Brian Morton's novel *The Dylanist* (New York: HarperCollins, 1991)—was finally released officially in 2007 on the soundtrack album for Todd Haynes's film of the same name (Columbia) which also included a version by Sonic Youth. "Sign on the Cross" (an addled Primitive Baptist testament), "See You Later, Allen Ginsberg," the hilarious "Get Your Rocks Off"—all in all, 140 covers, uncompleted experiments, alternate takes, fragments, and abandoned masterpieces—were finally collected, under the name of Bob Dylan and the Band, in their original form, in 2014 as *The Basement Tapes Complete: The Bootleg Series Vol. 11* (Columbia). The sessions were loose, playful, at times startlingly sober and quiet, in others madly unhinged, with Dylan sometimes offering typescripts of lyrics to Danko or Manuel, thus resulting in his first cocomposer credits (Danko for "This Wheel's on Fire," Manuel for "Tears of Rage"). The Hawks often sang backup to Dylan's leads, or joined him as duos or trios; with Levon not yet on hand, Manuel or Robertston played drums when arrangements called for it. The music was funnier and more distant than what Dylan and the Hawks had made onstage, just right for tunes divided about equally between the confessional and the bawdy house, and which seemed to draw their deepest inspiration from the fated ballads of the Southern mountains and the nonsense of ancient folk standards like "Froggy Went A-Courtin'" ("ZOOLOGIC MISCEGENY ACHIEVED IN MOUSE FROG NUPTIALS, RELATIVES APPROVE," wrote Harry Smith in his notes to "King Kong Kitchie Kitchie Ki-Me-O," the variant he used for his *Anthology of American Folk Music*; his notes were the inspiration for the headlines in my Epilogue, and I'm happy to acknowledge him). I tried to follow that theme in *The Old, Weird America: The World of Bob Dylan's Basement Tapes* (New York: Picador USA,

2011, first published in 1997 as *Invisible Republic*), but most of all I like a line from Paul Nelson's September 11, 1975, *Rolling Stone* review of *The Basement Tapes*: "If there are tests, they've all been passed, and what you're hearing are the results."

On January 20, 1968, Dylan and the Band showed up for a Woody Guthrie memorial concert in New York; the album taken from the performance was badly recorded, and most of the performances were maudlin at best. Dylan and the Band tore out a lean, grimy rockabilly; on "Grand Coulee Dam" they came across. (See *A Tribute to Woody Guthrie*, Warner Bros. "Grand Coulee Dam" can also be found on the superb Dylan collection *Live 1961–2000*, Sony Japan; the not-so-hot "I Ain't Got No Home" is on *History*.) The official recordings of their show at the Isle of Wight Festival late in the summer of 1969 were atrociously produced, with the Band shoved far into the background and Dylan's muddled, unsure singing forced up front. A planned live album was killed, but four muddy-sounding numbers were spliced into Dylan's slapdash 1970 *Self Portrait* (Columbia). It was a buried-in-plain-sight error salvaged in 2013 with *Another Self Portrait* (Columbia). An expanded edition included the entire Isle of Wight show, but both that and the conventional release rescued (along with the previously unknown Basement version of "Minstrel Boy") the highlight of the day, a gleefully inflamed "Highway 61 Revisited," with Garth leading the way around hairpin turns while the rest screamed "OUT ON HIGHWAY 61!" like PCP junkies hustling tourists into the worst whorehouse in Tijuana.

Late in 1973, gearing up for a joint comeback tour, Dylan and the Band cut *Planet Waves* (Sony; originally on Asylum), mostly first takes of songs the Band had not heard before they walked into the studio. They came up with a rangy sound—"stray-cat music," Robert Christgau called it—nothing like the past music they had made, and nowhere near as good, either. *Planet Waves* was Dylan's first number one album: a kind of proof that in pop music, or in the cultural depression of the early seventies, legend, or a working nostalgia, was replacing any commitment to the present moment. The shows that followed made *Planet Waves* irrelevant.

Before the Flood (Sony, number one; originally on Asylum), recorded almost entirely on February 14, 1974, in Los Angeles, on the last night of the tour, caught the guts of the performance Dylan and the Band offered the country (*History* catches a "Highway 61 Revisited" supposedly recorded at Madison Square Garden; it sounds more like it was the Bonneville Salt Flats). Separately, neither Dylan nor the Band did anything extraordinary. The Band's eight numbers on *Before the Flood*

("Après moi, le déluge"? Sure, right) included an old, unreleased number called "Endless Highway," no more imaginative than its title (studio versions are on the 2000 version of *Cahoots* and the 2001 *Moondog Matinee*), but in general their music was a lot more raucous than on *Rock of Ages*; "Up on Cripple Creek" was a party of falling-down drunks. Together, Dylan and the Band cut loose with a noise that made the Rolling Stones' concerts of the time seem as orderly as they were, and yet within the clatter was an emotional paradox that often went beyond Dylan's words. Roaring with resentment and happiness, riding Levon's enormous beat, fusing all parts into a collective momentum, the music touched rock 'n' roll at its limits—a drama I reached for at the time in "Heavy Breathing" and "Highway 61 Revisited Revisited," both from *Creem*, and "A Moment of Panic," drawn from pieces in *City* and the *Village Voice*, collected in *BD by GM*.

With Dylan there to take the heat, that side of the Band that was scared of the crowd, that sought shelter in craftsmanship and careful arrangements, disappeared, replaced by the chaos and intensity of those old Howlin' Wolf records. With the Band around him, Dylan broke through the strictures of false casualness that had weakened his music after *John Wesley Harding* in 1967. He was forced to use most of what he had just to keep up, and so he became that stray cat, howling for the moon.

The music, as I heard it in concert, was hard and angry, payback for the boos of 1965 and '66, with Levon—sometimes Manuel joined him on a second set of drums—at the center (there was no booing, but the applause for Dylan's solo set of acoustic numbers was still far louder than for anything else). On record, the textures in the sound were primary, with Garth shifting the rhythms, darting in and out of every song like a phantom horn section, sometimes wrestling the tunes away from the other five and tossing them back like lit firecrackers. The earlier, studio versions of "Highway 61 Revisited" and "All Along the Watchtower," both singular, fully realized recordings, were momentarily blown away as Dylan and the Band charged through the songs as if they had little idea what route they were traveling, let alone where they were headed, playing with the good-humored, nervy conviction that the journey would return in surprise whatever it cost in doubt.

The music was made in a particularly American spirit: loud, crude, uncivilized. It was an old-fashioned, back-country, big-city attack on all things genteel—all things genteel in the audience, in Bob Dylan, in the Band, an up-to-date version of Walt Whitman's YAWP.

SLY STONE

Ben Fong-Torres's "Everybody Is a Star: The Travels of Sylvester Stewart," *Rolling Stone*, March 19, 1970, a history of Sly and the Family Stone up to that time (collected in Fong-Torres's *Not Fade Away: A Backstage Pass to 20 Years of Rock & Roll*, New York: Backbeat, 1999), is one of the finest profiles of a musician I have ever read, and I relied on it for much biographical information, not to mention inspiration. Thanks, Ben.

In his essential book *Sly and the Family Stone: An Oral History* (New York: For the Record/Avon Music, 1998), Joel Selvin cites Sly Stone's first record as "On the Battlefield of the Lord" b/w "Walking in Jesus' Name" (Church of God in Christ, Northern California Sunday School Dept., 78–101), made with his siblings in 1952 under the name of the Stewart Four. Sly, recording a year before Elvis first stepped into a studio, played drums and guitar. He was eleven. The performance was not included on the 2012 four-CD anthology *Higher!* credited to Sly and the Family Stone (Epic/Legacy), with extensive track notes and interviews by Edwin and Arno Konings, and a career survey by Jeff Kaliss (author of the authorized *I Want to Take You Higher: The Life & Times of Sly & the Family Stone*, New York: Backbeat, 2008, which is too authorized—censored not from the outside but from the inside), but there is a snapshot of the group, along with the basic career highlights, oddities, and many unissued recordings.

Thanks to tapes provided by the music historian Steve Propes, Sly's early secular discography can be pieced together. "The Rat" b/w "Ra Ra Roo" (Ensign 3-4032) and "Sleep on the Porch" b/w "Yum Yum Yum" (Keen 8-2113), both made in Los Angeles in 1959 under the name of the Stewart Brothers, all four tunes written by Sly, are fully arranged, sophisticated novelty discs complete with horns and complex vocal parts. They follow the paths of the Coasters and the Olympics (credited to Sly and the Family Stone, *In the Still of the Night*/Music Masters, a mishmash of early Sly material, includes a terrible early recording of the Coasters' "Searchin'"), with "The Rat" a standout: a loud combination of "The Signifying Monkey" and "The Purple People Eater." There is perhaps a hint of racial metaphor: "The rat made the cat scratch his back." The tunes were very much of their time, but for all the rough singing and guitar, what's notable is the care that went into the music: the will to get it right.

"A Long Time Alone" b/w "I'm Just a Fool" (Luke 1008), released in 1961 under the name of Danny Stewart (later issued as "Long Time Alone" b/w "Help Me with My Broken Heart" under the name of Sylvester Stewart, G&P 901), is a complete shift—to late doo-wop, echoing Little Anthony, Shep and the Limelights, and, with baion rhythm and strings, the Drifters of "This Magic Moment." None were written by Stewart ("Why did we have to part?" asks "A Long Time Alone"), and none were good—but all were all business. And what other twenty-year-old black singer without connections or backing had talked no-where labels into recording him with strings, horns, choruses?

In Vallejo, California, with Joey Piazza and the Continentals and the Viscanes, where Sly made common cause with future Family Stone horn-man Jerry Martini, Sly was part of the Viscanes' 1961 "Stop What You Are Doing" b/w "I Guess I'll Be" (Tropo 101—the latter cut bearing one of the more sublimely existential, or anyway incomplete, titles in the annals of rock), and the unwieldy Viscanes and the Continental Band's "Yellow Moon" b/w "Uncle Sam Needs You" (VPM 1006, 1961, later issued as "Yellow Moon" b/w "Heavenly Angel."). These three cuts, "Long Time Alone," and "Help Me with My Broken Heart"—plus other pseudo-doo-wop tunes and two weird, minimalist demos that may date from the formation of the Family Stone—can be found on the misleadingly titled and credited Sly and the Family Stone, *Dance to the Music* (Thunderbolt). "Yellow Moon" was a local hit; the noted food writer Michele Anna Jordan, an alumnus of Hogan Senior High in Vallejo, still gives it pride of place on her 1954 Seeburg Select-o-Matic 100.*

Three years later, in 1964, Sly was at the heart of what passed for the music business in San Francisco: one-song-per-group fifteen-act package shows at the Cow Palace, AM radio, tiny local labels, and North Beach topless clubs. He worked as a disc jockey for both KSOL (see airchexx.com for a sample of his work) in San Francisco and KDIA in Oakland ("Why don't you sing the whole show tonight?" Jerry Martini remembers asking him one evening. "And he did just that. He sang all the commercials, everything"). He produced shows and sessions for Tempo Productions and Autumn Records, and cowrote Bobby Freeman's "C'mon and Swim" (a dance-craze homage to a local topless queen) with ruling DJ and concert promoter Tom Donahue (famed through the early sixties for his signature line on KYA, the leading Top 40 outlet—"This is Big Daddy Tom Donahue, here to clean up your

* "Three of the first four Zodiac victims went to Hogan High," Jordan notes—"the first two" killed at Lake Herman Road, "where I used to park with my boyfriend; we all did, it could have been any of us."

face and mess up your mind"—Donahue's later work on KSAN-FM can be heard on *The Golden Age of Underground Radio featuring Tom Donahue*, DCC). "C'mon and Swim" was a national smash (#5, 1964), but Sly's own "I Just Learned How to Swim" b/w "Scat Swim" (Autumn, 1964), both awful, barely made local noise. Both are collected on *Higher!* along with the 1965 Autumn singles "Buttermilk (Part One)," "Temptation Walk (Part One)," and the unissued "Dance All Night." As collected on *Sly Stone—Recorded in San Francisco: 1964–67* (Sculpture LP), there is one bizarre anomaly in the wash of bad funk, cheap jazz, and stripper blues: a flat, pious reading of T. Texas Tyler's 1948 "Deck of Cards," a country gospel recital. "I was that soldier," Sly says, concluding the uplifting tale of a grunt who found God in a front-line poker game—and you almost believe him. Other collections covering this period include the interesting *Precious Stone—In the Studio with Sly Stone, 1963–1965* (Ace), which along with Sly's own recordings (the "Swim" numbers, "The Jerk," "On Broadway") features his productions on gospel singer Gloria Scott, nightclub act George and Teddy, and other local hopefuls—plus a radio spot and various collaborations with Billy Preston, and the less interesting *Listen to the Voices: In the Studio with Sly Stone, 1963–1970* (Ace). Preston's 1965 *The Wildest Organ in Town* (Capitol), which included Sly's "Advice" and an early version of "I Want to Take You Higher," marked Sly's major-label debut; he played piano.

By 1966 Sly had taken over as house producer for Autumn and its spinoff, North Beach. A remarkable selection of his more obscure work with the Mojo Men, the Vejtables, the Spearmints, the US, and the Even More Forgotten is on the anthology *Nuggets from the Golden State: Dance with Me—the Autumn Teen Sound* (Big Beat). His more noticed discs— actually released—are best heard on the anthology *San Francisco Nights* (Rhino), which collects the Beau Brummels' "Laugh, Laugh" and "Just a Little," the Mojo Men's "Sit Down, I Think I Love You," the Vejtables' "I Still Love You," and most notably the original recording of "Someone to Love," by the Great Society, Grace Slick's first band, credited as the Great!! Society!! (North Beach 1001). With the Jefferson Airplane, Slick would retitle the song "Somebody to Love" and take a soaring performance to #5 in 1967; with a B-side of "Free Advice," the Great Society gave the song a strong chant, still falling far short of the fury and dissolution the band found in the tune onstage. The North Beach "Someone to Love" can also be heard on the Great Society's *Born to Be Burned* (Sundazed), a disc filled out with fifteen additional Autumn tracks that had stayed justifiably missing for nearly thirty years; as caught in a recording made at a 1966 Great Society show at the Matrix, now included on the four-CD anthology *Love Is the Song We Sing: San Francisco Nuggets 1965–1970* (Rhino), "Someone to Love" is the fabled San Francisco Sound at its limit. Legend has it that Sly drove the band through more than two hundred takes of "Free Advice" ("It was only fifty-three," composer Darby Slick insists), not because the song was worth it, but because he didn't like rich hippies.

Cutting loose from Donahue, Sly formed the Stoners, staying out of the city, playing bars in the nether regions of the Bay Area. They turned into Sly and the Family Stone—Sly, guitar, organ, other instruments; Rosie Stone (Stewart), piano; Freddie Stone (Stewart), guitar; Larry Graham, bass; Jerry Martini, saxophone; Cynthia Robinson, trumpet; Greg Errico, drums—and released "I Ain't Got Nobody (For Real)" b/w "I Can't Turn You Loose" on the local Loadstone label (collected on *In the Still of the Night* and on the must-to-avoid Sly and the Family Stone, *Slyest Freshest Funkiest Rarist Cuts*, Magical Mystery, which also includes twenty outtakes of the mid-sixties Sly solo number "Life of Fortune and Fame").

In 2007 Epic Legacy reissued the first seven discrete Sly and the Family Stone albums, both individually and as the boxed *Collection*, with extensive liner notes and mostly redundant additional tracks, many of them instrumental demos. Jess Harvell's superb overview can be found on pitchforkmedia.com—he looked back from a time when "people my age are almost born suspicious" of an era when dramatic change seemed not only necessary but inevitable. That was the clarion call of the band's first album, *A Whole New Thing* (Epic), which appeared in 1967. It missed the charts, and while the 1968 *Dance to the Music* (Epic) did little better (#142), the title song—which really was a whole new thing—made the top ten. *Life* (Epic), also 1969, did poorly (#195), but the band broke through with "Everyday People," a number one single in early 1969.

Stand! (Epic) appeared in mid–1969 and changed black popular music—not to mention Miles Davis's. Among mainstream white American bands, only cross-bay Creedence Clearwater Revival, from El Cerrito, was left with a shred of credibility; the Golden Age San Francisco bands from the Jefferson Airplane to Quicksilver Messenger Service were left for dead. Casting the group's earlier album-chart rankings in doubt, *Billboard* never placed *Stand!* higher than #13, but it sold more than two million copies and stayed on the charts for two years. From it came the songs that made the Family name: "Stand!" "I Want to Take You Higher," "Sex Machine," and "Everyday People," all suffused with determination and delight. They were spread across the country from the Woodstock Festival, where "parting the Red Sea" (Harvell) performances of "I Want to Take You Higher" and "Dance to the Music" confirmed the band's ability to set a crowd on fire—or, as the thankfully late Albert Goldman had it, turn a rock concert into a fascist rally (see the anthology *Woodstock*, Cotillion).

Next came the mild "Hot Fun in the Summertime" (Epic) #2 in 1969 (the Beach Boys did summer better), and the straight, pre-*Riot* version of "Thank you falettinme be mice elf Agin" b/w the transcendent "Everybody Is a Star" (Epic) number one in 1970. Sly announced the next album, "The Incredible and Unpredictable Sly and the Family Stone"; unpredictably, it did not materialize. For the reasons why not, and for an unmatched portrait of the personal and professional troubles behind *Riot*, see Timothy Crouse's "Sly Stone: The Struggle for His Soul," *Rolling Stone*, October 14, 1971, collected in *What's That Sound?* edited by Ben Fong-Torres (Garden City, New York: Doubleday Anchor, 1976), and in *Reporting: The Rolling Stone Style* (Garden City, New York: Doubleday Anchor, 1977).

To fill the dry spell between releases, Epic assembled *Greatest Hits* in late 1970, and it reached #2, eventually selling more than three million copies. Earlier in the year, on July 13, the band had appeared on *The Dick Cavett Show*, where a notorious interview with Sly fueled tales of meltdown, but what transpired now looks like a set-up. After many live, on-camera delays (at one point, as Cavett stalled, fellow guest Debbie Reynolds offered to sing "Tammy"), and, finally, the late-arriving band's performance of "Thank you falettinme be mice elf Agin," Sly, wiping glistening liquid from his nose, sat down with Cavett, Reynolds, and Pancho Gonzales. Cavett baited the laconic Sly, whose responses to every question were direct, interesting, and, apparently unforgivably, questioning. Asked in what sense the band was a family, Sly listed the various family members in the band, and then everybody else. Cavett reacted as if Sly had answered in Latin. Asked how he composed, Sly explained that he wrote in a mirror, so he could judge his own, usually negative reactions to any line or melody. "When you say writing, you don't mean, literally, writing—" Cavett said. When Sly said that was precisely what he meant, Cavett responded with cocaine jokes. Finally Cavett asked if he could dress as he was, in a suit and tie, were he himself to play in Sly and the Family Stone. "Any way you like," Sly said. "Would I look funny, dressed like this?" Cavett asked. "To people who judge by the way you dress," Sly said. For the rest of the show, Cavett insulted him in every way possible, not even trying to hide his contempt; the whole sorry affair can be seen on the DVD set *The Dick Cavett Show—Rock Icons* (Shout).

A few weeks later, on August 30, 1970, a kind of counterpoint to the Cavett appearance was played out at the Isle of Wight festival, but it was far more telling. The band took the stage for the last night of the festival at seven in the morning, following Miles Davis, the Doors, the Who, and, of all crowd-killers, Melanie. The half of the audience that wasn't asleep was ready to leave. The group began roughly, hit its stride, and the audience woke up; the music reached a peak with "You Can Make It If You Try" and "Dance to the Music," the crowd was moving and shouting, but the moment on which the day turned—turned toward the future, turned toward the past—had already taken place. In the middle of the set, Sly had stepped forward to introduce "Stand!" He spoke slowly, and his voice seemed to swirl, as if he were telling three stories at once. The band set down a brooding, constant sound that almost immediately slipped away under Sly's words.

"People believe in a lot of different things," he said. "Through our universal thoughts, in general. I mean, the people who believe that what's up is up and down is down, simple things, you know. It's very easy to be fair, and don't kill nobody, and those things—first, if you step on my toe: 'Ouch.' A lot of things happened in the sixties. A lot of people *stood* in the sixties. A lot of people went down in the sixties—for standing. That's unfair"—and then he went into a clear, cool, floating a cappella "Stand . . ." as voices came in behind him, then instruments making nothing but the most distant, quiet vamp, raising the image of a small group of people, dressed in white as they were that morning, gathered in a circle, and then there is a drum beat, and the song begins, even though Sly has already said its piece. It's remarkable how, a few months after the end of 1969, Sly speaks of "the sixties" as if he's referring to an already fading, already historicized past. As he calls up a time completely gone, when once things were possible and no longer are, when once people acted and, by the casting of some strange spell, or its lifting, no longer can, it is more unsettling to hear how fragile his invocation of that past is, at least for these few suspended seconds, suspended between a vanished then and a shapeless, meaningless now.

There's a riot goin' on (Epic) reached back to the chorus of the Robins' (later the Coasters) 1955 hit "Riot in Cell Block #9" for its title: "Scarface Jones said it's too late to quit," convict Richard Berry drawled, as Jerry Leiber and Mike Stoller wrote: "Pass the dynamite, 'cause, uh, the fuse is lit / There's a riot goin on—" Hear the original on the Coasters'

50 Coastin' Classics, a superb Rhino Atco collection—or, if you favor closing circles, on *There's a Riot Goin' On!—The Rock 'n' Roll Classics of Leiber and Stoller*, which includes everything from the Robins' "Riot" to Tom Jones's "I (Who Have Nothing)." *There's a riot goin' on* emerged out of a swamp: to follow the story day by day, breakdown by breakdown, Joel Selvin's above-mentioned *Sly and the Family Stone: An Oral History* and his August 2001 *Mojo* story, "Lucifer Rising," collected in his anthology *Smart Ass* (Berkeley: Parthenon, 2011), are more rewarding than Miles Marshall Lewis's workmanlike *There's a Riot Goin' On* (New York: Continuum, 2006).

Riot shared its time with George Jackson's *Soledad Brother* (New York: Bantam, 1970), a book that, while now almost as discredited as its author, certainly had its effect on my ideas about Sly Stone and Stagger Lee. The great study of Jackson, the breakup of the Black Panther Party, and the collapse of radical left politics in the U.S.—and, in its way, kin to *Riot* in terms of its palavers with death—is Jo Durden-Smith's *Who Killed George Jackson?* (New York: Knopf, 1976). Completely ignored or misconstrued on publication by both leftist and mainstream reviewers (something I tried to redress in "Martyr in the Promised Land," *New West*, November 8, 1976), the book provides no comfort to anyone—and no excuses. James Carr, Jackson's closest friend, fellow convict, and, after his release from prison, Jackson's most trusted deputy, was shot to death by two hired killers across the street from my grandparents' house in San Jose in 1972; the political milieu of *Riot*, what Jess Harvell calls an "ashen nihilism," is re-created in *Bad: The Autobiography of James Carr*, edited by Dan Hammer and Isaac Cronin (New York: Herman Graf). Many years on, *Riot* can seem to reach much further back than the Coasters; there are nights when "Thank you for talking to me Africa" can feel as if it's speaking the same language as Skip James's "Devil Got My Woman," sounding the high, faraway moan of one man calling out from the dead, telling another man not to join him. "What led you to make that particular kind of album?" Nelson George asked Sly in 2012, during an interview that made up part of George's documentary *Finding the Funk* (VHI, 2014); they were speaking in Sly's daughter Novena's house in Culver City, California. "'Cause there were a lot of riots going on," he said. "That's probably it. There were a lot of riots going on. All kinds of riots, too. There were racial riots, and there were economical riots, and then, just—*riots*."

Riot was an immediate number one when it was released in late 1971, as was the first single taken from it, "Family Affair," which was about families breaking up (perhaps more important to *Riot* than Family Stone contributions were the guitar playing and arranging of R&B veteran Bobby Womack). No other album by Sly and the Family Stone ever went so high. Whether Sly's many white listeners were more open to his difficult new music than his white critics, who almost unanimously dismissed it, is a question chart positions will not answer: by this time, the black album-buying public was big enough to put an album over the top all by itself.

Fresh (Epic), complete with Richard Avedon cover portrait (the curse of rock—the Band's *Cahoots* had one too), arrived in 1973, and promptly settled into the top ten (#7); its single, "If You Want Me to Stay," topped out at #12. *Fresh* documented conflicts within the group: Rusty Allen replaced Larry Graham on bass (Graham went on to a successful career as a purveyor of bland funk), and Andy Newmark briefly replaced Greg Errico on drums. Added were Pat Rizzo on sax and Little Sister, a female trio headed by Sly's sister Vaetta, an uncredited singer on the previous albums, on backing vocals. Rumors of Doris Day accompanying Sly on "Que Sera, Sera" did not pan out.

In 1974 Sly and Kathy Silva celebrated their marriage (they were later divorced) and the birth of their son with a sold-out wedding at Madison Square Garden; arriving about the same time was *Small Talk* (Epic). By way of further personnel changes and failed music, it testified to the disintegration of whatever Family was left. The album peaked at #15, a good deal higher than it deserved to go.

From there the road was downhill—and I must acknowledge Martha Bayles's comment in her *Hole in Our Soul: The Loss of Beauty and Meaning in American Popular Music* (1994; Chicago: University of Chicago, 1996) that in contradistinction to my reference to Sly's problems with "bad dope," "Stone himself knew perfectly well that his problem was *good* dope." In 1975 came *High on You* (Epic—why not go all the way with "High on Life"?), credited to Sly alone, a pointless set that reached #45. By 1976 Sly was beholden to George Clinton and Parliament-Funkadelic for a spot as an opening act; he had to leave the tour after only a few gigs. There were no bookings; *Jet* magazine reported Sly was broke and in hiding—from whom it did not say. He did release the optimistically titled *Heard Ya Missed Me, Well I'm Back* (Epic), complete with unusual sleeve augmentations—an apology-by-proxy through the pop writer Al Aronowitz, an endorsement from the producer Kenny Gamble, and a cover photo of a happy-faced, one-man-band Sly that placed him at most two degrees from minstrelsy—but the album did not live up to its title, or make the charts. The last cut was

"Family Again"; no one was fooled, or rather no one would have been, if anyone had paid attention.

In 1979, as the disco craze was fading, Epic released *Ten Years Too Soon*, an album of old Sly hits remixed disco-style. Hadn't Sly anticipated the entire movement? Not really—and in any case it was three years too late. Later that year, Sly "and the Family Stone" (a few original members returned, for the moment) issued *Back on the Right Track* (Warner Bros., #152). Though it was a more than decent album, the "Hey, I'm *fine*, don't believe the rumors, I'm *O.K.!*" titles had begun to drag, and the record had no impact at all. In 1981 Sly collaborated with George Clinton on Funkadelic's excellent *The Electric Spanking of War Babies* (Warner Bros.), and also collaborated with Clinton by getting arrested for drug possession (charges were later dropped). Further touring was documented on the P-Funk All Stars' *Urban Dancefloor Guerillas* (Sony). The 1981 demo "Who the Funk Do You Think You Are?" rescued from oblivion on George Clinton and the P-Funk All Stars' *Go Fer Yer Funk* (Jasrac), suggested not the future but the past—the pre–Family Stone past. In 1982 there was another Sly Fam Stone bid, *Ain't But the One Way* (Warner Bros.), which featured a cover of the Kinks' "You Really Got Me" and "High Y'all," a rewrite of "I Want to Take You Higher"; a few stumbling, aborted shows in small clubs led the record into nowhere. Both Warner Bros. LPs were collected on CD as *Who the Funk Do You Think You Are: The Warner Bros. Recordings* in a 5,000-copy edition on Rhino Handmade; it is out of print.

There were more arrests, numerous stays in rehab clinics, "performing therapy" with Bobby Womack, then bench warrants issued after failures to appear in court, two years spent as a fugitive, arrests compounded by arrests. In 1985 A&M announced the *real* comeback, promising that Sly had tracks in the can that would blow Prince and all the hip-hop pretenders to Sly's throne right off the charts over the course of his new, long-term contract—which, as it turned out, guaranteed only a guest spot on Jesse Johnson's "Crazay" (A&M 2878) and one single under Sly's own name, "Eek-a-Bo-Statik" (A&M 2890, 1986). After the latter appeared on the soundtrack of the racist movie *Soul Man* (A&M—a white college student with bad grades dyes his skin black and gets into Harvard Law School through an affirmative action program), the deal fell apart; the sordid story is in Edward Kiersh's "Sly Stone's Heart of Darkness," *Spin*, December 1985. In 1986 Sly was a fugitive from cocaine charges in Los Angeles; he was arrested in Connecticut in 1989, extradited to California, and finally sentenced to fourteen months' incarceration in a rehab center. In 1990 he took the lead on "Good Times," a track on Earth, Wind & Fire's *Heritage* (Columbia); in stray moments he was spidery and elusive, but by the end he was barely audible, buried in the mix, as if he had only one take to give and could not get through even that.

In 1993, in Los Angeles, Sly appeared along with the rest of the Family Stone to be inducted into the Rock & Roll Hall of Fame; he smiled, but spoke hardly at all to the old friends around him. Rumors continued to circulate—of unspeakable dissipation, or unfettered creativity. In 1998 Sly contacted a fan who had set up a Sly Stone Web site, and brought him to Los Angeles; the unreleased work Sly played for him, Jon Dakss told *Rolling Stone*, brought tears to his eyes: "Nothing has changed—the talent is still there. I think he hasn't made a comeback because he doesn't want to. He could take the world by storm right now if he wanted to." But as Dakss spoke, Sly's music was once again on the radio, and had been for more than a year: in the form of commercials for Toyota, which in the course of a long-running campaign spun out the tagline of "Everyday People"—"*I-I-I-I am . . .*"—millions upon millions of times, all benefit to Michael Jackson, to whom Sly had sold rights to his songs years before.

It would be eight years before the curtains parted again.

On February 8, 2006, for the forty-eighth annual Grammy Awards, rumors were floated that Sly Stone would perform. It was one of the worst shows in memory, drowning in John Legend's smarm, with the post–Mariah Carey melisma of Kelly Clarkson, Mary J. Blige, Christina Aguilera, and Joss Stone functioning not as a sign of passion but of insincerity, to the point that what at first seems to be meant to appear as a loss of control is revealed as its imposition, the style forcing any woman feigning autonomy into practicing a pimp aesthetic. The Family Stone appeared—as so many said, despite the presence of Cynthia Robinson and Vaetta Stewart it was more a tribute band than anything else. Grammy swells swirled in the foreground, dancing to the music, singing Sly Stone's songs—and then there he was, apparently twelve feet tall, in a gold lamé top coat and a towering blond Mohawk glued to his bald skull, looking like a cross between Wesley Snipes and a sea monster. He mimed a few passes on organ, did not appear to actually sing, but there was something in the way he held his body that said he was alive, that he was not impersonating himself, that he was merely biding his time. He was gone almost before anyone could register that he had been there at all.

Very oddly, the drama continued. He appeared again, briefly, with the Family Stone at a club in Southern California, then in 2007 in Las

Vegas; in July, as David Kamp's interview with him appeared in the August issue of *Vanity Fair*, there was a headlining show in San Jose, cut short not by Sly but by the promoter. In *Vanity Fair*, Sly made jokes ("Still sporting the blond Mohawk under there?" Kamp asked, as Sly was wearing a motorcycle helmet. "Most of it growing *under* the skin," he said.) He quoted lyrics to new songs, including a startlingly hard verse from "We're Sick Like That": "Give a boy a flag and teach him to salute / Give the same boy a gun and teach him how to shoot / And then one night, the boy in the bushes, he starts to cry / 'Cause nobody ever really taught him how to die." "The obvious allusion to the current war jars me," Kamp wrote—despite the "bushes" that called up Vietnam, not Iraq—"and I soon realize why: Stone has been absent from the scene for such duration that it's hard to imagine that he was with us all along, experiencing all the things we experienced over the years— the fall of the Berlin Wall, the collapse of the Soviet Union, Nelson Mandela's release from prison, the rise of the World Wide Web, the attacks on 9/11, the invasion of Iraq."

An actual tour of Europe began in Italy; there for the *Guardian*, Sean O'Hagan struggled on July 15 to find good words to pass on, but O'Hagan always tells the truth. "The gaunt figure that shuffles unsteadily towards the keyboards centre stage is just about recognizable as Sly Stone. The signature afro is long gone, and, with it, the flamboyant stage clothes, replaced by an odd red, white and black ensemble that is a cross between a track suit and some old-school Formula One leathers. Sly does not look well. In fact, he looks like a broken man, old and infirm, the swagger that once bordered on arrogance replaced by a tentative, almost fumbling vulnerability." Video from a July 7 performance at the North Sea Jazz Festival posted on YouTube began with a meandering onstage orchestration of will-he-or-won't-he: "Look, up in the air!" "The first person to find him will get—two euros." Sly appeared in a T-shirt to his knees, baseball cap, necklace, huge shades, and everything stopped. He tried out a vocal distortion device. In a thin voice, he sang a very slow "Stand!" almost unaccompanied save for his own organ. His voice grew thinner as he moved on—he sounded country, like Charlie Pride—taking one word of a song at a time, as if each meant something. "I'm an old man," he said, "gotta go take a break, I'll be fucking back." He returned at the end of "Thank you falettinme be mice elf Agin," and there was soul in his voice that no one else mustered. The words inevitably took on a new meaning: "Thank you for letting me be myself, again . . . again . . . again . . . again."

From afar, you could wonder at the courage it took to mount even

a single stage—inevitably as a freak, not a human being, let alone someone with a song to sing and a reason to sing it. "So what if you can
destroy a person's career with the stroke of a pen," Sly wrote in a fax he
sent David Kamp just before the *Vanity Fair* piece was to appear, shifting back and forth between contempt for the writer and respect, all but
disavowing his apparently antiwar song with a defense of the Iraq war
and the president who made it. "I'm invincible," he signed off. "No, Sly,
you're washable and rinseable." The story stumbled on. There were
published reports that Sly was homeless and living in a van in Los
Angeles—countered by claims that the van was actually a recording
studio, or anyway a rehearsal space. In 2010 he appeared with Rufus in
Japan; that same year, at the Coachella festival in California, he broke
his songs, asking the crowd how long he had to play to get paid, railing
against thieving managers. In 2011 he was arrested again, and sentenced to a ninety-day rehab; in between he released *I'm Back! Family
and Friends* (Cleopatra). Aren't tribute albums terrible? Yes, and especially self-tribute albums. With new versions of old songs festooned
with guest stars—Ray Manzarek of the Doors, Ann Wilson of Heart,
Jeff Beck, Johnny Winter—the record wasn't terrible; there was just
no reason to listen to it.* The most illuminating chronicle of these of
Sly Stone's times is Dan Booth's "@higherslystone: I HAVE BEEN
LEARNING THINGS ABOUT MYSELF THAT WILL MAKE
THE MOST INTERESTING BOOK EVER" (Experience Music
Project Pop Conference, Seattle, 2014), a reading of Sly's Twitter account, beginning in 2011 and continuing to 2014, through *There's a
riot goin' on* and vice versa, each as a version of the same speech, in
content and form. Skipping through the puns, blank stares, and non
sequiturs that make up both sides of the discourse as Booth recon-
structs it ("THIEVES ARE BEING SURROUNDED" "IS IT TRUE
THAT EVERY HONEST MAN WILL LIE WHEN HE NEEDS
TO"), you come face-to-face with the fact that, in some ways, nothing
has changed, and it's the past, not the future, that's called into doubt,
that refuses to reveal itself, to be reduced to facts, dates, or eyewitness
testimony.

In his interview with Nelson George in 2012, Sly Stone appeared

---

* There was reason to listen to Steven Bernstein's Millennial Territory Orchestra's *MTO Plays Sly*
(Royal Potato Family), released at about the same time. While on *I'm Back!* everything is obvious,
here very little is: not Martha Wainwright throwing herself into "Que Sera" as if it were a Mayan
well, the disturbing moans all through "Sly Notions 2/Fun," Dean Bowman and Vernon Reid's
discovery of the blues hiding in "Time." The musicians seem to be chasing the music down, not
remotely sure they'll catch it, or that they deserve to.

small and thin—a far cry from the robust and mohawked stomper who showed up at the Grammys six years before. He truly did look like someone who'd been living on the streets for years. He was dressed in an old parka, as if he were always cold, and a black cap reading CALIFOR-NIA, with brown-blonde curls and a white beard under a black mustache. Even though he's sitting in a well-kept room, in your mind's eye you can see him sitting on the sidewalk next to a packing case. He can seem addled, but his demeanor is relaxed, protective, good-humored, wary, his eyes constantly twinkling, at first blunt, becoming more lucid and charming as he goes on. "What was your goal?" George asks. "Make people get along," Sly says directly. "And I thought maybe if I had that people, black people, white people, girls, all that, and we're playing, and we're having a good time, the audience would just have to get in there. There's just no way around it. Like *that*"—he gestured happily with one hand—"and I thought I was right."

"I'm looking for albinos now," he said. "I mean, that's the only really legitimate minority group goin' on." As Constance Rourke wrote in 1931 in *American Humor: A Study of the National Character*, "The story of Rip van Winkle has never been finished."

STAGGER LEE

"Stack-o-Lee" or "Stagolee" was one of several post–Civil War or turn-of-the-century ballads about semi-legendary characters (they were real, or with John Henry might have been, but their legends were more so): figures like Tom Dula ("Tom Dooley"), Casey Jones, Railroad Bill, Frankie and Albert (or Johnny). Endless variants were popular among blacks and whites; they were first recorded in profusion in the 1920s, by such songsters as Mississippi John Hurt, Furry Lewis, and countless others (see the *Anthology of American Folk Music, Vol. 1, Ballads* and *Vol. 3, Songs*, compiled by Harry Smith, 1952, reissued in 1997 by Smithsonian Folkways). These tunes form a special genre, or map their own country: characters sometimes jump from song to song. Furry Lewis put Alice Fry (source of the trouble between Frankie and Albert) into his 1928 "Kassie Jones"; in the country singer Tom T. Hall's 1972 "More About John Henry," John Henry meets up with Stackerlee, kills him, and throws his body into a river.

The facts about Stagger Lee were always present, in the public record, in the newspapers—but even after they were collected, in 1976, they remained unpublished. The story, it turned out, was more about forgetting than remembering. Just as once-celebrated, then shameful, public events can, in a conspiracy of silence, vanish from the common memory in less than a generation (in America, usually lynchings or racist pogroms), the imperatives of folklore are a means to changing history back into fable. Thus a sense of mystery became part of the Stagolee song; the song itself became a mystery, despite a few folklore facts that clung to the tale. Most versions share certain details. Stagolee fights Billy Lyons over Stack's Stetson hat (in a version collected by John Lomax, Billy spits in it; as Jeff Bridges's Wild Bill Hickok mutters all through Walter Hill's 1995 *Wild Bill*, "You just don't mess with a man's hat"); Billy begs Stag not to kill him because he has a wife and children to support; Stack-o-lee invariably kills him anyway. In many versions, the crime occurs on Christmas night; always a gun is used (usually a .44), never a knife. But beyond that the story, and Stacker Lee's fate, were up to the singer.

John Lomax seems to have been the first to publish the song; it was given to him in 1910 by one Ella Scott Fisher of San Angelo, Texas, as an account of a murder she said had taken place in Memphis about ten years earlier. At the time, some Memphians bragged that their town had the highest murder rate in the world; carnage among blacks was so great that meat wagons were stationed at the end of Beale Street on Saturday nights. When I wrote this book in the mid-1970s, I didn't yet understand that the unanswerable but irreducible question of folk song is that of how it is that one commonplace event becomes a locus of narrative while all those like it vanish as if they never were; it seemed odd to me that a single incident, no matter how colorful, would stand out from every other. That thought, plus the confusion in some early versions of the song as to whether Stagger Lee was black or white, made me wonder if a reversal was hidden in the shadows of the story. Perhaps, I speculated, a white man—Stacklee—killed a black man— Billy Lyons. Stagolee was no doubt never even charged, let alone hung. So blacks might have fought back through myth, first exacting justice in song, and then, wishing for a freedom and mastery they could never possess, identifying with their oppressor, seizing his identity and sub- suming it into their own culture, taking his name, and sending him out to terrorize the world as one of their own. Inversions of this sort are what myth is all about (in his notes to his *Anthology*, Harry Smith wrote that Frankie Baker, who in 1899 shot Albert Britt in St. Louis, was herself shot and killed by Britt)—but proof that the original Stagolee was white would have constituted almost as deep a smearing of cultural identity as Freud's claim that Moses was an Egyptian, so in 1974 I asked my friend Patrick Thomas, a Kentucky journalist, to go to Memphis and try to dig up the facts. Despite the fact that we were off by three hundred miles, Thomas was able to establish that there were two Stacker Lees: a black man he could not identify, and a white man whom he did.

Samuel Stacker Lee was born on May 5, 1847; he died on April 3, 1890. He was the son of James Lee (1808–89) of Memphis, who founded the Lee Steamship line, which ruled the Mississippi from St. Louis to New Orleans after the Civil War. "Father of the river packet service," James Lee began his career as a river man in 1833, on the Cumberland. He was a friend of Jefferson Davis and Nathan Bedford Forrest, a Confederate hero and a founder of the Ku Klux Klan; in 1863, at the age of sixteen, Samuel Stacker Lee went off to fight at Forrest's side, black manservant slave in tow. According to Shields McIlwaine's *Memphis Down in Dixie* (New York: Dutton, 1948), which was researched by William McCaskill, Stacker Lee came out of the war ready for bear: a rounder, a hell-raiser, an all-around tough guy and ladies' man, known up and down the Mississippi once James Lee gave him a boat of his own. James Lee liked the boy, McCaskill told Thomas; the rest of the Lee family, perhaps because his women were mulatto as often as they were white, spurned him. And though Stacker Lee did have at least one legitimate son—Samuel Stacker Lee, Jr., whom Memphians lost track of when he "moved west"—into the 1970s many black Memphians believed there was a second Stacker Lee, Samuel Stacker Lee's son by a mulatto mistress: according to legend, his father's son in every way.

The second Stacker Lee, Thomas was told by Thomas Pinkston ("the last man alive to have played with W. C. Handy," Pinkston said), was a roustabout, a waterfront gambler, a legend in his own time; when someone threw a seven, it was called "a Stagolee roll." But Pinkston could offer no more details.*

An early version of the song places Stagger Lee in "The Bend"—the Tennessee penitentiary—but that was a common ending to ballads of the 1910s and '20s. In *Memphis Down in Dixie*, McIlwaine identified Stag-o-lee as a small, dark man from St. Louis who worked the Anchor

---

* Pinkston (1901–80) was a legendary raconteur, and the flavor of his storytelling, as recorded in 1977 by Memphian Jim Dickinson, can be heard on Dickinson's anthologies *Beale Street Saturday Night* (Memphis Development Foundation LP), for "Ben Griffin Was Killed in the Monarch . . ." and "Mr. Handy Told Me Fifty Years Ago . . ." and *Down Home* (Fan/Jasrac) for "Policy Talk: True Story of Machine-Gun Kelly and the Memphis Blues," plus Pinkston's backroom, between-the-wars versions of "Dozens" and "Same Man All the Time." "This is bad," he says. "I can't sing this like I want to . . . but it's too nasty for me."

steamship line, and who took the name of the first Stacker Lee to give himself an aura of superiority ("And so it came about that the glamour about the white man's name among Negroes passed to a black with a bad eye who was celebrated in the ballad"), but there was no documentation; in his *Anthology* notes, Harry Smith wrote that the famous murder "probably took place in Memphis about 1900," and that "Stack Lee seems to have been connected by birth or employment with the Lee family of that city," but this too was only river drifting, even if it occasionally touched shore.

The year 1900—whether Smith's date or Lomax's—seemed too late as a date for Stacker Lee's encounter with "Billy"; Furry Lewis (1893–1981), who was singing the song in Memphis well before he recorded it in 1927, recalled nothing of any specific incident. Lawrence W. Levine noted in his *Black Culture and Black Consciousness* (New York: Oxford, 1977) that "Charles Haffer of Coahoma County, Mississippi, remembered first singing of Stagolee's exploits in 1895, while Will Starks, also a resident of the Mississippi Delta, initially heard the Stagolee saga in 1897 from a man who had learned it in the labor camps near St. Louis." No one seemed to recall anything very clearly about a Billy Lyons, or (as some variants had it) Billy the Lion, or Billy the Liar, though he too traveled on the legend line. Billy Lyons, William McCaskill told Pat Thomas, might have been a recasting of Sam de Lyon, a Memphis police officer famous for killing five men in one night. That would have turned my imagined reversal on its head: if the Stagger Lee ballad truly incorporated de Lyon, that would mean that in the fantasy of the song a black man, Stagolee, killed a white policeman. McCaskill also suggested that in legend de Lyon might have been conflated with "Wild Bill" Latura, a notorious white Memphis craps cheat and racketeer—who, Kenneth Neill wrote in "Beale Street Remembered," *R.P.M* magazine, January 1984, "blew away five black patrons at Hammitt Ashford's saloon on the corner of Beale and Fourth on December 10, 1908"—an event that could have entered the song after it had taken its initial shape. "'I just shot 'em,' shrugged Bill when the police arrived, 'and that's all there is to it.' Despite the statement, the all-white jury before which he was tried handed down a verdict of not guilty." For that matter, Thomas discovered years later, there was a gunman named Billie Lyons who in the 1880s operated out of a bar called the Bear Dive in Jellico, Kentucky, on the Tennessee line. In his memoir *Seventy Years in the Coal Mines* (privately published 1945; see geocities.com/seventyyearsinthecoalmines), the mine foreman Philip Francis describes finding one victim in the Bear Dive: "a middle-aged colored man lying on his back and shot through the neck. He motioned feebly with his hand to a white man named Tom Brennan as if he wanted to speak. Brennan kneeled down by him and placed his ear close to the dying man's lips. Suddenly Brennan cried out as if in pain. The dying negro had sunk his teeth into his neck. It was his last dying effort." After killing a marshal on the Tennessee side of the border, Lyons was killed by a sniper during a shootout in Jellico; there is no evidence that Lyons's name traveled up and down the Mississippi as a bad hat, but you never know.

What happened to Stagger Lee? Thomas asked Pinkston. "He just disintegrated; old Joe Turner took him up . . . he took 'em all up." By that Pinkston meant to prison in Nashville; Sheriff Joe Turner was infamous for running black prisoners, or sometimes simply black men rounded up off the streets, from Memphis to Nashville, where the state sold their labor to white planters. "They tell me Joe Turner came to town, brought one thousand links of chain," Lead Belly sang in "Joe Turner," a song he called the foundation stone of the blues: "Gonna have a nigger for every link." But Thomas's search in Memphis and Nashville through prison records, birth records, death records, and burial records turned up nothing. "The Bend," after all, was also "the ben'," as in the river, and as in a song about a "Stack O' Lee" riverboat, quoted by W. C. Handy himself, in his autobiography, *Father of the Blues*:

> *Oh, the Kate's up the river, Stack O' Lee's in the ben'*
> *Oh, the Kate's up the river, Stack O' Lee's in the ben'*
> *And I ain't seen my baby since I can't tell you when*

As it happened, though, there were hints of a true story in the haze that surrounded Thomas every time he asked a question, or received an answer: "St. Louis," "bad eye," and that most unlikely detail from certain versions, "Christmas night."

It was John David of St. Louis University, in his unpublished Ph.D. dissertation, "Ragtime Tragedies: Black Folklore in St. Louis," who in 1976 first assembled the legal and forensic facts of the historical events behind the legend of Stagger Lee (David's work is available on microfilm, or by individual copy in bound form, from UMI Dissertation Services). His path was retraced, and greatly extended, by novelist (*The Life and Times of Mr. Jiveass Nigger*) and memoirist (*Coming Up Down Home*) Cecil Brown with *Stagolee Shot Billy* (Cambridge, Masschuetts: Harvard, 2003), a landmark study of the world the song came from and the worlds it made. Brown agrees that the history of the Lee family of Memphis is part of the saga; the name had to come from Samuel Stacker Lee. But the rest of the story goes far past anything anyone ever dared to invent.

In his reconstruction of events, Brown describes how, at about ten p.m. on December 25, 1895, in St. Louis, at Bill Curtis's saloon, one Lee Shelton—alias Stack Lee, as it reads on the document charging Shelton with murder, but also known as Stagolee—a small man with a crossed left eye, born in Texas in 1865, raised in St. Louis, shot and killed one William Lyons. A bar dustup, one might think: too much liquor, an everyday story. It wasn't that by half.

The incident made the papers—the *Globe-Democrat*, even the German-language daily—but it was in the December 29, 1895, issue of *St. Louis Star Sayings* that Brown found his first hints of a new story. The article centered on a secret society, the "colored 'Four Hundred'" (the name came from the then-current term for New York high society); following the killing, authorities claimed Lee Shelton was the president of the society, and that Lyons's death was the result of a "negro vendetta," with roots in a feud going back to 1890. One J. C. Covington, identifying himself as the financial secretary of the "400," admitted that Shelton was a member of the society (formed only on December 6 of the year, "for the moral and physical culture of young colored men"), indeed its captain, its third-ranking officer, but denounced talk of a feud: "This vendetta is all bosh, as no such idea has ever been conceived." What, exactly, was being claimed, and what was Covington denying?

"The two negroes," the *Star Sayings* piece began, "were in the saloon drinking and discussing politics" when they "began skylarking. Shelton snatched Lyons's hat and broke it. There was a dispute over this, during which Lyons threatened to kill Shelton. The latter returned Lyons's hat, and then Lyons snatched Shelton's.

"This caused a renewal of the argument and it was said that Lyons was in the act of putting his hand in his pocket threateningly when Shelton stepped back a few paces, drew a forty-four caliber revolver and fired. The bullet entered Lyons's stomach.

"Lyons fell to the floor, and Shelton coolly took his hat out of the prostrate man's hand and walked out of the room."

Shelton was arrested the next morning; Lyons, who though not married did indeed have three little children, died later that day. A crowd of three hundred gathered for the inquest—held, as was the custom, in front of the corpse—and there were fears of a lynching: a

black-on-black lynching. Why, for the killing of a notorious local en-
forcer by a well-known bar owner and pimp?*

Brown sets the scene, re-creating the saloon culture of turn-of-the-
century black neighborhoods: saloons were clubs, often highly politicized, with bitter rivalries, businesspeople tying their ships to one
political party or the other. Stack Lee and the 400 were headquartered
in Bill Curtis's saloon, where gathered the "hot stuff," men and women
dressed to the ceiling (and, matching Bobby Seale's version of the tale,
just down the street from a whorehouse called the Bucket of Blood)—
but the ceiling was higher at nearby Bridgewater's, where the real quality held court. Bridgewater's was the headquarters of the black caucus
of the Republican Central Committee, and of course almost all blacks
voted Republican, faithful to the party of Lincoln since Emancipation;
at Curtis's one found renegade black Democrats, those who believed
the Republicans took blacks for granted, and who thought they might
have more leverage with the other party. It was at Bridgewater's that, in
1890, a friend of Lee Shelton's was shot to death by a friend of William
Lyons's; Shelton had vowed revenge. The owner of Bridgewater's, Marie Brown, had powerful political connections; she was also considered
Lyons's mother-in-law. But Shelton had the feared Nat Dryden: "the
first lawyer in the state of Missouri," Brown writes, "to gain a conviction of a white man for murdering a black." Ordinarily, a black-on-
black killing might have merited little if any jail time; with Marie
Brown turning the screws, Shelton was looking at death.

In 1896 Dryden got Shelton a hung jury, with three votes for an
outright acquittal. But Dryden died of alcohol and morphine addiction
soon after the judge declared a mistrial. When Shelton was tried again
in 1897 he was convicted and sent to prison—and by that time, Brown
writes so magically, with a sense of art overtaking life, "he must have
heard the Stagolee songs many times. He would have heard them in the
Valley [the nightlife district of black St. Louis], where he had a bar, and
he would have heard them when he went to the Silver Dollar saloon,
where all the ragtime musicians hung out. Reigning over the group was
Tom Turpin, whose father ran the Silver Dollar . . . a few years later
Turpin himself would open the Rosebud, the most famous ragtime café

---

* In "The Original Gangsta" (*Boston Globe*, June 1, 2003), Mark Shone takes issue with Brown's portrait
of Shelton as a strutting brothel mogul, calling it vastly inflated and romantic; as a historian, Shone says,
"Brown has a nostalgic allegiance to what Stagger Lee signified in the '60s, and an inability to see that his
hero is more tragic than revolutionary." It is true that part of Brown's portrait of Shelton, down to mirrors
on his shoes, is speculative; it isn't true that his book is remotely naïve about who Shelton was, what
Stagolee became, and where Stagger Lee has gone.

in St. Louis. Turpin and Lee Shelton must have become good friends because after Shelton was in prison for a few years, Turpin petitioned the governor to give him a pardon."

The case didn't die. Year after year, advocates on both sides pressed one governor after another for pardons and refusals of pardons. Petitions for Shelton were signed by a state senator and ten of the twelve jurors who convicted him. Finally, in 1909, Shelton was set free. Arrested again for robbery, he was returned to prison, deathly ill from tuberculosis. The Democratic governor granted parole; the attorney general objected.

"Stack" Lee Shelton died in the prison hospital on March 11, 1912. By then he was already a specter in culture, a body irrelevant to the abstractions of his own myth, and nowhere near as real as his legend, with people in Memphis, New Orleans, Chicago, and New York already saying, "Oh, Stacker Lee? Bad man, bad man, lived right here, don't know where he's gone."

The timing was appropriate; black and white sides of the story remained on parallel lines, with the first phases of the tale ending nearly in tandem. In 1902, twelve years after the first, white Stacker Lee was buried (not, for what it's worth, in the Lee family plot), James Lee, Jr., put a boat named for his brother on the Mississippi: the *Stacker Lee*. It was the crack boat of the Lee line, 223 feet long with a 43-foot beam, the most famous boat on the river, known not only as "Stack O' Lee" but, for its gambling and traveling prostitutes, as "Stack O' Dollars"— in his novel *Another Good Loving Blues* (New York: Viking, 1993), Arthur Flowers has his hero remember "when there weren't no such thing as blues," when he first started out playing piano, on the *Stacker Lee*. In 1916 the boat dragged a landing and went down. James Lee, Jr., was the last riverman in the family, and he died in 1905; he left well over a million dollars, and relatives fought over the money for thirty years. There was a strange match in Southern California almost fifty years after the Lee will was finally settled, with black and white lines long since crossing: "The parents of a college football player who died in 1981 in a jail cell will receive about $1 million in a legal settlement," the *New York Times* reported in 1983; it was Stagger Lee who forced the deal.

Ron Settles, a twenty-one-year-old black man, was arrested for speeding in the private, white community of Signal Hill, and taken to jail; later he was found dead in his cell. His parents, represented by the late Johnnie Cochran, later world-famous for winning an acquittal for O. J. Simpson on double-murder charges, sued for $62 million, charging that Settles had been beaten and then strangled to death by Signal Hill police; the police claimed suicide. There never was a trial. The parents settled out of court, "as a result of a high-school composition written by Settles his father provided in a deposition" a few days before the case was closed—so said Stephen Yagman, the Signal Hill attorney. "Yagman called the composition 'highly damaging,' saying it demonstrated Ron Settles was 'aware of the notion of jailhouse suicide,' had contemplated it and, in fact, 'admired it,'" the *Times* went on. "Yagman said the composition, which Settles reportedly wrote about four years before his death, concerned the legend of Stagger Lee, a black folk hero of the South. According to legend, Stagger Lee enjoyed superhuman powers. In the paper, Yagman said, 'Settles said he admired Stagger Lee because people had shot at him and he didn't die, but particularly that he had hung himself in a jail cell and hung there for 30 minutes and in the end lived to laugh at everybody.'"

Still, the fight over Stacker Lee's legacy is a fight over meaning, not money; in 1987 blacks tried to take the legend back with the off-Broadway musical *Staggerlee*, written by Vernel Bagneris with a score by Allen Toussaint. Set in New Orleans in the late '50s, during Mardi Gras, the production starred Ruth Brown, a top fifties rock 'n' roll singer. Employing a *Rashomon*-style narration ("Stackolee shot Billy Lyons"—"Stag-o-lee fighting with Billy the Lion over a Stetson hat"—"Staggerlee shot Billy Bottom"), the script turned the story around until it swallowed its tale: not only was Bagneris's Stagger Lee innocent of any crime, his "dissatisfaction with his lifestyle and the possibility of being thought a criminal" leads him "to seek redemption" and try "to 'straighten up.'"

The play closed quickly; the legend had never sold tickets to heaven. But there were other plays.

In 1977, in Washington, D.C., a man named Mike Malone was fired as arts director of Western High School for the Performing Arts. Relying on his ties with the virtually all-black student body, he responded with a street play called *The Life and Times of Stagolee* (the play was originally meant to be staged in a nightclub, but shortly before it was to open, the owner was shot to death and the club closed). The *Washington Star* told the story: "Malone's adaptation of the Stagolee ballad is [a] somewhat allegorical view of the problems at Western ... To Malone, Stagolee 'represents that part of each of us that strives to be free to live our lives as we wish.' And more than that, said one teacher who worked closely with the production, Stagolee represents Malone himself, who fought unsuccessfully to lift the school for the arts out of the institutional constraints of the school system.

"The symbolism comes out strongest when Stagolee, who has 'shot poor Billy dead' over a gambling argument, is called before the Lord to answer for his sins. The teachers pointed out that the Lord took on the image of Superintendent Vincent E. Reed, who dismissed Malone. The Lord's chief advisor in the play consults a female St. Peter, who was said to represent Superintendent Dorothy L. Johnson, who bumped heads with Malone throughout the Western controversy. In the play, the Lord tells Stagolee: 'You have been disruptive and insubordinate and you ain't got no respect for nothing. So we gone have to get rid of you because if there's one thing we cannot have, it's disorder.' But down on earth, Stagolee's mentor, the Voodoo Woman, complains that the powers that be don't understand Stagolee, because they have 'stopped up their ears and closed their minds,' a charge Malone's supporters have often leveled at school authorities.

"Whether or not the audience understood the allegorical connections, they clearly enjoyed the play, despite the poor acoustics and faulty sound system. The audience was made up mostly of residents and regulars of the 14th and T Street area—children, teenagers on bikes, winos, and prostitutes. Some T Street residents had box seats at their bedroom windows and front stoops. Some stood on milk crates or trash cans to watch the action.

"Assistant D.C. Police Chief Tilman O'Bryant, one of the Street Theatre's strongest supporters, says he attends the opening performance every year. 'It takes the kids out of the ghetto, develops their talent, and then brings it back to the ghetto,' he said. 'Who else has the nerve to bring something into the ghetto? They're all scared to come down here.'"

Year after year, the story returned to its source, the progenitor archetype forgotten, the tale surfacing in the papers as an ordinary crime report—except that even then, as in an account from the April 15, 1993, edition of the *Virginian-Pilot*, some hint that the story was more than ordinary, that it demanded more from a writer than facts, was almost always present. Laura LaFay's "Man Guilty of Murder in Dispute over Stetson" (passed on to me by the critic Ricky Wright) had a Norfolk dateline: "Roy Tolbert couldn't find his black cowboy hat at the Fox Trap nightclub last summer," LaFay began. "But he did find his gun.

"It was a .44 Magnum pistol. He used it to murder 21-year-old Kerry Bright, one of three men he suspected of stealing the hat. Before collapsing in the Fox Trap parking lot, Bright took out his gun—a .357 Magnum—and shot once at the fleeing Tolbert, hitting him in the back of the leg.

"Both men were sailors. Both were at the Fox Trap with friends Aug. 21. And both were armed. On Thursday, a jury convicted Tolbert, 24, of second-degree murder and use of a gun.

"'This is something that, 20 years ago, would have ended up in a fistfight, a punch in the nose,' said prosecutor Catherine Dotson. 'But now, with the proliferation of guns, it ended up a . . . murder.'

"According to testimony during the two-day trial, Tolbert was partying at the Fox Trap in the 800 block of E. Little Creek Road, when he noticed that his Stetson was missing. Told by other patrons that Bright and his friends had stolen the hat, he went outside and confronted them.

"'He asked us, like three times,' testified Osmon El-Wahhibi, a friend of Bright's who was with him at the Fox Trap that night. 'He was like, "I know one of y'all have my hat. I saw you take it off the table." And we were like, "Man, we don't have your hat. Go ahead on."

"Tolbert, who was stationed aboard the guided missile cruiser San Jacinto, then went to his car and got a gun. A few minutes later, Bright approached him in the parking lot.

"'Hey bitch,' he said. 'You know you want to talk to me about your hat?'

"Tolbert shot Bright in the chest and ran away.

"He did it, he said, in self-defense. He was afraid Bright was going to shoot him.

"'I didn't think I was going to make it through the night and I was scared,' he said.

"'This was not about a hat,' said Tolbert's attorney, Jeffrey Russell.

"'This is about macho-ism. It was about some need to prove something. But not on Mr. Tolbert's part.'

"Dotson didn't see it that way.

"'It wasn't self-defense,' she said during closing arguments. 'It wasn't even close to self-defense.'

"'Kerry Bright got shot point blank in the chest because Roy Tolbert couldn't handle being called a bitch by someone he thought took his hat.'

"'We don't want people like Roy Tolbert walking around our community with a loaded .44.'

"The jury recommended a sentence of 12 years. Circuit Judge William F. Rutherford will officially sentence Tolbert on June 17.

"Bright, who was from Greenville, N.C., had been stationed at the Norfolk Naval Base.

"'Obviously, my client will live to see another day,' Russell said of Tolbert. 'In that respect, at least, he was the more fortunate of the two.' "Tolbert's hat was never found."*

Tracing the shape of the Stagolee ballad to the African-American folk song "The Bully of the Town" (or "The Bully"), Cecil Brown has surmised that the Stagolee ballad emerged in 1895 or 1896 as a "slow drag" ragtime number, but nothing of the sort was recorded. "'The Bully Song,' a form of the coon song, is about a bully who beats up 'the bully of the town' and is rewarded by the authorities," Brown writes. "The plot of the Bully Song and of some variants of 'Stagolee Shot That Bully' are the same. In both, one bully kills another and becomes the 'boss bully.' This plot mirrors St. Louis politics, where bullies were hired to go out and get votes and do 'dirty' work. If one bully got into trouble for killing another, he would get support from the whites he worked for." In 1907 the white singer and actress May Irwin recorded a rousing version of "The Bully" where the melody and rhythm anticipate the earliest recorded versions of "Stagolee"; onstage, she would pantomime a fight between herself and a little black boy (see the invaluable nine-CD set *American Pop: An Audio History—From Minstrel to Mojo—On Record, 1893–1946*, compiled by Allen Lowe, West Hill Audio Archives). Brown is more compelling when he moves from sociology to art. In "We Did Them Wrong: The Ballad of Frankie and Albert," his account of how the St. Louis street singer Bill Dooley likely composed the original "Frankie and Albert" ballad before Albert's body was in the ground (see *The Rose & the Briar: Death, Love and Liberty in the American Ballad*, ed. Sean Wilentz and GM, New York: Norton, 2004), he suggests that Dooley might have done the same four years before. "We often think that folk songs spring from the anonymous public, or the folk," Brown said. "But in time, place, and style, the 'Frankie' ballads, like the 'Stagolee' songs, point to a single author. This doesn't mean that the people didn't help produce them, by contributing to their transmission. It may be that, yes, to create a great folk ballad, you need a village—but you may also need an untaught genius."

The first recorded version of the song—of its melody, headed by the title "Stack O' Lee Blues"—may have been by Frank Westphal and His Regal Novelty Orchestra, an "instrumental foxtrot" released in 1923 on Columbia. The sheet music version, credited to Ray Lopez and Lew Colwell, appeared in 1924, but despite elaborate lyrics it had noth-

* © 1993 *Virginian-Pilot* (Norfolk, Virginia). Used by permission.

ing to do with anything remotely connected to Lee Shelton: it was a name-of-the-dance number ("Stack O' Lee Blues / I don't know what it means / Come on honey let's be stepping / 'Cause my feet won't keep still . . . I long to hear them play that Stack O' Lee") combined with a racist playground chant. What was memorable was neither the words nor the weak tune, but the art, by the leading sheet music illustrators William and Frederick Starmer: in red, blues, white, black, and pink, a swirling abstraction made up of dozens of circles, dots, and rectangles, a perfect match for the dada experimental films being made at precisely the same time. Look and you see the solar system; look again and you see only the vortex of a black hole. Despite the encouraging "Get This Number for Your Phonograph and Player Piano," the first hit came the same year with the instrumental of the same name by Fred Waring and His Pennsylvanians on Victor (Waring's 1928 version, collected on *The Fred Waring Memorial Album*, Viper's Nest, has some of the swing of Handy's "St. Louis Blues" and none of the conviction). The earliest recording by a black performer seems to be Ma Rainey's 1925 "Stack O' Lee Blues" on Paramount, a full jazz-band orchestration with Fletcher Henderson on piano and Coleman Hawkins on bass sax (see *Ma Rainey's Black Bottom*, Yazoo). But these were only records.

Frank Hutchison (1897–1945), a white slide guitarist from the West Virginia mountains, cut "Stackalee" in 1927 for Okeh; remarkably, its details (not merely the Stetson hat but the barking bulldog, the fight in the alley) seem to reappear more clearly in Lloyd Price's 1958 pop hit than in any of the countless versions put down in the years between. Hutchison makes a good joke out of the story: "God bless your children, I'll take care of your wife," Stack says after Billy begs for mercy. "They taken him to the cemetery," Hutchison sings in his bone-dry drawl. "They failed to bring him back." But as the song ends we find Stack in jail—haunted by Billy's shade crawling around his bed. See *Frank Hutchison: Complete Recorded Works in Chronological Order, Volume 1, 1926–1929* (Document), or Bob Dylan's leaping cover of Hutchison— as "Stack A Lee"—on his 1993 *World Gone Wrong* (Columbia). "what does the song say exactly?" Dylan wrote in his liner notes. "it says no man gains immortality through public acclaim. truth is shadowy. in the pre-postindustrial age, victims of violence were allowed (in fact it was their duty) to be judges over their offenders—parents were punished for their children's crimes (we've come a long way since then). the song says that a man's hat is his crown. futurologists would insist it's a matter of taste. they say 'let's sleep on it' but they are already livng in the sanitarium. No Rights Without Duty is the name of the game & fame is a

282 NOTES AND DISCOGRAPHIES

trick. playing for time is only horsing around. Stack's in a cell, no wall phone. He is not some egotistical degraded existentialist Dionysian idiot, neither does he represent any alternative lifestyle scam (give me a thousand acres of tractable land & and all the gang members that exist & you'll see the Authentic alternative lifestyle, the Agrarian one). Billy didn't have an insurance plan, didn't get airsick yet his ghost is more real and genuine than all the dead souls on the boob tube—a monumental epic of blunder & misunderstanding. A romance tale without the cupidity."

Beale Street singer Furry Lewis made the delicate "Billy Lyons and Stack O'Lee" (notable for its placing of Billy before Stag), also in 1927, on Vocalion; the knowing, stolid refrain, "If you lose your money, learn to lose," kept company with Charlie Poole and the North Carolina Ramblers' "If I Lose, I Don't Care" (for Lewis's version, see his *Complete Recorded Works in Chronological Order, 1927–1929*, Document; Poole's Columbia recording, which follows the best-known "Stagolee" melody, and is in its way as cavernous as any of Robert Johnson's tunes, can be found on many collections, most strikingly on the cigar-boxed set *"You Ain't Talkin' to Me"—Charlie Poole and the Roots of Country Music*, Columbia Legacy). The year 1927 also produced the otherwordly "Original Stack O'Lee Blues" by Long Cleve Reed and Little Harvey Hull—Down Home Boys on Black Patti, collected on the anthology *The Songster Tradition: 1927–1935* (Document): recording in Chicago for Black Patti, a Chicago label, they naturally, or with good commercial instincts, set the story in Chicago. Mississippi John Hurt's "Stack O'Lee Blues," featuring a dramatically hurried, irresistibly pretty guitar intro, is one of the most seductive of his many recordings (see his *Avalon Blues: The Complete 1928 Okeh Recordings*, Columbia Legacy). The 1946 performance by Memphis Slim, Big Bill Broonzy, and the original Sonny Boy Williamson (John Lee Curtis), with their accompanying conversation on the ballad as nothing more than a version of the next day's labor (on *Blues in the Mississippi Night*, Rykodisc), is probably the most chilling. The most influential post–World War II version, before that of Lloyd Price, was by the New Orleans singer Archibald; his "Stack-A-Lee I & II" was a top ten R&B hit in 1950 on Imperial (see his *New Orleans Sessions*, Krazy Kat LP, or the anthology *Piano Power—Gettin' Funky—The Birth of New Orleans R&B*, Proper). Archibald offered the complete scenario of Stagger Lee's fight with the devil: here we find not Stack haunted by Billy's ghost, but Stagolee chasing Billy's soul down to hell, where Billy suffers still further tortures. New Orleans R&B singer Dr. John covered Archibald's "Part II" on *Gumbo* (Atlantic), his 1972 Crescent City tribute, retaining the complex lyrics and adding the classic guitar solo from Guitar Slim's 1954 "The Things That I Used to Do," plus a horn intro that can break your heart.

Lloyd Price, also from New Orleans, put the tale on jukeboxes and car radios all across America in 1958 and 1959. "Everybody had a Stagolee version," Price told Cecil Brown in 2005, speaking of growing up in the forties. "They never called it Stagolee, but something like Smack-o-lee. We would just stand on the corner and make up things. That's the kind of genre we put Stagolee in." "Stagger Lee" was Price's first and only number one pop hit, topping the charts for four weeks straight; he had a number one R&B hit in 1952 with his floating "Lawdy, Miss Clawdy (see Price's *Lawdy! 1952–1956*, Specialty). Soon after he was drafted; in Korea, he put on a forty-five-minute Stagger Lee play. "I even had a thing that looked like a dog," Price told Brown. "I had two big sets of craps made up." A few years later, it all came together.

Judging strictly by lyrics, Price's version takes the prize, if only for his completely original introduction: four lines that with the perfection of a haiku set the scene with extraordinary tension and grace. What was that street corner where Price made up his Stagger Lee lines? In Florence there's an intersection made of Inferno and Purgatorio streets; New Orleans has Desire and Pleasure.

> *The night was clear*
> *And the moon was yellow*
> *And the leaves . . . came . . . tumbling*
> *Down*

"I had soldiers acting out the words I was saying," Price told Brown of the play he staged in Korea. "[I had them] point at the sky. 'And the leaves came tumbling down'? That refers to the play. There were no leaves in Korea. So we had to imagine leaves come tumbling down. 'The night was clear'—well, we had clear nights, but no trees. After the Army, two-and-a-half years later, I recorded it . . . that was a play, when I said the lights change. It was like a movie. I got [the arranger] Don Conte to make the voices sound like instruments. I was using white singers because I didn't want that doo-wop sound."*

---

*Brown, "Lloyd Price and 'Stagolee,'" unpublished, 2005. Courtesy Cecil Brown. Brown's "Wer Hat Angst Vorm Schwarzen Mann?" which includes comments by Price on his friendship with "Stagger Lee" fan Muhammad Ali, was published in *1958: Ein Jahr und Seine 20 Songs*, ed. Philipp Oehmke and Johannes Waechter (Munich: Süddeustsch Zeitung GmbH, 2005). "He still *loves* 'Stagger Lee,'" Price said, remembering how, in 1958, when Price passed through Ali's hometown of Louisville, Kentucky, a teenage boy

Price's record was all momentum, driven by a relentless saxophone, and in retrospect his manic enthusiasm seems to be what many earlier versions lacked. However, an interesting thing happened. As "Stagger Lee" was rising up the charts, Dick Clark booked Price onto *American Bandstand*—and then realized he could not possibly expose his millions of young viewers to a song that celebrated gambling and murder, especially with payola investigators breathing down his neck. Without missing a beat, Clark had Price change the lyrics. Price's label pulled the original record, had Price record the *Bandstand* version, and the result was a story wherein Stack and Billy "argue," not gamble, about a woman, not money or a hat. Stagger Lee and Billy go home, suffer remorse for all the mean things they've said to each other, and then apologize. "Stagger Lee was no more sore," Price concluded. Paradoxically, Price sounded even more impassioned than he had in the first place, and his band outdid itself. Though Price (or Dick Clark) had succeeded in turning the great tradition not only on its head but inside out, the tradition, as one might expect, won in the end: ever since 1959, when the radio has called up Price's hit it is only the once-banned version that is played (both the original and the *Bandstand* variant are on Price's *Greatest Hits—The Original ABC-Paramount Recordings*, MCA).

Stella Johnson countered with the answer record "Trial of Stagger Lee" (Night Train, 1959; courtesy Dave Marsh), where Stack's claim that "I didn't know the gun was loaded" ("*He didn't know!*" chirp the women in the courtroom) doesn't make it past the judge: "You knew the gun was loaded / When you fired that second shot." Wilbert Harrison's 1970 version on Sue, which follows Price's story line, is unique among modern treatments for its cautionary tone: "That'll teach ya 'bout gambling," he warns. The Isley Brothers may have added to the

---

ran up to him outside the Top Hat Lounge. "I'm Cassius Marcellus Clay," Ali said, using the birth name he would refuse when he joined the Nation of Islam. "I'm the Golden Gloves champion of Louisville, Kentucky; someday I'm going to be the heavyweight champion of the world; I love your music and I'm going to be famous just like you." "Stagger Lee" was "one of Larry Holmes's favorites, too," Price said. "They see themselves in the role and image of Stagolee?" Brown asked. "Obviously so," Price said, "because Stagolee is a bad guy—a good bad guy. He wore the white hat. That's how they see themselves, as the same kind of guy. He didn't start the trouble, but he ended it." The song took in more heavyweight champions than Ali and Holmes. As Mike Marqusee writes in *Redemption Song: Muhammad Ali and the Spirit of the Sixties* (New York and London: Verso, 1999), regarding the 1974 meeting of then heavyweight champion George Foreman and the supposedly washed-up Ali in Kinshasa, Zaire, in 1974, "Eight days before the scheduled fight, Foreman sustained a cut above the eye while sparring. The bout was postponed from 25 September to 30 October ... The music festival, a celebration of the African diaspora organized by Lloyd Price, could not be postponed. The first night was poorly attended, but the government gave away tickets and the final night drew a huge crowd. When Price himself mounted the stage to perform 'Stagger Lee,' Ali was on his feet"—just as, it seems, Stagger Lee held his robe when Ali finally entered the ring and took Foreman's crown by a knockout in the eighth round.

subtradition of Billy's "sickly" wife when in 1963 they cut a raging stomp (withering guitar fire courtesy of a young Jimi Hendrix) that, Dave Marsh swears, has Billy trying to talk Stack out of the inevitable by hinting, "I got four little children and a very *shapely* wife" (on the Isleys' *Complete UA Sessions*, EMI—"I got three hundred little children and a very horny wife," Elvis would insist at a 1970 rehearsal). Ike and Tina Turner's 1963 "Stagger Lee and Billy," on Sue, tells the story from the perspective of the innocent bystander: when the trouble starts, Tina hides under a table and puts her hands over her ears, but somehow misses nothing. The most striking recent treatment is by the Brooklyn bluegrass band the Felice Brothers: their "Dream On," from their *God Bless You, Amigo* (thefelicebrothers.com, 2012) is a dream of regret. "Stagolee," it begins, the name standing still like a statue, but the following "Why'd you do that?" puts the story square into the present. The music begins to move like a quietly turning stream, carrying the killer farther and farther away from the life he could have lived if, just that once, he hadn't pulled his gun. At the same time, the dream pulls back, so what you see is Stagger Lee in the moment before his act, seeing all the way into the half-life he will live from the next second on: the half-life of prison, and the half-life of a real person who disappeared into legend so long before he actually died that you can imagine him forgetting his own name.

I hear Tina Turner's witness under the table as a shadow character in Ace Atkins's *Leavin' Trunk Blues* (Thomas Dunne/St. Martin's, 2000), which centers around a man who, in the 1950s, is given a contract to kill a Chicago R&B producer, one Billy Lyons, and who thus takes the street name Stagger Lee. He becomes a drug lord; in his sixties, he's still a killer, with a long trail of bodies behind him and new ones piling up, but his legend is his mask. "We got all kinds of stories on the street," a community activist tells the man tracking Stagger Lee. "Lots of folks blame their lives on Stagger Lee . . . Your car's stolen? Stagger Lee did it . . . Stagger Lee's the man who haunts our dreams in the South Side. He runs gangs, right? He brought crack to the housing projects? And started turf wars? Hell, I even heard he organized Saturday night dog fights back in the sixties. They'd throw the loser onto church door steps. Usually a church who was tryin' to clean up a neighborhood. Those tales keep people from getting involved . . . Yeah, if Stagger Lee was one man, all our lives would be much easier." But thinking never undressed the archetype. "The hustlers were our heros," Lloyd Price said in 2005: "the ones who hung out at bars, drove big white Cadillacs, whitewall tires, and wore Stetsons. Any of those guys were Stagolees."

"There was many a pimp named Stack, and many a card hustler named Stakdollar," Dr. John wrote in 2004 in his notes to *N'Awlinz: Dis Dat or D'Udda* (Blue Note), where "Stakalee" was a pimp song. "We mixed the story up. All this is folk music. An epic saga of death and char-ak-ters." Cecil Brown continued his pursuit of the story with his novel *I, Stagolee* (Xlibris, 2004), which had its effect on Derek McCulloch and Shepherd Hendrix's irresistible graphic novel *Stagger Lee* (Berkeley: Image Comics, 2006)—part folklore, part love story, part thrilling *Law & Order* episode with a deadpan denouement (Lee Shelton hears a guitarist in the next cell playing "Stagolee": "That song about me," Shelton says. No, says the singer: "I think Stackalee from Memphis"). Percival Everett raised the stakes with his novel *Erasure* (2001; Minneapolis: Graywolf, 2011). Appalled by the nearly totalitarian success of *We's Lives in Da Ghetto*, a novel about the degradation of the African-American woman by the African-American man that confirms the nation's simultaneous impulses toward social work and concentration camps as answers to all questions of race, Everett's narrator, an African-American experimental novelist and professor of critical theory named Thelonius Ellison ("Call me Monk") begins to hear voices: "My mouth opened and I couldn't help what came out: 'Why fo you be axin?'" Out of his rage comes *My Pafology*, a nearly illiterate novel about the all-American degradation of African-American life by one Stagg R. Leigh and starring one Van Go Jenkins as a nineteen-year-old black man with four children—Aspireene, Tylenola, Dexatrina, and Rexall—by four different women. "The work inhabited no space artistically that I could find intelligible," Ellison says after emerging from a writing trance, but America will pay anything to hear the story it tells, and Ellison finds that his identity is being erased by a specter that, no matter how unintelligible, he somehow carries within himself.

Because Jamaican rock 'n' roll began in the fifties partly in response to R&B broadcasts originating in New Orleans, it's no surprise Stagger Lee made himself felt in ska, rock steady, and reggae—but in fact he nearly took the music over, ruling its symbolism at least until the late sixties, when he was ousted by Natty Dread and the Rastafarians, much as Big Red Little was finally buried by Malcolm X. The years between were spent in a long and frequently hilarious cultural struggle, as Stagolee, in the person of the rude boy—the Kingston hooligan who terrorized his own community—claimed his rights, celebrated his prowess, and fought off the inevitable answer records that called for his rehabilitation (or, failing that, his demise). Of the hundreds of discs that tell this story, the most striking are the 1967 tunes that make up Prince

Buster's "Judge Dread" trilogy ("Judge Dread," "The Appeal," and "Barrister Pardon," the latter also known as "Judge Dread Dance," all collected on *Judge Dread Featuring Prince Buster—Jamaica's Pride*, Melodisc/Blue Beat LP; there must be a CD with all three numbers, but I haven't been able to find it), which were naturally accompanied by numerous rudie-talks-back 45s. Buster (who in 1966 himself recorded a version of "Stagger Lee") produced a set of three-minute morality comedies: a black judge arrives from Ethiopia to clean up the Kingston slums, sentences various rude boys to hundreds of years in prison ("I am the rude boy now," he crows), jails their attorney when he has the temerity to appeal, and then, having reduced all wrongdoers to tears, sets everybody free and steps down from the bench to dance in the courtroom. The final lines—"I am the judge, but I know how to dance"—pretty much sum up the ethos of post–rude boy reggae. Prince Buster was years ahead of his time, but the wheel turns; today he is ahead of ours.

Mixing Jamaica's cultural work with the street life of punk-era Great Britain, in 1979 the Clash used the Stagger Lee–rude boy conflict as the underpinning of their epochal *London Calling* (Epic/CBS). Changing names, faces, and races, the old troublemaker appears in "Jimmy Jazz," "Rudie Can't Fail," "The Guns of Brixton," and most powerfully in the shattering "Death or Glory," which was Stagger Lee brought down to earth and made domestic. "Every cheap hood strikes a bargain with the world," Joe Strummer sang, piercing the Stackerlee aura with a realism it had always deflected. "And ends up making payments on a sofa or a girl / Love 'n' hate tattooed across the knuckles of his hands / The hands that slap his kids around 'cause they don't understand / How death or glory / Becomes just another story." Stack had surfaced under his own name just a cut earlier, in "Wrong 'Em Boyo," originally a 1967 rock-steady hit by the Rulers, who begin with a New Orleans–piano cover of Lloyd Price's "Stagger Lee" and then break into a slow, sad lament: "Don't you know it is wrong / To cheat the trying man?" (included on the anthology *Radio Clash*, Mojo). The Clash redid the number with a singular introduction—"Billy said, 'Hey, Stagger! / I'm gonna make my big attack / I'm gonna have to leave my knife / In your back'"—somehow pulling the knife the real Billy Lyons always carried out of the confusion before making the Rulers' heartfelt plea for good behavior.

Those seem to me the most memorable Stagolees, though I've omitted many of the more famous recordings (the website staggerlee.com estimates that, as of 2008, since 1927 a new version of the song has been recorded every ten weeks), from Duke Ellington's 1928 "Stack O'Lee Blues" to Cab Calloway's 1931 "Stagger Lee" to P. J. Proby's 1969 "Stagger Lee" (well, the latter not exactly famous, but certainly demented). A version of the tale close to that offered by Bobby Seale can be found on *Get Your Ass in the Water and Swim Like Me!—Narrative Poetry from the Black Oral Tradition* (Rounder, 1974, recorded by folklorist Bruce Jackson), and, skipping over numerous prison recordings of male and female black inmates by Alan Lomax and others, on Nick Cave and the Bad Seeds' "Stagger Lee" from their 1996 *Murder Ballads* (Mute) and Samuel L. Jackson's stomping "Stackolee" in the 2006 film *Black Snake Moan* (the soundtrack is on New West; the stunning dance floor the performance creates is on YouTube). They come from the tradition of prison toasts—ritualized declamatory insults and stories that in some cases have changed barely a word in a hundred years. Nearly all such toasts, not the least Stagolee's, whether in the form of Bruce Jackson's jailhouse field recording, Cave's almost Shakespearean rant (which if it takes off from Johnny Otis's 1969 "The Great Stack-o-Lee" from *Snatch and the Poontangs*, Kent, doesn't stay there), or Samuel L. Jackson sounding as if prison is precisely where he learned the piece, are so obscene they can sound like an assault not merely on rational discourse (Cave's Stag Lee orders "Billy Dilly" to perform fellatio on him, then shoots him dead as he complies) but on English itself—though, today, for whites, that may be because few understand Elizabethan obscenity as well as Cave, or enjoy it half so much. "I'm using the Nick Cave version," the porn producer Benny Profane said in 2007 of his film *Ballots and Bullets: The Deviant Life of Stagger Lee*, notable for its setting in 1832 (based on a misunderstanding of the lines "It was back in '32 when times were hard / He had a Colt .45 and a deck of cards / Stagger Lee"—presumably Profane had not heard of the Great Depression, or that there were no Colt .45s in 1832), and for actress Sasha Grey giving birth to a pig.

It's out of the toast tradition as much as from the ballad line that the overwhelming reemergence of the Stacker Lee archetype in gangsta rap came: thousands of dope-king brags and gun-thug taunts and dares, self-affirmation all mixed up with the purest nihilism, among them, at the start, Schoolly D's "Gangster," Ice Cube's "AmeriKKKa's Most Wanted," and the Geto Boys' "Mind of a Lunatic," until Tupac Shakur and Biggie Smalls could catch the whole odyssey in an album-cover stare. "Just like Stagger Lee himself," Nick Cave said, "there seem to be no limits on how evil this song can become." Not that Lloyd Price himself was done testing those limits. In 1998, on *a body with nobody* (Kjac), he released his own gangsta "Stagger Lee," with a rap by Freddie Foxxx over a slow, meandering pulse that felt like nothing so much as Sly's "Thank you for talkin' to me Africa." "The night was young and the moon was black, as I think about these two cats it's bringing me back, thug style in their Stetson hats, as I listen to this old man's story of fame and street glory intact," Fox chanted at the start; Price knew where his song came from, and he knew where it went.

As for the Stagolee reflection in rock 'n' roll, the records referred to in the text are "Crawling Kingsnake," by John Lee Hooker, first recorded for Crown in 1949; Tommy Johnson's "Canned Heat Blues," Victor, 1929; Muddy Waters's "Rollin' Stone," Chess, 1950; Chuck Berry's "Brown-Eyed Handsome Man," Chess, 1956; Bo Diddley's "Who Do You Love?" Chess, 1956; Wilson Pickett's "I'm a Midnight Mover," Atlantic, 1968; the Rolling Stones' "Midnight Rambler" (the studio version on the 1969 *Let It Bleed* is weak; the definitive, live performance is on the 1970 *Get Yer Ya-Yas Out!* both Decca/London); Howlin' Wolf's "Back Door Man," 1960, and "Going Down Slow," narrated by Willie Dixon, 1961, both Chess; and Bobby Marchan's "There Is Something on Your Mind, Pt. 1 and Pt. 2," Fire, 1960.

RECORDS BEFORE AND AFTER "RIOT"

The crunch of fear and repression under Richard Nixon (see the late Jonathan Schell's originally unsigned *New Yorker* editorials, collected in his *Observing the Nixon Years*, New York: Pantheon, 1989) and the growing tension between black movies and black music that emerged in the early seventies brought a realistic necessity to the pop charts—but realistic social commentary has not been particularly common in black American music. One could point to the occasional blues about the Great Depression or Lead Belly's Party-line "Bourgeois Blues," a few tunes about Korea (updated for Vietnam)—not much more. Many of the Coasters' records—"Riot in Cell Block #9," "What About Us?" ("He's got a car made a' suede . . . If we go out on dates, we go in a box on roller skates"), "Framed," "Hongry," and the cryptic "Run Red Run" (a monkey, who may represent the Negro, pulls a gun on his master, who may represent the white man)—are notable partly because in the fifties they were so anomalous. All were strictly white inventions, or white fantasies about black life, written and produced by Jerry Leiber and Mike Stoller—though it should be noted that when asked about their work in the 1950s as white producers of black artists, to the end of his life Leiber would insist that, then, "We weren't white."

More typically, black voices have channeled the emotions kicked up

by political exclusion and social despair into songs of sexual and romantic tragedy. It took the civil rights movement (and the riots in Watts,
Harlem, Newark, and Detroit in the mid-'60s, plus the riots that broke
out all over the country following the assassination of Martin Luther
King in 1968) to make black protest acceptable on the radio, not that
protest was always needed: for the 1967 Detroit riots, Martha and the
Vandellas' 1964 "Dancing in the Street" served as a ready-made anthem. Sly's "Everyday People" was a turning point, along with Jerry
Butler's saddening "Only the Strong Survive," #4 on Mercury in 1969,
and the Temptations' "Cloud Nine," #6 on Gordy in 1968. The last was
the first black pop record to hit dope head-on—as far as the singer was
concerned, with open arms.

Butler's hard look at the world at large—even if still couched in
terms of love and loss—and the Temptations' tour of the streets led
Paul Kelly into the church to cast out the money-changers: his "Stealing in the Name of the Lord" (Happy Tiger), #49 in 1970, #14 on the
soul charts, was a sharp attack on shyster preachers preying on the
misery of the black community. "Step right up, drop a buck," Kelly
chanted over a fast blues guitar. Even more impressive was Swamp
Dogg's *Total Destruction to Your Mind* (Canyon, 1970), one of the great
lost albums of the last fifty years, which brought together a weird selection of protest songs, among them Joe South's "Redneck," with soul
arrangements of unsurpassed elegance. ("Redneck" is on *The Best of 25
Years of Swamp Dog . . . Or F**k the Bomb, Stop the Drugs*, a Pointblank
Classic set that also includes "If It Hadn't Been for Sly," an increasingly
disturbing tribute that combines Swamp Dogg's incessant, squeaky
background cheerleading, a deep lead vocal that grows colder with every chorus, and, emerging out of the murk of the music, ever more
awful moans of self-loathing and despair—Sly's part, perhaps, and I
don't mean metaphorically.) Other seminal discs included Edwin Starr's
"War," number one in 1970 on Gordy, with its nicely understated cho-
rus: "WAR! Good God! What is it good for? ABSOLUTELY
NOTHIN'!"—and, all from 1971, the Chi-Lites' brooding "(For God's
Sake) Give More Power to the People," #26 (Brunswick); Marvin
Gaye's historic "Inner City Blues," #9 (Tamla); Undisputed Truth's
"Smiling Faces Sometimes (Tell Lies)," #3 (Gordy); and the Staple
Singers' "Respect Yourself," #12 (Stax).

If the breakthrough came in 1971 with *There's a riot goin' on*, the
takeover came in 1972 with Curtis Mayfield's soundtrack to *Superfly*
(Curtom; see also *Superfly Deluxe 25th Anniversary Edition*, an expanded
two-CD version released in 1998 on Rhino, a fabulous package adver-

tised as a "time-capsule of '70s chic," though it did not include a DVD of the movie, which in its freedom from Hollywood censorship—i.e., the bathtub sex scene between Superfly and his strong black woman— caught a moment of cinematic jailbreak that passed almost as quickly as it appeared). With the Impressions and later as a solo artist, Mayfield had been exploring a somewhat bland progressivism for years, complete with open heart, boundless optimism, tortured lyrics, and brotherhood speeches to nightclub audiences; he sang buoyant numbers like "We're a Winner," sticky ones like "Choice of Colors" ("Which one would you chose, my brother?"). With "Freddie's Dead," #4 on Curtom in October, and the sardonic yet sympathetic "Superfly," #8 in December, Mayfield found a new voice, and the new-thing music to go with it. His triumph was complete when the *Superfly* album hit the top of the charts. Paralyzed in an onstage accident in 1990, Mayfield died in 1999 at the age of fifty-seven; his work was collected on *People Get Ready: The Curtis Mayfield Story* (Rhino).

Along with *Superfly* came the deluge: the O'Jays' "Back Stabbers," #3 (on *Back Stabbers*, Philadelphia International); War's "Slipping into Darkness," #16 (the complete version is on War's *Grooves & Messages: The Greatest Hits of War*, Avenue, which also includes an 8.46 "Darkness" remix); Stevie Wonder's "Superstition," number one (on *Talking Book*, Motown); Johnny Nash's shimmering "I Can See Clearly Now," number one (on the album of the same name, Epic); the Staple Singers' "I'll Take You There" (Stax), number one (on *The Best of the Staple Singers*); and the Temptations' "Papa Was a Rolling Stone" (Gordy), number one—most of them crammed into the last months of 1972.

Contrasting most sharply with the heroes of the new black inner-city Westerns—a replicating genre best captured in Darius James's unfettered *That's Blaxploitation!* (New York: St. Martin's Griffin, 1995)—were the Chi-Lites and Al Green. They were vulnerable, unsure, searching for new ways to define what it meant to be a man. Green's string of hits began in 1970, with his "Tired of Being Alone," #11; "Let's Stay Together" was quickly number one in 1971, and "Look What You've Done for Me," likely his best, was one of three top ten hits in 1972. Recorded for Hi in Memphis, his records continued and expanded upon the fundamental Memphis pop aesthetic, as defined at Sun and redefined at Stax: a direct, uncluttered sound, a small, intimate ensemble of musicians, a single, naked voice. The hits (as collected on Green's *Greatest Hits*, Hi, or the four-CD *Al Green Anthology*, Right Stuff/Hi) did not tell the whole story; Green's superb albums from this period, topped by *Call Me* in 1973 (Hi), drew on Hank Williams as easily as gospel. Following a scandalous incident in which a woman killed herself after covering Green with scalding grits, Green turned ever more surely toward sanctified music, in 1977 producing one last masterpiece, *The Belle Album* (Hi); he then opened his own church and began recording for the Myrrh label, a subsidiary of Word, Inc., the giant religious conglomerate that later provided the born-again testimony of, among others, Eldridge Cleaver and Watergate felon Charles Colson. The Chi-Lites' more extreme and at times even more moving music is best heard on their *Greatest Hits* (Rhino), which collects "Have You Seen Her," #3 in 1971, "Oh Girl," number one in 1972, plus "A Lonely Man" and "The Coldest Day of Her Life," all originally on Brunswick.

The chart positions of these post-*Riot* records were extraordinary. They represented the most politicized black music in the history of rock 'n' roll and the most commercially potent. Never before, and never since, have black voices so dominated American radio.* But even as this unique outburst of creativity and capitalism was peaking, a retreat was under way—as if those most responsible for the new music trusted neither themselves nor their audience.

The Chi-Lites' "We Need Order" (Brunswick), which died at #69 in 1972, was joined in anti–Stagger Lee over-compensation by the Four Tops' "Keeper of the Castle," #10 in 1972 (Dunhill 4330), which linked *Superfly* street life to politics and damned both: "While you're worryin' about society / The leaves are witherin' on your family tree." Such rational conservatism was matched in a completely idiotic way by Brighter Side of Darkness's "Love Jones," #16 in 1973 (20th Century 2002), and more subtly by the Gamble-Huff labels. The contingent social vision of the O'Jays' "Back Stabbers" was undercut by the sentimental social vision of "Love Train," a brotherhood anthem (and a wonderful sound—see *Back Stabbers*); when the group's next few releases flopped, they returned with *Ship Ahoy* (Philadelphia International), #11 in late 1973, and almost an answer record to Randy Newman's "Sail Away"— because the ship in question was a slave ship. The album was tied to a single, "For the Love of Money," that rather tiredly pegged all evil to filthy lucre, but the killer was the title tune, a ten-minute Middle Passage epic. It was pretentious, overblown, and powerful.

---

* With the importance of radio in the pop world reduced in the 1990s and after, when dance clubs, video channels, ringtones, and downloads superseded simple airplay as a means to pop lingua franca, black voices, whether romantic or assaultive, whether hip-hop or neo-soul, were at least as prominent in American music a quarter century and more after *Riot* as in its time—and that after long periods in the 1980s and after when the radio might have led one to believe that black Americans had ceased to exist.

Most black groups, writers, and producers continued to step back from the work of 1971–72, or trivialized that work with poor self-imitations; their music, like Sly's *Fresh*, though formally well-made, lost much of its feeling. Still scoring in 1973 were Marvin Gaye, who turned to pure sex with "Let's Get It On," number one (see his album of the same name on Motown, its anti-politics summed up with a quote from T. S. Eliot: "Birth, copulation and death, that's all the facts when you get down to brass tacks"), and Stevie Wonder, who continued his mastery of the charts with "Higher Ground" (#4) and the deathly "Living for the City"—wherein a young man from the South leaves his no-where hometown for New York, is set up for a bust by a black "brother," and years later emerges from prison trying to remember what brought him to the city streets he now walks, his search reduced to an endless circle. The top ten version of the tune stopped with a description of the man's ambitions—you have to go to the album for his fate—but it was to Wonder's credit that the song worked either way (see *Innervisions*, Motown). In all but melody, rhythm, and words—as soul transmission—the number reappeared nine years later in the form of Grandmaster Flash and the Furious Five's "The Message" (Sugar Hill; see *Message from Beat Street: The Best of Grandmaster Flash, Melle Mel & the Furious Five*, Rhino).

Four other albums deserve mention; they fell into no genre, but played in the gap between the imperatives of the new black movies and the songs on the charts. First and most important was Diana Ross's much sneered-at soundtrack to *Lady Sings the Blues*, number one in 1972 (Motown), a personal and vital piece of music that served as a backdrop, and a necessary historical anchor, for the records of the era. It was also perhaps the first time the Stagger Lee story had been revised and publicly acted out by a woman ("Stagger Lee headed for the ball-room strapped bout to set it off, standin at the bar, singing like Diana Ross," Freddie Foxxx said in Lloyd Price's 1998 "Stagger Lee" remake)—though not the first time Ross kept company with Stack. In 1961, as a member of the Primettes, she backed Don Revel on their "Return of Stagger Lee" (Lu–Pine).

The Credibility Gap's comedy album *A Great Gift Idea* (Warner Bros., 1973) featured a trailer for the ultimate blaxploitation flick: "Black Ivory Productions' *King Pin*, the first movie that has dared to be suggested by the life of the late Dr. Martin Luther King, Jr.—a film of great importance not only to the Afro-American community, but to all Negroes." Opening with an uncanny imitation of the *Superfly* soundtrack ("He's a king, he's a pin"), the piece offered the audience

"Dever Deveroll, eighth-round draft choice of the New York Jets, who *is* King Pin." "He's got a plan—to stick it to the Man—they call him the Doctor—and he's got a special treatment—for whitey!" Executive producer Samuel Hirschorn, of course. Also on the album was an "Evening with Sly Stone" in the form of William F. Buckley's then-current PBS salon show, where one could find Sly discussing the most arcane points of black culture with the embodiment of intellectual droit du seigneur, embarrassing the ignorant Buckley into a shamed apology, and then begging off because he has to get to bed by ten so as not to be late for the next day's "recital."

Taj Mahal's music for *Sounder*, variations on traditional themes played on traditional instruments, was to me the finest album by a black performer released in 1972 (the Columbia soundtrack is worth seeking out, though some of the numbers were included on *Taj's Blues*, Columbia). The movie could not have been more different from every other black film on the market: this was a story (based on a white writer's book for children) about sharecropping, family life, oppression, education, and death. Taj's music and the performances of Cicely Tyson and Paul Winfield spoke for a kind of strength and pride that have everything to do with love between a few people—the mother, father, and children of *Sounder* do not stand only for their race, or as victims of racism, they stand for and as themselves. The movie was more painful than the big-city romances that outflanked it; Taj's music had more joy than the records that were hits.

And there was *Hustlers' Convention* (Douglas), a 1973 production by Lightnin' Rod, a former member of the Last Poets who now goes by Jalal Mansur Nuriddin: a long, rapped version of the story implicit in all the blaxploitation films. In first-person monologue, with music from Billy Preston and Kool and the Gang in the background, Lightnin' Rod recounted the adventures of Sport, a black street kid who reaches the top of the hustler's heap. About halfway through the opus, Lightnin' Rod moved to a detailed account of Sport's climactic poker game. Sport is way ahead—about $100,000 ahead—when an opponent accuses him of cheating; Sport pulls his pistol, grabs the pot, and flees. The losers give chase; Sport shoots two dead, but the rest follow—and duck out when the cops arrive. Sport is shot, caught, sent up, and spends twelve years on death row in Sing Sing. "But I kept coppin' a stay / Til the death penalty was done away / And after a retrial they let me go." It cost him all that time, Sport says as the record ends, to discover that he has lived exactly as the white world wished him to. No one picked up the movie rights—at least not until 1994, when the vogue for gangsta rap made *Hustlers' Convention* the hot property it had never been. The movie was never made. Lightnin' Rod made the sequels *The Hustlers' Detention* and *The Hustlers' Ascension*; they were never released. In 2014 the filmmaker Mike Todd was working on a documentary about *Hustlers' Convention*; you never know.

Randall Roberts's "Original Gangsta" traces the life of Stagger Lee from historical fact to the penetration of '90s black music by the archetype (see *Riverfront Times*, St. Louis, May 5–11, 1999). I met Roberts in the fall of 1998 in St. Louis, where I had come to give a talk on "The Birth of the Cool"—on the 1949–50 Miles Davis sessions, moving on to the Gerry Mulligan band that grew out of and extended the music, especially with Chet Baker on trumpet. I talked about the scene in the film *L.A. Confidential* where, at a party to celebrate a show about the Los Angeles police force, you can glimpse a band playing: the Mulligan band, a band of junkies, playing for the city establishment. I wasn't thinking about Stagger Lee, but it was a Stagger Lee moment.

I was meeting Roberts for dinner. "We've got a little time," he said when he picked me up. "Anywhere you'd like to go in St. Louis?" I couldn't think of anything; he looked at me with amusement. "How about the spot where Stagger Lee shot Billy Lyons?" he said. I almost jumped out of my seat. By then I knew the facts, but somehow the idea that behind the history was a real place, a place you could stand, had not occurred to me.

Roberts pulled out a page from the St. Louis Visitors' Guide: right there under "Places of Historical Interest" was the original site of Bill Curtis's saloon, Eleventh and Delmar streets. Not long ago no one knew; now the spot is not only known, it's official. So we drove through downtown St. Louis in the early evening; just outside the main business district was a quiet intersection, with a modest, modern office building on the northwest corner and a block of old, seemingly empty warehouses across the street. The office building was it; unlike the building that held the Cabaret Voltaire in Zurich, where on a twisting street in the old city, across from a house where Lenin lived at the same time, dada was discovered, a building the walls of which carry a plaque and graffiti from dada pilgrims from all over the world, and which since 2002 has been occupied by a thriving experimental nightclub of the same name, there was no aura left in St. Louis. The building was just a building. It could have been anywhere—but it was the place. From this spot, because of what happened between two men on a certain night, came a story-song that for more than a hundred years has told itself again and again: a free story, open to anyone's inventions, anyone's fantasies, a story that defines the country as well as *The Searchers* or *The Adventures of Huckleberry Finn*.

"I now have a mental picture of the way the corner looked at the time," Roberts wrote me after a visit to the St. Louis Historical Society, where he looked through fire insurance maps from 1893. "Brick buildings, three and four stories, lined the streets in every direction. No open space. Huge warehouses all around: Globe Pickle Co., Columbia Incandescent Lamp Co., Beckfold Printing and Book Mfg. Co., Mound City Wood Novelty Co. The area at that time was thriving; St. Louis was a huge city then. Within a five-minute walk was the river, and there were railways stations and off-loading warehouses—I counted something like thirty tracks side by side. It's no wonder the song spread so rapidly, and that so many cities laid claim to its origin. A dockworker could hear the song one night, hop on a train or a boat to Memphis or New Orleans and share the song with others the next night."

In Normandy, a cemetery town just outside of St. Louis, you can find the grave of Billy Lyons—or rather you can find the unmarked plot on findagrave.com, which allows you to "Leave flowers or a note" for the decedent in question, or for that matter a cigar or a beer. Photos posted in 2001 by Connie Nisinger, a high-school librarian, show a bouquet of flowers on a steep, bare hillside—and not a headstone within yards of Lyons's sec. 5, lot 289, as if the ground itself is dead. That is chilling. But back on Delmar and Eleventh, the corner resolutely refused to surrender any atmosphere. If it wasn't here it would have been somewhere else, one view of history would tell you, but I don't believe history works like that. So I looked around for a souvenir, and settled on a few sprigs of flowers growing in a small bed in front of the office building. They were yellow and red, before long they turned brown, and going on twenty years later, now resting below a 78 of Dock Boggs's "Pretty Polly," they naturally look just like blood.

RANDY NEWMAN

Randy Newman seems to have taken his first small steps toward world renown in 1962, when the Fleetwoods recorded his "They Tell Me It's Summer" as the B-side of "Lovers by Night, Strangers by Day" (see the wonderful *Come Softly to Me: The Very Best of the Fleetwoods*, EMI). Much beloved for such masterpieces of white doo-wop as "Come Softly to Me," "Mr. Blue," and "(He's) The Great Impostor" (like the Band's

"Ferdinand the Impostor," inspired by the exploits of Ferdinand De-mara), the Fleetwoods vanished from sight almost immediately.*

Thanks to Steve Harvey's "Randy Newman" (*Goldmine*, November 1981) and the exhaustive "The Invisible Randy Newman: The Metric Music to Reprise Years," by Scott Montgomery with Gary Norris and Kevin Walsh (*Goldmine*, September 1, 1995), the dimmer corners of the Newman discography glow with the energy of a sixty-watt bulb. The story begins at Metric Music, where a teenage Newman signed on as a contract songwriter; Metric was a division of Liberty Records, which passed Newman's compositions on to artists on the label and its subsid-iaries, though soon enough Newman's tunes went further afield. Some-times aided by his father, Irving, a physician who dabbled in songwriting (one of his tunes was recorded by Bing Crosby), Newman turned out formula pop songs, quirky, Kurt Weill–influenced pop songs, made his own demos, and recorded a single teen-market disc under his own name: "Golden Gridiron Boy" b/w "Country Boy" (Dot 16411), coproduced by Pat Boone ("The first person who ever liked my voice," Randy said) and issued as a promotional 45 in November 1962. "Golden Gridiron Boy" today has a certain poignancy, with Randy singing in the voice of one who is "too small" to make the team. "I can only play in the band," Randy moans as his girl goes running off after the football hero, "but I'm big enough to have a dream." "HOORAY!" chirps the female chorus, presumably the pom-pom squad. "Be True to Your School" it was not. Never much more than a rumor, in 1998 "Golden Gridiron Boy" led off the "Odds & Ends" disc of the four-CD retrospective *Guilty: 30 Years of Randy Newman* (Warner Archives/ Rhino). After thirty-six years, it sounded god-awful.

While Randy tried to emulate such Brill Building writers as Carole King—"She was my hero," he mentioned to me in the course of a con-versation we had in 2003. "The only one I've had"—and longed for a

* Despite F. Scott Fitzgerald's dictum about there being no second acts in American lives, Gary Troxel, the lead singer of the Fleetwoods, was featured in all major media on January 12, 2000, seen before the Supreme Court as the plaintiff in *Troxel v. Granville*. The case concerned the right of a grandparent—in this case Troxel—"to visit with a child over the objection of parents who have not been shown to be unfit," as Linda Greenhouse put it in the *New York Times*. Troxel, sixty, was bald, stocky, tight-lipped. "I saw him at an oldies concert about five years ago," the critic Charles Taylor wrote, stunned to see Troxel all over the news. "'The Fleetwoods' were on the bill—I have no idea if the women were the same. I fully expected it to be another depressing act. And he was wonderful. The voice was the same, and suddenly I was looking at a middle-aged man for whom none of the uncertainty of those songs had ever been settled." But on the evening news hours, Troxel—whose son had killed himself in 1993, leaving two children with their mother, with whom Troxel and his wife were now in dispute—only looked bitter, as if he had settled all ques-tions in his heart and knew no one would ever feel as he did, as if he had nothing to say to anyone. The Supreme Court later ruled against the Troxels.

chance at a Bobby Vee B-side, Gene McDaniels cut "Somebody's Waiting" as the flipside of "Spanish Lace" (Liberty 55510), also in 1962; Newman considers it his first "big record," probably because it brought him his first measurable royalty check ("Spanish Lace" topped out at #32). Of the many singers who recorded Newman's early songs, perhaps most worthy of mention are Irma Thomas ("While the City Sleeps," on her classic *Wish Someone Would Care*, Imperial, 1964), the Fleetwoods again, and off the charts ("Lovers' Lullaby," "Who's Gonna Teach You About Love," and "Ask Him If He's Got a Friend for Me," the latter two on their *Buried Treasure* LP, EMI Liberty), Spike Jones ("Stoplight," Liberty 3349), Martin Denny ("Scarlet Mist" on *The Versatile Martin Denny*, Liberty, 1963), Jerry Butler ("I Don't Want to Hear It Anymore," 1964, Vee-Jay, 598), Billy Fury ("Baby Do You Love Me," 1967, Parlophone 5658, Mala 595), Billy Storm ("Baby, Don't Look Down," 1964, Loma 2001), Harper's Bizarre ("The Debutante's Ball," Warner Bros. 7028, plus "Happyland" and "Simon Smith and the Amazing Dancing Bear" on their *Feelin' Groovy*, Warner Bros., 1967), Rick Nelson ("Wait Till Next Year" on *Perspective*, Decca, 1968; the Ace package *Another Side of Rick/Perspective*, includes "I Think It's Going to Rain Today," "Love Story," and an apt "So Long Dad" / "Love Story" medley, recognizing two parts of the same song), P. J. Proby ("Straight Up" on *Phenomenon*, Liberty, 1967, the C-Five package *Phenomenon/Believe It or Not* includes "Mama Told Me Not to Come"), Frankie Laine ("Take Her," Columbia 42884, 1963), Ricardo Montalban ("La Campanilla," "With Orchestra by Randy Newman," A&M 847, 1968), Claudine Longet (the prophetic "Snow," 1968, on *Love Is Blue*, A&M), Little Peggy March ("Leave Me Alone," RCA 8357, 1964), the O'Jays ("Friday Night," Imperial 66197), Erma Franklin (the superior "Love Is Blind," Epic 9610, 1963), Cilla Black ("I've Been Wrong Before," Capitol 5414, 1965, in its time covered by Jerry Butler, H. P. Lovecraft, Julius LaRosa, and Dusty Springfield, and, covering Springfield, Elvis Costello, on *Kojack Variety*, Warner Bros., 1995), the Everly Brothers (the promisingly titled and utterly bland "Illinois," on their acclaimed *Roots*, Warner Bros., 1968), and the Beau Brummels (the promisingly titled "Bless You California," a sarcastic ballad of dependency and self-loathing upended by out-of-control Kurt Weillisms and Sal Valentino's horrible vocals, on *Bradley's Barn*, Warner Bros., 1968). He cowrote "She Don't Understand Him Like I Do" with the great Jackie DeShannon (it appeared along with Newman's "Did He Call Today, Mama" on her 1965 *You Won't Forget Me*, Imperial); their "Hold Your Head High" came out with Newman's "Take Me Away" in 1968 on DeShannon's *Lonely Girl* (Sunset).

Newman got a tune into *The Lively Set*, a 1964 beach movie starring Doug McClure and James Darren (there was a soundtrack album on Decca; somewhere, a copy survives); "Galaxy A-Go-Go! (Leave It to Flint)" turned up in *Our Man Flint* in 1966, though not on the soundtrack album. As a moonlighter he contributed background music to the CBS series *The Many Loves of Dobie Gillis*. He composed background rock functionals for the ABC series *Peyton Place* ("Something for Betty and Rodney to dance to"); in 1965, without Newman's knowledge, but no doubt with the hope the public might confuse Randy with his famous film-scoring uncles Alfred and Lionel, the results were assembled into *Original Music from the Hit Television Show Peyton Place by the Randy Newman Orchestra* (Epic). Reports that Newman also wrote theme music for the 1963 Girl Scouts Cookie campaign, the 1964 Republican convention, and a December 7, 1965, meeting of the Croatian-American Benevolent Society ("Dead Serb Blues") have never been verified.

Newman's first real notoriety came in 1966, with Judy Collins's recording of "I Think It's Going to Rain Today" on her arty *In My Life* (Elektra). In 1967 there was Van Dyke Parks's fey chamber music version of "Vine Street," a Hollywood "On Broadway" (Newman conducted, but did not release the number himself; see Parks's *Song Cycle*, Warner Bros.). The year 1968 brought Alan Price's *The Price Is Right* (Parrot), which featured five Newman songs, including the perfect sweet-sixteen fantasy, "The Biggest Night of Her Life" (she has "a promise she must keep"—presumably, to sleep with her boyfriend, unless she's saving herself for "The Biggest Day of Her Life").

Randy Newman Creates Something New Under the Sun (Reprise) also appeared in 1968, decked out with a cover photo that pictured Newman as a throwback to the thrilling days of, say, 1951; Reprise later substituted a picture of Randy with longer hair, but it had no impact on sales. Overproduced, occasionally musically cute, the album lived up to its title anyway. "Love Story," the first cut, clinched the game. Here was an American romance, from proposal to the grave, with every warm promise undercut by a darker promise. When the kids are grown, Randy-the-suitor tells his bride-to-be, "They'll send us away, to a little home"—and that's all part of the dream, or the deal.* There was "So

---

* "When I wrote it," Newman said in 2003, "I thought it was just such an impoverished dream to have. I look at it now and think, that's not all that bad considering what can happen to you. At least you make it to today. You make it to Florida. A lot of people didn't."

Long, Dad" ("Love Story" sung from the point of view of Dad's grown-up son: "Drop by anytime," he assures his father. "Just be sure and call before you do"), "Living Without You" (marvelously covered in 1972 on *Manfred Mann's Earth Band*, Grapevine/Polygram), "Davy the Fat Boy," and "The Beehive State" ("Utah is known as the Beehive State," the *San Francisco Chronicle* sportswriter John Crumpaker wrote in a report on the 2002 Winter Olympics in Salt Lake City, "for the archaic hairdos worn by waitresses in time-warp coffee shops"), a weird little masterpiece about the forgotten territory between L.A. and New York. At some grand national convention, the delegate from Utah rises. "We gotta tell this country about Utah," he says with all his courage, "because nobody seems to know."

Along with a good deal of dross, the *Guilty* "Odds & Ends" disc collected several unique and striking demos from the *Sun* sessions: the damning, miserabilist "Love Is Blind," "The Goat" (in which, perhaps anticipating Newman's early patron Gary Troxel, an incorrigibly criminal animal winds up braying to the Supreme Court), and, most memorably, recorded in 1968, Newman's own solo piano version of "Vine Street." The melody stretches, yawns, and then begins to twist and crawl like someone waking up in a huge bed in the middle of the afternoon. By its words, the song is about a band that didn't make it, but the words come off as an excuse for something to sing. By feeling, the song is about desire and the pleasure of putting off doing anything about it—about, as the title of an L.A. novel once put it, the weather tomorrow. *Viiiiiiiiiiine Street*, Newman sings, until you can feel the plant the street was named for curling around the gates and mailboxes. The famous Hollywood and Vine is there just as a reminder of the fame the singer will never get; where the song takes you is an ordinary street where people live.

12 Songs (Reprise), released in 1970, was a better album than the first. Randy's voice and piano were up front, the orchestration stripped down and muted. *Something New* was a showbiz fantasia with dim echoes of Charles Ives buried in Broadway kitsch; *12 Songs* leaned on the blues and New Orleans. Newman's imagination went wild within his tight little structures, producing "Let's Burn Down the Cornfield" ("And I'll make love to you, while it's burning," Newman added), "Suzanne," "Lucinda" (victim of the beach-cleaning machine), "Yellow Moon," "My Old Kentucky Home," his version of the 1932 hit "Underneath the Harlem Moon," and a few other perfect pieces. All but hiding from the rest of the album was the last track, "Uncle Bob's Midnight Blues," the sound of a man staring at a hole in his wall: "Had a great idea the other night," he says, and that's all he says about it. Three Dog Night got a number one hit out of a Stepin Fetichity version of "Mama Told Me Not to Come" later in 1970.

Randy Newman Live (Reprise) was Newman's first chart entry, fading away at #191 in 1971. Despite "Lonely at the Top," it's not a good record; originally pressed as a promotional item for disc jockeys, the sound is thin, and little of Newman's stage personality came across. "Tickle Me" and "Maybe I'm Doing It Wrong," neither much more than one-line jokes, were thankfully left off other albums—until a 2002 "Expanded and Remastered" version of *Sail Away* (Rhino/Reprise) picked up a studio take of the former to accompany "You Can Leave Your Hat On," the latter best covered, with unstoppable glee, by Tom Jones (on the anthology *Party at the Palace: The Queen's Concerts, Buckingham Palace*, Virgin, 2002).

Sail Away (Reprise) was issued in 1972, and rose to #163. It included "Lonely at the Top," "Burn On," "Political Science," and "Memo to My Son," a song about fatherhood that insisted on the locker-room motto "When the Going Gets Tough, the Tough Get Going" as an absolute non sequitur. The album closed—and felt as if it were closing down the world—with "God's Song (That's Why I Love Mankind)"—fiercely covered by the great soul singer Etta James on *Etta James*, also known as *Only a Fool* (Chess, 1973). But "Jesus in the Summertime," a 1972 demo included on *Guilty*, made even this sound like a happy ending; anyone willing to write a tune as serious as "God's Song" must care about *something*. "Bring him back!" Randy shouted, as if calling for a revival of the Twist. "Bring him back!"

No doubt because of its melody, "Sail Away" was covered by many singers; Linda Ronstadt accomplished the most uncomprehending version, while Salvation was responsible for changing "little wog" to "little child"—as if such a term, addressed to African men and women, would be less offensive (Bobby Darin used "little one"). Newman's ironies were compounded geometrically when the tune was cut by veteran black songsters Sonny Terry and Brownie McGhee: they sang "Sail Away" as the lament of two former slaves reminiscing about the good old days before the Yankees came and ruined their happy home, and it was not for the tenderhearted (see *Sonny & Brownie*, A&M, an album that promoted some ironies of its own when it showcased archetypal British bluesman John Mayhall on "White Boy Lost in the Blues"). Ironies compound ironies, especially when history rewrites songs: Dave Marsh suggests that "Sail Away" may have begun as "Uncle Sam's Farm," a paean to westward expansion written in Boston in 1850 by

Judson J. Hutchinson and Jesse Hutchinson, Jr., of the Hutchinson Family Singers. Harriet Tubman sang it when in 1863 she led Union troops up the Combahee River in South Carolina—as a call to slaves to leave their chains behind. "Come along! Come along! Don't be alarmed," Tubman cried. "Uncle Sam is rich enough to give you all a farm." A 2005 YouTube performance by the fiddler Truman Price gets the point across. "Come away," he shouts in the chorus. "Come away, come away, from every nation."

The 2002 edition of *Sail Away* includes an early version of the title song where, behind Newman's watery piano, percussion by the great New Orleans drummer Earl Palmer brings out a kinship between "Sail Away" and Sam Cooke's 1964 "A Change Is Gonna Come"—on which Palmer also played—more fully than the master cut. In a painful way, it's a lumbering performance, as if Newman isn't ready to get all the way into the slave-trader character—as if he's still afraid of him. "I've always felt the characters in my songs, as dark as they get—I think the audience is going to recognize these people as defective in some way or wrong in some way, and that the people in the audience are better than the people in my songs," he said in 2003. "I know they are. I'm expecting [the audience] to be able to laugh or at least notice bigotry or a lack of self-awareness—it's that these characters know themselves less well than I expect the audience to know them." But as for the racism, stupidity, or greed of the characters? "You have to make your best case."

In 1974 Newman unveiled a project he'd been threatening for years: *Good Old Boys* (Reprise), a picture of the white American South that spanned half a century. The ethos Newman aimed for was one of pride undercut by guilt, guilt driven off by pride—or whiskey. Included were love songs, work songs, and a few tabloid adventures involving whites disguised as blacks, rural degeneration, exhibitionism, and the like. There was as well a cover of a tune by Huey Long: "Every Man a King," done as the sing-along the Kingfish wrote it to be*—though he probably hadn't imagined a couple of the Eagles in the chorus—and not as the strange piece of soul music Newman singing alone might have made it. ("I had an aunt who said she worked for Huey Long at his office in New Orleans," Randy wrote in his notes to the 2002 reissue of *Good Old Boys* (Reprise/Rhino). "She said he came to work in pajamas sometimes. Well, who doesn't?") Whenever Newman has performed

---

* There are two clips of "Every Man a King" in Ken Burns's 1985 documentary *Huey Long* (PBS): one with a male pianist and Huey singing along, another with a female singer and a female band, with Long waving his hand in time.

the album's travelogue of racism, "Rednecks," he's gotten predictable hometown response; as Mark Athitakis put it in *SF Weekly* in 1999, it was still "probably not in good taste for audience members to shout 'Woo-hoo!' when he sings, 'The Negro's . . . free to be kept in a cage in the Fillmore in San Francisco . . .'"

"Louisiana 1927" was the album's moment of triumph. A lovely string intro that called up both Virgil Thomson's 1937 *The River* and Walt Disney's 1946 *The Song of the South* kicked it off, and then piano notes from the side of "Sail Away" drifted in, guiding a first line that in its mystery and simplicity—"Art," to quote Kathleen Cleaver, "that conceals art"—is as pure an American language as anyone will ever speak. "What has happened down here, is that the wind have changed," Newman sang, beginning a song about a flood—and then, as one of the people that happened to, he tried to tell you what it meant. It was, the song struggled to say, no accident: the country, Providence, nature, or God was taking revenge on the South. The great Mississippi flood of 1927 inspired dozens of songs—Blind Lemon Jefferson's "Rising High Water Blues," Vernon Dalhart's "The Mississippi Flood," Kansas Joe McCoy and Memphis Minnie's "When the Levee Breaks," covered by Led Zeppelin as if the flood were a tornado, Charley Patton's "High Water Everywhere," and, looking over its shoulder, Bob Dylan's "High Water (For Charley Patton)" among them—see Richard M. Mizelle, Jr.'s *Backwater Blues: The Mississippi Flood of 1927 in the African-American Imagination*, Minneapolis: Minnesota, 2014, for a more complete chronicle—but Newman's is the best, because it has the strongest sense of place. In 1989 it made a quiet end to *Blaze*, a film about the 1959 love affair between the stripper Blaze Starr and Governor Earl Long, Huey's damned, heroic brother. John M. Barry missed mentioning the tune in his *Rising Tide: The Great Mississippi Flood of 1927 and How It Changed America* (New York: Simon & Schuster, 1997), which takes the flood and the response to it as a key to federal/state relations and class politics over the following fifty years, but Percival Everett ran his own number on the "Little Fat Man" Newman put next to President Coolidge in his novella *Grand Canyon, Inc.* (San Francisco: Versus, 2001). Everett was writing about one Rhino Tanner, a titanic con artist: "Daddy Tanner drove his son to southern Iowa one spring to see the devastation caused by a major flood. There was a huge crowd of people standing near the edge of a sandbag dike and they joined in and it turned out that President Truman had come down to see the devastation too. The great man kept saying things to a little fat man beside him and the little fat man would write those things down on his notepad.

The sight of pigs, cows, barns and a sleigh bed floating away did not impress young Tanner, but he was impressed by the idea of having a little fat man with a notepad by his side."

Newman's original idea for *Good Old Boys* was an entire album in the voices of a Birmingham steelworker, Johnny Cutler, and his wife, Marie. Recorded in early 1973 as a full-length demo session, or a pitch where a screenwriter acts out every line in every role, *Johnny Cutler's Birthday* made up a second disc on the 2002 reissue. As Randy talks his way through the songs, sitting at his piano, you hear how the project could have taken any form—album, novel, play, film, epic poem, or a Southern version of "The Cremation of Sam McGee." He adds background, bringing out Marie as her own character, filling in others, singing his way through songs familiar and not (Marie's "Shining" and "Good Morning," "If We Didn't Have Jesus," "The Joke," "My Daddy Knew Dixie Howell," "Doctor Doctor"). "Rolling" is an incomplete version of "Guilty" ("We'll fix it in the mix")—but also a reach for the spiritual "Leaning," at least as Robert Mitchum and Lillian Gish sang it at the end of *Night of the Hunter* in 1955. What comes across is an artist in a bad mood, at once gloating over his ideas and half-convinced they aren't worth pursuing, his misanthropy and self-loathing undisguised, his sense of humor something to use and throw away, like a styrofoam cup. Throughout Newman played and sang directly, with the empathy of someone still understanding his own songs—empathy for his own foibles as well as those of his characters—and without a trace of condescension or distance. He was there, just as on the official version he was often somewhere else. That might be why *Good Old Boys* fell short of its subject. Many of the songs on this concept album are part of the concept only by fiat, and the orchestration is sometimes out of control, as if to hide the real action, or lack of it. Still, the concept sold the record, which did well for a Newman set, reaching #36 in the U.S., and even winning Randy a gold record—in the Netherlands. "I think they like me there because they think I hate America," Randy said. "How depressing." A seal for the whole project came in 2014 with David Kastin's effectively illustrated and linked e-book *Song of the South: Randy Newman's Good Old Boys* (Turntable Publishing): an excavation of the entire severed corpus of the work and a deep dive into the history—musical, social, economic, political, sectional, and waterborn—Newman both drew from and recast.

In 1977 Newman got his hit: the notorious "Short People," which, climbing to #2 on the *Billboard* charts and to number one on others, pulled the accompanying *Little Criminals* (Warner Bros.) to #9, enough to achieve all-American gold record status. The single, which remains Randy's sole dent in the top ten, or for that matter the Top 40, could have been taken as a slap at the irrationality of prejudice, which is how Newman has always insisted it was meant ("No one's as nuts as the guy in 'Short People'"); some heard it as a pleasurable indulgence hiding in its own irony. The singer Graham Parker and the novelist John Irving, both certified short people, told me how impressed they were that "a short person like Randy Newman had the nerve to write a song like that";* both were visibly unhappy to learn of Randy's excessive height. "Short People" was actually "banned in Boston," whatever that means ("*One* phone call," Newman says). Addressing the controversy, Dave Marsh, himself once known as the teenage dwarf—"I can see if you were in junior high school at the time or something, that it might have been hard," Randy said in 2003—formulated the unassailable doctrine that no one was short who was taller than he. He also coined the word "sizist," which was immediately put into use by organizations representing people with the appropriate physical deficiencies (it was only a few years later that certain medical researchers proposed classifying less-than-tall stature as a "disease"). Not that the argument Newman started ever stopped. In 1999, in the *International Herald Tribune*, Brian Knowlton reported on a *Scientific American* piece by Thomas Samaras. "The best way to save world resources, and to live longer?" According to Samaras, Knowlton wrote, "Be short." The point was that smaller people eat less, produce less garbage, put less pressure on their hearts, and fall down with less impact than taller people, thus apparently inflicting lighter bruises on the earth. "Of course," Knowlton said, the theory was without practical application: "People could not get short, even if they wanted to. But Mr. Samaras feels he has cut down to size the idea behind the Randy Newman song, 'Short People,' which says 'short people got no reason to live.'"

Randy Newman Live aside, *Little Criminals* was Newman's poorest album. With such tunes as "Jolly Coppers on Parade," "In Germany Before the War," "Sigmund Freud's Impersonation of Albert Einstein in America" (inspired by E. L. Doctorow's puerile novel *Ragtime*), the music was pallid, and Newman's indirection seemed more than anything a blithe substitute for a commitment to his material. Backing vocals by the Eagles didn't just sound smooth, they were highlights.

---

* "It took more nerve to write 'My Country,'" Newman said in 2003, referring to the opening song on his 1999 *Bad Love*, an album that maps a nation where TV sets keep playing even after people shoot them out.

Born Again (Warner Bros.), released in 1979, was a rebound—perhaps significantly going no higher than #41. The sleeve pictured Randy in Kiss-style makeup, with dollar signs painted over his eyes. "It's Money That I Love" was a number Fats Domino would have appreciated, if not sung. "I don't love Jesus, he never done a thing for me," Randy proclaimed. "Short People" had clearly made Newman suspicious of his audience, and of himself—not, perhaps, an ideal position for a popular artist, but the only position Newman can work from. ("Everything I write," he said in 2003, "I think, oh, people will really like this. Not everything anymore because I know better—but I was always under the misguided impression that, oh, 'God's Song,' it's not that hard. It's not like it's physics I'm doing up here. You just have to listen to it.") If nothing else on *Born Again* matched "Money," at least "The Story of a Rock and Roll Band," "Half a Man" (an unfashionable dramatization of homophobia), and "Pretty Boy" (an unfashionable assault on, depending on how one heard it, John Travolta or Bruce Springsteen) kept the pace. The disc ended in a tailspin with "Pants," another kinky-sex number, and there were easy-target tunes throughout—but it was, as Newman said, "a nihilistic, no-human-feeling album . . . a comedy record."

Though "It's Money That I Love" might have seemed to set up Newman perfectly for termite work in the Reagan years, it was 1983 before his next album appeared, and it was disappointingly vague. *Trouble in Paradise* (Warner Bros., #64) was loosely based on the concept of the falsity of sun-drenched utopias: there were songs about Cape Town, Miami, and Los Angeles, but they didn't hurt. "I Love L.A.," despite its line about the town's attractions including the sight of bums throwing up on the street, was appropriated by happy Angelenos as a new city song; Randy obligingly made a popular video of himself cruising the boulevards in an open convertible. The album included the then-requisite guest spots by pop heavyweights: Linda Ronstadt, Bob Seger, Don Henley, Rickie Lee Jones, Lindsey Buckingham, Christine McVie, on and on down to Paul Simon. The year 1983 also saw the release of a Newman concert video, *Live at the Odeon* (RCA Columbia Pictures).

Newman's first film score was for the 1971 Norman Lear satire *Cold Turkey* (to win a contest, a town gives up smoking; one number, "Rev Running," is included on the Film Music disc of *Guilty*); that same year he contributed "Let Me Go" to Lear's *The Pursuit of Happiness*. His only attempt at sustained TV work, at least since *Peyton Place*, was with the almost immediately cancelled *Cop Rock*, Michael Mann's disastrous *Miami Vice* spinoff, which nevertheless brought him an Emmy for "He's

Guilty." (In 2004 he contributed the "It's a Jungle Out There" theme for the equally contrived but far more popular *Monk*, which can be found on *Monk—Original Television Soundtrack*, Varese Sarabande); in 2007, joining the ranks of Elvis Costello, the Shins, Billy Bob Thornton, Donovan, and Englebert Humperdink, he sang Malvina Reynolds's sneering 1962 protest song "Little Boxes"—"the most sanctimonious song ever written," the late Tom Lehrer once said—to open an episode of *Weeds*. But throughout the 1980s and '90s Newman made his living principally with movie soundtrack work, scoring and winning an Oscar nomination for Milos Forman's *Ragtime* (Elektra, #134, 1981; the album included a Newman vocal omitted from the film, "Change Your Way"), scoring Barry Levinson's *The Natural* (Warner Bros., 1984), and writing ditties (sung by Steve Martin, Chevy Chase, and Martin Short) for the instantly forgotten *Three Amigos* (Warner Bros. LP, 1987). Such production—which continued with soundtracks for *Parenthood* (Reprise, 1989, with Newman's slotmouth account of his "I Love to See You Smile": "Made more money for me than anything else I've done," Randy said in 1997. "I sold it to toothpaste companies, mule-packing teams"), Levinson's *Avalon* (Reprise, 1990), *Awakenings* (Reprise, 1990), *The Paper* (Reprise, 1994, with a decent New Orleans shuffle pumping Newman's vocal on "Make Up Your Mind"), *Maverick* (Atlantic, 1994, #35, with Newman's vocal on "Ride Gambler Ride" accompanying the crawl), and *Toy Story* (Walt Disney, 1995, #94, featuring a duet between Randy and Lyle Lovett on "You've Got a Friend in Me")—made the irreducible substance of Newman's *Land of Dreams* (Reprise, #80) a shock. Released in October 1988, it featured Randy singing as himself for the first time—if "Dixie Flyer" and "New Orleans Wins the War" were not exactly autobiography, they were presented as such. As the work of a man who had always sung as a character actor, they threw the listener off, made the listener listen in a new way. In these two songs, there was no level on which Randy Newman was kidding.

He was singing about what it meant to be a Jew in the Deep South, to feel like a foreigner in your own country ("Jews want to be American real bad," Newman told Chris Bourke in 1994. "Dylan ran away from it as far as he could. Irving Berlin wrote Alabamy. I know I'm American but I feel . . . they could *turn* on me at any moment"). He was singing from memory, no self-pity, only confusion. On a light, easy-swinging piano, "Dixie Flyer" opened up a tricky map, too tricky for a child to follow; "New Orleans Wins the War" inked it in. "Mama used to take me to Audubon Park, show me the ways of the world," Randy sang happily, with no irony at all: "She'd say, 'Here comes a white boy, there goes a black one . . .' " Racism becomes part of the song not as an issue, not even as a subject, merely as a fact the singer couldn't understand, and still can't. Perhaps the best moment comes when Newman's father returns to New Orleans—in 1948—to tell everyone the news of the Allies' victory over the Axis ("Maybe they'd heard about it, maybe not," Randy remembers. "Probably they'd heard about it, just forgot"—and the way he sings "maybe not" and "just forgot" is as deep as anything in "Sail Away"). A huge celebration breaks out: "New Orleans had won the war." You can sense what it must have felt like to win a war, to win a war worth winning—but in a way *Land of Dreams* was about a war that in 1948 was just beginning, a war that would be fought in America by blacks and whites in the decades to come, a war that is worth winning, and that hasn't been won. Anchoring the happiness of "New Orleans Wins the War" to the portents in "Dixie Flyer," Newman made *Land of Dreams* an answer record to Ronald Reagan, his parents, and to himself.

There was as well the single "It's Money That Matters," at once a first-rate driving song and a tougher, painful version of *Born Again*'s "It's Money That I Love"—though, hitting the air on the eve of George Bush's election to the presidency, it seemed the country would turn the tune's no into a yes as easily as Angelenos did with "I Love L.A." (which, to be fair, was a big yes and a little no). Newman raised his head out of his soundtracks in 1991 with "Lines in the Sand," a tune about Bush's triumphalist Gulf War. Never actually released, but included on *Guilty*, the piece, passed on to radio stations, offered an out-of-fashion stoicism: an elegy in advance of victory. It was quiet, cold, and defeatist.

I heard it on the radio, once. Far more airplay went to "Voices That Care," the result of a gathering of movie stars under the same name for a "We Are the World" reprise that should have been called "We Are the War." For an answer record to "Voices That Care" (Giant 19350, #11)—an explicit apology, from the likes of Kevin Costner, Luther Vandross, Meryl Streep, Richard Gere, and Little Richard, for failing to support the Vietnam War (the Gulf War, after all, had a great deal to do with "putting Vietnam behind us")—Lenny Kravitz and Sean Lennon organized "The Peace Choir," for a recording of a rewritten version of John Lennon's "Give Peace a Chance" (Virgin, #54). Newman was there, along with Yoko Ono, Peter Gabriel, Tom Petty, LL Cool J, Iggy Pop, Bonnie Raitt, and, not missing a beat, Little Richard again. Perhaps even more than with "Lines in the Sand," Newman was playing with fire; in October 1998, as a warning to anyone considering attending an upcoming Kravitz/Lennon double bill, the Toronto Web site "rolling eye" documented the startling fact that "most of the Peace Choir members had "suffered irreparable damage to their careers"— noting not only Kravitz and Lennon but the commercial collapse of Cyndi Lauper, Sebastian Bach, Michael McDonald, Bruce Hornsby, Bros, and MC Hammer.

Randy Newman's Faust (Reprise, 1995)—shades of *Gore Vidal's Caligula*—was Newman's first musical, not counting the off-Broadway cabaret-style revues *Maybe I'm Doing It Wrong*, directed by Joan Micklin Silver in 1982, *The Middle of Nowhere*, directed by Tracy Friedman in 1988, and various other failed like-minded efforts. (In 2000, Newman himself was involved with *The Education of Randy Newman*, a musical that, the South Coast Repertory Theater of Costa Mesa, California, announced, "follows a Newmanesque Everyman from childhood in Louisiana to his arrival and adult years in Los Angeles. Using the classic turn-of-the-century autobiography *The Education of Henry Adams* as a model, it offers a picaresque walk through 20th century America . . ."—and that "picaresque" is the dead giveaway of why it was never heard of again.) *Faust* was a move many thought overdue, and thus much ballyhooed (features in all major print media, full-page ads in the *New York Times* and *Time*), but despite James Taylor as the Lord, Randy as Lucifer, Don Henley as the callow Notre Dame student Henry Faust, Linda Ronstadt as the virginal Margaret, and Bonnie Raitt as the siren Martha, the disc went nowhere commercially or aesthetically. The music was timid, as if afraid to overwhelm the stringing of the narrative line or the jokes dropped along the way (the biggest joke was Newman, who once made so much of how poorly his records sold compared to James Taylor's, now being in a position to give the then-washed-up Taylor work). The lyrics were too carefully wrought and often too carefully sung (while Henley consistently broke free, Ronstadt was a disaster: on "Gainesville" she turned the word "university" into a final exam). Taylor perhaps filled out Newman's vision of his role too well (the Lord, Randy explained to an interviewer, is "a big, relaxed guy to whom everything comes easy, like Gerald Ford or George Romney"): he was so bland he never began to work as Newman's foil, and thus Newman never began to work as Taylor's. (An "Expanded" version of the album, released in 2003 on Reprise/Rhino, included a second disc of demos, with Randy talking and singing all the parts; the contrivance of the project was no less killing.) The promises of Newman's liner notes ("Margaret has Henry's child, and crazed with grief and shame, drowns it in a creek," he wrote after Susan Smith's drowning of her two young sons scandalized a pious nation. "This is the high point of Goethe's original play, and one of the most delightfully urbane moments in all of German literature") remained unkept by theatrical productions, first at the La Jolla Playhouse, contemporaneously with the *Faust* release, and later in Chicago. In 2014, for a one-night revival at the New York City Center, Randy played the Devil in the flesh.

The soundtrack work, and the Oscar nominations, never ceased. "Newman obviously gets a perverse kick out of composing exclusively for stomach-turning treacle," Rob Sheffield wrote in *Rolling Stone* in 1999: "pick a Top Ten of the most revolting movies you've ever seen, and the odds are Randy worked on at least one of them … His soundtracks might be fine for what they are, but in the rock & roll scheme of things, writing a good song for *Babe: A Pig in the City* is even more pathetic than writing a bad one."* Sheffield might have been thinking of the 1996 *Michael*, featuring John Travolta as an angel, which carried a soundtrack that included the Newman–Valerie Carter duet on "Heaven Is My Name" (Revolution). There followed the animated productions *James and the Giant Peach* (Disney, 1996, which included a Newman vocal on "Good News"), *Cats Don't Dance* (Polygram, 1997; an unused track, the maniacally depressed "Laugh and Be Happy," is on *Guilty*), the aforementioned *Babe* (with the Newman compositon "That'll Do," sung by Peter Gabriel on the 1998 Geffen soundtrack), *A Bug's Life* (Disney, 1998, with Newman's vocal on "The Time of Your Life"), and the inevitable *Toy Story* 2 (Disney, 1999). Newman's most memorable soundtrack work of the time came with *Pleasantville*, probably the best American movie of 1998, which brought one of Newman's three 1999 Oscar nominations: with the lightest touch, he broke sunshine over the film's climactic scene, offering the sort of smile you can only get in the movies—offering what people go to the movies for. So it was in the theater; listening to the soundtrack album (Clean Slate/Work), it was plain this was a trick Newman knew by heart.

In June 1999, on *The Tonight Show*, host Jay Leno brought up Newman's latest Oscar nominations ("Lost for all three," Newman said) just after Newman premiered the thoroughly unpleasant *Bad Love*, his first non-soundtrack, non-theatrical album in eleven years (Dreamworks, #194). "Like, when you did *A Bug's Life*," Leno said, "did this attract younger fans?" "Yeah, it does!" Newman said with the happy enthusi-

---

* "No," Newman said in 2003 after reading Sheffield's charge. "Writing a good song for anything isn't pathetic. It's an assignment. Irrespective of the quality of the picture, almost, if it offers me a musical chance that interests me, I'll take it. And it has nothing to do with rock 'n' roll, it's not the same. If you want to look at the world in a rock 'n' roll sense—I don't know what you'd make of it. What does that even mean?"

asm his fans have learned to trust like a car salesman's handshake. "I played a thing where I had a four-year-old coming up to the stage and heckling me 'cause I didn't do 'You've Got a Friend' "—the Newman/ Lovett hit from *Toy Story*—"and I couldn't, I had to leave. I couldn't say anything too foul to the little guy. And they couldn't get him away from the stage. *You've Got a Friend! You've Got a Friend!*" "Just whack him and leave," Leno offered. "Well, I couldn't," Newman said. "Not while the audience was there."

The little riff was like Newman's sun in *Pleasantville*—he can play the misanthrope in his sleep. *Bad Love* was insomnia: a messy, powerful piece of work about, as the historian Robert Cantwell, who is two years younger than Newman, puts it, the sense that one's world is about "to go into the past." That means the contempt older men feel from the younger women who want to live in the world of their money, and the way one's whole frame of reference—taking in expressions like "two bits" and events like the Second World War—changes from lingua franca to a dead language. You can go out on the street and speak it, but not only will people give you a wide berth because you're talking to yourself, you'll feel like a foreigner in your own country.

On "Shame," a man who long ago would have been called a sugar daddy conducts a hateful dialogue with a female chorus singing the title word over and over again: he just wants sex and flattery, he can give the woman a good life in exchange, he's not talking about leaving money on the bed, and the chorus acts as if he wants her to lick her own shit off his dick. Really, he asks decently, what's so terrible about what I want? The song rolls along easily, with the singer's embarrassment and self-loathing nowhere near the surface until the song blows up, as if the singer has just realized the women sneering at him from the chorus have no right to mock him. "SHUT UP!" he says, just as suddenly realizing that's the worst thing he can say. In seconds he's on his knees apologizing—and begging for kindness. Don't you think I know what a fool I am? But this is a free country!

Whatever that means, says the rest of *Bad Love*, telling a story of a country where greed has replaced idealism but cannot kill it, tracing a landscape in which to think of anyone but yourself is to experience a kind of mental illness. Leading off *Randy Newman Creates Something New Under the Sun* more than thirty years before, "Love Story" insisted that the clichés of American life were so powerful there was no life to be lived outside of them. It was a notion Newman would echo in "Sail Away," with "In America, every man is free / To take care of his home and his family," itself echoed in that most chilling line in Kenneth Starr's 1998 special prosecutor's report urging the impeachment of President Bill Clinton on the Congress: "All Americans, including the president, are entitled to enjoy a private family life." That means there is no other sort of privacy that need be respected, and none at all if you are not part of a "family"—just as, in America as Newman had described it, freedom stops when you walk out your front door.

"DO YOU KNOW WHAT IT FEELS LIKE TO BEG A LIT-TLE BUM LIKE YOU FOR LOVE?" So says the man in "Shame"; so says Newman to his audience, whoever might be in it, promising that sooner or later everyone will feel the same. As he put it without irony on *Land of Dreams*, "I Want You to Hurt Like I Do." "I would like to be in the Rock & Roll Hall of Fame," he told Dan Ouellette of the *San Francisco Chronicle*, promoting *Bad Love* amid a shower of rave reviews. "But rock critics are very Bolshevik. They're very strict. If you don't use the right chords, you're out. If you use the wrong chords, like any that aren't in Led Zeppelin tunes, then forget it."

He was right; in 2000, James Taylor was inducted, and Randy stayed home. He did go to the Oscars, as usual; as usual, he lost. He finished the year with soundtrack performances for *Meet the Parents* (Dreamworks)—which, combining his vocals on his own "A Fool in Love" (a second version, with Susanna Hoffs of the Bangles providing a heavy-breathing lead, was included as a hidden track) with dead-fish covers of Fats Domino's "Poor Me" and Muddy Waters's "Got My Mojo Working," the latter the sort of paint-by-numbers white-blues bash that was already a national embarrassment in 1967, comprised the nadir of his career. (Even his soundtrack to the sequel, the 2004 *Meet the Fockers*, Varese Sarabande, with Newman carrying "We're Gonna Get Married" and "Crazy 'bout My Baby," was better.) In 2001, dueting with John Goodman, he came up with "If I Didn't Have You" on his soundtrack for *Monsters, Inc.* (Disney), which brought him his sixteenth Oscar nomination—and his first win. "Thank you," he said as he took the statuette from Jennifer Lopez in 2002. "I don't want your pity. I want to thank, first of all, the music branch for giving me so many opportunities to be humiliated over the years. I have nothing. I'm absolutely astounded that I won for this, though the picture deserves recognition. They made four pictures in a row that were good, and Peter Weir did that once, but I can't remember another instance, exactly. All four of the Pixar Disney movies were good." He turned to the orchestra pit, trying to stop the walking-off music: "Wait. Are you really going to play in four seconds? Don't play. It's been so long . . .

"I have something," he said. "I would like to thank Milos Forman and Barry Levinson—no, I'm very grateful. I would like to thank John Lasseter [of Pixar], Pete Docter [director of *Monsters, Inc.*], all these musicians"—again looking to the orchestra—"many of whom have worked for me a number of times and may not again. Walking out here and having someone this beautiful give me an award—I'll never get to heaven, but that's as close as you get, I think."

The story went on: in 2003 Newman was for the first time in memory not nominated for an Oscar. Instead there was the commercial for Ford where, as never before, he sang an advertiser's jingle rather than composing his own ("If you haven't looked at a Ford lately—look again") and, after fidgeting over the question, left his name on themes as distinctive as temperature-gauge adjustments for *Seabiscuit* (Decca) in 2003.* "Our Town" from the 2006 *Cars* (Disney/Pixar) brought a seventeenth Oscar nomination; Newman appeared on the 2007 telecast with James Taylor, who looked like a cadaver and sounded like a whiney fourteen-year-old. It was a lousy song, but it had to have been embarrassing to lose to a save-the-planet number by Melissa Etheridge. Film work continued with *Leatherheads* (Varese Sarabande, 2008), *The Princess and the Frog* (Disney, 2009), *Toy Story 3* (Disney, 2010), and *Monsters University* (Disney, 2013).

"It isn't a measure of merit," Newman said a year after his Oscar went up on a shelf. "I always have known it as I watched my uncle go, and he won nine of them. And he lost for things he should have won for and won for things maybe he shouldn't have won for. I was never bothered, except when something really bad beat me. When I lost sixteen times in a row and when I won I didn't think it would mean that much. I figured it would just be my time—perhaps that's what it was, I don't know. It was just another shuffle. But when I went out there and the orchestra stood up—that's sort of what I always wanted. Musicians that I saw when I was five years old, when I would go to Fox and see my uncle doing *The King and I* or *All About Eve*—and people who know music, like the rock critics who are always better educated than anyone

---

* "The worst experience of my life," Newman said. "Gary Ross [the director, who also made *Pleasantville*] wanted everything *slowed down*." He quit the project with the soundtrack unfinished, and then went to the theater to see the result: "It was just absolutely *grazing* the music that was written for it. It was like taking body blows. The person sitting next to me must have thought I was crazy. I was like, 'Uhhh. Ohhh.' I mean," he said, as if trying to convince a judge, "it's a *horse racing* movie. It's about a *horse*. He wouldn't let me play the races at all . . . My uncles used to complain about how hard writing new music really was," he said. "And my other uncle who was an agent said, 'It's better than threading needles.' Well—sometimes it isn't. I like doing an assignment and doing it well. Not to the point of being a concentration camp guard, but almost. You get paid off when you see where you're helping the movie a little bit. Even in the cause of evil. But when that gets taken away from you, it really hurts."

in rock 'n' roll. I think I wanted people who knew what they were talking about to like me almost more than I wanted a big audience—for a while I did, anyway. It's kind of a snotty thing to want, and I don't know whether anyone wants that now, but I got it, and then I would rather have sold two million records."

Two million people weren't going to hear *The Randy Newman Songbook Vol. 1*, Newman's first album for the refined Nonesuch label, an austere set of piano remakes from tunes from all across his career released in 2003. With the orchestration of past albums dropped like fancy dress, there was nothing on the record that couldn't have been written and recorded then and there. "Lonely at the Top" was sung in the wasted voice of a Sinatra-like legend spewing contempt for his fans; "The World Isn't Fair," originally on *Bad Love*, a lament for the failed dreams of Karl Marx, was brought down to the level of poolside gossip, and "Louisiana 1927" was a folk song. And then for a vanished country it was the national anthem.

"In 1927 the Mississippi flooded, and the levees broke in the state of Mississippi, above Clarksdale," Randy wrote in 2002 in his notes to the augmented version of *Good Old Boys*. "The Bosses in New Orleans probably were behind the decision to let it flood up there diverting the water away from their city. Anyway, the cotton fields were wiped out, changing America forever, disemploying hundreds of thousands of black field workers, most of whom held executive positions in the cotton industry, meaning that they were permitted to wear gloves while picking. They all moved North and were greeted with open arms right across America."* In 2005, when Hurricane Katrina destroyed New Orleans, those words blew back in Newman's face, just as Katrina blew by the rest of the country, which turned its face away. "Louisiana 1927," as a friend said, was suddenly a song "*everybody* knows." It was everywhere, on newscasts, radio specials, rushed documentaries, telethons, charity concerts.

"The river have busted through clear down to Plaquemines," people mouthed as a news photo captioned "Coffin Floating at Plaquemines"

---

* In a 1932 German radio broadcast, as part of a series on disasters and con artists, the critic Walter Benjamin detailed the efforts of farmers to resist the holocaust New Orleans was planning, which President Coolidge backed with the U.S. Army: forming militias, arming themselves with machine guns, even an assassination attempt on the visiting Secretary of Commerce Herbert Hoover, who would be elected president in 1928 partly because of his reputation for dealing with disasters. "And so, stay tuned," Benjamin said after quoting a page of devastating testimony from a survivor, "for the Ku Klux Klan and Judge Lynch and other unsavory characters that have populated the human wilderness of the Mississippi, and still populate it today." See "The Mississippi Flood of 1927," *Radio Benjamin*, ed. Lecia Rosenthal (London: Verso, 2014).

appeared on their computer screens. The song became part of the weather; then it turned into a sentimental, 't'was-ever-thus gloss on the erasure of a great city, until you could almost believe it was God who didn't care, not the president of the United States. But the song took on a new body with *Our New Orleans* (Nonesuch, 2005), a collection of performances by refugees and expatriates, all of whom, recording in such diasporas as Houston, New York, or Maurice, Louisiana, must have heard the same thing from the producers: You have to do your best work now.

Irma Thomas, "Soul Queen of New Orleans," for decades after "Wish Someone Would Care" and "It's Raining" a hard-working, dedicated woman of noble mediocrity, sang Bessie Smith's 1927 "Back Water Blues"—always associated with the Mississippi flood, but written and recorded before it hit—as if she were digging a trench. With "A World I Never Made," Dr. John caught the feeling of a man staring at a wall in an SRO hotel. Buckwheat Zydeco led eight minutes of "Cryin' in the Streets" across guitar solos by Ry Cooder that were so blasted you couldn't immediately tell what they were. The Wardell Quezergue Orchestra took Louis Armstrong's "What a Wonderful World," which since 1964 every hotel pianist in New Orleans has had to sing whenever a drunken tourist shoved a $10 bill into his snifter, and turned it into a moon hanging over the ruins, refusing to set. Inevitably, the album closed with "Louisiana 1927"—but unlike the dutiful performances of the song Newman had been doing since the levees broke, what he offered now had no mastery. Recording in the fall of 2005 in New York with the Louisiana Philharmonic Orchestra and members of the New York Philharmonic, Newman sang as if what had finally hit home was how cheap the conceit of the song had always been—until, this time, he sat down to play it. He used a great historical event for a song, he made a lot of money from it, and then the event in which the song began came full circle and said, *You called the tune, now it's time to pay the piper—and you thought you were the piper, didn't you?*

The abandonment of New Orleans had to lie behind "A Few Words in Defense of Our Country," the broken manifesto Newman addressed to the nation and the world in 2006. Contemplating George W. Bush's half-decade of crime and lies, bullying and contempt, the "war president" and war profiteering, Newman searched history for leaders lower than his own ("The worst that we've had"), but Caligula, Torquemada, King Leopold of Belgium, Hitler, and Stalin were cold comfort. Newman pulled off his mask of craft and elegance, shrugged Gershwin and Arlen off of his shoulders, and, to the tune of "Columbia, the Gem of the Ocean," in a verse the *New York Times* omitted when it ran his lyrics as an op-ed piece, said what he meant: "You know it pisses me off a little / That this Supreme Court is gonna outlive me / A couple of young Italian fellas and a brother on the court now too / But I defy you, anywhere in the world / To find me two Italians as tightass as the two Italians we got." You could watch Randy sing it on YouTube; you could buy it on iTunes. You could imagine the Dixie Chicks covering it as a hidden track on *Taking the Long Way*, their last album. You couldn't hear it on the radio, but while Newman could have had no illusions about the power of a song even to give a country a moment's pause, no one writes solely to hear the sound of his own voice. The number appeared on Newman's 2008 *Harps and Angels* (Nonesuch), which despite leading off with the title song, about physical collapse and near-death experience (and reprieve: God says there's been a clerical error), had Randy sounding perhaps more relaxed than he ever had. The highlight was "A Piece of the Pie," a tune about income inequality, and also Randy's fullest embrace of Kurt Weill orchestration. The words spit out bitterness—"There's a famous saying someone famous said / As General Motors goes so go we all / Johnny Cougar's singing it's their country now / He'll be singing for Toyota by the fall," Newman offered in a vicious swipe at John Mellencamp, who had dropped the record-company teen-idol name nearly twenty years before, not to say a vicious swipe of the purest hypocrisy, coming from Mr. Looked at a Ford Lately—and the music crashed and burned like a soundtrack to the end of *Metropolis*. "And no one gives a shit but Jackson Browne," Randy sang of the hitmaker whose politics all but got him blacklisted. "The country turns its lonely eyes to who? Jackson Brown, Jackson Browne . . ." The words were out of control, and the song held together with implacable conviction. In 2011, Newman released *Live in London* (Nonesuch), a double album drawn from performances with the BBC Concert Orchestra, with tunes ranging from "The Great Nations of Europe" to "I Think It's Going to Rain Today"; it was hard to hear the British audience embrace "A Few Words in Defense of Our Country" with such enthusiasm, as if their own Margaret Thatcher had never been born. The same year saw *The Randy Newman Songbook Vol. 2* (Nonesuch), with such obscure numbers as "Same Girl," "Last Night I Had a Dream," and "Cowboy" quieted down to the mood of someone thinking them over while lying in bed in the middle of the night, and "Kingfish" as it always should have been: Newman alone, on piano, not soul music, just, in the voice of Huey Long, right. The set reached its height with "Dixie Flyer." The tale of Newman's mother leaving Los Angeles for her native New Orleans during World War II, when Newman's father was overseas, took on a weight the original from *Land of Dreams* never had. The regret in the opening notes as Newman looks back nearly seventy years is awful: as he sings now his father is dead, his mother is dead. This is his attempt to feel for himself the dilemma the world dropped on them like a bomb, and they will never hear him, never understand how fully he understands. The train crosses the country, and even as a baby Newman feels the journey, hears what it means to be Jewish in the South. He flinches, pushes harder, takes a stand, draws a line in the sand, and he leaves who he is now behind that line, because he knows he would have made the same choice his mother did. What is new, now, is the depth of the compassion, and the hate: "Trying to do like the gentiles do / Christ, they wanted to be gentiles too / Who wouldn't, down there, wouldn't you? / God damn!" Then in September 2012, as the presidential election race turned a corner toward the first debate between Barack Obama and Mitt Romney, Randy put a video of "I'm Dreaming" on YouTube. "I think there are a lot of people who find it jarring to have a black man in the White House and they want him out," he said of his little intervention, or witnessing, partly sung to the tune of "White Christmas," this time "dreaming of a white president." "You won't get anyone, and I do mean anyone, to admit it." The performance was placid, unashamed, the singer disappearing into his character so fully he could suck you in, whoever you are.

A year later, along with Rush, Heart, Albert King, Public Enemy, Donna Summer, Lou Adler, and Quincy Jones, Randy Newman was inducted into the Rock & Roll Hall of Fame. As part of a self-tribute band that also included Jackson Browne, John Fogerty, and Tom Petty, Newman performed "I Love L.A.," and then gave his acceptance speech. "It's hard for me to express a genuine emotion," he said, "as you can tell from my writing. But I'm very happy to receive this award. And I hope the fact that I rushed my own song a little earlier doesn't mean I get kicked out on my first night in."

He might have been embarrassed to walk in with a number that, as far as his own albums went, was on the level of one of his movie tunes; if Newman's bile is directed only at himself, the world gets off easy. When his first *Songbook* appeared in 2003, Randy was a guest on the NPR show *Morning Edition*, where host Bob Edwards homed in on Newman's new recording of "Sail Away"—slowed down, every note and word seemingly suspended in its own falsehood. The character sweet-talking Africans onto his slave ship wasn't exactly in the historical record, Edwards said—why such indirection? "What am I supposed to say?" Newman said. "'Slavery is bad'? It's like falling out of an airplane and hitting the ground, it's just too easy. And it has no effect." "But the contrast is so strong," Edwards said. "That beautiful melody—" "It worked out well," Newman said finally. "It ended racism in this country. Kids today don't remember, now that it's gone."

Of Newman's more fugitive recorded vocal work, most memorable is his charge through "Gone Dead Train" on the soundtrack to the ep-ochal fin-des-années-soixantes film *Performance* (Warner Bros., 1970, included on *Guilty*), a near-hysterical rocker titled after a 1932 King Solomon Hill blues. Among other one-shots, he contributed a straight cover of Fats Domino's 1956 "I'm in Love Again" to the soundtrack for the underrated East Coast beach movie *Shag* (Sire/London/Rhino, 1989) and a hard "Blue Monday" to *Goin' Home: A Tribute to Fats Domino* (Tipitina's Foundation, 2007; when Randy sings "I hate blue Monday," you hear a lifetime of them); "I've Been Working on the Railroad" to the anthology *Disney—For Our Children—The Concert* (Disney, 1993); "Re-member" to the anthology *For the Love of Harry: Everybody Sings Nilsson* (Music Masters, 1995), finishing a loop that began twenty-five years before with *Nilsson Sings Newman* (Buddha); and in 2004 came up with a full-throated, feet-on-the-ground vocal for "I Ate Up the Apple Tree" ("A story from the Bible," Randy said in one of several spoken passages. "I didn't read it, but some people *have* read it") on Dr. John's *N'Awlinz: Dis Dat or D'Udda* (Blue Note). In 2013 he answered Peter Gabriel's one-dimensional version of "I Think It's Going to Rain Today," from Gabriel's covers album *Scratch My Back*, with a tough little reading of Gabriel's "Big Time" on a faux-Gabriel's *And I'll Scratch Yours* (Real World)—Gabriel had enlisted all the people he'd covered to cover him. That same year Newman visited the Gershwin Room at the Library of Congress and sat down at Gershwin's piano to play "Outdoors But Not the Red River Valley," which he'd written as a tribute to his uncle Alfred, who, Randy explained, "wrote the music for a number of John Ford's films. In every one of them, the great director wanted to use 'Red River Valley.'" This wasn't that, but Ford could have used it in *My Darling Clementine*. Of songs Newman wrote for others but never recorded him-self, Dusty Springfield's ethereal versions of "Just One Smile" and "I Don't Want to Hear It Anymore" (both on her great *Dusty in Memphis*, Atlantic, 1969, augmented version on Rhino) are likely the best. New-man's piano and arranging credits are legion; he received no credit for his remarkable arrangement of Peggy Lee's 1969 recording of Jerry Leiber and Mike Stoller's nihilistic art song "Is That All There Is?" (Capitol; the album *Is That All There Is?* included Newman's "Linda" and a terrible version of "Love Story"), which brought Miss Lee back from the dead, and from the late '70s has worked as an almost secret punk air. Franklin Bruno's "'Is That All There Is?' and the Uses of Disenchantment," collected in the anthology *Listen Again: A Momentary History of Pop Music*, ed. Eric Weisbard (Durham, NC: 2007), sees not only all the way into the song but all around it.

The book on Newman is Kevin Courrier's *Randy Newman's American Dreams* (Toronto: ECW Press, 2005). My thanks go to the late Susan Lydon for the help she gave me with the Newman chapter here; I had the benefit of her unpublished conversations with Randy, and I have taken some quotes and much biographical information from her profile "Randy Newman—Out of Cole Porter, Hoagy Carmichael, Bob Dylan, Groucho Marx, Mark Twain, and Randy Newman" (*New York Times Magazine*, November 3, 1972). We had a good time trading ideas one night at the Palace Theatre in San Francisco, as Randy played God up on stage and the audience gave him the cheers he deserves, an occasion that turns up in Lydon's *Take the Long Way Home* (New York: HarperCollins, 1993).

CAMEOS: RAYMOND CHANDLER, NATHANAEL WEST, THE BEACH BOYS & OTHERS

All of my quotes from Chandler come from *Raymond Chandler Speaking* (Berkeley: University of California, 1997, first published 1962), an indispensable collection of letters, articles, and fiction fragments. Chandler's mysteries, especially *The Big Sleep* (1939) and *Farewell, My Lovely* (1940), shaped my picture of Los Angeles; Nathanael West's 1939 *Day of the Locust*, though inferior to Chandler's best, belongs to the same "There's nothing wrong with Southern California that a rise in the ocean level wouldn't cure" (Ross Macdonald) genre—the difference being that Chandler would have expected to go under along with everybody else. From the mid-seventies on it was the late Warren Zevon more than any novelist who took up the noir side of the city's tale, from "Desperados Under the Eaves" to "Mohammed's Radio" to "Run Straight Down" (all on the bottomless *I'll Sleep When I'm Dead (An Anthology)* (Elektra Traditions/Rhino).

The other side of the Southern California story ("There's nothing wrong with surfing conditions that a rise in the ocean level wouldn't cure") is best told by Jan and Dean and the Beach Boys. The former's heart-rending "Surf City," number one in 1963 and co-written by Beach Boy Brian Wilson, can be easily found, but is best heard on Jan and Dean's *Anthology Album* (United Artists), a crazed set that comes with a concordance matching the duo's discs with the car and girl-friend each had at the time any given 45 was released. Richard Compton's insistently quotidian 1978 TV biopic *Dead Man's Curve* (CBS, based on Paul Morantz's "The Road Back from Dead Man's Curve," *Rolling Stone*, September 12, 1974), which is best seen along with *Behind the Music: Jan and Dean* (VH1, 1998), is a priceless portrayal of denizens of California subcultures as real people in a real place; "Jan & Dean as Purloined Letter" in my *The Dustbin of History* (Cambridge: Harvard, 1995; London: Picador, 1996) is an attempt to pin down what makes it different from all other pop music movies. The Beach Boys' wonderful mid-'60s work is available in numerous packages, though I stick with *The Best of the Beach Boys, Vol. 2* (Capitol, 1967). A common prize in the vinyl graveyards of the digital age, it includes "409," "Let Him Run Wild," the touching-'n'-true what-if-summer-doesn't-last-forever lament "When I Grow Up (To Be a Man)," "the immortal 'California Girls'" (Camille Paglia), and the never-topped "I Get Around." *Beach Boys Party!* (Capitol, 1965), to which Dean of Jan & was luckily invited, and the suburban *Wild Honey* (Capitol, 1967), are essential.

The Beach Boys wanted more out of life than cars and surf could give them, and like many they went from easy questions to easy answers. When they recorded "Cease to Exist" (retitled "Never Learn Not to Love" as the flipside of "Bluebirds Over the Mountain" and on *20/20*, Capitol, 1969), a composition by the aspiring Los Angeles singer-songwriter Charles Manson—a pal of Beach Boy Dennis Wilson (who took songwriting credit), and a shaman who combined in equal parts the displaced lumpen proletariat Nathanael West found crusted beneath the Hollywood sign and the high-rent Dr. Feelgoods Raymond Chandler seemed to hate more than any other species of L.A. con artist—the Beach Boys were truly faced with the challenge of growing up, a challenge they failed to meet. Ed Sanders's *The Family* (unexpurgated edition, with a chapter on the Process, New York: Dutton, 1971; revised, censored, and updated edition, New York: Thunder's Mouth, 2002), a terrifying investigation of Manson loose in post-surf Hollywood, lays out the facts of the Southern California synthesis of sun and horror, just as Newman's songs capture its soul.

Unlike so many L.A. groups that come from somewhere else, the Beach Boys were not fakes. Empty, tired, desperate, stupid, and even insane as they were through the next decades, singly or as a group, for a time they nevertheless performed life as some people actually lived it. The Beach Boys celebrated California hedonism, looked for its limits, and found them. Their pleasures, as opposed to those offered by such latter-day inheritors as the Eagles, always radiated affection—perhaps because those pleasures were rooted in friendship, or its memory, or its fantasy.

THE KINKS

The Kinks will likely be remembered as one of the oddest rock 'n' roll bands, and as one of the best. For crude, brutal hard rock, their early singles sometimes outran those of the Beatles and the Rolling Stones, probably because the resentment and rage such music communicates were exactly what Kinks leader Ray Davies felt: he really didn't like it here, wherever that happened to be. Davies was genuinely at home only in his fantasies of a simpler day, when class lines were clear, when everyone knew everyone else and everyone else's place; when, presumably, there would have been a place even for him. His search for a phantom paradise took him as deeply into the throes of nostalgia as a pop artist can travel—thus his dull pleas for the preservation of village greens, and the power to make records as disturbing and haunting as "The Way Love Used to Be" and "I'm Not Like Everybody Else."

"I'm Not Like Everybody Else" appeared in 1966, on *Face to Face* (Reprise/Pye), which also included "Sunny Afternoon," and can also be found, along with the Kinks' initial 1964–65 smashes (the rockers, like "You Really Got Me," and the first attempts at social satire, like "A Well Respected Man"), on the Kinks' *Greatest Hits* (Reprise, 1966). "The Way Love Used to Be"—the highlight of *The Great Lost Kinks Album* (Warner Bros., 1973), which is itself now lost—first shone through the English mist on the band's soundtrack to the 1971 film *Percy* (Pye). Davies's finest work came in 1968, with *Something Else* (Reprise/Pye), which sings to a close with the ineffable "Waterloo Sunset."

That album disappeared commercially, but *Arthur, or the Decline of the British Empire* (Reprise/Pye, 1969) and *Lola versus Powerman and the Moneygoround* (Reprise/Pye, 1970) brought the Kinks new fans even as Davies's songs grew more coarse. The unforgettable "Lola" is best heard on *The Kink Kronikles* (Reprise), a collection of '67–'71 album cuts, non-hits, and unreleased numbers. The best criticism is probably Robert Polito's "Bits of Me Scattered Everywhere: Ray Davies and the Kinks," collected in the anthology *This Is Pop: In Search of the Elusive at the Experience Music Project*, ed. Eric Weisbard (Cambridge: Harvard, 2004).

They wrote their own books. First was guitarist Dave Davies's *Kink: An Autobiography* (New York: Hyperion, 1997), ultimately a genre piece; following a stroke, Davies published *Heal: A Guide to Meditation* (Meta-media/Amazon), also a genre piece. Ray Davies's *X-Ray: The Unauthorized Autobiography* (New York: Viking, 1994, was an unbreakably coded mix of real life and fiction, with the burden of corruption, sleaze, and shame nearly unrelieved, no matter what you thought you were reading; *Waterloo Sunset: Stories* (New York: Hyperion, 2000) covered the same territory, with all the blame on somebody else. But *Americana: The Kinks, the Riff, the Road: The Story* (New York: Sterling, 2013), was different: there was a plainness, a lack of tailored style, and you could believe the places Davies had been, and why he left. Ever campy, disgusted, fed up, worn out, occasionally even trendy, the Kinks rolled on through the decades. They broke up. They reformed. They stopped speaking to each other. The original bassist Pete Quaife died in 2010. In 2014 there was, as always, talk of one more go.

A WAVE

In the writer-director John Carney's 2014 film *Begin Again*, Keira Knightley's hopeful singer-songwriter is talking to Mark Ruffalo's fallen record man. "I just think that an A & R man telling people how they should dress, or come across, is total *bullshit*," she says. "People don't want that, they want *authenticity*."

"OK, babe," Ruffalo says. "'Authenticity.' Give me the name of *one artist* who you think passes your authenticity test."

Knightley thinks for her answer, gets it, raises her head in a smug, that's-all-she-wrote toss: "Dylan."

"Dylan," Ruffalo says, as if he's heard it a thousand times. "That is the most cultivated artist that you could have thought of. Look at his hair, his sunglasses, he changes his look every decade—"

Knightley's face goes blank, then lights up: "*Randy Newman*."

"I fucking love Randy Newman," Ruffalo says. "You got me on that."

ELVIS PRESLEY

In 1974, RCA issued *Elvis: A Legendary Performer, Vol. 1*, a single album that illustrates, historically and aesthetically, virtually every side of the man's music. For my concerns it remains a perfect outline.

Legendary Performer begins at Sun, with "That's All Right," Elvis's first single, followed by "I Love You Because," the sentimental country tune with narration that was in fact his very first officially logged professional recording, though Sam Phillips never released it. Then immediately to "Heartbreak Hotel," altogether unlike any of the Sun sides (a concession to the cool jazz sound popular in the mid-'50s, if the truth be told), number one on pop and country charts and #3 on the rhythm and blues chart in early 1956. A snatch of interview from that time: a reporter asks Elvis if his success is due to luck or talent, and Elvis naturally answers luck. Without pause we are into "Don't Be Cruel," this time a three-chart number one sweep, and it gives the lie to Elvis's modesty: no one has ever sung with more confidence.

We hear "Love Me Tender," the title song from Elvis's first movie; we hear "(There'll Be) Peace in the Valley (For Me)," from 1957—Elvis's first, and perhaps best, gospel recording.* Then to the similarly parenthetical but otherwise utterly opposite "(Now and Then There's) A Fool Such As I," from 1958, where Elvis distances himself from his style with outrageous parody; then to "Tonight's All Right for Love," a ghastly number from the 1960 film *G.I. Blues*, where the parody has become the style.

Scattered through the album are three performances from the 1968 television comeback show, cut with a small combo in front of an audience: a joking "Are You Lonesome Tonight?"; a staggering "Love Me," with Elvis wavering between parody and passion until passion wins; and "Tryin' to Get to You," a song Elvis recorded at Sun in 1955. Thirteen years later, he sings it as a message to his listeners: his way of telling anyone who cared how hard it was for him to find his way back, and what the trip was worth. His singing makes his early classics seem

---

* A country hit in 1951, this remarkable song was written by the Rev. Thomas A. Dorsey, a man who might have understood the apparent contradictions in Elvis's music: in the '20s, as a bluesman with the accent on blue, he was widely reviled by religious black families throughout the South for his suggestive lyrics. Born in 1899 in Villa Rica, Georgia, and musically active almost until his death in Chicago in 1993, Dorsey became the "father of modern gospel" by combining blues and jazz modes with sanctified themes; drawing on the spiritual "We Shall Walk Through the Valley in Peace," Dorsey composed "Peace in the Valley" while riding on a train in 1939, thinking about the war that had just begun in Europe, measuring his fears against the suddenly comforting valley he found himself passing through. For his blues, see *Georgia Tom Dorsey, 1928–1932: Come On Mama Do That Dance* (Yazoo), or *Georgia Tom (Thomas A. Dorsey): Complete Recorded Works in Chronological Order, Vol. 1 (1928–1930)* and *Vol. 2* (Document); for his gospel, the 1934 "Singing My Soul" on the unmatched anthology *The Prewar Gospel Story: 1902–1944* (Best of Gospel/France Telecom) and *Say Amen, Somebody* (DRG), an augmented soundtrack to the 1982 film about Dorsey's life and work (augmented DVD on Rykodisc), which includes performances by him, and *Precious Lord: New Recordings of the Great Gospel Songs of Thomas A. Dorsey* (Columbia, 1973). For an inspired essay on Dorsey, Elvis, and much more, see Tom Smucker's "Precious Lord" in *Stranded*, ed. GM (1979; New York: Da Capo, 2007).

immature, unfocused, even hesitant. They weren't, but this music—all drama, fury, and glamour—is not like anything else in rock 'n' roll.

Legendary Performer ends, as in 1974 it had to, with "Can't Help Falling in Love," from the *Blue Hawaii* soundtrack of 1961—the song that became Elvis's touchstone in the '70s, at least until the end, when it was replaced by "My Way." Here, it sounds like a hymn.

On this album, Elvis's career makes sense, it has shape. You can hear the artist grow, the god fail, the King return, the man endure and change. As a version of American possibility and American limits, it is the equal of Robert Johnson's *King of the Delta Blues Singers*; given hindsight, a version of "Hellhound on My Trail" is all that is missing.

With *Legendary Performer* as a map, we can turn to Elvis's music in detail.*

SUN, 1953–55

All of Elvis's master recordings at Sun (with the apparent exception of lost masters for covers of Sister Rosetta Tharpe's 1945 "Strange Things Happening Every Day," Martha Carson's 1951 gospel hit "Satisfied," and Ray Charles's 1955 "I've Got a Woman")—plus Elvis's four amateur Sun acetates, two sides of a demo cut in 1955 at a radio station in Lubbock, Texas, and several live 1955 Louisiana Hayride performances—can be found on *Sunrise* (RCA). Alternate takes can be found all over the place.

Elvis's first recordings were made in June 1953 by the Memphis Recording Service, a cut-your-own disc operation ("$3 one side, $4 two sides") Sam Phillips set up to supplement the uncertain income of the pre-rock Sun label. According to legend, Elvis showed up to make a birthday record for his mother; Hans Langbroek, author of the pioneering self-published booklet *The Hillbilly Cat*, was perhaps the first to argue that since Gladys Presley's birthday fell in April, Elvis really made the record for himself, hoping someone would notice him. (Langbroek was also the first to break the news—outside of the Netherlands, anyway—that Col. Tom Parker, Elvis's manager, was not born in West Virginia with carny in his soul, but was rather an illegal immigrant born in Breda, in Holland, as Andreas Cornelis van Kuijk.)

---

* Since Elvis's death he has received a simultaneous would-be resurrection and all-but second burial as a result of an endless stream of excavated recordings, special box sets, Byzantine and redundant repackagings. Those needing more information than I can provide here should consult Ernst Jorgensen's *Elvis Presley: A Life in Music—The Complete Recording Sessions* (New York: St. Martin's, 2000).

Whatever his motive, Elvis recorded two songs, with Phillips's co-manager Marion Keisker (1927–1989), according to her, or Phillips himself, according to him, running the machines: "My Happiness," a 1948 hit for John and Sandra Steele, Ella Fitzgerald, and the Pied Pipers, and "That's When Your Heartaches Begin," a country weeper in its 1951 version by Bob Lamb and a ballad as done by Billy Bunn and His Buddies in 1952, but also recorded by the Ink Spots in 1941, in a performance released in 1952. Long believed forever lost, the original acetate surfaced in 1988 in the possession of Edwin S. Leek, a high school friend of Elvis's. He claimed that Elvis brought the disc to his parents' house to play it, having no other means to hear it, and then forgot about it—a nice story contradicted by Peter Guralnick's discovery, as chronicled in his scrupulously researched and sourced *Last Train to Memphis: The Rise of Elvis Presley* (see below, in "Elvis in Print and in the Grave"), that far from forgetting about his first recording, Elvis actually tried to make it public, convincing the owner of Charlie's, Elvis's local record shop, to put the single copy on the store jukebox.

Both sides of the acetate were included on the essential reissue *The King of Rock 'n' Roll—The Complete '50s Masters*, a five-CD set that collects the primary versions of all of Elvis's 1950s solo studio recordings (RCA). While "That's When Your Heartaches Begin" suggests a novice, with "My Happiness" Elvis's style, his musical personality, even his personal culture, are almost completely present—and, as one listens, it's almost impossible to disbelieve the story about Gladys's birthday. The performance drips with devotion, piety, a sentimentality taken to the point of desperation. Writing in *The Wire* in September 1992 under the name Hopey Glass, Mark Sinker went all the way into the music: "Sung to Gladys or himself, or the young Gladys in himself, [the song] says quiet gentleness can also be an unearthly force."

Whoever first recorded Presley, Keisker heard something unusual in his voice ("I felt the hair on the back of my neck begin to prickle in some way" she told her friend John Bakke, then a professor of communications at the University of Memphis, in 1977), secretly taped some of his singing, asked for a number where he might be reached (the Presleys had no telephone), and pushed her boss to give the boy a formal audition. Phillips demurred, but on January 14, 1954, Elvis was back, this time with Phillips definitely at the controls, to record "I'll Never Stand in Your Way," a then-recent hit for Joni James, plus "It Wouldn't Be the Same Without You," a country number first recorded in 1950 by Al Rogers and His Rocky Mountain Boys—though until 1993 the tune was always listed in Elvis literature as "Casual Love Affair" (an odd pseudo-fact, since no one had ever discovered anything about a composition titled "Casual Love Affair"). The correction emerged when Elvis's second acetate, also considered lost, was purchased by Elvis collectors Sean and Tracy O'Neal as part of a grab-bag of Elvisiana they saw advertised in a local newspaper while on vacation. These recordings were a step back: "his lack of confidence betrayed him," Guralnick writes, "and he sounds more abrupt, more insecure . . . He was at an impasse—unlike the hero in comic books and fairy tales, he had not yet discovered his true guise, underneath his outer rags." Elvis's "It Wouldn't Be the Same Without You," sung in a very high, pleading register, was first released in 1997 on *Elvis Presley Platinum: A Life in Music* (RCA), an interesting four-CD career retrospective featuring numerous alternate takes and previously unreleased performances.

Not long after, on June 26, Elvis got his chance.

Phillips had secured a demo recording of a tune called "Without You" from a Nashville music publisher, who had recorded it in the state penitentiary. The song was eerie—with a stronger voice, it might even . . . who knew? Again, Keisker and Phillips disagree: "Why not try the boy with the sideburns?" Keisker said. ("Why not try the boy with the sideburns?" Phillips thought to himself.)

Elvis was called back into the studio; Phillips played him the demo. The original Nashville demo has never been released or bootlegged; Keisker kept the only copy, which a few years before her death in 1989, at seventy-two, she gave to John Bakke, who has written extensively on Keisker, Phillips, and the recording in "It's a Mystery! The Story of Elvis Presley and 'Without You'" (2012). A bit can be heard in the 1987 BBC radio documentary *Presley: "I Don't Sing Like Nobody"*; heard entire, the performance is ghostly, demanding to be played again and again, as if by so doing one could get to the bottom of it. To listen, now, is to be transported back to the very instant before the beginning of the present age. The unnamed singer's voice is full of pain and full of acceptance, gliding along the stately lines of the song, reaching for solace, falling short, reaching again. It's pure Sisyphus—and as Camus said of Sisyphus, one must imagine the singer happy.

Though Guralnick hears a white singer, I hear Sonny Til of the Orioles, Bill Kenny of the Ink Spots, and the gospel tones of Johnny Bragg and the Prisonaires (Marion Keisker told Jerry Hopkins, Elvis's first serious biographer, that "Sam couldn't find out who the singer was"; much later Phillips asserted that it was in fact Johnny Bragg). Still, most of all, anyone who listens hears Elvis—and as soon as one seems to identify what, it seems, Elvis must have taken from the demo, the element vanishes. Then it creeps back. What could Elvis have heard? Was it a shock of recognition, hearing what, in his head, in his fantasies, he sounded like himself?

All through the afternoon, Elvis tried to sing "Without You." He couldn't do it; take after take ended in shambles. He turned away from the mike and pounded his fists on the wall, shouting at the man sitting in prison in Nashville: "I hate him! I hate him!"

The session may not have been a total loss: singing "every song he knew" after Phillips asked him if he could sing anything else, Elvis is sometimes said to have taped a lost version of "Rag Mop," a 1951 novelty first recorded by Johnny Lee Willis, and popularlized by Lionel Hampton, the Ames Brothers, and Joe Higgins and the Honeydrippers—that is, by a jazz band, a white-bread vocal group, and a jump blues combo. Phillips was intrigued; he brought Elvis together with Scotty Moore and the bass fiddle player Bill Black (1926–65) and bid them rehearse. Phillips was looking for a distinctive sound; on July 5, supposedly only a day after Elvis met his bandmates, the sound was found. Elvis's Sun singles* followed in this order:

"That's All Right" b/w "Blue Moon of Kentucky," released July 19, 1954 (Sun 209). Original version of "That's All Right" by Mississippi blues singer Arthur Crudup ("I wanted to be as good as Arthur Crudup when I saw him, back in '49," Elvis told the Dutch critic Jip Golsteijn in the early seventies), 1946 (see *Elvis Classics*, P-Vine, a 26-cut set of blues and R&B originals of songs recorded by Presley, or *Arthur "Big Boy" Crudup: Complete Recorded Works in Chronological Order, Vol. 2: 1946–1949*, Document; for Crudup's originals of "So Glad You're Mine" and "My Baby Left Me," which Elvis recorded soon after leaving Sun for RCA, see *Vol. 1* and *Vol. 3*, respectively; "My Baby Left Me" is on *Elvis Classics*). Original version of "Blue Moon of Kentucky" by Bill Monroe and His Bluegrass Boys, 1946 (see Monroe's *Blue Moon of Kentucky*, Country Stars, *The Essential Bill Monroe and His Bluegrass Boys*,

---

* Elvis's first two singles featured "Scotty and Bill" (as the labels read), but some later Sun recordings included drums (on the "country" sides more often than on the "rhythm" sides, interestingly enough—drums were almost standard on post-war blues and rhythm and blues recordings, and all but banned on country recordings, and the idea at Sun was clearly to bridge if not erase any difference between the languages spoken on either side of an Elvis record). The drummer was not D. J. Fontana, Elvis's first onstage and RCA studio drummer, but teenage jazz drummer Jimmie Lott, on "I'm Left, You're Right, She's Gone," and Western swing musician Johnny Bernero on "I Forgot to Remember to Forget" and "Tryin' to Get to You" (with Elvis on piano on the latter). Lott and Bernero soon vanished into oblivion, where they are no doubt trading tales of what might have been with Jimmy Nicol, who replaced an ailing Ringo Starr when the Beatles toured Australia in 1964. "Sam asked me if I would be interested in working with the group," Lott told Nicol years later (well, Colin Escott, anyway, in his *Good Rockin' Tonight: Sun Records and the Birth of Rock 'n' Roll*, New York: St. Martin's, 1990), "and I told him I had another year of school and couldn't."

Columbia box set, and *The Roots of Presley*, Catfish, a strong collection of mostly country recordings). Elvis's first, "that's a pop song, now!" version of "Blue Moon of Kentucky" is included on *Sunrise* ("What you have there," pronounced Memphis bandleader Jim Dickinson when he identified the tape, "is what it sounded like ten minutes before rock 'n' roll was invented"); the "*Damn*, nigger!" studio dialogue is included, unidentified, between tracks eight and nine on disc two.

"Good Rockin' Tonight" b/w "I Don't Care If the Sun Don't Shine," released September 22, 1954 (Sun 210). Original versions of "Good Rockin' Tonight" by jump blues singer Roy Brown (who wrote it), 1947, and Wynonie Harris (who had the bigger hit), 1948 (for Brown's version, see *Good Rocking Tonight: The Best of Roy Brown*, Rhino, or *Elvis Classics*; for Harris's, see *Bloodshot Eyes: The Best of Wynonie Harris*, Rhino, or *The Roots of Presley*). "I Don't Care If the Sun Don't Shine" written by Mack David, a hit for Patti Page in 1950, and recorded as well by Dean Martin (fabulously—included on his eight-CD Bear Family set *Memories Are Made of This*, and on Martin's more fly-by-night *Rare Records*, Favorite Classics). Percussion on Elvis's version, possibly bongo drums, or hands slapped on cardboard to simulate bongo drums, by Sun singer Buddy Cunningham, unless it's Elvis banging on his guitar.

"Milkcow Blues Boogie" b/w "You're a Heartbreaker," released January 8, 1955, Elvis's twentieth birthday (Sun 215). Original versions of "Milkcow" by many singers, most relevantly Georgia country bluesman Kokomo Arnold, 1934, as "Milk Cow Blues" (see *Elvis Classics*, or *Kokomo Arnold: Complete Recorded Works in Chronological Order, Vol. 1, 1930–1935*, Document), Johnny Lee Wills and His Boys, 1941 (see "Milk Cow Blues," with Arnold credited as composer, on the anthology *From the Vaults: Decca Country Classics 1934–1972*, MCA), and Western swing orchestra leader Bob Wills and His Texas Playboys, 1946, as "Brain Cloudy Blues" (see *The Bob Wills Anthology*, Sony). "You're a Heartbreaker" written by Jack Sallee, first recorded by Elvis.

"Baby Let's Play House" b/w "I'm Left, You're Right, She's Gone," released April 25, 1955 (Sun 217). Original version of "Baby Let's Play House" by R&B singer Arthur Gunter, 1955 (see *Elvis Classics*, *The Best of Arthur Gunter*, Excello, or the fine anthology *Southern Rhythm 'n' Rock: The Best of Excello Records, Vol. 2*, Rhino). "I'm Left, You're Right, She's Gone" written by Stan Kesler and William Taylor, first recorded by Elvis; seven takes of "My Baby Is Gone," the slow, torchy version Sam Phillips sent to DJs, are collected on *The Complete Sun Sessions*, an RCA set otherwise superseded by *Sunrise*. "Baby Let's Play House" was

Elvis's first record to make the national charts, reaching #5 on the *Bill-board* country list.

"Mystery Train" b/w "I Forgot to Remember to Forget," released August 1, 1955 (Sun 223). Original versions of "Mystery Train" by the Carter Family, as "Worried Man Blues," 1930 (see the Carter Family's *Worried Man Blues*, Rounder), and by Little Junior's Blue Flames (blues singer Junior Parker), 1953 (see *Elvis Classics*, or the anthology *Mystery Train*, Rounder). "I Forgot to Remember to Forget," written by Stan Kesler and Charlie Feathers first recorded by Elvis, was a number one country hit.

All of Elvis's unreleased Sun production passed to RCA along with Elvis's contract in 1955; five numbers were used to fill out *Elvis Presley*, Elvis's first album, in 1956. "I Love You Because" was recorded by Leon Payne in 1949 and Eddie Fisher in 1950; "I'll Never Let You Go (Little Darlin')" by Jimmie Wakely in 1943; "Just Because" by the Shelton Brothers in 1942 (if one has a horror of blandness, these numbers are the soundtrack to a horror movie); "Blue Moon" by Shirley Ross for the 1934 film *Manhattan Melodrama* (the movie John Dillinger watched just before he was ambushed by the FBI), in 1935 by Glen Gray and Benny Goodman, and in 1949 by Billy Eckstine (a big hit, and likely the proximate source of Elvis's unearthly treatment; see Eckstine's *Everything I Have Is Yours: The Best of the M-G-M Years*, Polygram), and in 1952 by Ivory Joe Hunter; "Tryin' to Get to You" was first recorded in 1954 by the Eagles, a black harmony group from Washington, D.C. (see their *Trying to Get to You*, Bear Family).

Other Sun moments, including studio dialogue, fragments, and completed takes, surfaced more slowly, on RCA LPs, bootlegs, or on scattered reisssues. "Harbor Lights," first recorded by Rudy Vallee in 1937, featured in John Ford's 1940 film *The Long Voyage Home*, and cut as well by Sammy Kaye, Guy Lombardo, Bing Crosby, and Harry James and His Royal Hawaiians, comes from Elvis's first session; "To-morrow Night" is a 1948 ballad by bluesman Lonnie Johnson (see *The Roots of Presley*, or the superb anthology *1948—The R&B Hits*, Indigo, for Johnson's scratched vocal and odd timing) also covered by Bob Dylan (on *Good As I Been to You*, Columbia, 1992); "When It Rains, It Really Pours," with Carl Perkins on guitar, is a first halting, then messy, then searingly erotic reading of Sun singer Billy "The Kid" Emerson's 1955 original (see "When It Rains It Pours" on *Elvis Classics*, or Emerson's *Red Hot: The Sun Years, Plus* Bear Family).

Those seeking more from this period should start with the lively radio cuts from Lubbock, Texas, made early in 1955 (it was common for touring performers to make recordings at the local stations they visited to promote their shows): an expansive cover of Joe Turner's "Shake, Rattle and Roll," with what could be, but isn't, Buddy Holly and the Crickets chanting the chorus in the background (for Turner's epochal 1954 original, see *Elvis Classics* or *The Very Best of Big Joe Turner*, Atlantic, and for commentary, my "Atlantic Records 1947–54" in the anthology *What'd I Say: The Atlantic Story*, New York: Welcome Rain, 2001), and a fine run through the Clovers' 1951 "Fool, Fool, Fool" (see *Down in the Alley: The Best of the Clovers*, Atlantic). *Sunrise* collects live recordings, from 1955 Louisiana Hayride performances (with Leon Post on piano and Sonny Trammel on steel guitar to soften the sound), of the Drifters' "Money Honey," LaVern Baker's "Tweedle Dee," and the Jewels' "Hearts of Stone." The misleadingly titled three-CD set *The Louisiana Hayride Shows* (Goldies) includes performances and interviews from 1954 through 1956, from Louisiana to Texas; the waves of screams that surge over "Hound Dog" are thrilling. You can hear Elvis loosen up, step away from himself ("I'd like to shake around here for you all night," he says at Eagles Hall in Houston in 1955, "but we're booked into Alcatraz tomorrow night—got a long drive ahead of us"), and you can hear, so spookily, way back in 1956, the words that in 1977 would end the public life of the Hillbilly Cat: "Elvis has left the building."

There is more, though what there is is spectral. *First Filmed Performance: Elvis, August 7, 1955* (originally released by Tapeworm Video, partially accessible on YouTube in colorized footage as "First Ever Elvis Presley Performance") catches an outdoor show in a setting that seems no more formal than a family picnic, at Magnolia Gardens in Sheldon, Texas; Lois Robertson brought her home movie camera. The brief soundless footage she got is lengthened by present-day interviews (Robertson's son says he was once told this was the second-most important piece of film in history, "after the Zapruder film") and teasing intercuts, and by the time you're allowed to watch the performance whole, you can't take your eyes off of it. Girls are sitting on the stage; Elvis could not be more relaxed. He pulls up his pants mid-song, and that's his most outrageous gesture. But the performance is all about movement; Elvis's singing is something to get over with on the way to a chance to dance through the guitar solo. At several points Elvis throws back his head and laughs—and it's painful to see, knowing how the story would play out. Just as resonant is the 1990 ABC TV series on the Sun years, *Elvis*, produced by James Parriot, with Priscilla Presley as executive producer. Starring Michael St. Gerard as a stunningly convincing, underplayed young Presley, the episodes were made with a painstaking but never heavy-handed attention to period detail. Some shows were carefully based on real events, some made up out of whole cloth (a couple of singles under his belt, Elvis returns to Tupelo to visit a black friend who taught him guitar; local whites leave "NIGGER LOVER" painted on his car, so Elvis joins his mentor's son's band as they stomp through a set in an all-black juke joint), and every one made sense. The series attracted few viewers, and was soon cancelled; never released on video or DVD, you might still find it on TNT during Elvis Week—that is, the week of August 16.

The Sun story ends on December 4, 1956, when Elvis, already a national hero/antichrist, returned to Sam Phillips's "chicken shack with the Cadillacs out back" and fell into an informal country sing with Carl Perkins and Jerry Lee Lewis. Phillips recorded the session, which though it remained unheard became legendary as "The Million Dollar Quartet" (Johnny Cash, who was thought to have completed the quartet, appeared in group photos that day, but did not sing). It was only after Elvis's death that the music appeared; *The Complete Million Dollar Quartet* (RCA) collects forty-seven pieces spread over seventy-nine minutes. Suddenly, Presley, Perkins, and Lewis were in your living room, throwing sound in your face; you were part of their conversations, you got their jokes. Each sound is a physical fact as the trio starts songs, fails them, realizes them, or tosses them aside, moving through gospel to Chuck Berry to "Don't Be Cruel" (Elvis recounts seeing Jackie Wilson singing it in Las Vegas with the Dominoes, with Wilson utterly outclassing Elvis's original, Elvis now trying to follow Wilson's version, giving up, going on to "Paralyzed," attempting to match Wilson just one more time), then Lewis emerging from his piano-man role to challenge the King, taking over, trying to turn the meeting into a cutting contest, except that Elvis won't play. There is a hilarious, stirring version of "Don't Forbid Me": "Hey, have you heard Pat Boone's new record?" Elvis says, to laughter all around. "It was written for me, stayed around the house for ages, never did see it, so much junk around—" So they wail on.

THE TRIUMPH, 1956–59

Elvis's first record for RCA was "Heartbreak Hotel" b/w "I Was the One"—and "Heartbreak Hotel," released on January 27, 1956, did in the world. In Ian McEwan's *The Innocent* (New York: Doubleday, 1990), Leonard, a young man at the British embassy in Berlin, listens to Armed

Forces Radio every chance he gets. He's in love with Little Richard and Screamin' Jay Hawkins; jive-dancing is king. And then the stakes are raised: "In April came a song that overwhelmed everybody . . . It was no use at all for jiving. It spoke only of loneliness and irresolvable despair. Its melody was all stealth, its gloom comically overstated. He loved it all, the forlorn, sidewalk tread of the bass, the harsh guitar, the sparse tinkle of a barroom piano, and most of all the tough, manly advice with which it concluded: 'Now if your baby leaves you, and you've got a tale to tell, just take a walk down Lonely Street . . .' The song's self-pity should have been hilarious. Instead it made Leonard feel worldly, tragic, bigger somehow."

The explosion of the song coincided with Elvis's first national television appearances (Elvis was rejected in 1955 by *Arthur Godfrey's Talent Scouts*, then the country's premier showcase for unknown performers), and the exposure did much to divide the nation into friends and enemies. The U.S.A. initially saw Elvis on Tommy and Jimmy Dorsey's *Stage Show* (six appearances over the first three months of 1956); audio recordings of these performances, and extensive selections from the other TV appearances noted here, can be found on *Elvis—A Golden Celebration* (RCA), an essential box set. Kinescopes are presented in sequence in the expanded version of *This Is Elvis* (Warner Home Video), a biopic by Andrew Solt and Malcolm Leo composed of documentary footage and scenes reconstructed with actors that was first released theatrically in 1981; much TV footage is also used in Alan and Susan Raymond's 1987 production *Elvis '56—In the Beginning*, narrated by Levon Helm (Warner Vision). Highlights from the Dorsey shows include covers of Carl Perkins's 1956 "Blue Suede Shoes," Little Richard's 1955 "Tutti Frutti," Joe Turner's 1955 "Flip, Flop and Fly," and the Drifters' "Money Honey"—Elvis's musical personality was suddenly narrowing, and intensifying. In April and June there followed two appearances on *The Milton Berle Show*.

It was at about this time that Ed Sullivan, then king of American television, declared that "Elvis will never appear on my show." However, since Elvis turned up on the upstart *Steve Allen Show* on July 1— the notorious appearance where Allen humiliated Presley by forcing him to dress in tails and sing "Hound Dog" to a dog—opposite Sullivan's presentation of an interesting tribute to John Huston capped by soporific readings by Gregory Peck of Captain Ahab soliloquies from Huston's film of *Moby-Dick*, and, not unlike Melville's monster, sunk Sullivan in the ratings, "never" meant only a few months—probably about as long as it took to negotiate Elvis's fee. The three appearances

Elvis made on *The Ed Sullivan Show* (September 9 and October 28, 1956, and January 6, 1957; all three shows, including commercials integrated into the presentations so that one can hardly tell them from the entertainment, are collected on the DVD set *Elvis—The Sullivan Shows*, Image Entertainment, with my liner notes) put Elvis over the top as a national figure; the first show pulled 82.6 percent of the viewing audience. Songs included "Don't Be Cruel," "Love Me Tender," "Love Me," "Too Much," and an amazingly kinetic "Ready Teddy" (not up to Little Richard's 1956 original, but it was Richard's greatest performance—see his 18 *Greatest Hits*, Rhino, *The Specialty Sessions*, Specialty, a four-CD gold mine, or *Elvis Classics*). It was only on the 1957 date that Elvis was televised "from the waist up"; the previous shows displayed him in—as the vaguely pornographic phrase generally used has it—"full body shot." "Ed Sullivan is standing on the sidelines," Elvis said onstage in Las Vegas in 1969, "going 'sumbitch, sumbitch.'

"They arranged to put me on television" he said. "At that particular time, there was a lot of controversy—you didn't see people moving—out in public. They were getting it on in the back rooms, but you didn't see it out in public so much." A single look at *This Is Elvis* or *Elvis '56* makes it plain why Elvis's early TV performances caused so much trouble: Elvis, clearly and consciously perceiving the limits of what Americans had learned to accept as common culture, set out to shatter them. He turns toward the camera, and suggests a body in freedom for which, at the time, there was no acceptable language; he turns away, and suggests that he is only kidding; then he moves in a manner so outrageous memory cannot hold the image—a drama caught with grace and power in Jonathan Rhys Meyers's performance in the first part of the 2005 CBS television production *Elvis—The Miniseries* (Anchor Bay). Were Elvis to appear on TV today, for the first time, with the world somehow still changed as he changed it, the spectacle would be no less shocking. "My God," I said to myself as I watched him move twenty-five years after the fact. "They let that on television?"

Earlier, Elvis had played the New Frontier Hotel in Las Vegas (it seems Mafia moll Judith Campbell wasn't all JFK picked up there), third-billed under the Freddy Martin Orchestra and comedian Shecky Greene as "The Atomic-Powered Singer," no doubt to absorb some of the glamour of the nuclear testing the government was conducting nearby; his show from May 6, 1956, is included on *The Complete '50s Masters*. The music isn't bad (though D. J. Fontana plunges into nightclub shlock with unnerving enthusiasm); Elvis does his best to mock the setting, the audience, and himself.

There are three notable accounts of Elvis facing his true audience. On the four-CD box set *Today, Tomorrow & Forever* (BMG Elvis), a twenty-one-year-old Elvis takes the stage of the Robinson Memorial Auditorium in Little Rock, Arkansas. It's May 16, 1956, and local DJ Ray Green is on the air for a live broadcast: "He's winding up his legs, and here he goes with—'Heartbreak Motel'!" "Here's a song that's real hot around the nation and some parts of Africa," Presley says to introduce the next number. "A song here recorded by a—friend of mine," he says, bending the last three words with an odd inflection, almost twisting them. The friend is Little Richard ("I never met him"), the song is "Long Tall Sally," and Elvis is instantly ripping it to shreds, rushing far out ahead of his band. Little Richard told a funny story, watching from the alley as Uncle John chased Sally out of her wig and Aunt Mary caught them; Elvis lets you know it's the man singing and no one else who has his hands all over Sally, and who's not letting go. "We've been doing this song for about twenty-five, thirty years around the country," Elvis says to introduce "Blue Suede Shoes." It was a riff he would use from the beginning of his career to the end ("One of the first records I recorded, back in 1927, I think it was," he says in Las Vegas in 1969. "Just before the stock market crashed"), as if it signified that the new music he was making was nothing new, that it had always been present—or that he had. "You can burn my wife, steal my car, drink my liquor from an old fruit jar," he laughs in the middle of the song, and with a momentum that stops you cold: did he just say *that*? For "Money Honey"—in the 1953 original, as heard best on the Drifters' *Let the Boogie-Woogie Roll* (Atlantic), as explosive a record as early rock 'n' roll produced—the shouts that Elvis shoots over the dark guitar chords that start the tune clear the ground, and with an open spirit, a confidence, so strong it hardly makes sense. "Very good, Elvis," the DJ shouts as Presley leaves the stage. An aura of unlikeliness comes through the rough performance and the holes in the audio. You hear a young man taking steps that did not have to be taken; you hear him communicating pleasures for which there was no tongue but his own. You hear the screams from the crowd, and in a certain mood you can hear the person behind each scream, and you wonder: *Did she know? Did she understand? Was she changed? Did she change back?*

Live recordings made at afternoon and evening shows at the Mississippi-Alabama Fair and Dairy Show in Tupelo on September 26, 1956—on *A Golden Celebration*—combine sometimes distant sound with an excitement and fervor that dissolve all distance. Elvis had placed fifth at a talent show at the same fair in 1945 for his rendition of "Old Shep"; now the mayor gave him the key to the city, Governor J. P.

Coleman gave him a scroll, and twenty thousand people listened on the verge of riot. At one point Elvis seems genuinely afraid the crowd will go out of control, worrying from the stage over casualties in the audience, introducing "Blue Suede Shoes" as "a song that says you can do anything—but don't. Just don't." Given what he and Scotty Moore had already done with "I Got a Woman," he had only himself to blame if his fans burned down the fairgrounds in appreciation.

Best of all, in its way, is Gordon Bowker's "Rock!" (*Seattle* magazine, February 1970; my thanks to Ed Leimbacher for providing it), which places several teenagers at Elvis's concert at Sicks' Seattle Stadium on September 1, 1957, and then catches up with them twelve years later—two years before Bowker himself cofounded Starbucks. His concluding paragraphs sum up the moment:

"The rosy glow had gone from the cap of Mount Rainier, and the infield was bright with the best night-baseball lights in the minor leagues. The noise from the 15,000 people was immense. Finally the crowd grew quiet.

"'I alluz like to begin mah concerts with the national anthem,' the King said, into the mike. 'Will y'all please rise?' Boyd Grafmyre and Willie Leopold and Ted Shreffler and Dennis Lunde and Merrilee Gunst [as Merrilee Rush, she would score a top ten hit in 1968 with the shimmering "Angel of the Morning"] and Tom Hullet and Pat O'Day who had driven over from Yakima with his wife to celebrate their second anniversary and the other 15,000 people all stood up. Also on his feet was Jimi Hendrix, then a Seattle schoolboy.

"Elvis picked up his guitar, twitched once more, took a breath, and groaned: 'You ain't nothing but a hound dog . . .'

"The crowd was stunned. Then it erupted into a frenzy that dwarfed the one a few minutes earlier. The grandstands seethed back and forth like a huge sea anenome. Not even Elvis could be heard above the roar."

On TV, onstage, and on his early RCA recordings, Elvis was backed by Scotty Moore, Bill Black, D. J. Fontana, and (usually) the Jordainaires on vocals. In the studio, pianists Shorty Long and Floyd Cramer, guitarist Chet Atkins, and others were brought in. Though Atkins was nominally in charge, in effect Elvis acted as his own producer. While every official release from this period appears on *The Complete '50s Masters*, it's still worth hearing Elvis's music as it came forth, and that can best be done with his fifties albums in their original configurations—though reissues now follow the original track sequence with hits and B-sides, which at the time were not included on LPs, and alternate takes.

Elvis's first album, *Elvis Presley* (RCA), number one in 1956, added covers of recent rock 'n' roll hits to the Sun leftovers. His second album, *Elvis* (RCA), also number one in 1956, was quite mild (this was the "folksinger" album)—as if Elvis were in retreat from the furor he'd kicked up. But neither album contained the singles of the period, most of which are on *Elvis's Golden Records* (RCA), #3 in 1958, an interestingly annotated set that includes "Heartbreak Hotel," "Don't Be Cruel," "Jailhouse Rock," "All Shook Up," "Treat Me Nice," "Any Way You Want Me (That's How I Will Be)," and the song with which Elvis was perhaps identified more than any other, "Hound Dog."*

Elvis' Christmas Album (RCA) was number one in 1957; to predictable Christmas standards Elvis added "Peace in the Valley," an R&B recasting of Ernest Tubb's 1949 "Blue Christmas," a version of "White Christmas" based on the 1954 imp-of-the-perverse rendition by the

---

* "Hound Dog" was controversial in the 1950s because it was so sexy, so funny, and so vehement—pretty much a burlesque onstage, on record it was a way of life, or, as Elvis sometimes said to introduce it, "a philosophy lesson." The performance was if anything even more controversial in the following decades, as a supposed example of white expropriation of black culture, given the tune's original 1952 recording by Willie Mae "Big Mama" Thornton (see her *Hound Dog: The Peacock Recordings*, MCA). Co-composer Jerry Leiber (1933–2011) agreed: "It wasn't about anything," he told Geoffrey Himes forty years later ("Some Cats Know," *City Paper*, December 4, 1996). " 'Big Mama' Thornton's version is about a woman kicking a gigolo out of her house, and she's doing it with a lot of style. Elvis' record sounded like nonsense by comparison. It was nervous; it was too fast; it was too frenetic; it didn't have any groove. It sounded like a lot of white boys trying to get in on the action." In Alice Walker's story "Nineteen Fifty-five" (collected in her *You Can't Keep a Good Woman Down*, New York: Harcourt, 1981), the good-hearted Elvis figure gains wealth and fame from a black woman's song, but because the song can never truly be his, he is destroyed by his alienation from his own false creation; if only it were that simple. Elvis certainly knew Thornton's record, a number one R&B hit in 1953, but brought the song into his repertoire only after seeing it performed in Las Vegas by Freddie Bell and the Bellboys, a white novelty act. ("We stole it straight from them," Scotty Moore told Peter Guralnick of the arrangement Elvis used live; on record his version resembled Bell's hyped treatment—see *The Leiber & Stoller Story—Volume One: Hard Times*, Ace, which also includes the original "Kansas City," aka "KC Lovin'," by Little Willie Littlefield—no more than Thornton's cooler take.) Perhaps at the urging of her producer, Johnny Otis, the white man who ruled the Los Angeles R&B world while passing for black, Thornton claimed authorship of the song, thus allowing Otis to claim the then-common producer's courtesy of coauthorship, not to mention control of publishing rights. But not only did Jerry Leiber and Mike Stoller write "Hound Dog," teaching their arrangement to Thornton in the studio—when they wrote it, in a Los Angeles where cohabitation between unmarried blacks and whites was a matter for the police, Leiber was a member of an interracial, male-and-female communist commune (Stoller was a hanger-on: "He never got me roped all the way into that," he said in 2007), and their glee over Thornton's success with their composition brought forth from Leiber's comrades not praise but a condemnation of commodity fetishism. "We walked in full of excitement," Stoller said twenty years later, in 1973, in an unpublished interview with the editor Michael Roloff and the art critic Barbara Rose, recalling a commune party the night "Hound Dog" became what the world would remember as the first Leiber–Stoller smash, "and they went through this whole lecture on why our excitement had no real social value, and that we were falsely elated and stimulated falsely about what we were doing and I can remember how dragged I was." "I felt it wasn't an honest response to what had happened," Leiber added. "You felt maybe they were jealous," Stoller said. "There was envy involved," Leiber said. "There was," Stoller said. "There damn well was. I drank a lot of wine and I got very sick and was throwing up in the yard. That's how I came to remember that night so well."

Drifters, plus Leiber and Stoller's hard blues "Santa Claus Is Back in Town," which gave the Big E the chance to leer, "Santa Claus is coming—in a big black Cadillac." It was, in Charles Perry's phrase, like finding a hamburger in a medicine cabinet.

50,000,000 Elvis Fans Can't Be Wrong—Elvis' Gold Records, Vol. 2 (RCA), with Elvis in his gold lamé suit on the cover, the image the U.S. Postal Service really should have used for its 1992 Elvis stamp, #31 in 1960, collected chart entries from 1957 through 1959. It was during this period, as Langdon Winner put it, that Elvis "sold out to girls," by which Winner meant that Elvis stopped threatening—not only girls, but the whole of the social order—and began pleading. Already, the music was somewhat hackneyed, and even the parodies ("Wear My Ring Around Your Neck") communicated as the real thing. The highlight was a comparatively small hit, the 1958 "One Night," a cleaned-up cover of New Orleans R&B singer Smiley Lewis's 1955 "One Night of Sin" (see *Smiley Lewis, Vol. 2*, K.C., or *Elvis Classics*; Elvis's rehearsal version, with Lewis's words and title, is on *The Complete '50s Masters*). As with Lloyd Price's sanitized "Stagger Lee," repression put the edge on; the take RCA released was far more intense than the lyrically more transgressive cut that stayed in the can.

By the time "The Elvis Diary," by one Robert Johnson, appeared in the July 1957 issue of *16*, Elvis was devoting himself almost strictly to the movies; soundtracks to *Loving You* (1957; the 2005 reissue of the soundtrack includes "One Night of Sin") and *King Creole* (1958) offered dubious rock and ineffectual ballads. Elvis's best movie, the 1957 *Jailhouse Rock*, also contained his best movie music, partly because Leiber and Stoller were writing the songs (see *Essential Elvis: The First Movies*, RCA, for both studio and soundtrack versions of the movie songs, plus fine alternate takes, from *Love Me Tender*, *Loving You*, and *Jailhouse Rock*; for a particularly congenial setting for *Jailhouse Rock* tunes and other numbers, from such underrated gems as "Don't" to mistakes like "Just Tell Her Jim Said Hello"—Elvis could not have been less convincing as a "Jim"—*Elvis Presley Sings Leiber and Stoller*, RCA). "Young and Beautiful" and "(You're So Square) Baby I Don't Care" still sound perfect; Elvis left for the Army still on top.

THE DECLINE, 1960–67

RCA filled Elvis's Army years with repackagings, giving his original Sun releases national currency for the first time, though Elvis made informal recordings while stationed in West Germany—after his death, five home-taped tunes, highlighted by a version of the Penguins' 1954 "Earth Angel," were collected on *A Golden Celebration*. He returned in 1960 and immediately made *Elvis Is Back!*, #2 in 1960 (RCA; see also the alternate takes collected on *Such a Night*, RCA). Though the record is uneven, every minute of it screams release and relief. And what better way to affirm that rules and regulations were behind him than to cut loose with the blues? The sound Elvis and his band got from these sessions was nothing like the country blues of the Sun singles, but full-blown Chicago menace, driven by Elvis's super-miked acoustic guitar, brutal playing by Scotty Moore and guitarist Hank Garland, and demonic bebop saxophone from Boots Randolph. Elvis's singing wasn't dirty, it was obscene. A cover of the Drifters' 1954 "Such a Night" stood out, but the clincher was "Reconsider Baby." Lowell Fulson recorded the tune in 1954, on his knees (see his *Hung Down Head*, MCA Chess, or *Elvis Classics*), Elvis himself had sung it at the Million Dollar Quartet session, but now, pushing the band like a ringmaster cracking his whip, first coolly, then as if nothing but the pleasures of suspense could hold him back, he sang the song as a slow, measured dare, and it was unbearable to hear him let it end.

With that burst of passion out of the way, Elvis settled down to work. He made two, sometimes three movies a year, with full soundtracks for each. He was more successful than ever—"It's Now Or Never" (1960) sold nine million copies; the *Blue Hawaii* soundtrack sold five million straight off—and counted for less than ever before. As a contract player in his own movie factory, he quit his night job for his day job. There were echoes of humor and excitement, even of genius, but they were only echoes.* *Elvis's Golden Records, Vol. 3* (RCA) collected hits from 1960 through 1963, but there was a soullessness in the music (even "Little Sister," formally a tough pop blues, is slick) that he escaped only with the lovely "Fame and Fortune" and a remake of Chuck Willis's 1954 "I Feel So Bad" (see *Let's Jump Tonight! The Best of Chuck*

---

* Though looking back in 2014 at the 1960 *Flaming Star*, directed by Don Siegel, where Elvis plays Pacer Burton, "a variant of the American stock character known as the tragic mulatto"—Burton's father is white, his mother is Kiowa—J. Hoberman found much more. "The Presley persona was produced at a moment when America's self-image was in flux," Hoberman wrote. "The King achieved his televised apotheosis in 1956, a year that brought *The Searchers* and began with the Montgomery bus boycott. *Flaming Star* opened amid lunch-counter sit-ins, little more than a month after the United States elected its first Roman Catholic president. Although the movie is explicitly concerned with the conflict between white settlers and Native Americans, its coded casting, as well as the moment at which it was released, bespeak an even larger historical issue.

"America 'has a powerful disintegrative influence upon the white psyche,' D. H. Lawrence wrote in his *Studies in Classic American Literature*. The land is 'full of grinning, unappeased, aboriginal demons,' and 'it persecutes the white men, like some Eumenides, until the white men give up their absolute whiteness.' Such is the meaning of Elvis Presley." "Elvis, Brooding and Alienated," *The New York Times*, November 26, 2014.

Willis, 1951–1956, Epic/Okeh, or *Elvis Classics*), a frenzied piece that owed more to Boots Randolph's sax than to Elvis's fine vocal, and which sounded like nothing so much as a cut left over from *Elvis Is Back!* "It had been years," Bob Dylan wrote in 2004, "since he had taken his songs to other planets."

"I made *G.I. Blues*, lemme see, what else did I do, *Blue Hawaii*, *Viva Las Vegas*, and, uh, *Girls Girls Girls*," Elvis said in Las Vegas in 1969, "and a little eight-millimeter black-and-white underground film that hasn't come out yet," a statement that should still have people combing Andy Warhol's archives, though Bruce Conner's would be a better bet. Dream on: one must look long and hard through *Elvis for Everyone*, and soundtracks to the likes of *Roustabout*, *Girl Happy*, or *Paradise, Hawaiian Style*, for even a glimmer of style. One such moment comes on a non-soundtrack cut on the *Spinout* album (RCA, 1966), with Elvis's version of Bob Dylan's then-unreleased "Tomorrow Is a Long Time," which Elvis apparently heard on the 1965 RCA album *Odetta Sings Dylan*. ("Are there any particular artists you like to see do your songs?" Jann Wenner asked Dylan in 1969. "Elvis Presley," Dylan said. "He recorded a song of mine. That's the one recording I treasure most.") Invariably, Elvis's best music in this period was gospel. *His Hand in Mine* (RCA), #13 in 1961, was straightforward and convincing; *How Great Thou Art* (RCA), #18 in 1967, which included a profound "Crying in the Chapel," a 1953 hit by the Orioles (on *Elvis Classics*; Elvis's version was recorded in 1960, but left unreleased until 1965, when it came out as a single), was enough to make you convert. But there was little more. When *Elvis' Gold Records, Vol. 4* appeared in 1968, reaching #38 (RCA—really, somebody at the place could have decided if it was "Gold" or "Golden"), the disc contained not a single interesting track. The story can be heard in reverse on *The Home Recordings* (RCA, 1999); beginning in 1956 ("When the Saints Go Marching In"), the collection includes fifteen tapes from 1966 (a cool "After Loving You," a soft "Dark Moon"). It was parlor music, a nineteenth-century tone, an escape through music from a career in music.

The one priceless document of this era is an impeccably pressed and packaged bootleg LP, *Elvis' "Greatest Shit"!!* (on the Dog Vomit label—the logo shows Nipper, the RCA dog, throwing up into RCA's trademark ear horn). This triumph of conceptual art features a picture of Elvis in his coffin on the sleeve, production credit to Albert Goldman, a facsimile of Elvis's last prescription from Dr. George Nichopolous ("Dilaudid—50, Quaalude—150," etc.), a complete lyric sheet, and released and unreleased versions of Elvis movie classics: "Old MacDonald Had a Farm," "Song of the Shrimp," "Yoga Is as Yoga Does," "The Bullfighter Was a Lady," and, among eighteen others, "Can't Help Falling in Love." "What's that doing here?" said a friend. "That's not shit." "Aaaaaaaahhhh, *shit!*" Elvis immediately replied, as the take collapsed. Advertised on the back were a number of other albums (which, unfortunately, have yet to surface, though *Cut Me and I Bleed—The Other Side of Elvis Presley,* Double "G" bootleg, catches a slew of profanity-driven, sometimes rage-driven performances, most indelibly, from 1969, in a take that has since turned up on YouTube, a journey through Percy Mayfield's "Stranger in My Own Home Town"). Among the promised LPs was "Vocal Duets," with the famous picture of Elvis and President Richard Nixon on the cover; tunes were to include "How Much Is That Doggie in the Window?" (presumably to make Nixon comfortable, though it was Nixon who brought Duke Ellington to the White House, not Mr. Cool JFK) and the once-fugitive Elvis track "King of the Whole Wide World."

That last can now be found on *Elvis: From Nashville to Memphis— The Essential '60s Masters* (RCA five-CD set), which collects all of the best-known sixties releases, minus gospel and material from movie soundtracks, plus a desultory selection of mostly uninteresting rarities (an exception is a heavenly treatment of "That's Someone You Never Forget," which Elvis supposedly asked his bodyguard Red West to write about his late mother). It's an altogether unshapely set, mashing periods of junk into outbreaks of ambition, worst of all omitting the crucial live comeback performances from 1968. The set makes no more sense than the entirely odd three-CD *Collectors Gold* (RCA), a jumble of live and studio material from the '60s and '70s distinguished mainly by a great deal of in-studio patter and bad jokes, yet with every dull moment redeemed by the shockingly gnostic pronouncement Elvis issues before launching into the otherwise unremarkable "Going Home": "Papa oo mau mau, papa oo mau mau . . . Be talking in unknown tongues in a minute. Ah-*oooommmmm* . . ."

That was January 1968, and in truth Elvis had already begun speaking in a tongue that was both untranslatable and undeniable. Starting in 1967, in short order he released covers of blues singer Jimmy Reed's 1961 "Big Boss Man" and of country rocker Jerry Reed's 1967 hits "Guitar Man" and "U.S. Male." They weren't big records ("U.S. Male," the most successful, reached only #28, in 1968), or even particularly good; all had a gruff, obviously contrived toughness, but even that was about to make those who heard them wonder if something wasn't about to change.

THE COMEBACK, 1968–69

Thanks to producer Steve Binder, Elvis reappeared on December 1, 1968, before a national television audience, and saved his career. The show—*The Singer Special*, named for the sponsor, not the performer—opened with "Trouble" and closed with "If I Can Dream," a roughly sung ballad; in between were the pretaped live performances that proved Elvis really was the King.

There were two sorts of live performances: those done with a large studio orchestra ("Jailhouse Rock" with a prominent flute part worked into the arrangement, etc.) and those done informally, with a small audience, as Scotty Moore, D. J. Fontana, a couple of Elvis's pals, and the man himself casually made history. ("Casually" is perhaps not strong enough a word; Fontana kept time banging his sticks on a guitar case.) Except on the first few numbers, Elvis took over on electric lead guitar—the first time he had ever been seen in public playing the instrument—and he did so with the same violent emotion he put into his singing.

These performances—taken from two invitation-only concerts held in a Burbank studio auditorium on June 27, 1968—are collected on *Memories: The '68 Comeback Special* (RCA), the six p.m. show, plus three rehearsals from June 25, and on *Tiger Man* (RCA), the eight p.m. show. *Burbank '68* (BMG) collects a dozen rehearsals; *Let Yourself Go! The Making of "Elvis"—The '68 Comeback Special* (Sony BMG) includes rehearsals on "When It Rains, It Really Pours" and "That's My Desire." The TV show as broadcast can be found as *Elvis—The '68 Comeback Special* (Lightyear); *One Night with You* (Lightyear) captures one full small-combo session. *Elvis—The '68 Comeback Special Deluxe Edition* (BMG), a three-DVD set for which I was lucky to write notes, includes the show as broadcast, both small-combo concerts, and what seem like days, if not weeks, of rehearsals. The payoff comes in the long whorehouse sequences, when Elvis (hey, he's the Guitar Man, he's just looking for a job) doesn't actually get off as cleanly as he's supposed to—still, with all the costume changes, the gospel production numbers, the skits and dances, the small sessions are a pagan temple in a shopping mall.

Working from memory, not a song list, Elvis goes back to Rufus Thomas's 1953 Sun hit "Tiger Man," rolls through a few versions of Jimmy Reed's 1960 "Baby, What You Want Me to Do," playing with the tune until he abandons the words, presses hard on his electric guitar and hammers the rhythm into fire, charges through "One Night,"

"Lawdy, Miss Clawdy," "Blue Christmas," "Tryin' to Get to You," so many more, with Elvis's buddies shouting for another chorus or Elvis forcing one. As a body of work it is the equal of the Sun sides, and in some ways much superior: the feeling is more raw, desperate, and alive. The Sun sides leave you satisfied; this leaves you in a state of disbelief, satisfied and nervous. As Elvis said—hoisting his mike stand like a harpoon, thrusting it out over the crowd, perhaps remembering a TV show of some twelve years before: "Moby Dick!"

Elvis TV Special (RCA) reached #8 in 1969, the first top ten Presley album in three years; "If I Can Dream," the single from the special (inspired by Martin Luther King's 1963 Address to the March on Washington for Jobs and Freedom, the peroration of which Elvis often recited, and by the 1968 assassinations of King and Robert F. Kennedy), reached #12. In May came *From Elvis in Memphis* (RCA)—Elvis's first non-soundtrack, non-gospel, non-random, non-greatest hits album since *Elvis Is Back!*—and it reached #13. There were no weak spots. "Long Black Limousine" and a cover of Eddy Arnold's 1947 "I'll Hold You in My Heart (Till I Can Hold You in My Arms)" were powerful, mature performances, but the best was "Any Day Now," a Burt Bacharach–Bob Hilliard composition Elvis sang with a naked passion—a naked piety, really—that cannot be found in any of his other recordings.

"Suspicious Minds" was number one in the fall of 1969, Elvis's first claim on the top spot in seven years. Along with it came *From Memphis to Vegas/From Vegas to Memphis* (RCA, #12), a two-LP set now retrievable in pieces from numerous repackagings. One disc was made up of decent but unexciting studio material left over from the *From Elvis in Memphis* sessions (see also *Suspicious Minds: The Memphis 1969 Anthology*, RCA); the other was the first of the seemingly countless live albums—this one drawn from the initial comeback shows at the International Hotel in Las Vegas—that in the '70s would serve the same function soundtrack albums had in the '60s: blind product. One would do better with the August 24, 1969, International Hotel show, three weeks into the engagement that would define the last stage of Elvis's career, as collected on *Today, Tomorrow & Forever*, if only for "Elvis Talks About His Career," the only true autobiography he ever offered. "Welcome to the big, freaky International Hotel," he says. "This is my first appearance in nine years, live—I appeared dead a few times"—*dehhhhhhd*, he says, all but putting the word in a coffin—"but this is my first live appearance. Before the evening's over I will have made a complete and total fool of myself. And I hope you get a kick out of watching it."

THE APOTHEOSIS, 1970–77

His resurrection assured, Elvis settled into a public state of grace; in Bob Dylan's words, his only sin was his lifelessness. He played New York City for the first time (not counting TV shows) in 1972; reviews were ecstatic (jaded rock critics went mad for El's version of "Bridge Over Troubled Water"), and the marketing even better, with *Elvis as Recorded at Madison Square Garden* (RCA) in the stores a week after the concerts. Twenty songs were crammed onto the vinyl, "American Trilogy" among them, but clearly a good part of the magic must have come from the fans, and they took most of it home with them. (*Prince from Another Planet*, a stuffed repackaging titled after the headline of Chris Chase's *New York Times* review of the first of four shows, collecting two full concerts, onstage performances retrieved from a fan's video footage, video of a press conference, and fine notes by Lenny Kaye, appeared on BMG in 2012). Elvis reversed field later in the year with "Burning Love," an aching 45 that fought past records by Chuck Berry and Rick Nelson on its way to number one (on some charts; *Billboard* stopped it at #2). "The most exciting single Elvis has made since 'All Shook Up,'" Robert Christgau wrote in *Newsday*. "Not only that, it's dirty. Who else could make 'It's coming closer, the flames are now licking my body' sound like an assignation with James Brown's back-up band?" Some said "Burning Love" reached the top only because of a brief vogue for the fifties, but they couldn't have been listening; this was a rare sort of record, a natural hit, on the order of "I Heard It Through the Grapevine," "You're So Vain," or "Don't Be Cruel." Typically, RCA made it available on an RCA Camden drugstore LP called *Elvis Sings Burning Love and Hits from His Movies, Vol. 2* (the company title factory working overtime as usual). It is now a highlight of *Elvis: Walk a Mile in My Shoes—The Essential 70's Masters* (RCA), a five-CD box set with numerous surprises, the deepest being a forty-second studio warm-up on Bob Dylan's basement tapes tune "I Shall Be Released." It was 1971, with six years to keep the promise.

His rocker's dues paid off with "Burning Love," the King floated on with numerous gruesome ballads, and in 1973 launched another live opus, *Aloha from Hawaii via Satellite* (RCA), now augmented, in a frenzy of posthumous redundancy, by *The Authentic Aloha*, i.e., the rehearsal (RCA). Issued to commemorate a planet-wide TV special, *Aloha from Hawaii* featured a map of the world emblazoned with "WE LOVE ELVIS" in twenty-nine languages, if my count is accurate. There was one song for each language, more or less, though all were in English, except for "Ku-u-i-po" ("sweetheart" in Hawaiian). *Aloha* was Elvis's first number one album in nine years—the last, appropriately enough, had been *Roustabout*.

And they kept coming, album after album, the sloppy, mindless releases all too accurately reflecting the drugged and helpless off-stage life of the man himself. Occasionally the songs changed, but not often. Elvis gained and lost and gained weight; saw his wife leave him for a karate instructor; bought Cadillacs for, it seemed, anyone who would take one; and made the papers when, as began to happen regularly, he checked into a hospital for "rest." One was left to pore through the records for hidden gems—proof that, against all odds, the *truth* was still to be found—and it was, mostly in the form of old R&B hits. *Fool* (RCA), issued in 1973, contained a beautiful version of Ivory Joe Hunter's "I Will Be True"; 1974 brought a thrilling ride through Chuck Berry's 1964 "Promised Land," Presley's first successful cover of a Berry tune, though the disc should have gone much higher than #14. It was followed by the bizarre *Having Fun with Elvis Onstage* (RCA, followed, posthumously, by three more volumes), a Col. Parker dada work that consisted mainly of the King saying, "Well ... well ... *wellllll*" for thirty-seven minutes. In 1975 there was *Elvis Today* (RCA), which offered a magnificent reading of Faye Adams's magnificent 1953 "Shake a Hand" and a priceless version of Billy Swan's 1974 country hit "I Can Help" ("Have a laugh on me," Elvis changed the lyric to say, "I can help"). In 1976, on *From Elvis Presley Boulevard, Memphis, Tennessee* (RCA—the road ran past Graceland, which was to say that by this time Elvis was not leaving the house to record), there was an apocalyptic attack on Timi Yuro's 1961 "Hurt." In 1977, on *Moody Blue* (RCA), Elvis sang Johnny Ace's "Pledging My Love," a song that had spelled death since 1955, when a bullet went through Ace's brain as his record was climbing the charts. Luck held: Elvis's version too was rising the day he died.

No matter how ruined, Elvis retained the power to be as exciting or as dull as he chose; that was always the rhythm of his career. In some ways, then, an album that appeared in late 1971, *Elvis Sings the Wonderful World of Christmas* (RCA), was the truest statement of all—for here, in the midst of ten painfully genteel Christmas songs, each one sung with sincerity and humility, one could find Elvis (as one can hear on *The Essential 70's Masters*) tomcatting his way through almost six blazing minutes of "Merry Christmas, Baby," a raunchy 1947 Charles Brown blues. That was the philosophy lesson: if Elvis's sin was his lifelessness, it was his sinfulness that brought him to life; even something very much like a sense of sin may have finally done him in.

ELVIS IN PRINT AND IN THE GRAVE

While countless "I knew the King" books have appeared since Elvis's death at Graceland on August 16, 1977, until 1994 Jerry Hopkins's *Elvis* (New York: Simon and Schuster, 1971), supplemented by his *Elvis: The Final Years* (New York: St. Martin's, 1980), remained the most useful biography. The book lacks any real point of view; it's wrong on Col. Parker, but it's neither sensationalistic nor sycophantic, and I certainly couldn't have worked without it. Most helpful for detail, among many scholastic compendiums, discographies, concordances, logs, and other reference works is Fred L. Worth and Steve D. Tamerius's encyclopedic and entertaining *Elvis: His Life from A to Z* (Chicago: Contemporary, 1988). Far more inspiring, for me, were these pre-death essays: Stanley Booth's 1968 "A Hound Dog, to the Manor Born" (so titled when it originally appeared in *Esquire*; with an *Esquire*-censored preface restored, it is included in Booth's *Rhythm Oil: A Journey Through the Music of the American South*, 1991; New York: Da Capo, 2000, as "Situation Report: Elvis in Memphis, 1967"), a moving account of Elvis's emergence in Memphis in 1954 contrasted with his mid-'60s limbo; Jon Landau's "In Praise of Elvis Presley" (in Landau's *It's Too Late to Stop Now*, San Francisco: Straight Arrow, 1972), a report on a 1971 Boston concert (the piece was found among Elvis's effects after his death); Stu Werbin's "Elvis and the A-Bomb" (*Creem*, March 1972), a cosmic attempt to place Elvis in a cosmic context, written following the same concert Landau attended; Robert Christgau's "Elvis Presley: Aging Rock" (in Christgau's *Any Old Way You Choose It*, 1973; expanded edition New York: Cooper Square Press, 2000), an analysis based on Elvis's shows in Las Vegas in 1969 and his Madison Square Garden concerts in 1972; Nik Cohn's chapter on Elvis in *Awopbopaloobop Alopbamboom* (1969, as *Pop from the Beginning*; London: Palladin and New York: Da Capo, 1996—"His voice sounded edgy, nervous, and it cut like a scythe, it exploded all over the place. It was anguished, immature, raw. But, above all, it was the sexiest thing that anyone had ever heard"). Also essential are Peter Guralnick's "Elvis Presley" in *The Rolling Stone Illustrated History of Rock & Roll*, ed. Jim Miller (New York: Rolling Stone Press/Random House, 1976, in the form the book was written and designed to have, and re-edited and redesigned in 1992 as a lump), and his "Elvis Presley and the American Dream" in his *Lost Highway: Journeys & Arrivals of American Musicians* (1980; New York: Back Bay Books, 1999).

Elvis's death resulted in a frenzy of hucksterism, most of it licensed by Col. Parker, until all rights were taken over by Elvis Presley Enterprises, Inc., sole heir Lisa Marie Presley's corporate parent, which under Priscilla Presley's direction had by 1988 so effectively worked, or built, the market that Elvis made the cover of *Forbes* as the highest-paid dead entertainer of the year. (Lisa Marie, having long since achieved her majority, and for that matter having put out her own albums, *To Whom It May Concern*, EMI International, 2003, and *Now What*, Capitol, 2005, and in 2012 reissued Elvis's 1954 "I Love You Because" as a BMG single with herself offering a strikingly intimidated vocal accompaniment, and married and divorced Danny Keough, Michael Jackson, and Nicolas Cage, in 2005 sold everything to CKX Inc., after which she left for Japan and married Michael Lockwood.) But right from the beginning, the marketplace opened into realms of spiritualism and morbidity, realms no trademarks or copyrights could control. Ads in British tabloids offered videos of the autopsy performed on Elvis's corpse; teams of collectors tried to dig it up. In the tradition of James Dean, Elvis spoke frequently from the Beyond, usually through the magic of the *Star* and the *Weekly World News*. Elvis impersonators roamed the land, the most interesting being the masked singer "Orion," whom Nashville record magnate Shelby Singleton, who at the time of Elvis's death owned the Sun catalog, promoted as a prophet to make the blind see and the lame walk, the suggestion being that Elvis had faked his death (and changed his name, face, and voice) in order to commune with his followers while escaping the pressures of fame. Scores of cripples and other unfortunates from across the South duly appeared at Orion's concerts, waiting patiently for the laying on of hands. Appalled, the Seattle filmmaker John Myhre produced the six-minute *He May Be Dead But He's Still Elvis* (the phrase first appeared as graffiti on the walls surrounding Graceland)—in which, *Rolling Stone* reported in 1979, "The King's decaying body is exhumed and brought back for one last concert tour (unfortunately, it keeps falling off its stool and collapsing onstage in a heap). The corpse is trotted out for record-store and autographing sessions . . . Finally, slices of flesh are hacked off and sold in 'Piece o' Presley' packages." The notion of a king in hiding—a replay of similar legends about King Arthur, Frederick the Great, Bonnie Prince Charlie, or Jim Morrison—mushroomed into a national craze in 1988, when Elvis was sighted repeatedly in a supermarket in Kalamazoo, Michigan, a discovery pumped up by well-made photographs, taped telephone conversations (swiftly put on sale), and a new single, the uncredited "Spelling on the Stone" (collected on the anonymous and shamelessly fraudulent album of the same name released by Mike Curb, in better times, for him at least, lieutenant governor of California).*

Immediately after Elvis's death, dozens of tribute records were rushed onto the country market, including Misty's "Dead on Arrival," Leigh Grady's "Blue Christmas (Without Elvis)," and Billy Joe Burnette's "Welcome Home, Elvis," which, sung as it was in the voice of Jesse Garon Presley, Elvis's stillborn twin ("El, I been waitin' forty-two years ... Not long ago, Mama joined me here ... She's waitin' for ya, Elvis. Yeah, she's right over there. And soon our daddy will take our hand, and we'll be a happy family once more"), defied credence. Yet over the decade there were even more punk songs about Elvis (as a stiff, Elvis was, in the aesthetics of punk, alive); by the end of the 1980s, especially given the international commemoration ("celebration" is really the word) of the tenth anniversary of August 16, most of these tunes seemed to be about sin and redemption, excess and spiritual starvation. The whole discourse was perhaps caught in the beginning, with X's 1981 "Back to the Base" (on *Wild Gift*, originally on Slash, later available on a single PolyGram CD with X's corrosive debut, *Los Angeles*): a batteringly naturalistic account of a psychotic bus rider raining curses on the King ("Presley's been dead / The body means nothing / Man in the back says Presley sucked dicks / With a picture of Li'l Stevie over his head / I'm in the back with a hole in my throat"). Not only was it likely the best song about Elvis up to its time (Bill Parsons's 1958 "The All-American Boy" was the only decent competition), it was, as Tom Carson wrote, "about how culture shapes lives—as indiscriminately as water shapes wood." That is the theme of my *Dead Elvis: A Chronicle of a Cultural Obsession* (New York: Doubleday, 1991, with color illustrations, and Cambridge: Harvard, 1999, without them), and, I think, of Gilbert B. Rodman's *Elvis After Elvis: The Posthumous Career of a Living Legend* (New York and London: Routledge, 1996), though whether Elvis is water or wood depends on when and where the question comes up.

Millions upon millions of bad books swiftly made their way into

---

* The only spawn of the Elvis-lives hullabaloo worth treasuring is Bono's spooky, heart-rending treatment of "Can't Help Falling in Love," from *Honeymoon in Vegas—Music from the Original Soundtrack* (Epic Soundtrax, 1992), accompanied as it was by an old on-tour Elvis interview, from Lubbock or Cleveland, Charlotte or San Francisco, running in the background. As Bono climbs the golden ladder of the song toward a falsetto so desperate it's all too obvious who he can't help falling in love with—the man himself—or the boy; Elvis sounds very young, and completely guileless—talks about a book called *Poems That Touch the Heart*. After two minutes, Bono fades into the ether, and from out of it comes that familiar voice: "Yessir, I'll be looking forward to coming back. Yessir, I'm looking forward to it."

print—and, in most cases, just as swiftly out of it. (For a careful and frequently hilarious wrap-up of the first wave, see Robert K. Oermann and Al Cooley's review of *Elvis Presley: King of Kings* and thirty-seven other titles, in the *Journal of Country Music*, vol. IX, no. 2, 1982.) *Elvis: What Happened?* (New York: Ballantine, 1977), by former longtime Presley bodyguards Red West, Sonny West, and Dave Hebler, with Steve Dunleavy (the model for the tabloid journalist played by Robert Downey, Jr., in *Natural Born Killers*) as "As Told To," was the first of many scandal-bios, appearing only days before Elvis's multiple-drug overdose; while in many places self-evidently inaccurate or overin-flated, the book is worth reading. Less so are any number of memoirs by friends, distant relatives, Memphis mafiosi, ex-wife, ex-wife's ex-lovers, a nurse, a gatekeeper, and so on, though occultist Jess Stearn's *The Truth About Elvis* (New York: Jove, 1980)—heralded as "the book Elvis planned to write" (as with the Col. Parker product Always Elvis, "The Wine Elvis Would Have Drunk, If He Drank Wine"*), and writ-ten with Larry Geller, Elvis's hairdresser and "spiritual advisor"— de-serves mention for its barely hedged thesis that the man we knew as Elvis was in truth none other than . . . yes, the Son of God himself, back for another look. More unsettling was Lucy de Barbin and Dary Ma-ters's *Are You Lonesome Tonight? The Untold Story of Elvis Presley's One True Love—and the Child He Never Knew* (New York: Villard, 1987), in which de Barbin recounted every detail of the affair she shared with Presley—beginning in 1954, lasting until his death, producing two pregnancies and one child, who of course de Barbin never mentioned to Elvis (she respected his "position"—Bill Clinton should have been so lucky)—an affair that, a reader had to conclude, began in 1954 in de Barbin's unconscious, which became her ego, and is her ego still. ("The way I see it," John Kordosh wrote in his *Creem* review of the book, "we're *all* Elvis's children. So where's my money?") Dee Presley upped the ante in 1992, with a *National Enquirer* scoop from a forthcoming book (which never appeared): "OWN STEPMOM REVEALS SHOCKING TRUTH AT LAST—ELVIS AND HIS MOM WERE LOVERS," though Vernon Presley's second wife at least made no claims for off-spring. As for Albert Goldman's *Elvis* (New York: McGraw-Hill, 1981), he did good work on Col. Parker; otherwise the best-seller—which de-

---

* Prompting widespread fantasies of the likes of Elvis Kibbles, "The Dog Food Elvis Would Have Eaten, If He'd Been a Dog," and later superseded in real life by Priscilla Presley's Graceland Cellars, which started off in 1995 with an expensive Napa Valley Chardonnay ("We invite you to enjoy the alchemy now," Priscilla said on the label, "or savor the mystery for years"), but quickly cut back to the likes of Blue Christmas Cabernet Sauvignon.

spite countless errors, inventions, and racist smears, academics continue to cite—was no more than a 598-page attempt to discredit Presley, the culture that produced him, and the culture he helped create. "Like most country boys of his time," Goldman wrote of Elvis, "he was uncircumcised . . . he saw his beauty disfigured by an ugly hillbilly pecker."

Though Goldman's work will live on in the popular imagination, in many ways it ruled historically until the appearance of Peter Guralnick's *Last Train to Memphis: The Rise of Elvis Presley* (Boston: Little, Brown, 1994). Guralnick's research led to the abandonment of any number of treasured Elvis stories, and as well to unprecedented candor from many of Elvis's early associates, especially his girlfriends. Guralnick insisted on a distinct lack of drama, allowing (or, given the mythic haze that by the 1990s had taken over the story, forcing) the tale to emerge according to its own rhythms, trying, as he put it, to let Elvis and those around him "breathe their own air." In this he succeeded—this history played itself out on roads and in houses, not in a theater—and yet the essential strangeness, the unlikeliness, of Elvis's arrival remained. Bob Dylan, in his unencumbered way, may have best summed up Guralnick's achievement: "Elvis as he walks the path between heaven and nature." Isn't that the whole story, right there in ten words? It wasn't, of course. Guralnick's beautifully titled *Careless Love: The Unmaking of Elvis Presley* (Little, Brown, 1999) reinhabited the airlessness of Presley's life through the sixties to the end, to the point that the reader could feel as trapped as Elvis was.

Good books on Elvis were published before and after Guralnick's. Albert Wertheimer's *Elvis '56: In the Beginning* (1979; New York: Pimlico, 1994), superseded but thankfully not replaced in 2006 by the treasure chest of Wertheimer's collectors' production *Elvis at 21: New York to Memphis* (San Rafael, CA: Insight Editions), is a photo-journal by the only photographer ever given complete access to Elvis: it combines historic, kinetic images of Elvis in the studio, on tour, behind the scenes, and at home with a serious, witty memoir (Wertheimer on Col. Parker: "He looked like a football referee from the Panama Canal Zone"). Just as indelible, and also indelibly subversive of whatever images one might bring to it, is *Private Elvis* (Stuttgart: FEY, 1978), a conceptual work by Diego Cortez that brings together a probing text by Duncan Smith with accidentally discovered photos by Rudolf Paulini: photos of Elvis consorting with whores, junkies, actresses, and strippers in a Munich nightclub in 1959. It's Elvis in montage, after the manner of Michael Lesy's *Wisconsin Death Trip*: a seamy, erotic smashup of American health and postwar European decay, and a version of the porn film (that "little eight-millimeter black-and-white underground film"?) Elvis's fans had dreamed of for more than twenty years. Most important are two books by the late Ernest C. Withers, the great Memphis photographer whose subjects from the 1940s on included the early civil rights movement, the assassination of Martin Luther King, Jr. (Withers's picture of the fetid bathroom from which James Earl Ray fired his bullet is unforgettable), and the last days of the Negro baseball leagues—mostly in *Pictures Tell the Story* (Norfolk, VA: Chrysler Museum of Art, 2000)—and Memphis musicians of the fifties, the latter gloriously collected in *The Memphis Blues Again*, with a strong text by Daniel Wolff (New York: Viking Studio, 2001). All of the famous shots of Elvis with Rufus Thomas, Junior Parker, and Bobby Bland—including one where a Hollywood Elvis is back in town and posing as if he's already slept with everyone in it—are Withers's; so is *Coretta Scott King with Family and Mourners, Main Street, Memphis, April 8, 1968*, which shows the King funeral procession passing by the State Theater, where the marquee reads "ELVIS PRESLEY AT HIS BEST—'STAY AWAY JOE.'" It makes you ask: why wasn't Elvis back in his hometown to walk with those he'd stood with onstage decades before? Withers was there, too, in 1957, in Little Rock, a year after Elvis's show at the Robinson Memorial Auditorium, when nine black students, protected, on the order of President Dwight D. Eisenhower, by the National Guard, braved racist mobs to enter Central High School, one of whom, fifteen-year-old Melba Pattillo, wrote in her diary of being assaulted by "side burners," boys she speculated were trying to turn themselves into "James Dean and Elvis." Pete Daniel notes in *Lost Revolutions: The South in the 1950s* (Chapel Hill: North Carolina, 2000, with Withers's picture of Elvis and B. B. King on the cover) that one of the white girls who stood against Pattillo and the rest of the Little Rock nine appeared in *Look* magazine in a Confederate cap, waving a Confederate flag, over the caption "Likes Elvis Presley," and you had to wonder if she was there the year before to hear Elvis proclaim "Long Tall Sally" a hit in both the U.S.A. and Africa, or if Pattillo was, or if as social life music does anything more than orchestrate the songs people are already playing in their heads.

Elvis: Images and Fancies (Jackson: University Press of Mississippi, 1979), edited by Jac L. Tharpe, is a collection of essays by academics and fans; at its heart is Linda Ray Pratt's "Elvis, or the Ironies of a Southern Identity," which challenges this book and goes it one better. I wrote, Pratt says, "that Elvis created a beautiful illusion, a fantasy that shut nothing out. The opposite is true. The fascination was the reality always showing through the illusion—the illusion of wealth and the psyche of poverty; the illusion of success and the pinch of ridicule; the illusion of invincibility and the tragedy of frailty; the illusion of complete control and the reality of inner chaos." Also rising above the water level were Elaine Dundy's *Elvis and Gladys* (New York: Macmillan, 1985), a sensitive study of ancestry and legacy with many coups of research, and David Adler's unsurprisingly funny and surprisingly empathetic *The Life and Cuisine of Elvis Presley* (New York: Crown, 1993), which in 1995 the director James Marsh turned into the down-home surrealist documentary *The Burger and the King* (BBC/Arena)—a picture Marsh followed ten years later with the relentlessly disturbing feature film *The King*, starring Gael García Bernal as Elvis Valderez; William Hurt as Pastor David Sandow, his father; and Pell James as Malerie Sandow, his sister and lover (Velocity/Thinkfilm DVD).

Two pieces and two photographs should be mentioned: Dave Marsh's "Elvis: The New Deal Origins of Rock 'n' Roll" (*Musician*, December 1982, first delivered as a talk in Memphis in 1982), and Lester Bangs's "Notes for Review of Peter Guralnick's *Lost Highway*" (unpublished in Bangs's lifetime, but collected in his posthumous *Psychotic Reactions & Carburetor Dung*, ed. GM, New York: Knopf, 1987). Bangs (1948–82) "begins slowly, mulling over rather humdrum notions about producer Sam Phillips's shamanhood," Mark Moses wrote. "But he quickly tires of one-step-after-another thinking, and lurches toward more scabrous observations like 'There was always something supernatural about him. Elvis was a force of nature. Other than that he was just a turd.' After he stews and steeps along these lines for a page or two, Bangs hits critical mass and launches into a fixated fantasy about eating essence-of-Elvis-soaked drugs left in the King's corpse-belly. Reincarnating the departed spirit, Bangs becomes the terminal Presley of *Elvis: What Happened?*, sweltering in an ennui imposed by Las Vegas but colored by Franz Kafka. Bangs/Elvis ponders whom to shoot out on a TV screen, decides singing and sex are not options anymore, and descends to a quivering moment of blankness and mystery: 'The point is that something I started doing to make people know I existed started rubbing out my existence, a little at a time, day by day. I could feel it going, seeping away, steady and calm . . . and nothin' comin' in to replace it. And I knew nothin' ever would.'"*

---

* As Peter Fonda's Dr. Van Helsing puts it in Michael Almereyda's 1995 film *Nadja*, after finally driving a stake through the heart of Count Dracula (whose middle name is Ceausescu, and who has been operating in the present day in downtown New York), there was no satisfaction in the victory, it was all too easy: "He was tired, he was lost. He was—he was like Elvis in the end. Drugs; confused; surrounded by zombies; just going through the motions. The magic was gone. And he knew. I didn't kill him. He was already dead."

"Elvis was on *welfare*," Dave Marsh had insisted to a suddenly angry crowd in Memphis. With "Elvis as a Teen? See a Never-Before Published Photo from His Hometown in Tupelo, Mississippi," Vanityfair .com, January 8, 2014, Alanna Nash accidentally placed Elvis in Marsh's Depression context: as it happened, James Agee's *Cotton Tenants: Three Families*, with photographs by Walker Evans, was published for the first time just months before (Brooklyn: Melville House, 2013). This was the long-believed-lost 30,000-word essay that turned into Agee and Evans's 1941 *Let Us Now Praise Famous Men*. In contrast to the sweep and scope of that book, which rides the same American wind as *Moby-Dick* once the *Pequod* ships off, *Cotton Tenants*—a never-printed 1936 assignment by *Fortune*—pitches between fastidiousness and rage, coldly matter-of-fact summaries of infant mortality and flatly reported accounts of family economies, snide dismissals of individuals turned into types, and, for individuals who for moments escape all typology, an awestruck respect that Agee seems almost desperate to suppress. Agee never finds an even keel because he didn't want one. But Evans did want a stable perspective, a certain distanced, confident stance that allowed his subjects—men, women, children, their houses, their beds, their walls decorated with magazine advertisements—to appear as both iconic and ordinary, as objects and individuals, as poor people smashed by the cotton economy, and as art. It was this—as Agee, in the more than four hundred pages of *Let Us Now Praise Famous Men*, dove so far down into the lives he chronicled that it's not clear he ever completely came up—that allowed Evans's pictures to enter the common American imagination as images that were not made but found, and that allows anyone to see them anywhere, as if Evans's camera were a mirror and his eye not his but that of the country itself, dreaming its fractured, free-associating dream. For example: the 1936 Evans picture of the farmer Floyd Burroughs and three children from the neighbor Tengle family in Hale County, Alabama, that appears on the cover of *Cotton Tenants*, Burroughs in store-bought overalls and with his hat at a rakish angle, leaning with casual dignity against a support beam of a shack, the kids in flour-sack clothes with their wet hair slicked back to look nice for the camera, and the recently surfaced photo, by an unnamed photographer, of a thirteen-year-old Elvis Presley, born a year before Evans's picture was made but now standing with his bike on a Tupelo street in 1948, his blond hair slicked back, his face proud, and what can look to be the same man in the first picture standing just to Elvis's right, the same hat, the same physical demeanor, maybe slightly better clothes. You don't have to know that Evans took photos of soil erosion

NOTES AND DISCOGRAPHIES   353

in Tupelo in 1936—or to imagine that he came back years later to follow up and had his eye caught by a boy on the street who reminded him of children he'd shot before—to know that in the deepest sense he made both pictures.

The most interesting novels about Elvis were published before his death and remain little known. Harlan Ellison's *Spider Kiss* (Milwaukie, OR: M Press, 2006), originally published in 1961 as *Rockabilly*, was the first, and it's still the best, even if Ellison, as he says, modeled the main character "after the Killer, Jerry Lee Lewis." At once a roman à clef, a trash rock novel, a prescient version of *Elvis: What Happened?* and a clear look at the sources of American culture, it chronicles the rise and inevitable fall of a Southern flash: principals include a soul-searching flack (the narrator), a Col. Tom–style manager, and "Stag Preston," né Luther Sellers, a rockabilly hero who is not only a craven hype and a vicious thug, but a natural artist whose genius no evil, including his own, can ever quite snuff. Out of this material comes a story that makes sense ("Elvis's management people once took an option on *Spider Kiss*," Ellison wrote in the introduction to the 1990 edition. "Either they wanted to style it as a vehicle for him, or they wanted to make sure no one else made the movie") and an ending with some real tragedy to it.

Nik Cohn's *King Death* (New York: Harcourt, 1975) offers an English promoter (probably the same one who appears in the last verse of Bob Dylan's "Highway 61 Revisited") who turns a professional killer, first glimpsed at work in Tupelo, into America's biggest star—as a professional killer, in what one can now see as the original reality show. This was the first step down a major byway of Elvis fiction, where Jesse Garon Presley stands in for Elvis—for "King Death," as he's known to his fans, is no other, though Cohn buries the identification as deeply as he can. Nick Tosches picked up the theme in his otherwise nonfiction (or merely legend-mongering) *Unsung Heroes of Rock 'n' Roll: The Birth of Rock in the Wild Years Before Elvis* (1984; expanded edition New York: Da Capo, 1999), with "Esau Smith: The Hairy and the Smooth," wherein Esau, né Jesse Garon, explains that he was not born dead, but as was not unheard of among desperately poor families during the Depression had been passed on to relatives to be raised as their own (Gladys Presley's relatives, the Smiths), after which Vernon and Gladys contrived the story of a stillbirth to cover their shame; naturally, as Esau grows up, a certain musical affinity makes itself felt. The sub- or pseudo-archetype broke loose when Sarah Shankman merged it with that of the Elvis impersonator (no stages, no singing, as in Gerald Duff's *That's All Right, Mama: The Unauthorized Life of Elvis's Twin*, Dallas: Baskerville, 1995, merely gestures and speech) in her sexy, creepy mystery *The King Is Dead* (New York: Pocket Books, 1992), a Tupelo class study that by the end has the reader praying for Jesse Garon's demise. Ace Atkins's 1998 mystery *Crossroad Blues* (New York: Thomas Dunne/St. Martin's) pitted Jesse Garon (real name, different person) against Robert Johnson (still dead, but embodied by the missing records everyone is after).

Though there have been any number of attempts at Elvis fiction as such (sort of as-such: usually Elvis survives his own death or is reincarnated in spirit form), they have yet to produce memorable results, with the uncanny exception of Louie Ludwig's *The Gospel of Elvis* (Arlington, TX: Summit, 1994), no Elvis-as-Godhead treatise (there are piles of those, from academic to coy to cute to drooling), but a revisioning of Elvis's story in biblical form (the postwar context of Elvis's emergence has never been rendered more completely, and Col. Parker has never appeared as more sinister), humor running wild, irony cackling and cracking like a whip, tragedy always waiting in the wings, never mind that Ludwig presents the book as a found document, attributing it not where it belongs, to the Church of the Subgenius, but to "the spurious 'wash-'n'-wear mystery cult' known as Sol's Big and Tall Men's Church—As Seen on TV." Mark Childress's *Tender* (1990; New York: Ballantine, 1998), is "the story of Leroy Kirby, a poor white boy from Tupelo, Mississippi, who . . ." The tale collapses under the weight of its literalism ("Leroy," *le roi*, "the King," get it?), not to mention its length (566 pages in its first edition); nevertheless there are magical imaginings of Elvis bringing a picture he's torn out of a movie magazine to a beauty parlor so he can get his hair fixed just like that, and of his first visit to the Lansky Brothers' haberdashery on Beale Street—and *Tender* remains the only place where you can read a story (never mind *the* story) of how Elvis lost his virginity. The Elvis impersonator is a safer theme, as in William McCranor Henderson's quite literary and unsatisfying *Stark Raving Elvis* (New York: Dutton, 1984), or P. F. Kluge's *Biggest Elvis* (New York: Viking, 1996), about three impersonators plying their trade in Olongapo, in the Philippines, for American servicemen and villagers alike, all joining, as Sarah Ferguson put it in the *New York Times*, in a "dreamy, melancholy tale of economic and pop-cultural imperialism."

The element of domination Ferguson identifies in Kluge's novel— the urge in the Elvis drama that in its most diffused and abstract form is an irreducible lust for power—is at the heart of perhaps the trickiest Elvis theme: emotional and even political fascism. Girls who became

Elvis fans in the fifties have described how, even as they grew up, married, and had children, Elvis continued to embody life so fully they felt dead, or alive only in his thrall; as one such woman has written, they worshipped him as he wanted them to. It's this element in Elvis that led Jim Jones of the People's Temple to style himself after the post-'68 Elvis, and that sparked the Elvis fixation of David Koresh of the Branch Davidians, both of them fiends, devourers of souls and bodies. The same factor animates the black humor of the Elvis-Hitler identification one can find all through Elvis's posthumous career, from the band Elvis Hitler to Bill Barminski's comic strips, which present Hitler swooning over "Do the Clam" and calling on Elvis "to give me strength to crush my foes," while El, uncertain but, as always, polite, returns the favor by raising his right hand and tentatively mouthing "Heil Hitler" (seek out *A Bar-min-ski CD-ROM*, De-Lux 'o Consumer Productions, 1995). The theme was taken to something like its limit in John Paxson's *Elvis Live at Five* (New York: Thomas Dunne/St. Martin's, 2002), where at a Dallas TV station looking for a new angle on the twenty-fifth anniversary of Elvis's death, a producer and a computer wizard create a virtual Elvis, and, making no pretense that it is anything but an image, a joke the viewer is in on, make him, or it, into a talk show host. Then the station manager takes over—and, shifting to a new format, turns Elvis into a version of Michael Savage, attacking homosexuals, immigrants, Hare Krishnas, his denunciations backed by footage created by the same means that keep Elvis talking. Soon homicidal mobs roam the land, driving their victims before them, until the end of America looms up, the whole country one long Trail of Tears: "Thousands of men, women and children in a long snaking line of misery and fear stumbling through the winter snows of Nebraska."

One might hope that it is a more benign incarnation of Elvis-as-ruler that in 1992 led to the half-joking, half–deadly serious identification of Bill Clinton with Elvis, and, more interestingly, Elvis's startlingly ubiquitous presence throughout the year's presidential campaign. It was, after all, a campaign that ran on sometimes parallel, sometimes crossing tracks with the Elvis stamp election, which began with voters choosing between a "Young Elvis" and a "Mature Elvis," and ended with the stamp's issue only days before Clinton's inauguration. Beginning in 1992, I tried to follow this story into the last year of Clinton's presidency in pieces collected in my *Double Trouble: Bill Clinton and Elvis Presley in a Land of No Alternatives* (2000; expanded edition New York: Picador USA, 2001), but the Clinton-Elvis saga may not have been the half of it. Was it Elvis's legitimation of primacy, of absolute dominion within democratic borders, or his affirmation that one must step out of the history that, for any individual, has putatively already been made—the way, in so many moments, he did try to affirm the promise that "All the world's a stage . . . and each of us must play a part"—that, with an elected leader facing a coup against his government and facing as well his own execution, had already affected the fate of a great nation? For the following tale, here in the words of John Heileman (from his "Rouble Without a Cause," *Modern Review*, Autumn 1991), is true: "It is past midnight, August 20, and Boris Yeltsin is hunkered down in the bowels of the Russian White House. Outside, several hundred members of the resistance militia man the hastily assembled barricades. Three of them will die later in the night. In his sanctuary, Yeltsin sits alone, pondering the possibility that time, for him, is running out. His situation is impossible for us to imagine. But it gives rise to an impulse that is instantly recognizable. For in that moment of fear and isolation, Yeltsin yearns for a soundtrack, for a song that will both envelop him and render his situation more dramatic still. He puts on 'Are You Lonesome Tonight?' by Elvis Presley. It is not one of Elvis's best—none of his ballads are. Still, if you listen closely, you can almost hear what Roland Barthes called 'the grain of the voice.' Taking comfort there, Yeltsin is one of us."

It's that *us*—concrete or spectral—that led to the finest, or the most final, words of obituary spoken on the occasion of Elvis Presley's death. Lester Bangs was writing in the *Village Voice*, August 29, 1977, in a piece titled "How Long Will We Care?" (collected in his *Psychotic Reactions & Carburetor Dung* as "Where Were You When Elvis Died?"): "If love is truly going out of fashion, which I do not believe, then along with our nurtured indifference to each other will be an even more contemptuous indifference to each other's objects of worship. I thought it was Iggy Stooge, you thought it was Joni Mitchell or whoever seemed to speak for your own private, entirely circumscribed situation's many pains and few ecstasies. We will continue to fragment in this manner, because solipsism holds all the cards at present; it is a king whose domain engulfs even Elvis's. But I can guarantee you one thing: we will never agree on anything as we agreed on Elvis. So I won't bother saying goodbye to his corpse. I will say goodbye to you."

THE CARTER FAMILY, JIMMIE RODGERS & HANK WILLIAMS

The Carter Family—A. P. (1891–1960, producer and song-catcher), his wife, Sara (1898–1970, vocals, autoharp), and his sister-in-law "Mother" Maybelle Addington Carter (1909–78, vocals, guitar)—came from the Clinch Mountains in western Virginia, near the Tennessee border. Ralph Peer of Victor recorded both the Carters and Jimmie Rodgers for the first time in August 1927 (see the anthology *The Bristol Sessions*, Country Music Foundation; for a fictional version of the event, Lee Smith's novel *The Devil's Dream*, 1992; New York: Berkley, 2011). Together they dominated country record sales and country radio until the Depression all but destroyed the new market, but not before the Carters' songs (traditional folk material, gospel, blues, nineteenth-century sentimental standards, and such topical numbers as "No Depression in Heaven") had begun their journey all over the world. Their *Complete Victor Recordings* (Rounder) collects the most important material, eight CDS that range from *Anchored in Love: 1927–28* to *Last Sessions: 1934–41*; someone else can choose between them. For detail on the Carters' career, see John Atkins's "The Carter Family," in *Stars of Country Music*, edited by Bill C. Malone and Judith McCulloch (Urbana: University of Illinois, 1975). Mark Zwonitzer and Charles Hirshberg's 2004 *Will You Miss Me When I'm Gone? The Carter Family and Their Legacy in American Music* (New York: Simon and Schuster, 2004), a sort of white-minstrel show that has likely drained the market for a major book on the Carter Family for years to come, cannot be recommended. After the original Carter Family broke up, Maybelle Carter formed Mother Maybelle and the Carter Sisters (her daughters Helen, June, and Anita); in 1956 and '57 they toured with Elvis as an opening act.

Jimmie Rodgers (1897–1933) was born in Meridian, Mississippi, and spent a good part of his youth on the railroad, listening to black minstrels and work gangs; when tuberculosis forced him off the rails in 1925, he turned to music. By the time he began to record, he had mastered a unique blues style: the "blue yodel" that Howlin' Wolf said taught him how to howl. Deserving of reissue on their own are *My Rough and Rowdy Ways* (RCA), which collects "Blue Yodel No. 1 (T for Texas)," Rodgers's first big hit, "Blue Yodel No. 9" (backing by Louis Armstrong and Earl Hines), and "Long Tall Mama Blues," and *Never No Mo' Blues* (RCA), featuring "California Blues," Rodgers's tribute to the dispossessed Okies and Arkies who sang his songs all the way to the coast. Still, Rounder's eight-CD series is a deep mine, from *First Session* to *Last Sessions*, and there is nothing like the latter, cut just before Rodgers's death. On "Blue Yodel No. 12," Rodgers fades the word "home" in the line "I know she's never coming home." He's trying to disguise the awful rasp in his chest, but his technique and his commitment to the song are such that he produces something very different: a moment of absolute blues, where a certain word, a certain signifier, is so hurtful language can't carry it. The conventional blues device is to drop the word and play up its absence on guitar. Rodgers lets the word surface—and then, as if by hoodoo, makes it disappear. But with "Yodeling My Way Back Home" he can make nothing disappear. Neither the formal structures of the song nor Rodgers's persona can contain the fear and acceptance in the death sound he's making. It's not easy to listen to; the vibrations in his voice unbalance the room. It's like the last shots of F. W. Murnau's 1931 *Tabu*, with Matahi swimming to his death against the tides, chasing the skiff that has taken his beloved Reri—which, as Pauline Kael wrote, "is headed for nothing so commonplace as land." The most complete Rodgers biography is Nolan Porterfield's *Jimmie Rodgers: The Life and Times of America's Blue Yodeler* (Urbana: University of Illinois, 1979). *Waiting for a Train: Jimmie Rodgers's America*, an anthology edited by Mary E. Davis and Warren Zanes (Cambridge, MA: Rounder Books, 2009) and Barry Mazor's *Meeting Jimmie Rodgers* (New York: Oxford, 2009) are strong attempts to clear the territory and start the story over, but a more aesthetically oriented, modernist, impressionist treatment is called for.

Hank Williams was born in 1923 in Georgiana, Alabama; he left home to sing in 1937, and first recorded commercially in 1946 (a single demo or radio transcription, "I'm Not Coming Home Anymore," dates to 1942), almost precisely a generation after the first recordings by the Carter Family and Jimmie Rodgers. He was the first country singer whose music reached every corner of the United States; in terms of music and impact, he was a white Ray Charles ("country" Ray Charles won't do; Charles was country himself). Dragged down by chronic pain, alcoholism, drugs, and divorce, Williams saw his career dissolve into the chaos of his life; by the end, the Grand Ole Opry had banned him for his sins. He died in the early hours of New Year's Day, 1953, only twenty-nine years old, though the coroner refused to believe it; should you take the chance to watch the 1980 *Hank Williams: The Show He Never Gave* (Echo Bridge, 2008), you will. Written by Maynard Collins, directed by David Acomba, the film opens with Williams in his Cadillac, his driver rushing through the night to a show in Ohio. A bar looms up; Williams imagines calling his driver to stop, then sees himself getting out of the car. He goes through the door, takes the band-stand, his band already warming up the crowd: Hank Williams, right here, in our nowhere bar, on New Year's Eve! All right!

Playing Williams, the Canadian country singer Sneezy Waters doesn't look like him, doesn't necessarily sound like him, but within minutes he is him, running through the hits and making each one into an event the people in the crowd (you can catch Jim Carrey) will never forget. They mill around the foot-high platform that serves as a stage, as close to Williams as pogo dancers were to the Buzzcocks, but without starlust, as if it's just a special night in a long life. After jokes about drinking and divorce—complex, plainly rehearsed, and seemingly spontaneous stories—Williams/Waters ends his first set with "Alone and Forsaken." Recorded in 1949 by Williams alone, with only an acoustic guitar tuned in to the melody of "Buffalo Skinners" for accompaniment, it is as anomalous in Williams's songbook as "Hellhound on My Trail" is in Robert Johnson's: that bereft. In *How Bluegrass Music Destroyed My Life* (Chicago: Drag City, 2000), the abstract blues guitarist John Fahey (1939–2001) imagined himself at a last Williams concert, this time on a riverboat on the Potomac, in 1953: "At some point in the show he sang 'Alone and Forsaken,' and while he did that many of us almost died of grief and fright." He quotes the first line of "the greatest song of despair ever written": "We met in the springtime." "By the fifth word," he says, "you know it's all over." Here Williams's words fail to fit into the philosophical borders of "Cold, Cold Heart" just as the messy architecture of "Hellhound" breaks up the order of "Me and the Devil Blues"; the cadence of "Alone and Forsaken" damns the melody of "I'm So Lonesome I Could Cry" as a cheat, a sedative, just as the antibeat of "Hellhound" destroys the rhythm of "Terraplane Blues." It seems that nothing could follow this performance, but after a short time in a dressing room, shooting up, Williams comes back for a second set, and it's time to pay the piper.

This same man is caught in Ralph J. Gleason's "Hank Williams, Roy Acuff, and Then God!" (the title was Gleason's addition to Williams's "For drawing power in the South, it was Roy Acuff and then God!"), a piece about an evening Gleason spent in 1952 with Williams, in his hotel in Oakland, then in a bar up toward Vallejo, collected in *The Rolling Stone Rock & Roll Reader*, edited by Ben Fong-Torres (New York: Bantam, 1974). The best book is *Hank Williams: The Biography*, by Colin Escott with George Merritt and William MacEwen (Boston: Little, Brown, 1994). Avoiding the Hunter Thompson–like sensationalism of Chet Flippo's harrowing 1981 *Your Cheatin' Heart* (New York: Simon and Schuster), Escott—facing down a figure who in terms of conventional biography is a specter beyond scandal, and yet who remains "almost desperately alive through his music"—ends up in a graveyard far more terrible. "There's the notion that the writer or poet calms his troublous soul by reducing it to rhyme," Escott finishes, ready to seal the case he's made. "For Hank Williams, though, as he pulled off his boots and eased himself gingerly onto his bed, the little verses scratched out in his untutored spidery handwriting almost certainly offered no relief at all." If you want to hear Williams laugh about it, you have to go to the grave, at least as he speaks from it ("by virtue of that special privilege granted to dead hillbilly singers on the occasion of their having been dead longer than they were alive") in Dave Hickey's "A Glass-Bottomed Cadillac," in his *Air Guitar: Essays on Art & Democracy* (Los Angeles: Art Issues Press, 1997).

The basic collection is *40 Greatest Hits* (Polydor); the monument, rivaling the Williams monument that sits just across the lane from that of my great-grandparents Jacob and Mena Greil in Oakwood Cemetery in Montgomery, Alabama, is *The Complete Hank Williams* (Mercury Nashville). The sunny afternoon is in the radio broadcasts collected on *Health & Happiness Shows* (Mercury); the last breath is on *Alone & Forsaken* (Umvd), which begins with the title song, moves through the Gothic "Ramblin' Man," and ends with "Angel of Death."

CAMEOS: FROM CHARLIE RICH TO "LOUIE LOUIE"

Charlie Rich's "I Feel Like Going Home" was released in 1973 as the flipside of "The Most Beautiful Girl" (Rich's first, and last, number one hit) and again in 1974 on *The Silver Fox* (Epic), a bizarre superstar package that showed Rich striding onto a Vegas stage trailing a line of prancing showgirls. This harmless version of the tune had nothing to do with the performance I saw Rich dedicate to Richard Nixon. Producer Billy Sherrill buried the vocal in choruses and horns, and smoothed away the broken melody and confusing chord changes that gave the music its power; the baroque rendition on the wildly overpraised 1992 *Pictures and Paintings* (Sire) was no better. Rich (1932–95) did record the song as it was meant to be heard, on a rehearsal tape that for years his label denied even existed; Rich's piano was the only accompaniment, a strange wedding of Skip James's free hand and stately country gospel. The recording, perhaps the most distinctive of Rich's long career, finally saw the light of day in 1981 on the misnamed anthology *Rockabilly Stars, Vol. 1* (Epic). In

1997 it served as the title song for the excellent two-CD career retrospective *Feel Like Going Home: The Essential Charlie Rich* (Epic Legacy), which nevertheless does not supersede the now likely fugitive collections noted directly below; liner notes include comment by Sam Phillips, Rich's wife Margaret Ann Rich, and Peter Guralnick, and excerpts from Terry Gross's 1992 interview with Rich on her WHYY/NPR show *Fresh Air*.

The most convincing of all white soul singers—Ernest Withers's *The Memphis Blues Again* includes a shot of B. B. King flanked by the twin pianos of Rich and Jerry Lee Lewis—Rich's 1957–62 work for Phillips International (a Sun subsidiary) is collected on his *Lonely Weekends* (Avi/Sun), and on the more interesting *Don't Put No Headstone on My Grave* (Zu Zazz), which combines an unreleased 1962 session with better-known numbers remixed to omit overdubbed strings and choruses. Rich's far more expressive mid-'60s recordings, cut with producer Jerry Kennedy in Nashville ("I Can't Go On," "Down and Out," "Everything I Do Is Wrong," "Blowin' Town," and the odd Tennessee-beatnik celebration, "Mohair Sam," which Nik Cohn termed "a work of genius"), are on *The Complete Smash Sessions* (Mercury). The Epic albums *Set Me Free* (1968) and *The Fabulous Charlie Rich* (1969, with the stoic, blasted "Life's Little Ups and Downs," by Margaret Ann Rich) define how far a country singer whose spirit comes from the blues can go. Peter Guralnick's chronicle of Rich's career can be followed in "Lonely Weekends," in Guralnick's *Feel Like Going Home* (1971; New York: Back Bay Books, 1999), an account of Rich's commercial failure, and in "Snapshots of Charlie Rich," in *Lost Highway*, an account of Rich's commercial success.

Dolly Parton's "My Blue Ridge Mountain Boy," released as a single in 1969 and included on Parton's *The RCA Years, 1967–1986* (RCA), is best heard on the hard-to-find *A Real Live Dolly Parton*, a 1970 RCA LP recorded at Sevier County High School, Parton's alma mater, which also features "Bloody Bones," a ditty about orphans who burn down their orphanage. The Allman Brothers' "Blue Sky" is on their *Eat a Peach* (Capricorn, 1972); "Pony Boy" is on *Brothers and Sisters* (Capricorn, 1973). William Moore's timeless 1928 celebration, "Old Country Rock," can be heard on the anthology *Ragtime Blues Guitar (1927–1930)* (Document).

The saga of "Louie Louie" (in 1988, in an interview with Bob Greene, Richard Berry, 1935–97, finally confirmed—or, confronted with the age-old question, finally decided—that there was no comma in the song's title; there wasn't on the original label, but as for the copyright, well . . .) demanded a book, which Dave Marsh inflicted upon the world in 1993, part detective story, part tall tale, and altogether too good to be true, though all of it is: *Louie Louie—The History and Mythology of the World's Most Famous Rock 'n' Roll Song; Including the Full Details of Its Torture and Persecution at the Hands of the Kingsmen, J. Edgar Hoover's F.B.I, and a Cast of Millions, and Introducing, for the First Time Anywhere, the Actual Dirty Lyrics* (second rev. ed., Ann Arbor: University of Michigan, 2004); someday I hope to come across a copy of *Louie Louie: Me Gotta Go Now*, which Kingsmen drummer Dick Peterson published in 2005 (Bloomington, IN: Author House). A joke in the sixties, when bands like the Mothers of Invention would play it to make fun of the old-fashioned rock 'n' roll they had transcended, by the late '70s and '80s the tune was all-pervasive, like a law of nature or an act of God. College radio stations put on "Louie Louie" marathons, competing year by year to see who could find the most versions. The project reached its peak on KALX-FM in Berkeley, near the end of a twenty-four-hour no-repeat absurdity, when, because people were taping their own performances of the number as they listened to the broadcast, then taking them to the station, where they were immediately aired—my favorite was a version recorded on the keypad of a touch-tone telephone—it became clear that unless someone called a halt the show would never end.

The records that tell the story I tell are "Riot in Cell Block #9," by the Robins (later the Coasters), lead vocal by Richard Berry, 1955 (originally on Spark; see the Coasters' *50 Coastin' Classics*, Rhino Atco); "The Big Break," by Richard Berry (originally on Flair; see Berry's *Get Out of the Car*, Ace, though for some reason the spoken passages have been dropped; also included is "Next Time," Berry's second "Riot" followup); "Louie Louie" by Richard Berry and the Pharoahs, 1956 (originally on Flip, now on Berry's *Have "Louie", Will Travel: The 1956–62 Recordings*—that misplaced comma again—Ace); "Louie, Louie," by the Kingsmen, 1963 (originally on Jerden; see *The Best of Louie, Louie*, Rhino, which also includes a re-recording by Berry, plus versions by Black Flag, the Rice University Marching Band, and Rockin' Robin Roberts, the Seattle singer who rescued the tune from oblivion in 1961); "Louie, Louie" by Paul Revere and the Raiders, 1963 (originally on Sande; see *The Best of Louie, Louie, Vol. 2*, Rhino, which also includes the Russian band Red Square, the Kinks, and Mongo Santamaria); and "Brother Louie," by Stories (Kama Sutra, 1973).

The initial recording of the last tune was by the black and white U.K. band Hot Chocolate, 1973 (see *Every 1's a Winner: The Very Best of Hot Chocolate*, Capitol, or *The Essential Collection*, EMI Gold); in their version, "Louie" was black and his girlfriend white (with Alexis Korner, a founder of the British blues scene and mentor to the Rolling Stones, playing her racist father), while with Stories it was the other way around; there is no bottom to this tale. As for those who must hear the *real* lyrics (which Berry never wrote; as Ed Ward once remarked, they are the truest example we know of the folk process), Iggy and the Stooges sing them and then some on *Metallic KO* (Melodie/Skydog), cut in 1973, at the band's first last concert, in a hail of beer cans and bottles.

SAM PHILLIPS, SUN RECORDS & ROCKABILLY MUSIC

Sam Phillips (1923–2003), for those who haven't guessed it, is the secret hero of this book. I don't know if he was the right man in the right place at the right time, or much more than that, and I don't really care. "This is like Paris at the turn of the century," said Jim Dickinson in 1982, trying to explain. "We saw a change in Memphis that affected the whole world."

"My greatest contribution," Phillips said in 1978, "was to open up an area of freedom within the artist himself, to help him express what *he* believed his message to be. Talking about egos—these people unfortunately did not *have* an ego. They had a desire—but at the same time to deal with a person that had dreamed, and dreamed, and dreamed, looked, heard, felt, to deal with them again under conditions where they were so afraid of being denied again—it took a pure instinctive quality on the part of any person that got the revealing aspects out of these people . . . I don't care if it was me or somebody else. Because I knew this—to curse these people or just to give the air of 'Man, I'm better than you,' I'm wasting my time trying to record these people to get out of them what's truly in them. I *knew* this."*

* From Peter Guralnick's *Lost Highway*; his *Sam Phillips: The Man Who Invented Rock 'n' Roll*, is scheduled for publication in 2015. For more on Sun and related topics, see Margaret McKee and Fred Chisenhall's *Beale Black and Blue* (Baton Rouge: Louisiana State University Press, 1981); Nick Tosches's *Country* (1979; New York: Da Capo, 1996), a down-and-dirty account of America's lust for miscegenation as found in its music; Colin Escott and Martin Hawkins's *Good Rockin' Tonight: Sun Records and the Birth of Rock 'n' Roll* (New York: St, Martin's Griffin, 1992) and their *Sun Records: The Discography* (Vollersode, West Germany: Bear Family, 1987); for comment on Sun and the blues, see Robert Palmer's *Deep Blues* (New York: Viking, 1981); for Sun and R&B, see Louis Cantor's *Wheelin' on Beale: How WDIA–Memphis Became the Nation's First All-Black Radio Station and Created the Sound That Changed America* (New York: Pharos, 1992); and, for the Memphis music world from then to now as a secret bohemia, Robert Gordon's *It Came from Memphis* (Boston and London: Faber and Faber, 1994), with a soundtrack album on Upstart featuring contributions by the legendary disc jockey Dewey Phillips, Mud Boy and the Neutrons (Jim Dickinson and company, with the scarifying "Money Talks"), Othar Turner's Fife and Drum Corps, and the unknown Russ Johnson (the unforgettable, or unrememberable, "Wet Bar").

Gordon continued this side of the Memphis story with "Late Night with Sam and Dave" (*Oxford American*, Spring 1997)—a piece that could have been titled "America's Real Dada." It's a

Moonlighting from his jobs as a disc jockey and hotel big-band broadcast announcer, Phillips built a studio at 706 Union Avenue in Memphis—it was the town's first permanent recording facility—and in 1950 began recording local blues talent (along with speeches, weddings, commercials), leasing the results to Chess in Chicago and Modern in Los Angeles. The Sun label was founded in 1952. Interesting releases pretty much ceased by 1960; Phillips made his fortune less as a record man than as an early investor in the Holiday Inn chain.

After Phillips sold the label in 1968, a vast confusion of reissues began—hundreds of albums, on many labels, in many countries—and it continues today, with single or double CDs and back-breaking box sets competing on Charly, Bear Family, Avi, Rhino, and other labels in a sarabande of gross redundancy, usually with predictable sound quality.

The best place to start is *The Sun Records Collection* (Rhino three-CD set), which begins with Joe Hill Louis's "Gotta Let You go," picks up Harmonica Frank and the Miller Sisters along with Dr. Ross and the Prisonaires, covers Elvis and attendant rockabillies, and ends with Charlie Rich ("Don't Put No Headstone on My Grave") and Jim Dickinson's Jesters. *The Sun Blues Box: Blues, R&B and Gospel Music in Memphis 1950–1958* (Bear Family) is a great historical document, and also unfailingly listenable, offering hours of surprise, shock, and delight; present are Howlin' Wolf, the Prisonaires, B. B. King, James Cotton, Pat Hare, Junior Parker, Little Milton, "Hot Shot" Love, Billy "The Kid" Emerson, Rufus Thomas, Jackie Brenston (whose "Rocket 88," one of many "first" rock 'n' roll records, was a huge hit in 1951), and many more. What you hear is not a production style, though there is that, but the invention and testing of a creative milieu. *The Sun Country Box* (Bear Family) is of more academic interest. If the blues box is an epic, this is an everyday story. There is no hint of a change that could

---

priceless account of Sam Phillips's 1986 appearance on *Late Night with David Letterman*, where he reduced the smug and cynical talk-show host to a vat of bile and confusion. Letterman expected to "do to [Phillips] what he does with most folks," ran a line heading the article: "control him, make fun of him, and come out looking superior and hip." Phillips, acting as if he were from Mars—that is, as if he were *really* from Memphis—took control from the start. After a few minutes, "Sam [was] now producing Dave," Gordon wrote: all rules were broken. "Now," Phillips said before the nation, addressing its tribune of condescension, "how did you, with buck teeth, make a million dollars? You know, not a lot of people can do that." To most of the country, Phillips must have seemed drunk or insane: only Letterman himself was supposed to be allowed to talk like that. Letterman tried to come back, asking, as everyone always has, what kind of sound Phillips was after, how he found it, how he made his records. What he got was a long silence, a smile he couldn't read, and then a polite demurral: "You know," Phillips said, "I'm not going to give away my secrets because when this show goes under you might want to start recording. If I give away my secrets, what am I going to have to write about in a book and a movie? You could copy me and you're so young, I might drop off dead."

affect Memphis, let alone the rest of the world. The deep themes aren't desire and refusal, but acceptance and routine. There are gleaming anomalies, more effectively collected if less easily found on *Defrost Your Heart: Sun Country, Vol. 1* (Avi/Sun): Howard Serratt's quiet folk gospel ("Troublesome Waters"), the rare sound of a man at peace with himself, and Cash King and the Miller Sisters' "Can't Find Time to Pray," a piece so delicate it almost hides its sting: "You must find time to die." Sam Phillips never released it, fearing it was too strong for the market, and no doubt he was right. Another Sun country sampler, *Memphis Ramble*, is notable for "Try Doin' Right," a cut by Mississippi Slim (Carvel Lee Ausborn)—who in 1946, on *Singin' and Pickin' Hillbilly*, his weekly noontime show on WELO in Tupelo, hosted an eleven-year-old Elvis Presley, who "didn't know but two songs."

For Howlin' Wolf ("Where the soul of man never dies," as Phillips described him), see also *Howlin' Wolf Rides Again* (Flair), very early recordings from about 1950, featuring the explosive Willie Johnson ("Play that guitar," Wolf shouts in "House Rockin' Boogie," "'til it smoke") and the pianist known as "'Struction"; *Moanin' in the Moonlight* (Chess); and the wonderful *Memphis Days: The Definitive Edition*, *Vol. 1* and *Vol. 2* (Bear Family), with probing annotation by Jim Dickinson. *Delta Rhythm Kings* (Charly LP) collects Sun producer and talent scout Ike Turner's early powerhouse sessions, with Bonnie Turner's bizarre "Down in the Congo"; for the Prisonaires, the rhythm 'n' gospel singers Sam Phillips recorded when they were still incarcerated in the Tennessee State Penitentiary, see *Just Walkin' in the Rain* (Charly).

With Elvis, Sun changed. Blues vanished almost completely; Phillips went for the main chance, which meant white boys who could sing country rock. Malcolm Yelvington, who looked like an accountant attending an office Halloween party in a cowboy costume, but who could sing country rock, was the first to record after Elvis; his version of Stick McGhee's 1949 R&B touchstone "Drinkin' Wine Spo-Dee-O-Dee" is on *The Sun Records Collection*, while his cool "Rockin' with My Baby" is on *Rock Baby Rock It: Sun Rockabilly Vol. 2* (Avi/Sun).

When Elvis left Sun in the fall of 1955, dozens of new white singers were beginning to record in Texas, Nashville, Alabama, and other Southern centers; the rest were in Memphis, begging Sam Phillips for auditions. The best were Carl Perkins and Billy Lee Riley, who entered 706 Union in 1955, and Roy Orbison and Jerry Lee Lewis, who arrived in 1956.

Perkins (1932–98) made beautiful records for Sam Phillips—and all of them, plus numerous surprising alternate takes, are on his *Classics*, a five-CD set (Bear Family) that also includes 1958–62 recordings for Columbia and 1963–65 work for Decca, the latter highlighted by the sizzling "Big Bad Blues," cut in 1964 with England's Nashville Teens. The best single collection is *Up Through the Years* (Bear Family), which hits all the highlights: "Blue Suede Shoes," "Boppin' the Blues," the gentle re-creation of the Platters' "Only You," the jailhouse rocker "Dixie Fried," the rough "That's Right," the stomping "Matchbox," and Perkins's celebration of race envy, "Put Your Cat Clothes On." Perkins first told his own story in Michael Lydon's *Rock Folk* (1971; New York: Citadel Underground, 1991); his own *Go, Cat, Go! The Life and Times of Carl Perkins, the King of Rockabilly* (New York: Hyperion, 1996) suffers from the intrusion of coauthor David McGee.

Born in Arkansas in 1933, Billy Lee Riley cut "Trouble Bound" in 1955 in the Fernwood Studios in Memphis; it came out on Sun. He hit a dark, moody tone that only Elvis surpassed—and at RCA, not in Memphis. Riley was soon part of the Sun house band, with which he recorded two unforgettably scorching sides as Billy Lee Riley and the Little Green Men: "Flying Saucers Rock 'n' Roll" and "Red Hot," the former being one of the weirdest of early rock 'n' roll records, and early rock 'n' roll records were weird (see Riley's *Classic Recordings, 1956–1960*, Bear Family) or *Rock with Me Baby: 1956–1960* (Hoodoo). Riley continued as a session man in Los Angeles, Nashville, and Memphis, but he never stopped looking for another chance to hear his voice on the radio. He should have made it with his 1992 *Blue Collar Blues* (Hightone), cut with his old bandmates, a strong attempt to mix rockabilly heedlessness and blues fatalism ("Well, I heard the president talkin' / 'fore I hocked my TV set . . ."). In 2002, for his own Sun-Up label, he cut new versions of old Sun numbers for *One More Time*; far more valuable is *Shade Tree Blues* (Icehouse, 1999), a strong set of blues strung together by guitar-playing with a full life behind it. He died in 2009. An extensive interview with Jeanne Whayne can be found in the August 1996 number of the *Arkansas Historical Quarterly*; Ken Burkes's long talk with a sometimes fatalistic, often bitter Riley is collected in *Flying Saucers Rock 'n' Roll: Conversations with Unjustly Obscure Rock 'n' Soul Eccentrics*, ed. Jake Austen (Durham, NC: Duke University Press, 2011).

Roy Orbison (1936–88) and the Teen Kings of Wink, Texas, recording in Clovis, New Mexico, in late 1955, cut "Ooby Dooby" b/w "Tryin' to Get to You" (the latter based on an acetate of Elvis's then-unreleased version; Orbison is said to have listened to the demo on headphones as he sang into the mike) for the Jewel label; Sam Phillips signed the group and had them cut a far stronger version of the A-side, which hit #59 on the pop charts. The flip side, "Go Go Go," one of the most thrilling rockabilly records ever made, featured guitar work that formed Buddy Holly's hard rock style almost completely. The Teen Kings' *Are You Ready?* (Roller Coaster), recently discovered 1956 tapes from local TV performances, is a messy, utterly alive picture of the former Wink Westerners throwing themselves headfirst into the unknowns of a new music; Orbison's *The Sun Years, 1956–58* (Bear Family) is a well-mastered set that includes undubbed versions of Orbison's best-known early work plus the Jewel single. Orbison went on to many memorable pseudo-operatic hits in the '60s, (the best is "Crying") and occasional rockers (I can't choose between "Mean Woman Blues" and "Pretty Woman"), collected on *All-Time Greatest Hits of Roy Orbison* (Monument); he experienced a startling revival after his 1963 "In Dreams," as mimed by Dean Stockwell, was used as the centerpiece of David Lynch's 1986 horror movie *Blue Velvet*. Orbison made a classic video in 1988, *Black and White Night* (Image), collaborations with Elvis Costello, Tom Waits, Bonnie Raitt, and Bruce Springsteen that nearly burned up its own film stock with k. d. lang's backing action on "Mean Woman Blues"; he followed in 1989 with a new album, *Mystery Girl* (Virgin), again with contributions by Costello and Springsteen, plus Bono, George Harrison, Tom Petty, and others. Along with its hit single, "You Got It," the record was a great success, only weeks after Orbison's death. The 2006 film *Roy Orbison: In Dreams*, produced by Orbison's widow, Barbara Orbison, is a fine tribute (Sony Legacy); there are workmanlike biographies, but more interesting is Peter Lehman's *Roy Orbison: The Invention of an Alternative Masculinity* (Philadelphia: Temple, 2003). In his biggest hits, Orbison wept, he rent his garments, he walked alone in a desert of loss; he was not handsome. To the end, he wore a helmet of black hair, never moved onstage, and kept his shades on. "I knew his voice was pure gold," Sam Phillips is reputed to have said. "I also knew that if anyone got a look at him he'd be dead inside of a week."

Jerry Lee Lewis started off playing Al Jolson songs at home in Ferriday, Louisiana, snuck into black-only dives with his cousin Jimmy Lee Swaggart, studied for the ministry at a Pentecostal academy, and turned to rock 'n' roll full-time when he was expelled, he says, for sneaking too much boogie-woogie into the hymns. He recorded far more extensively than any other Sun artist, remaining with the label until 1963: highlights range from the audition-session roadhouse stomp of "Deep Elem Blues" and "You Are My Sunshine" to international hits, from the insanely salacious "Big Legged Woman" (when the song's publisher was sent the lyrics quoted in this book for permission to reprint, he declared he never had, and never would have, published anything of the sort) to the hurricane-level "Lovin' Up a Storm," through countless country renditions, novelty records, schmaltz, gospel, coon songs, and Stephen Foster. The best introductions are Lewis's *Up Through the Years, 1956–1963* (Bear Family) or *25 All-Time Greatest Sun Recordings* (Varese Sarabande); the monument is the eight-CD box *Complete Sun Recordings* (Bear Family), a houseful of banter, obscenity, philosophical disquisition, plus 240 performances, which, dauntingly, do not include Lewis's very first recordings, made in 1954 at the Louisiana radio station KWKH—or in any case such were the claims made for the versions of Hank Snow's "I Don't Hurt Anymore" and "If I Ever Needed You" collected in 1991 on *The Killer's Private Stash* (Electrovert). Lewis's 1957 career-making appearance on *The Steve Allen Show*, plus interviews at Sun, are on the DVD *Greatest Live Performances of the 50s, 60s, and 70s* (Time-Life).

After the scandal over his bigamous marriage to teenage cousin Myra, Lewis ultimately found his way to Nashville, producer Jerry Kennedy, and the Smash label; in repentance, he promised that he would record only country, abjuring the devil's music forevermore. He kept his promise on his singles, but broke it on his albums, issuing *The Greatest Live Show on Earth* (Smash, 1964) and a duet album with his sister Linda Gail so genteel it made you wonder what they were covering up.* The eight-CD box *The Locust Years* (Bear Family) covers the time, from "I'm a Lonesome Fugitive" to a long, revelatory, angry interview from 1976

---

* Far better is Linda Gail's 2000 collaboration with Van Morrison, *You Win Again* (Point Blank). By this time Linda Gail had been married eight times to her brother's seven, three times before she was sixteen—sibling rivalry takes many forms—and here she sounds as if she's daring Morrison to add a notch to her gun. With a much bigger voice, Morrison tries to walk all over her; she takes over the house on "Let's Talk About Us." Morrison is pacing the song, not matching the hot band, and then suddenly the whole feeling, the fast, rockabilly dance, changes. "Ahhhhhhhh," Lewis says, breathing right into the mouth of the song. As in her hilarious memoir *The Devil, Me, and Jerry Lee* (Atlanta: Longstreet Publishing, 1998)—the tales of someone who can no longer be surprised by anything ("Jerry Lee would probably not do a double-take if he were seated at the Last Supper," she says, meaning she wouldn't either)—you glimpse a woman more country than Dolly Parton, more of a punk than Corin Tucker, and who'd likely have nothing but contempt for either of them or anybody else. Or was that a wink? "It's a miracle we're not more fucked up than we are": Jerry Lee, who once tried to kill his baby sister Frankie Jean, Linda Gail's older sister, by throwing her off a hill, was no different from anybody else, she says; family was family. "When I was very young, my mother was always commenting on what pretty little hands I had. I think it finally got to the point when Frankie Jean really had heard enough about my beautiful hands, so naturally, she took me over to the oven and helped me to place them directly on the hot grates inside"—it's that "to" in "helped me to place them," slowing the description, making it more formal, that suspends the event in time, putting you right there.

that says as much about the complexities of desire, fame, and exile as do any of Lewis's records. Missing is the apogee (for me, anyway) of Lewis's post-Sun years, "Drinkin' Wine Spo-Dee-O-Dee," a single taken from a session with U.K. rockers that cut a swath through everything else on the radio in 1973 (see *The Revised London Session*, Bear Family). New albums, along with new wives, appeared sporadically through the next decades, up to *Young Blood* (Sire) in 1995, featuring the Coasters song covered that same year by the Band ("Does he still have it," the critic Sarah Vowell wondered, "or does he just want to fuck it?"). There was as well the 1995 set-to on "Whole Lotta Shakin' Goin' On" and "Great Balls of Fire" with Bruce Springsteen and the E Street Band (see the anthology *The Concert for the Rock & Roll Hall of Fame*, Columbia, and if you know, write and tell me what Melissa Etheridge was doing there) that recalled a similar television cutting contest from decades before, with Tom Jones (it was better). Lewis's death has been announced any number of times over the years, which gave him the chance, in 2006, to spit at the world with *Last Man Standing*, both an album (Artist First) and a TV special (Artist First) with Lewis, joined by Jimmy Page, B. B. King, Robbie Robertson, Bruce Springsteen, Mick Jagger, Ron Wood, Keith Richards, Ringo Starr, Merle Haggard, Kid Rock, Rod Stewart, George Jones, Neil Young, John Fogerty, Toby Keith, Willie Nelson, Eric Clapton, Little Richard, Norah Jones, Buddy Guy, Don Henley, and Kris Kristofferson, the last man standing because he was frozen solid. But he was there. Everyone else present for those million-dollar sessions fifty years before—Elvis, Perkins, Cash, Phillips—was already dead. He won.

And he wasn't shutting up. A 2010 follow-up, *Mean Old Man* (Verve Forecast) featured a suspiciously similar cast—that is, the likelihood of tracks leftover from the previous session—though the set also featured "Will the Circle Be Unbroken" with Mavis Staples, Robertson, and Nils Lofgren, and "Railroad to Heaven" with Solomon Burke. Better than either was *Rock & Roll Time* (Vanguard, 2014). Lewis was seventy-nine, and he came unfrozen. Unnecessary backing vocals tried to smear his singing, but that old laconic drawl, the most casual nihilism, was there in the curls he gave the lines in Chuck Berry's "Little Queenie" and Johnny Cash's "Folsom Prison Blues." The best tracks featured Robbie Robertson—anonymously, except for the liner credit. Still, it paled next to *The Knox Phillips Sessions* (Saguaro Road) recordings Sam Phillips's son made at Phillips Recording in Memphis in the late 1970s, which appeared only months after *Rock & Roll Time* in 2014. Lewis was angry, as always, misused, as always, looking for someone he could trust, for people who, unlike those sharks in Nashville, wouldn't tell him what to do, and the Phillipses, at least in the moment, were always the ones. It was therapy, not a session meant to produce anything that might be made into a record and sold to any fool with the money to pay for it, as if a few dollars were enough to buy a piece of Jerry Lee Lewis—as if Lewis weren't still under contract somewhere else. So night after night tapes rolled, Lewis pounded the piano, he ranted, he told cosmic jokes ("I have struck again," he said at the end of a seven-minute jam with himself and his demons on "Bad, Bad Leroy Brown," a performance that was never meant to see the light of day, "with a fourteen million selling underground record"). Songs from the 1950s (Chuck Berry's "Carol") to the 1910s ("Ragged But Right") were rewritten in the moment—with "Johnny B. Goode" the song just disappears, leaving in its place a parade down the main street that suddenly appeared in the middle of the studio. At the end came Stephen Foster's 1864 "Beautiful Dreamer," with a spoken introduction by Mack Vickerey: "They found him dyin' with thirty-eight cents in his pocket / A penny for each year of his life." Did Lewis care? Did anything matter but the fact that he was still there? As he began the song his voice was thick, a corny violin weeping behind him: "America's greatest poet," he said of Foster, but it all sounded canned. "He sang of the beauty of a steamboat," Lewis intoned. "The sorrow—my lord, the *sadness* of the black folks—you know, those people were treated so unfair," dragging out the last word into a trough of insincerity. "But what puzzles Jerry Lee Lewis, neighbors," he went on, "is that for all he had given, this great man, he died so young, my God, he was broke, he was drunk, he was all alone—I just can't understand it. I know how he must have felt—the night he wrote his last, and greatest, song. Listen to the words, now"—and as you listened, you realized Jerry Lee Lewis was in a cutting contest with Foster himself: a contest in heaven.

Also in 2014 came Rick Bragg's *Jerry Lee Lewis: His Own Story* (New York: HarperCollins). It wasn't an oral biography, but it was Lewis giving Braggs—a serious reporter, prone to clichés of his own making, but in tune with Lewis's landscapes—his goods. The book is a rich mine, lined with quartzite and silver, but the book to read—the best rock biography there is—remains Nick Tosches's *Hellfire: The Jerry Lewis Story* (1982; New York: Grove Press, 1998), Lewis's life rendered in bedrock American prose (typically, for Tosches, absolutely scrupulous about dates, labels, dollars, though including a scene where a young Jerry Lee and a black friend listen to Robert Johnson's "Hellhound on My Trail"). Along with *Deep Blues, Rock & Roll: An Unruly*

History, and his albums with the Insect Trust, the late Robert Palmer (1945–97) left *Jerry Lee Lewis Rocks!* (New York: Delilah, 1982), which combines fine photos and a vivid, personal essay beginning with a twelve-year-old Palmer in Little Rock at the time of the Central High battles. Myra Lewis's *Great Balls of Fire! The Uncensored Story of Jerry Lee Lewis*, written with Murray Silver (New York: Quill, 1982), is hard to read; in 1989 it was made into the film *Great Balls of Fire!* which featured a mugging, not unconvincing star turn by Dennis Quaid, an I-will-now-turn-to-stone expression on Winona Ryder's face as her Myra suddenly realizes she is actually getting married, fabulous performance sequences, and a superb soundtrack by Lewis himself, who re-recorded his music as if decades were minutes (see *Great Balls of Fire—Original Motion Picture Soundtrack—Newly Recorded Performances by Jerry Lee Lewis*, Polydor).

Those were the titans of rockabilly. Other singers, deified by misty-eyed collectors, are far less impressive. Certainly there are gems to ferret out, and some take the rockabilly style to places Sun never got to. There is Sonny Fisher's smoky sexual menace, authentically tough stuff from 1955 (six fine cuts are on the anthology *Texas Gold: The Starday Story, Vol. 2*, Texas Gold); the Lonesome Drifter, whose authentically strange stuff can be heard on the anthology *10 Years—Collector Records* (White Label); thrillingly pure Memphis country rock (i.e., no drums) from Junior Thompson and Wayne McGinnis (see *Meteor Rockabillies*, Ace, which also includes Charlie Feathers's addled "Tongue-Tied Jill"); and the blazing, Willie Johnson–influenced guitar playing of Paul Burlison (fronted by the far less convincing vocals of Johnny Burnette) with the very early Memphis combo the Rock 'n' Roll Trio (see the miscredited Johnny Burnette Trio's *Rockabilly Boogie*, Bear Family). But Warren Smith (1933–80) had no real affinity for the black rhythms rockabilly took off from (though Smith, in his heart an Appalachian balladeer, can be heard for the quirky delight he was on his *Classic Recordings, 1956–59*, Bear Family, an ideal Sun retrospective that includes the devastating "Red Cadillac and a Black Moustache," "Ubangi Stomp"—one of the only rockabilly records with the word "nigger" in it—"Black Jack David," and "So Long I'm Gone"). Charlie Feathers (1932–98), despite his unforgettable "One Hand Loose," cut in 1956 for King (see Feathers's *Get With It: Essential Recordings, 1954–69*, Revenant, which collects official releases on Flip, Sun, Meteor, King, Kay, WalMay, and Holiday Inn—the chain started in Memphis; at one time, every truly important business in town had to have its own label—plus numerous alternate takes and unreleased numbers, most notably Feathers's collaborations with bluesman and mentor Junior Kimbrough), was mostly a very odd country singer, though his sole major-label album, the 1991 *Charlie Feathers* (Elektra/Nonesuch Explorer), is a suite of unpredictabilities. (After canonization by rockabilly followers, Feathers released numerous third-rate true-believer albums in the '70s—and then, rather shockingly, came up with "Gone and Left Me Blues" and "Rockin' with Red," spooky, sensuous, fragile performances that have no parallels in rockabilly, but point to directions the music might have taken; see *Johnny Burnette's Rock and Roll Trio and Their Rockin' Friends from Memphis*, Rock-a-Billy, 1980—Johnny Burnette, dead since 1964, was not present, though Paul Burlison, Malcolm Yelvington, and Jim Dickinson were.) But for every Hasil Adkins (a lunatic one-man band with a penchant for love songs about decapitation; see *Chicken Walk*, Dee Jay Jamboree, which features the flying "Truly Ruly," and also Howard Hampton's "Bring Me the Head of Gordon Sumner," collected in Hampton's *Born in Flames* (Cambridge: Harvard, 2007), there were dozens of Carl Manns and Carl McVoys, not much more than fakes; Sonny Burgess, while wild-eyed enough, huffed and puffed more than he rocked (though see his Sun retrospective, *Classic Recordings, 1956–59*, Bear Family, his noble 1992 collaboration with Dave Alvin, *Tennessee Border*, Hightone, but not his dull 1996 collaboration with Gary Tallent of the E Street Band, *Sonny Burgess*, Rounder). Outside of originals like Buddy Holly, Gene Vincent, Eddie Cochran, and Ricky Nelson, most rockabilly singers weren't listening to that inner voice Sam Phillips wanted to hear, they were listening to Elvis. Fanatics call the likes of Alvin Wayne geniuses, but the aggression is full of doubt and the flash is almost always forced.

Rockabilly was a very special music. For all of its unchained energy and outrage, it demanded a fine balance between white impulses and black, country and city, fantasies of freedom and the reality that produced those fantasies. The sound Phillips got proves how well he understood this—but sometimes, working for that next hit, Phillips ran into mysteries in the music not even he could have expected.

In 1957, Phillips, engineer Jack Clement, Billy Lee Riley, and Jerry Lee Lewis were setting up to make "Great Balls of Fire," the follow-up to "Whole Lotta Shakin' Goin' On," Sun's biggest record up to that time. Suddenly, as one can hear on Lewis's *Sun Recordings* box, Jerry Lee objected. In 1949, as a kid in Ferriday, he had talked his way onto a bandstand for a chance to bang out "Drinkin' Wine Spo-Dee-O-Dee," but the road to Sun took him through an outbreak of glossolalia in

Ferriday to the Southwest Bible College in Waxahachie, Texas; like all Sun rockabilly ravers, he was raised on the gospel, and unlike most he knew it by heart. Sitting in Phillips's studio, reading over the lead sheet for "Great Balls of Fire," the meaning of the image must have hit him. "Great balls of fire": that was a Pentecostal image, that meant Judgment Day—and now Sam Phillips wanted Jerry Lee to turn that image into a smutty joke, to defile it. Jerry Lee said no.

JERRY LEE LEWIS: H-E-L-L.

SAM PHILLIPS: I don't believe it.

JLL: Great Godamighty, great balls of fire!

BILLY LEE RILEY: That's right!

SP: I don't believe it.

JLL: It says, WAKE, MAN! To the joy of God! But when it comes to worldly music—that's rock 'n' roll—

BLR: Rock it out!

JLL:—or anything like that, you have done brought yourself into the world, and you're in the world, and you hadn't come on out of the world, and *you're still a sinner*.

You're a sinner—and when you be saved—*and borned again*—and *be made as a little child*—

And walk before God—

And be holy—

And brother, I mean you got to be so pure! No sin shall enter there: *no sin!*

For it says, *no sin!* It doesn't say just a little bit, it says, NO SIN SHALL ENTER THERE—brother, not one little bit! You've got to walk and *talk* with God to go to Heaven. You've got to be *so* good.

BLR: Hallelujah.

SP: Alright. Now, look, Jerry. Religious conviction—doesn't mean anything—resembling extremism. [Phillips suddenly goes on the offensive.] *Do you mean to tell me* that you're gonna take the Bible, you're gonna take God's word, and you're gonna revolution*ize* the whole universe? Now, listen! Jesus Christ was sent here by God Almighty. Did He convince, did He *save*, all the people in the world?

JLL: Naw, but He tried to.

SP: *He sure did*. NOW, WAIT JUST A MINUTE! Jesus Christ—came into this world. He *tolerated* man. He didn't preach from one pulpit. He went around, and He *did good*.

JLL: That's right! He preached *everywhere!*

sp: Everywhere!

jll: He preached on land!

sp: Everywhere! That's right! That's right!

jll: He preached on the water!

sp: That's right, that's exactly right! Now—

jll: And then He done everything! He *healed!*

sp: Now, now—here's, *here's* the difference—

jll [speaking as if horns have sprouted on Phillips's head]: *Are you fol-lowin' those that heal?* Like Jesus Christ?

sp [confused]: What do you mean, I, I, what—

jll [triumphant]: Well, it's happening every day.
The *blind* had eyes opened.
The *lame* were made to walk.

sp: *Jerry*—

jll: The *crippled* were made to walk.

sp: Alright, now. Jesus Christ, in my opinion, is just as *real today,* as He was when He came into this world.

jll: Right, right, you're so right you don't know what you're sayin'.

sp [back on the offensive]: Now, then! I will say, *more so*—

blr: Aw, let's *cut it.*

sp: Wait, wait, wait just a minute, we can't, we got to—now, look. Now, listen. I'm tellin' you outta my heart. I have studied the Bible, a little bit—

jll: Well, I have too.

sp: I've studied it through and through and through and through and Jerry, Jerry, if you think that you can't, can't do good, if you're a rock 'n' roll exponent—

jll: *You can do good,* Mr. Phillips, don't get me wrong—

sp: Now, wait, wait—listen, when I say do good—

jll: YOU CAN HAVE A KIND HEART!

sp [suddenly angry]: I don't *mean,* I don't *mean* just—

jll: You can help people!

sp: YOU CAN SAVE SOULS!

jll [appalled]: No—NO! No! No!

sp: Yes!

jll: How can the *devil* save souls? What are you talkin' about?

sp: Listen, listen—

jll: I have the devil in me! If I didn't I'd be a Christian!

sp: Well, you may *have* him—

jll [fighting for his life]: JESUS! Heal this man! He cast the devil out, the devil says, *Where can I go?* He says, *Can I go into this swine?* He says, Yeah, go into him. Didn't he go into him?

sp: Jerry. The point I'm trying to make is—if you believe in what you're singin'—you got no alternative whatsoever—out of—LISTEN!—out of—

jll: Mr. Phillips! I don't care, it ain't what you believe, it's [as if explaining to a child], *it's what's written in the Bible!*

sp: Well, wait a minute.

jll: It's what is *there*, Mr. Phillips.

sp: No, no.

jll: It's just what is there.

sp: No, by gosh, if it's not what you believe [and Phillips pulls in his chips], *then how do you interpret the Bible?*

blr: Man alive—

sp: Huh? How do you interpret the Bible if it's not what you believe?

jll [confused]: Well, it's just *not* what you believe, you *just can't*—

blr: Let's cut it, man . . .

And so they did: *Good Rocking Tonight*, the bootleg on which this conversation first appeared, followed it with the furious take of "Great Balls of Fire" used in the forgotten film *Jamboree*—a take that, one could say, outsins the version Sam Phillips released to the public.

"Sam's crazy," Lewis told John Grissim many years later. "Nutty as a fox squirrel. He's just like me, he ain't got no sense. Birds of a feather flock together. It took all of us to screw up the world. We've done it."

GENERAL INDEX

*Songs are identified parenthetically by performer(s). Movies referenced are identified by director; movie soundtracks are identified by composer; when both movie and soundtrack are referenced, identification is by director/composer. Footnotes are identified by an *n* following the page number.

377

INDEX OF SONG AND ALBUM TITLES